YALE HISTORICAL PUBLICATIONS, MISCELLANY, 99

HSI-LIANG AND THE CHINESE
NATIONAL REVOLUTION

ROGER V. DES FORGES

NEW HAVEN AND LONDON
YALE UNIVERSITY PRESS
1973

Published with assistance from the foundation
established in memory of Philip Hamilton McMillan
of the Class of 1894, Yale College.

Library of Congress catalog card number: 73–77147
International standard book number: 0–300–01644–1

Designed by Sally Sullivan
and set in Times Roman type.
Printed in the United States of America by
The Colonial Press Inc., Clinton, Massachusetts.

Published in Great Britain, Europe, and Africa by
Yale University Press, Ltd., London.
Distributed in Latin America by Kaiman & Polon,
Inc., New York City; in Australasia and Southeast
Asia by John Wiley & Sons Australasia Pty. Ltd.,
Sydney; in India by UBS Publishers' Distributors Pvt.,
Ltd., Delhi; in Japan by John Weatherhill, Inc., Tokyo.

FOR ALISON WITH LOVE

CONTENTS

Maps

Illustrations

ACKNOWLEDGMENTS

It is a pleasure tinged with sorrow to acknowledge a great debt of gratitude to the extraordinary scholar and teacher Mary Wright. She first stimulated my interest in the Chinese revolution and suggested a look at Hsi-liang's career. Because she died before I began to write, I have tried to compensate for the loss of her critical comments by emulating her own high standards. Although an impossible task, it was brought nearer my reach by Jonathan Spence, who took over direction of the dissertation and guided it to completion. I should also like to thank Frederick Mote, who introduced me to Chinese history, and Arthur Wright, who taught me the importance of the earlier centuries. All three mentors graciously took the time to read and comment on various stages of the manuscript.

Thanks go also to many others: Li T'ien-yi and Parker Huang of Yale, who taught me to read Ch'ing documents; Wan Wei-ying of Yale, who assisted in locating important documents; Hsü Cho-yün and Chang Wei-jen of the Institute of Philology and History, Academia Sinica, who introduced me to libraries and archives; Kuo T'ing-yee, Chang P'eng-yüan, Su Yün-feng, Lin Ch'üan, Wang Erh-min, Shen Yün-lung, and Chao Chung-fu of the Institute of Modern History, Academia Sinica, who provided a congenial atmosphere for research and made suggestions of procedure and substance; Chao Yea-shu of National Taiwan University, who helped elucidate difficult passages; George Lin, who assisted with local histories; Chiang Fu-tsung and Ch'en Chieh-hsien of the National Palace Archives, who allowed access to some of Hsi-liang's original memorials; Liu Hang-ch'en, who kindly discussed his native Szechwan; Ichiko Chuzō of the Toyo Bunko, who facilitated research in Tokyo; my colleagues Show Shi-ping, Robert Kapp, Harold Metzgar, and Michael Hunt, who shared sources on areas of mutual interest; and my students at Middlebury College and Yale University who helped me refine some of my ideas.

I would also thank the staffs of libraries and archives where I carried on most of the research: the Sterling Memorial Library at Yale; Olin Library at Cornell University; the National Archives in Washington; the Public Record

Office in London; the Ministry of Foreign Affairs in Paris; Academia Sinica in Nan-kang; the National Palace Museum in Shih-lin; the Ministry of Education Archives in Musan; and the National Diet Library in Tokyo.

I would express, finally, warm appreciation to my mother-in-law, Sybil S. Liebhafsky, whose heroic performance as marathon typist and occasional editor has already earned her a Yellow Riding Jacket. I cannot convey in words my gratitude to my wife, Alison, for her constant assistance and devotion, or to our son, Alexander, for his welcome diversions and silences.

INTRODUCTION

In the past two decades our understanding of the complexity and dynamism of the Chinese national revolution has grown enormously. Intellectual historians have devoted great effort to clarifying the nature of Chinese nationalism. They long ago showed that it did not necessitate a rigid defense of all aspects of Chinese culture against Western influence. Some went so far as to see Chinese nationalism as a rejection of most of Chinese culture and an acceptance of the Western idea of the sovereign and equal nation state. Others have modified this view by suggesting that nationalism drew on certain aspects of the culture which lent themselves to the creation of wealth and power. Recent scholars have even portrayed some Chinese nationalists who had little difficulty in leaping almost directly from an old Confucian universalism to a new Marxist one.[1]

Political historians have traced the emergence of modern nationalism in the last decades of the Ch'ing dynasty (1644–1911). Several have studied the so-called pure criticism (*ch'ing-i*) of the 1870s and 1880s, which stood somewhere between traditional "culturalism" and modern nationalism. Another has divided late Ch'ing officials into three groups, the "mainstream" officials, "militant conservatives" (who were closely associated with *ch'ing-i*), and "radical reformers" who allegedly laid the groundwork for the development of real Chinese nationalism. Cultural historians have explored the nature of the traditional Chinese world order, especially in its Ming and Ch'ing forms. They have suggested that it was a highly flexible and efficient means for ordering relationships among East Asian states and societies. Others have found continuities between the early idea of world order and current Chinese concepts of international relations.[2]

Moving toward an increasingly precise analysis of rebellion and revolution, Sinologists have discovered some interesting secular changes in rebel ideologies and programs throughout Chinese history. Students of the more recent revolution have agreed that it was a response to new conditions in China, such as population growth, and new ideas from outside, such as social equality. Scholars have differed largely over whether the revolution came mainly from below, involving unprecedented popular participation in politics, or from above, entailing a new degree of state control over society. It has also been argued that the Chinese revolution has involved less an overthrow of one class by another than the addition of new classes to Chinese society.[3]

Political historians concerned with the development of the modern revolution generally hold that China moved from the conservatism of the T'ung-chih Restoration through the reforms of 1898, the reaction of the Boxers, and the radicalism of the first decade to the revolution of 1911. In this view the 1911 event was the first revolution, followed by another in 1927, and a third in 1949. Meanwhile cultural historians have looked at the broader sweep of the last three hundred years of Chinese history and have discussed the transition from the Ch'ing to the People's Republic as an adaptation of a rich heritage in a series of phases. According to these views, the revolution involved not so much secular change on a Western model as periodic efforts to regain the greatness achieved by China prior to the instabilities brought by population growth and Western impact.[4]

From all of these studies has emerged a kind of revisionist consensus. This consensus reacts against the Chinese Nationalists' claim that they represent the mainstream of Chinese nationalism and the Chinese revolution. It also challenges the Chinese Communists' claim that Chinese history was foreordained to develop from a bourgeois nationalism to a proletarian communism. The consensus disputes the earlier Western idea of an unchanging China by looking carefully for change at every stage in history. It also precludes recent suggestions that the Chinese Communists may be creating a culture which conforms to some of the highest ideals of early Chinese civilization. Perhaps because this consensus has offered an attractive alternative to so many other interpretations, it has won wide acceptance among American students of Chinese history. In its most current and revisionist form, it holds that both Chinese nationalism and the Chinese revolution appeared earlier and had deeper roots in the past than scholars had previously assumed. Both phenomena were so complex and involved that numerous shades of definition need to be employed in analyzing them.[5] Yet this consensus still suggests that China's identity developed in a line from traditional culturalism through antiforeignism to modern nationalism and that Chinese society passed through the successive phases of traditional conservatism, reform, and modern revolution.

Underlying this consensus is the continuing assumption that Chinese history may be sharply divided into so-called traditional and modern periods. The theory of modernization was supposed to free Western scholars from the parochial belief that the rest of the world was becoming Westernized, but all too often proponents of that theory have continued to operate on the same assumptions and to make the same judgments as earlier advocates of Westernization. Despite warnings from our most esteemed colleagues, many still hastily identify "traditional" with Chinese and "modern" with Western. Some take pains to specify "traditional Chinese" and "modern Western"— which should suggest at least the existence of the "traditional West" and "modern China"—but others hardly heed the distinction. As a result, most American students of China, including some of the most radical and revisionist, still believe that China fell behind in the march of world history; only now, through the revolution, is it learning to act like a modern nation state.[6] Underlying this view of modernity is the equally limiting premise that technological development and economic achievement are the main forces of history. Indeed, in the hands of too many scholars, they have become the chief indices of the ultimate worth of any particular civilization.

I undertook the present study believing that the analyses of Chinese nationalism and the Chinese revolution had to be further refined. The term *culturalism,* while sometimes useful, should be dissociated from any one country or any particular period of history. It should be used to describe a culture, whether Chinese or any other, existing in the past, present, or future, which remains free from any outside challenge. *Antiforeignism,* occasionally an indispensable term, should be distinguished clearly from culturalism, as has sometimes been done, and linked more closely with foreign imperialism, which scholars seem reluctant to do. In such a perspective, antiforeignism in the late Ch'ing becomes on balance a rational reaction against arrogant and racist foreigners who invaded China and tried to make it over in their own image. Nationalism then emerges not as the abandonment of culturalism and the transcendence of antiforeignism but as their incorporation into a more militant stand against foreign encroachment. Nationalism was less a simple Chinese "response to the West" than a reinterpretation of China's long history and culture in complex interaction with the West.

With regard to the Chinese revolution, too, there was some need for rethinking the use of terms. Some of the many rebellions in Chinese history may have come very close to being revolutions. A good number brought secular changes even while originating out of a cyclical pattern of development; some were led by members of the lower as well as of the upper classes and were precipitated by social as well as political causes. Chinese conservatism was in some ways very different from conservatism in the West. A conservatism based on belief in the innate goodness of man, on the possibility of his education, and on the need for state action to secure social justice may not have been as much of an obstacle to modernization as some have thought. Reforms for their part need not always be labeled moderate, for some could be moderate in the Chinese context and radical in others, or moderate in means and radical in goals. Finally, as the deeper currents of the Chinese revolution become clearer, its origins, course, and consequences may seem less novel than had been thought before.

To reexamine such questions naturally risks confusion, but it also opens some exciting new possibilities in the study of Chinese history. At the very least one should be able to free himself of his Western blinders and begin to look at history in more truly universal terms. One should be able to purge himself of the nineteenth-century concept of progress which has curiously persisted under other guises into the twentieth century. Once the historian has done these things, he may begin to approach the really fundamental questions of what constitutes civilization and how cultures change through history.

With these ideas in mind, I decided to test the current concepts of nationalism and revolution through the study of an individual who played a leading role in an already well-documented period of Chinese history. While the biographical approach has its own limitations, it offers perhaps the best opportunity for getting outside one's own mind and into that of a historical actor in a different time and place. To the extent that one is able to do this, one may even go beyond the present range of hypotheses to ask wholly new questions of Chinese history.

Although the name Hsi-liang rarely appears in published Western studies of China, it was familiar enough to Chinese of the day. Born in 1853, Hsi-liang became one of the most powerful provincial officials in China between 1900 and 1911. It was as an outstanding official that he was treated in his first biographies. Ch'ing dynasty scholars wrote a biography for the *Draft History of the Ch'ing* honoring his political loyalty and military achievements. Republican editors of the revised *History of the Ch'ing* confirmed the image of Hsi-liang as a Ch'ing loyalist by dropping his biography from their study. Communist scholars who compiled his papers in Peking restored him to a place of honor as an anti-imperialist leader, but they deplored his "naïve" diplomatic strategies and alleged upper-class outlook.[7]

Chinese biographers who knew him painted a more intimate but only slightly less hagiographic portrait. They depicted him as the exemplary upright and honest official, who declined to take the customary percentage of revenue for himself and refused to make the expected gifts to superiors. A private secretary who served him for three years recorded that this Mongol bannerman was more "frugal and pure" than most in the late Ch'ing. A leading commentator on official mores who seems to have known him well said that he was "honest and energetic, far above average; very strict in his private life, a pure scholar. He held office . . . and yet never gave presents; he was the only man in the late Ch'ing with important authority who was like this." A close friend who was also a leading Manchu scholar testified that Hsi-liang placed his integrity above his own career and even above the fate of the Ch'ing dynasty.[8]

From Hsi-liang's published papers, we learn more about his full career under three different reigns and in ten different provinces.[9] During the T'ung-chih reign (1862–75), he won the highest civil service degree (the *chin-shih*) and was named to his first minor posts. During the Kuang-hsü reign (1875–1908), he supported the Empress Dowager Tz'u-hsi and became one of her most trusted provincial officials. During the Hsüan-t'ung reign (1908–12), he attained the high rank of imperial commissioner and served the regency in its last fateful years. Moving slowly but surely up most of the steps of the bureaucratic ladder from lowly magistrate to lofty imperial commissioner, Hsi-liang held office in interior provinces such as Shansi and in frontier provinces such as Manchuria. During the last decade of the Ch'ing, he was the man who filled the key post of governor-general the longest.

These perspectives, while helpful, illustrate only a few facets of Hsi-liang's career. Even a casual perusal of the record shows that he was not so much loyal to the Ch'ing as he was devoted to what that dynasty could do for China in his lifetime. Further research reveals that while he was indeed outstandingly honest and frugal, he could at times waive his principles in the interests of retaining the power necessary to carry out his programs. While some of the stereotypes about Hsi-liang did not take account of all the facts, others did not go far enough in showing his true significance. For example, he served under three reigns and in ten provinces, but his impact went far beyond court policy or the provinces where he held office.

In searching for a perspective that was at once more comprehensive and more specific, I discovered the views of an American diplomat who was posted in Manchuria when Hsi-liang was there. This foreigner, who knew Hsi-liang well, characterized him as above all "patriotic." [10] I began to grapple with the difficulties of evaluating Hsi-liang's patriotism. What were the various criteria to be taken into account and how were they related to one another? How could one bridge the gap between a Chinese biographer's characterization of Hsi-liang as a "worthy" and an American diplomat's view of him as "patriotic"?

First, I needed to study Hsi-liang's world view—the working of his mind and the thrust of his ideas. This was sometimes difficult because he was a man of action deeply involved in managing everyday affairs, with little time or, one suspects, taste for theorizing. Unlike some of his towering intellectual contemporaries, he was not constantly preoccupied with explaining and defending his views. While occasionally less explicit in his statements than his purely scholarly friends, he was also often more sincere and honest. If his ideas proved unworkable, he had to modify them or risk impairing his effectiveness as a statesman. By the very nature of his role, he was forced to strive for those Chinese ideals of reconciling names with realities and thought with action. As a result, he may have been more representative of his time than better-known intellectuals. Such a likelihood adds even greater significance to Hsi-liang's ideas about critical relationships, such as those between an individual and society, between military and civil pursuits, and between Chinese and foreigners.

Second, I had to look at Hsi-liang's politics, or how he went about getting support for his ideas. While one can study an intellectual primarily through his ideas, one can describe a statesman only by treating his actions as well. Since Hsi-liang was a man of his times, the most important gauge of his success was his impact on those times. Hsi-liang's ideas were particularly important because he had power; his power rested not only on his authority but also on his political sense. This sense can be measured in terms of his relations with the court, his superiors and subordinates, the upper class (including the local elite, merchant-businessmen, and students), and the lower class (workers, peasants, and bandits). In trying to determine the extent of his influence, I have also weighed his contacts with adversaries such as the foreigners and anti-Manchu agitators.

Third, I tried to explore the actual policies which Hsi-liang devised to implement his ideas. To define the shape of these policies and to assess the relationships among them, I chose to divide them into the general categories of domestic, frontier, minority, and foreign affairs. Where necessary, I have further distinguished between purely domestic affairs and domestic affairs in a frontier area, and between simple minority policy and minority policy involving considerations of foreign affairs. In making judgments, I have compared official records with unofficial ones, broad statements of policy with day to day decisions, and Chinese accounts with foreign ones. Having delineated Hsi-liang's policies, I have sought to relate them to his world view and politics.

The resulting portrait is admittedly incomplete. Because Hsi-liang's biographies are hagiographic, his official papers are incomplete, and his personal records have not been published, we can recapture little of his character or of his private life. Although his rise to power and the best years of his career owed much to the empress dowager, scant evidence remains of his contacts with her. His connections with certain patrons and his militancy would suggest ties to the "pure party" (*ch'ing-liu tang*) and to their outlook of "pure criticism" (*ch'ing-i*), but there is no specific proof of any close links with this earlier movement and thinking. Nonetheless Hsi-liang was above all a public figure, his power rested on the total political situation, and his policies were responses to the circumstances in which he found himself: what we do know about his world view, politics, and policies enables us to take the measure of this man. He was very much an independent individual, yet he represented something far beyond his own particular experience.

The significance of Hsi-liang's life may be appreciated through an examination of the successive periods of his career. After a gradual rise to power, during which he became familiar with most of the major problems facing China, he entered on three main phases, each distinguished by its own special tone. During the first, from 1900 to 1903, he adopted a general strategy of resistance (*ti-k'ang*) in dealing primarily with foreign encroachment and to some extent with internal pressures. This strategy, although never explicitly articulated, emerges from the totality of his thought and action during this period. It was largely a negative reaction to outside forces pressing in on him, one which betrayed some sense of insecurity in dealing with major issues for the first time in his career. At the same time, this strategy drew upon a long-standing Chinese tradition of resistance to outside invasions and internal threats, a tradition which corresponded well to China's belief in her self-sufficiency and to the officials' faith in the power of self-cultivation. The overriding problem for Hsi-liang and his contemporaries was to resist the foreign invasion and to conduct internal affairs in such a way as to retain Chinese sovereignty.

The second phase, from 1903 to 1907, was dominated by a different strategy which might well be called expansion (k'uang-chang or hsing). This strategy represented a more positive reaction to foreign and internal problems, one which involved an effort to realize Chinese capacities in new as well as old ways. It may have resulted in part from Hsi-liang's newfound confidence in his ability to influence decisions on major policy. It drew also on certain traditions of expansion dating back into early Chinese history and philosophy. In the main, however, the various types of expansion which Hsi-liang undertook in this period were more reactions to the West. Hsi-liang reacted to foreign encroachment by trying to pre-empt certain fields through Chinese expansion. He also tried to secure political support by extending the political process downward to the lower classes and by involving more people in policies of economic expansion. In an effort to combat Western territorial expansion, he even took over some of its attributes. His programs of expansion differed from the real or presumed expansion over the centuries which had resulted from dynastic vigor, cultural assertiveness, economic development, population growth, or technological advances.[11] Hsi-liang's strategy of expansion and, even more, that of some colleagues, was heavily influenced by the Western threat and the Western model.

The third phase, from 1907 to 1909, was marked by different kinds of radicalism. The first, implying something fundamental (ken-pen ti), involved an effort to change current ideas or trends by realizing some basic concepts or goals. In taking this approach, Hsi-liang was aware of foreign influence and pressure, but he turned to the Chinese past as the ultimate source of inspiration. The second kind of radicalism, implying rapid progress (chi-chin ti), entailed an attempt to make changes in political and social institutions as quickly as possible. Here too Hsi-liang drew on some Western notions but was impelled primarily by earlier Chinese ideas about the theoretical and practical aspects of change. The third kind of radicalism, political and social reform (kai-ko and she-hui chu-i), depended more on foreign models and vocabulary but still represented a reaction against foreign pressure and a revitalization of values embedded deeply in the Chinese experience. Hsi-liang was aware of the

West and hopeful about the future but he took the Chinese past as the most reliable guide for successful radical action.[12]

These three strategies of resistance, expansion, and radicalism encompass the various tendencies in Hsi-liang's thought and action. Each phase seems to have led naturally to the next, with the overlap in most cases resulting from the continuity of the problems to which the strategies were answers. Further, while the three strategies can be easily distinguished, they might nonetheless be used simultaneously or in varying order depending on the time and circumstances. During the last phase of Hsi-liang's career, from 1909 to his death in 1917, he adopted elements of all three strategies and blended them in a most complex and significant way. I will discuss this complicated period further in the conclusion. But we note here that understanding it, as well as grasping the pattern of the whole career, will be essential to comprehending Hsi-liang's place in the Chinese national revolution.

1: THE RISE TO POWER, 1853–1899

Hsi-liang was something of the Chinese ideal self-made man. He was born in 1853 into an obscure Mongol family that had originally been part of the Buriat tribe of outer Mongolia. Although his father had served as a minor functionary in the Bordered Blue Banner garrisoned in North China, neither he nor other relatives could contribute much to Hsi-liang's career.[1] Hsi-liang had four brothers, of whom one, Chi-liang, obtained the Manchu licentiate degree, which required no knowledge of Chinese, and served briefly as a prefect in Kansu in the 1880s.[2] Hsi-liang married a woman who reportedly did her best to help him fulfill his ambitions, but apparently only by faithfully executing her household duties and keeping modestly from public view.[3] A brother-in-law, Shan-ch'eng, served as prefect in Honan but, far from advancing Hsi-liang's career, merely managed to embarrass him by serving in the same province at the same time.[4]

Hsi-liang's family did prepare him for a career by providing him with a good education. Although he spoke Mongol as a youth and would retain the language to his death, he learned Chinese both early and well.[5] A precocious student, he moved quickly through the lower levels of the examination system to take the highest examination (the *chin-shih*) in Chinese at the extraordinarily young age of twenty-one. Hsi-liang not only emerged among the 5 percent of the candidates who passed the examination, but also placed well (seventieth in the third class) and was one of only five Mongol bannermen to get the degree in 1874.[6] While skill in handling the Chinese language showed that he had already become partly Sinicized, his success in getting the *chin-shih* marked the beginning of a promising career.

Hsi-liang apparently did not indulge in the common practice of exploiting associations with classmates (*t'ung-nien*) to advance his ambitions. He later served in the same province with the Chinese Bannerman Chao Erh-sun, one of the most capable of late Ch'ing officials, but neither he nor Chao helped each other on the way up the official ladder (see below, chaps. 7, 11, 13). Nor did the young Hsi-liang form close ties with another classmate, the Manchu Bannerman Kuei-lin, with whom he later had brief contact (see below, chap.

8). Hsi-liang also neglected to cultivate the friendly relationship that often linked a student with his examiner (*k'ao-kuan*). His examiner, Wang Hsien-ch'ien, later became one of the outstanding classical scholars of the late Ch'ing, editing numerous works and wielding enormous academic influence. But when Wang asked Hsi-liang to place some of his other students in the administration, Hsi-liang refused, remarking to a friend simply that "It pains me that I have no way to oblige him." [7] He apparently felt he had passed the examination by his own efforts and was indebted to no one.

Given Hsi-liang's reluctance to use personal relationships to his advantage, he was fortunate indeed to obtain an official post within two years of receiving his degree. He followed the standard pattern for middle-ranking *chin-shih* by receiving an appointment at the local level. He was named acting magistrate in 1876 and was sent west of Peking to Shansi province where he would serve for nearly twenty years. In 1877 he was appointed to a more difficult post as supervisor of the likin tax collection in a commercial town. In this post, the fledgling magistrate faced his first administrative challenge. A famine spread over North China from 1877 to 1880, taking an estimated 13 million lives and creating widespread economic and social disorder.[8] According to his superior, he performed well during this crisis, showing himself "aware of right and wrong" in collecting taxes and "outstandingly meritorious" in managing relief.[9] He undoubtedly followed a trend of the time and tightened up the system of public security (*pao-chia*) to maintain peace and order. He probably also supervised public lectures (*hsiang-yüeh*) to restore the people's faith in the future.[10] He was so effective in fighting the famine that he was transferred from district to district to deal with its worst effects.

Hsi-liang's growing reputation as a "good magistrate" might have availed him little along the road to power had he not come to the attention of a higher official whose own career was on the rise. Chang Chih-tung, a brilliant Hanlin scholar who had distinguished himself in domestic administration and foreign policy, had recently come to the attention of the empress dowager. Now in 1881 he was made governor of Shansi.[11] After observing Hsi-liang's conduct in Yang-ch'ü, the capital district, Chang recommended him to the throne as one of five outstanding magistrates among the eighty-eight in the province. He praised him for having "completely wiped out the hoarders of grain and satisfied the merchants and people." [12] With the famine under control in 1882, Chang tried to reform the compulsory labor services that by this time involved oppressive monetary exactions on the people. He appointed Hsi-liang and Yü Lien-san, another of his favorite subordinates, to investigate abuses. Hsi-liang first helped to pinpoint the defects of the system throughout the province. When he then abolished the levies and made up for lost revenue by lending state funds to private banks, Chang praised him for his energy and ingenuity.[13] Chang also opened a campaign against opium and praised Hsi-liang for managing it "according to the laws." He first recommended him to the Grand

Council for preferment, then promoted him two full ranks to become magistrate of an independent department, and finally transferred him to an opium-rich department to enforce the new ban. Chang's confidence in Hsi-liang now became known in the capital.[14]

In addition to classical scholarship and administrative efficiency, Chang Chih-tung was noted for his integrity and frugality. In a letter to a friend at this time, Chang espoused loyalty to the state and valued public over private interests:

> My way of placing myself with regard to the dynasty is this: I respect those who are loyal to the state [kuo-chia], hate those who prey on it, help those who serve it, fight those who harm it. . . . [As for myself, I try] to follow a straight path without wavering, look after public needs without bothering about myself, and hope to assist without seeking fame.[15]

While perhaps a bit boastful, Chang's communication accurately described his private conduct. He wished his subordinates to follow his example and instructed them to cease giving presents to superiors in hopes of getting a promotion.[16] It was probably under Chang's influence that Hsi-liang came to dislike the practice of offering gifts to superiors. He may also have begun at this time to show the concern for frugality which marked his career. Much later, as a governor-general making a substantial salary, he startled a private secretary by appearing with a threadbare jacket covered with patches. "I first wore this," he explained with a chuckle, "when I was a magistrate in Yang-ch'ü over twenty years ago. How could it help being in tatters now?"[17]

When Chang Chih-tung left Shansi in 1884 he did not include Hsi-liang among those subordinates he took with him to deal with French aggression in Vietnam. Left to his own devices, Hsi-liang allowed a criminal to escape punishment and received his first reprimand but soon recovered sufficiently to secure a recommendation to the Grand Council.[18] After seven more years serving in three different departments he was promoted to the more substantial post of prefect in 1892. In the midst of another famine, he was placed in charge of administering relief in the northern part of the province outside the Great Wall. There he had his first experience in governing his fellow Mongols, but he showed the degree of his Sinicization by avoiding all comment on his own people. He later remarked simply that his relations with "subordinates" (who were mostly Manchu bannermen) had been "good."[19] Increasingly Chinese in his outlook and ever more experienced in administration, Hsi-liang continued his gradual rise up the bureaucratic ladder, headed, it seemed, for a career of solid accomplishment but no extraordinary excitement.

The Shantung Experience

In the winter of 1894 Hsi-liang was suddenly transferred to the coastal province of Shantung, which was suffering the full blast of war with Japan. For the next four years, the nearly middle-aged official faced the bitter reality of growing foreign control over China. The Shantung experience affected not only the progress of his career but the development of his ideas and the course of late Ch'ing politics.

Despite Hsi-liang's indifference to personal friendships, his appointment to Shantung resulted from the coincidence of past associations. One of his fellow officials (t'ung-kuan) in Shansi, Li Ping-heng, had gone south with Chang Chih-tung to Kwangsi to help conduct the war against France. Because he had proved himself both militant and capable, Li had been made governor of Shantung and charged with helping to defend Korea from the Japanese. Recalling that Hsi-liang had "hurried around saving lives, working until he was weary and worn" during the famine in Shansi, Li memorialized, asking for his transfer to the Shantung military secretariat (ying-wu-ch'u).[20] The court overlooked Hsi-liang's exclusively domestic experience and named him to the key military post located far out on the peninsula at Yen-t'ai (or Chefoo).

When Hsi-liang arrived in Yen-t'ai he found that the Ch'ing navy was being destroyed by the Japanese at Wei-hai-wei, only sixty miles away, and that the Ch'ing armies were falling back before Japanese ground forces. According to Li Ping-heng, Hsi-liang soon overcame his inexperience, "steadfastly fulfilled the duties of his office, and showed no fear in the midst of the crisis." Li said that he increasingly relied on Hsi-liang's "profound knowledge of military affairs."[21] As a bannerman, Hsi-liang belonged to an organization whose original purpose had been military, and, as a scholar, he was undoubtedly familiar with the Chinese military classics. Of even greater importance, perhaps, were his proved ability to master the details of any office that he held and his presumed concurrence in Chang Chih-tung's belief that a martial spirit could compensate for technical weakness.[22] Colleagues who took less militant stands during this period apparently felt uncomfortable in Shantung. For example, the rising young Ts'en Ch'un-hsüan, who doubted China's ability to resist the Japanese by force, soon left his post at the military secretariat on the excuse of "illness."[23] Whatever the reason, Li Ping-heng so valued Hsi-liang's services that he asked the court for permission to keep him in Shantung permanently. When the court replied by transferring him to another post within the province, Li obtained permission to keep him at Yen-t'ai temporarily so as to make use of his "experienced hand" in military defense.[24]

In his post at Yen-t'ai, Hsi-liang was intimately involved in China's humiliation at the hands of hitherto lightly regarded Japan. The Chinese armies that engaged the enemy in Shantung suffered 2,000 casualties in a few days. A colleague in the military secretariat was given the task of surrendering to the Japanese.[25] Since Hsi-liang's personal code of conduct differed greatly from that of Li Hung-chang, the powerful governor-general and veteran diplomat, he may have shared the widespread belief that corruption in Li's army and navy had contributed to the defeat.[26] Whatever the causes, the results of the disaster were clear. By the Treaty of Shimonoseki, China lost suzerainty over Korea and sovereignty in its own treaty ports. While the huge indemnity provided the foundation for Japan's industrialization, it further sapped China's resources and forced her to borrow from European powers in order to pay it off.[27] The defeat seems to have persuaded Hsi-liang that the foreigners wanted not only trade but also control over Chinese territory.

As Hsi-liang watched China's land slide under foreign control, he took refuge in China's culture, which had yet to suffer from foreign attack. Preoccupied until this time with the everyday matters of public administration, he now began to read the poetry of a scholar named Fan Tang-shih. Fan, who had served as a minor secretary under Li Hung-chang, reacted to defeat by quitting his post and devoting himself to writing melancholy odes on China's latest disaster.[28] Unlike Fan, Hsi-liang decided to remain in office, but he grew to appreciate Fan's poetry, the best of which has been compared with that of the great T'ang masters Li Po and Tu Fu. Hsi-liang also took the highly uncharacteristic step of sending Fan gifts and of asking him to become his personal secretary. Although Fan refused, apparently resolved to influence the world only through his poetry, Hsi-liang continued to read and admire his work[29] This turn inward to the poetic tradition suggested that Hsi-liang had become completely Chinese. It was as a Chinese that he reacted to the Sino-Japanese War and began to share in the nationalist thinking (*kuo-chia chih ssu-hsiang*) that he later traced back to this period.[30] He embraced one of the aesthetic expressions of Chinese civilization as an alternative to the predatory ethic of an increasingly Westernized Japan.

Appointed prefect of I-chou in western Shantung in 1895, Hsi-liang continued to live up to his reputation as the good official. Li Ping-heng repeated Chang Chih-tung's judgment that Hsi-liang was "pure and honest" and added that he was now "experienced in both local administration and military affairs." Li also said that Hsi-liang was "especially attentive to getting and using talent," and thus, by implication, capable of holding higher office. Li concluded that he was also "energetic in loving the people." In other words, he was establishing the rapport with local society that was essential to sound administration. Li lavished this praise on none of the other eleven officials whom he recommended at this time. For example, Hsi-liang's superior, the circuit intendant Yü-hsien, who wielded great financial and judicial authority in western Shantung, became famous for his harsh administration of the laws. Li said that Yü-hsien had gained only the "respect of the people." [31] When Yü-hsien vacated his post to become judicial commissioner of the province, Li acted on Hsi-liang's reputation for benevolence by promoting him to be the new intendant of the Yen-I-Ts'ao-Ch'i circuit.

In this post in western Shantung, Hsi-liang first learned about the growing impact of foreign missionaries on Chinese society. The Christian missionaries of the nineteenth century were much more aggressive than their seventeenth-century predecessors had been. They were apostles not only of Western religion but also of the industrial revolution; they relied not just on the strength of their arguments but also on the protection of foreign military force for their status in China.[32] Since Hsi-liang was loyal to the state and mindful of the people, who generally opposed the missionaries, he tended from the beginning to resent the foreigners' presence in China. His tendency was reinforced by the attitudes of his superiors, Li Ping-heng and Yü-hsien, who also disliked the missionaries. In 1896 Li submitted a famous memorial in which he asked the court to borrow nothing from the West except arms with which to fight the West. Yü-hsien made up for his harshness toward the people by taking their side against the missionaries.[33] These three officials nevertheless knew that, according to the Treaty and Convention of 1860, their duty was to defend the missionaries from attack. In 1896 the powerful secret societies in western Shantung retaliated against the abuses of Chinese converts by attacking missionaries and destroying churches. The loyal Li ordered a firm suppression of the agitation, and the obedient Yü-hsien and Hsi-liang immediately complied. These three officials thereby put down what has since come to be known as the first outbreak of the Boxer movement.[34]

In a second and more notable antiforeign incident, Hsi-liang again helped to carry out the treaties by suppressing the agitators. On 1 November 1897 some Chinese in Ts'ao-chou reacted to further convert abuses by killing two German missionaries. The local magistrate may have favored the agitation, but there is no evidence that Hsi-liang or his superiors encouraged the attack.[35] Since Ts'ao-chou was near the Kiangsu border, news of the incident was picked up first by the officials in that province and conveyed to Li Ping-heng via the Tsungli Yamen (Board of Foreign Affairs) in Peking. The Yamen ordered Li Ping-heng to arrest the agitators and to restore peace in the area. During the next two weeks, Yü-hsien and Hsi-liang complied with Li's instructions by arresting nine men suspected of the killings and by restoring order in Ts'ao-chou.[36] Even the *North China Herald*, the Shanghai English-language newspaper, which generally supported missionaries of whatever nationality, concluded that Hsi-liang and the others had handled the Ts'ao-chou case in complete accord with the relevant treaties.[37] Under ordinary circumstances the foreigners would have demanded an indemnity and considered the case closed.

Unfortunately for Hsi-liang and for China, circumstances in western Shantung were not ordinary—even for the imperialist period. The local bishop, Johann Anzer, had long ago set out to undermine Chinese respect for their own culture, hoping thus to open the way for conversion to Christianity. He had tried to do this by establishing a mission in Ts'ao-chou, the heart of the ancient state of Lu where Confucius was born. To deter the Chinese from harassing the mission, Anzer had earlier obtained the active protection of the growing German navy. A German imperialist as well as a Catholic priest, Anzer had gone so far as to call on the Reich to establish a naval base at Chiao-chou Bay, on the southern coast of Shantung, so as to be better able to protect the mission stations in that province. German commercial interests had gradually warmed to the idea. Since December 1896 the German navy had been waiting for the slightest incident against Germans anywhere in China as a pretext to seize the bay. When an incident occurred right in Shantung and involved some of Anzer's own priests, Kaiser Wilhelm himself called it a "splendid opportunity." [38] Within a week and a half of the killings at Ts'ao-chou, German ships were racing toward Chiao-chou.

Hsi-liang now witnessed a great debate over how to deal with the German advance. Anticipating German designs on the bay, Li Ping-heng had garrisoned it with 1,500 troops. On 14 November he ordered the local commander to deploy his troops and to resist the some 700 Germans who were about to land. The court, however, feared the German navy and countermanded Li's order, instructing the local commander to withdraw. Ignoring Li and obeying Peking, the Chinese troops withdrew and surrendered the strategic bay without firing a shot. Understandably enraged at the commander's retreat, Li pleaded for permission to create a new force under the Ts'ao-chou commander, Wan Pen-hua, who had distinguished himself in fighting the Japanese. When the court warned that hostilities would bring a "calamity," Li retorted angrily that passivity would bring "three calamities." Noting that his subordinates had arrested and punished the offenders at Ts'ao-chou, he characterized the German decision to occupy Chiao-chou as a "calculated insult." He argued that submission to the Germans in this case would set a precedent for others elsewhere. This was the first calamity. The second was that a concession to Germany at Chiao-chou would touch off a scramble among all of the powers to get similar bases until "none of the ports will remain in our hands." The third calamity would be the end of military morale as armies lost all confidence in the courage of their commanders and in their will to defend the country.[39]

The court ignored Li Ping-heng's call for military resistance and instead authorized the great statesman Li Hung-chang to try to save Chiao-chou through diplomacy. Li Hung-chang's first strategy was to wait for the Russians to intervene on China's side against the Germans, but it soon became obvious that they were not interested in pulling China's chestnuts from the fire. The second strategy was to concede all of the German demands on Ts'ao-chou in order to get them to withdraw from Chiao-chou. One of the German demands was the punishment of several local officials who supposedly had encouraged the massacre. The Court deputed Weng T'ung-ho, the influential tutor to the Kuang-hsü emperor, and Chang Yin-huan, a career diplomat associated with Li Hung-chang, to negotiate with the Germans. In December 1897 Weng and Chang secretly agreed to memorialize for the punishment of Li Ping-heng,

Hsi-liang, and Wan Pen-hua.[40] The following month the Grand Council publicly chastised these officials for "not preventing the . . . bandits from rising up." It ordered Li to be demoted two grades, Hsi-liang and Wan to be stripped of ranks, and all three to be transferred from the province.[41] This strategy of concessions on Ts'ao-chou failed when the Germans still refused to leave Chiao-chou.

The German occupation of Chiao-chou destroyed whatever faith Hsi-liang might have had in the good will of the Westerners. He became increasingly convinced that it would be necessary to use military force simply to hold the foreigners to the treaties (which were themselves unequal and which had been imposed on China by force). The Chinese troops that had fought the Sino-Japanese War had lost, but they had at least returned with some honor. The diplomatic strategy pursued against the Germans had failed miserably, and there was evidence that a firm military resistance might have been more successful.[42] Hsi-liang undoubtedly resented the role played by Weng T'ung-ho and Chang Yin-huan in his transfer, and he may have begun to question the patriotism of their patrons, the Kuang-hsü emperor and Li Hung-chang. Instead of being humbled by his transfer, he grew all the more determined to resist foreign intervention in China's domestic affairs.

In May 1898 Hsi-liang was transferred to Shansi, where he spent the summer as a circuit intendant without rank. During this time the imperial tutor, Weng T'ung-ho, and the scholar-philosopher, K'ang Yu-wei, in turn led the young emperor to decree far-reaching reforms to save the country.[43] Hsi-liang's past experiences probably made him highly skeptical of these court reforms. He had served under Chang Chih-tung, who saw the need for moderate reforms, but who was engaged in a covert power struggle with Weng T'ung-ho. Weng's acquiescence in Hsi-liang's transfer must have confirmed Hsi-liang's antipathy to his activities.[44] Hsi-liang had also served under Li Ping-heng, who saw the need for a new militancy to save China but who did not share K'ang Yu-wei's desire to change institutions. K'ang's tendency to enlist the assistance of foreign missionaries and to base his reforms on foreign models cannot have appealed to Hsi-liang, who had come to hate the missionaries and to reject foreign modes of behavior.[45] In more practical terms, as a self-made man who had climbed all the rungs of the official ladder, Hsi-liang had little in common with the eccentric scholar who had catapulted to fame overnight under the aegis ot the Kuang-hsü Emperor.

Hsi-liang was still in Shansi when the Empress Dowager Tz'u-hsi, fearing that K'ang's party was going to eliminate her, moved with her usual skill to reassert the full authority she had relinquished a decade earlier.[46] When K'ang arranged with the judicial commissioner of Chihli, Yüan Shih-k'ai, to assassinate the Governor-General Jung-lu, Yüan revealed the plot to the intended victim, who was loyal to the empress dowager. Jung-lu was thus able to strike first against the Reformers and to drive them from the country.[47]

Despite his obvious indebtedness to Yüan Shih-k'ai, Jung-lu was close enough to Hsi-liang to warn him that Yüan was a "hawk" and was "not to be trusted." [48] The empress dowager, who had retained authority over appointments, had earlier shown faith in Hsi-liang by naming him temporarily as financial commissioner. Now, two weeks after resuming the regency on 21 September, she promoted him to be judicial commissioner and restored his rank.[49] When Hsi-liang sent in the usual memorial of thanks, he received the highly coveted rescript: "Come in for an audience." [50] Whatever his attitude toward the Reformers, Hsi-liang obtained his first audience in the wake of their demise.

Hsi-liang went to Peking and attended audiences with the empress dowager three times. The sixty-four-year-old grand lady of the late Ch'ing must have been impressed with the forty-five-year-old Hsi-liang. She decided to use him to help fill the gap created by the purge of the Reform party. In February 1899 she appointed him judicial commissioner of Hunan to serve under his admirers, Governor Yü Lien-san and Governor-General Chang Chih-tung. Before he could leave Peking, she promoted him to the even more responsible post of financial commissioner. Hsi-liang was so confident of his new standing at court that he dared to ask for another audience, which was granted. This time he advised Tz'u-hsi to hold firmly to the regency. As he later recorded, he told her:

> When Her Majesty the Empress Dowager was living at I Ho Yüan [the palace in the suburbs of Peking], the people in the empire were uneasy. It was only after she returned to the capital in September that their minds were calmed again. I beg that hereafter Her Majesty remain in the capital and stop all construction [at I Ho Yüan] which is not critical.[51]

By this indirect means, Hsi-liang pledged to repay Tz'u-hsi's confidence in him by showing loyalty to her. At the same time, he chided her gently for spending badly needed military funds to reconstruct the imperial palace. Just as he had risen to power on his own merits, so he would now enter high office on his own terms.

Having climbed the bureaucratic ladder with little assistance from family, colleagues, or teachers, Hsi-liang remained apart from the coteries of officials around his patrons and superiors. Through education and experience he had become completely Sinicized and he obviously appreciated some of the higher forms of Chinese civilization. At home he had begun to acquire skill in handling subordinates and dealing with the populations under his control. Abroad he came into contact with foreign power and became antiforeign as the foreigners violated their own laws as well as China's to interfere in Chinese politics and seize Chinese territory. Immersed in Chinese culture and responsible for Chinese territory, Hsi-liang was learning more every year about the need to defend both from foreign power if he was to remain an effective official. By sheer force of circumstances, the worthy official was developing into a budding patriot.

Part 1: Resistance in North China, 1900–1903

As Hsi-liang was rising to power, the Chinese order that he treasured was succumbing to the superior force of foreign empires. The Ch'ing state, centuries old, was coming under criticism from some Chinese. Domestic administration, previously autonomous, was being encroached upon by the foreigners. Some vigorous approach was required if Hsi-liang was to defend Chinese order and autonomy.

The approach that Hsi-liang chose, resistance, was well suited to the circumstances of North China, where he served from 1900 to 1903. For millennia the central plain (*chung-yüan*) had been the cultural and political hub of China, rivaled only in recent centuries by the cultural and commercial center of the Southeast. North China boasted a centuries' long tradition of local military organization that could be utilized as a basis for popular resistance to foreign intrusion. At the heart of China, the central plain symbolized the autonomy of all of China. Should the outsiders successfully extend their influence there, the rest of China would have little hope for survival.

In three successive posts, Hsi-liang became an outspoken advocate of firm resistance against foreign encroachment. Named governor of Shansi in the wake of the Boxer movement, he led imperial armies from several provinces in resisting the Allied punitive campaigns against scores of villages in Chihli. Transferred to Honan just after the Boxer indemnity was imposed, he dealt with agitation against local indemnities and British mining concessions. Appointed military lieutenant-governor of Jehol, he sought to bring order to an area plagued by banditry and tried to resist foreign commercial penetration.

JEHOL

CHAHAR

□ Ch'eng-te

GREAT WALL

GREAT

□ Peking

Tientsin

Gulf of Chihli

Tai ●

Lu-Han Railway

● Pao-ting

CHIHLI

● Cheng-ting

T'ai-yüan □

P'ing-ting ●

● Huo-lu

SHANSI

Yen-t'ai
(Chefoo) ●

Wei-hai-wei ●

SHENSI

□ Chi-nan

SHANTUNG

Chiao-chou
(Kiaochow) ●

● P'ing-yang

Chang-te ●

● Yen-chou

YELLOW

RIVER

GRAND

I-chou ●

SEA

Wei-hui ●

Ts'ao-chou ●

Huai-ch'ing ●

K'ai-feng ●

CANAL

□ Sian

YELLOW

HONAN

Nan-yang ●

● Pi-yang

HUPEH

Map 1. North China

2: MISSIONS AND ALLIES IN SHANSI

Before his appointment to Shansi, Hsi-liang served briefly in Hunan under his patron Chang Chih-tung and his former superior Yü Lien-san. During this time, he opposed the remnant Reform movement of K'ang Yu-wei and sympathized with the Boxer movement sponsored by an important faction at court. The service in Hunan prepared him well for the coming responsibilities as governor when he would face both missionary demands for reparations in Shansi and Allied military campaigns in Chihli. Although his own attitudes and those of the court were clearly in flux, he ultimately would have to choose between maintaining his convictions and advancing his career.

The Hunan Period

As financial commissioner of Hunan with the right to memorialize the throne directly, Hsi-liang for the first time was able to express his reservations about the Reformers under K'ang Yu-wei, who had either fled the country or retreated into the provinces. In May 1900 he repeated his request that the empress dowager remain in Peking. This time he stated his reasons most forcefully:

> The danger lies not only with the foreign countries but is also hidden within. There are Chinese who profess to be officials and servants but who actually follow the barbarians and the revolutionaries. Moreover, they are everywhere. Only if we coerce them by strictly enforcing the law will we deter them from continuing their activities. We must strengthen the base area, guard scrupulously against them, turn danger into safety, and avoid any unexpected crisis.[1]

Hsi-liang's critique of the Reformers was in line with the empress dowager's position at this time. It also had some basis in fact. K'ang had not only associated closely with foreigners, but had even sought their assistance in returning to power under the emperor.[2] Other Reformers, such as T'ang Ts'ai-ch'ang, were planning a rebellion in Hunan that would break out three months later.[3] Hsi-liang apparently played no role in suppressing the Reformers in Hunan, but later as governor of Shansi he captured two

members of K'ang's party and executed them. He also asked rewards for the
local officials involved, an act that revealed his enthusiasm for carrying out the
empress dowager's wishes in this matter.[4]

Hsi-liang showed more sympathy for the Boxers who won court support
during the summer. Despite Hu-kuang Governor-General Chang Chih-tung's
commitment to defend the missionaries in the Yangtze valley, Hunan
Governor Yü Lien-san posted the court's declaration of war on all foreigners
in June 1900. Hsi-liang probably agreed with Yü that the missionaries should
be expelled, and he doubtless helped him post the declaration of war
throughout the province. When the declaration resulted in an attack on two
Italian missionaries in July, however, Hsi-liang had already left his post. When
the powers later investigated the incident, they called for the punishment of
Yü but allowed Hsi-liang to escape censure.[5] Thus Hsi-liang was not a
prominent pro-Boxer official. He seems to have felt that the times required
steady resistance against the foreigners, not a dramatic offensive which China
lacked the power to sustain. Later, in Shansi, he would crack down on Boxer
bands and would finally conform to the new court policy of considering them
"bandits."

Hsi-liang next became preoccupied with the large Allied expeditionary force
sent by twelve nations to relieve the Boxers' siege of the foreign legations in
Peking.[6] When the court called on the various provincial officials to send
forces to guard the capital against the 16,000 foreign troops, Hsi-liang wired
Governor-General Chang Chih-tung asking permission to go north to help in
the defense.[7] He thus followed the example of his erstwhile patron, Li
Ping-heng, now imperial inspector, and the governor of Kiangsu, Lu Ch'uan-
lin, who led troops to defend the capital. Although Chang Chih-tung, the
governor-general of Liang-Kiang, Liu K'un-i, and the commissioner of the
southern ports, Sheng Hsüan-huai, agreed to keep the southern provinces out
of the Boxer war, they remained loyal to the court and wished to show their
concern for its safety.[8] When Hsi-liang arrived in Wu-ch'ang, Chang ignored
his disclaimer that he "did not know anything about military affairs" and
praised him in a memorial as "loyal, brave, enthusiastic, and keenly aware of
the situation." He placed him in charge of the best troops in Hunan and
Hupeh, allowed him his pick of officers, and instructed him to go north to
protect the court.[9] The story was that Chang held a dinner in Hsi-liang's
honor, fell asleep over his wine, and was still snoozing soundly as Hsi-liang
slipped away, crossed the Yangtze with his troops, and headed off to find the
court.[10]

When Hsi-liang reached Chihli in August, the forces under Li Ping-heng
and others were being defeated. Peking itself fell to the Allies on 14 August.
On the next day the empress dowager, together with the emperor and a small
group of courtiers and officials, fled Peking and headed west through Chihli to
northern Shansi. Hsi-liang met with the Chihli Governor-General and Grand

Councillor Jung-lu, who had been left behind to deal with the foreigners. They decided to deploy their troops in western Chihli along the Shansi border to prevent the Allies from pursuing the court.[11] Hsi-liang then went west to the capital of Shansi, T'ai-yüan, to join Lu Ch'uan-lin and others in paying court to the empress dowager, who was quartered there. On 23 September Chang Chih-tung memorialized, recommending that Hsi-liang be appointed a guard (kung-wei) to assist the court as it retreated further westward.[12] Perhaps remembering Hsi-liang's outstanding performance as a Shansi local official, the empress dowager decided instead to name him governor of Shansi. She showed the extent of her confidence by charging him with concurrent responsibility for coordinating the defense of Shansi and Chihli as she withdrew deeper into the interior to Shensi.[13]

Hsi-liang thus became overnight the senior official in Shansi, with full authority over the province, as well as a military figure on the national scene with control over some 10,000 troops from six provinces.[14] He dedicated himself to defending Shansi not as an end in itself but as a "shield for Shensi" where the court—symbol of the nation—was now located. He also began to speak out regarding the larger defense of China. His new standing brought him into competition with the governors-general in the South and with the newly appointed imperial commissioner in Peking, Li Hung-chang, who favored conciliation of the foreigners in order to restore peace and prevent a harsh settlement.[15] When Liu K'un-i threatened to cut off funds to the Liang-Kiang forces under Hsi-liang's command unless the court sued for peace, Hsi-liang replied that Liu was "loyal to the essence of the country. . . . Certainly he will pay heed to the whole picture (lit. the whole situation, ch'üan-chü)." The court accepted Hsi-liang's suggestion and admonished Liu not to "allow provincial boundaries to divide you off." [16] In his first effort to invoke the national interest as the rationale for policy, Hsi-liang had registered a moderate success.

Militant Resistance

During his six months in Shansi, Hsi-liang faced the claims of the foreign missionaries and the threats of the foreign military to invade westward into Shansi. The previous governor, Hsi-liang's former superior in Shantung, Yü-hsien, had permitted the massacre of 178 foreigners and 2,000 Chinese converts and had even struck one old foreign missionary with his own hand. The missionary community had reacted with loud cries for revenge, and Queen Victoria had demanded that Yü-hsien be removed from his post.[17] Even after Yü-hsien was dismissed, the missionaries' demands for retribution continued to mount. On the military front the situation was also dangerous. Some 7,500 troops of the Allied expeditionary force were marching west from Peking, approaching Shansi along several routes. The recently appointed general commander, German Field Marshal Alfred Count von Waldersee, kept the Allies' purpose ominously vague, later noting only that "apart from punishing the Chinese our policy had no definite aims." [18] The missionaries' claims and the military expeditions were to be closely related.

Hsi-liang's general strategy was to treat the missionary claims and military threats separately and to pose militant resistance to both. He dealt first with his former superior, Yü-hsien, with whom he had earlier shared the humiliation of being transferred from Shantung at the foreigners' request. Liu K'un-i and Sheng Hsüan-huai wired the court that Yü-hsien alone had been responsible for the massacres and should be punished severely in order to keep the Allies from invading Shansi.[19] Chang Chih-tung adopted the same view and even informed the British that Yü-hsien had committed suicide by swallowing gold leaf. When this rumor proved false, Chang promised the British to press for his execution if the Allies refrained from invading Shansi.[20] In contrast to his southern colleagues, Hsi-liang was impressed by the extent of popular support for Yü-hsien in Shansi. According to a missionary, when Yü-hsien had left the province, he had been "escorted by the people, gentry and scholars, with every expression of regret and respect." [21] Hsi-liang wired the court that Yü-hsien had "captured the minds of the people" and stressed, in words reminiscent of those of the empress dowager in June, that during a crisis it is "most important to bind up and unify the minds of the people." [22] On these grounds and on the more practical one that Yü-hsien's return to Shansi would only attract the Allies to the province, Hsi-liang refused to take responsibility for the punishment of the dismissed official. He was supported in his stand only by a Hanlin compiler, Wang Lung-wen, who declared that Yü-hsien had merely carried out court orders and should not be punished for having done so.

While defending Yü-hsien, Hsi-liang moved decisively to suppress the Boxer secret societies that had led the attack on the foreigners and converts. He soon reported that he had executed eighty Boxers and had proscribed the display of Boxer symbols and placards. He ordered local officials in Shansi to protect the remaining foreigners and stated that as a result the "people . . . do not dare create further disturbances." [23] He responded favorably to British pleas to supply the remaining foreigners in Shansi with escorts to the coast and later reported that he had spent 2,500 tls. (or about U. S. $1,800.) for this purpose. He also took steps to aid the converts who had been driven from their homes and were suffering from the recurrent famine in the province. He stoutly refused, however, to discuss the matter of reparations until the foreigners ceased their advance and agreed to terminate hostilities.[24]

Hsi-liang was soon able to persuade the court to accept his point of view. The duty of punishing Yü-hsien and the opprobrium of angering the people of Shansi fell to others. In November Grand Councillor Jung-lu yielded to pressure from the southern governors-general and banished Yü-hsien to

Kansu; later he carried out Chang Chih-tung's promise and had him executed.[25] When Hsi-liang was pressured by the governor of Hupeh to provide more relief for the converts, he wired the court asking for a special edict "to demonstrate the real intention of the dynasty to protect [the converts], prevent disorders, and facilitate peace discussions." This time his effort to get the court behind him had mixed results. The Grand Council duly noted that he had restored the peace in Shansi but warned that "some local officials may have relapsed into carelessness and some bandit gangs may have created further disorders." It approved of the measures Hsi-liang had taken so far but urged him to go even further and punish local officials who failed to comply with the new court policy.[26]

Hsi-liang next turned to the Allied forces advancing on Shansi's border. Here again he had to contend with the views of those officials who favored conciliation and withdrawal. Liu K'un-i argued that the foreigners' modern weaponry rendered traditional strategic concepts outmoded; Chang Chih-tung doubted that the several thousand Chinese troops in Chihli could possibly resist the "large Allied army"; and Li Hung-chang advocated welcoming the foreign troops as they advanced and settling all outstanding cases with them on the spot.[27] Since Li Ping-heng had committed suicide with the fall of Peking, Hsi-liang was almost alone in advocating a firm military resistance against the foreign advance. Wiring Chang Chih-tung that he "could not allow [the Allies] to come through the pass and alarm the court," Hsi-liang stationed a large number of troops at the town of Huo-lu in Cheng-ting district, Chihli. He then memorialized:

> In my humble opinion, Pao-ting and Cheng-ting are interrelated like lips and teeth. Huo-lu is the doorway to the mountains. If arrangements at Pao-ting are amiss, Huo-lu will be shaken and T'ai-yüan endangered. If we do not send reinforcements to defend Huo-lu, we will not be able to bolt the door of eastern Shansi.[28]

Hsi-liang seems here to have followed the classical strategy of placing an army on "key ground" that would be highly dangerous for the enemy to attack.[29] At the time, this strategy was supported mainly by the president of the Censorate, P'u-liang, who by the very nature of his office was expected to speak frankly and who argued for total resistance no matter what the consequences.[30]

But Hsi-liang's strategy received partial endorsement from the court in late October when the Grand Council wired Li Hung-chang that the imperial army at Huo-lu would react to any Allied advance against it. The council continued:

> If the foreign troops first open fire with cannon and rifles, we have ordered all the battalions to resist with force. If this results in a disturbance to the peace, it cannot be said that we began the hostilities. . . . Presently we are in the midst of discussing peace, and yet the foreign troops continue to push westward. What, after all, can their motives be? [31]

The council then wired Hsi-liang asking him to assess the Allies' motives and to resist their advance.

> Although it is of course not permitted to undertake this business rashly or carelessly in a way that will damage the chances of peace, still we cannot allow them to advance to a point where the whole picture will be irreparably damaged.[32]

The council thus authorized the difficult strategy of resistance short of hostilities.

During the next several months of the fall of 1900 and the spring of 1901, Hsi-liang directed the resistance against scores of punitive expeditions undertaken by thousands of Allied troops in western Chihli.[33] In one of these incidents, Chinese converts helped guide a combined force of German and French troops along the middle route toward central Shansi. Hsi-liang sent the Shansi financial commissioner, Sheng-yün, out to stop them. Sheng-yün complied, but his raw recruits disobeyed orders and fled the scene of battle, causing the court to inquire who had opened hostilities and why the Chinese forces had disintegrated. Hsi-liang explained that the foreign commanders had ignored a Chinese envoy and opened fire first, that Sheng-yün had resisted valiantly and narrowly escaped death at the front, and that the troops had been incapacitated by a blinding morning sun. He noted that he had sent Sheng-yün back to hold positions in Chihli and concluded: "We can only defend [this area] even more carefully; we do not dare to allow them to advance further." The court ignored the fanciful explanation for retreat and supported Hsi-liang's firm strategy of resistance. It ordered him to "control and disperse the converts, all the while protecting them so as not to give the foreigners a pretext [for advancing]." It also showed its continued confidence in Sheng-yün by encouraging him to take "extreme precautions to hold his position." [34] The strategy of resistance survived its first test.

Hsi-liang's involvement in a second clash was indirect but nonetheless illustrative of his strategy. A French task force had gone to the Chihli provincial capital of Pao-ting in early October and had escorted from the area missionaries who had been protected from the Boxers by the Chihli financial commissioner, T'ing-yung. Despite this, another force of German and French troops entered the city later in the month. They refused to discuss a settlement with local officials but instead set up a military court, which sentenced four high officials, including T'ing-yung, to death. They also confiscated 240,000 tls. found in the provincial treasury, tore down temples and walls, imposed a fine of 100,000 tls., and garrisoned 3,200 troops in the city for the winter. The new governor-general of Chihli, Li Hung-chang, had earlier asked for T'ing-yung's demotion to forestall the expedition, and he now merely protested mildly when the Allies executed T'ing-yung in Pao-ting.[35]

Hsi-liang had previously displayed an attitude toward the Boxers quite similar to that of T'ing-yung, and he had recently met him in Pao-ting to discuss military strategy. He now memorialized, granting the need for caution but attacking Li's policy:

> When the people of Shansi survey the scene in Chihli, their righteous wrath boils up. Wherever we welcomed [the Allies] they killed and defiled, stirred up trouble and opened hostilities. The [Boxer] bandits are certainly an obstacle to negotiations and [their activities] relate directly to the safety of the imperial house. But by the same token, when many officials die, how does *this* bear on the general peace?—or on the welfare of millions of people? [36]

The court agreed with Hsi-liang's assessment of the Pao-ting affair. It assailed the executions of officials as "outrageous and saddening," rejected the foreigners' attempt to "encroach this way on our self-government," and later characterized the whole incident as "extremely damaging to our national prestige" (*kuo-t'i*).[37]

Three other incidents during November and December 1900 confirmed Hsi-liang in his strategy of militant resistance. The French commander at Pao-ting, General Voyron, recommended to the French minister in Peking that he be allowed to lead French forces west through Cheng-ting to put pressure on T'ai-yüan. The minister vetoed the recommendation, however, arguing that the continual Chinese build-up of troops at Huo-lu would mean stiff resistance against any such advance.[38] In another case further north, the Germans advanced toward the Shansi border only to be rebuffed by forces under the command of a general who ignored Li Hung-chang's advice to withdraw and followed Hsi-liang's orders to resist.[39] Such was the general momentum of Hsi-liang's policy that even when it suffered a setback he was able to persuade the court of its continuing validity. The French learned that the Chinese troops at Huo-lu were conveying supplies from South China northwest to the Chinese troops in Shansi. They decided to attack Huo-lu to interdict the flow of provisions and weaken the Chinese forces to the west. Hsi-liang interpreted their advance on Huo-lu, which he had called indispensable to the defense of Shansi, as evidence of "their clear intention to invade further west." Alarmed, he ordered a firm defense of the town. Although the Chinese troops apparently fought well, they lost the town and were forced to fall back to a nearby village. After the French took Huo-lu, they found the neighboring village "solidly entrenched by numerous troops supplied with modern arms." Partly because the French advance was largely a police action and partly because the Chinese were so well prepared, the French decided against any further advance and garrisoned their forces in Huo-lu for the winter.[40]

Hsi-liang faced his greatest crisis in early 1901 when the Allied general commander, von Waldersee, threatened a major invasion westward into Shansi. The Germans had been among the most avid advocates of punitive expeditions because they had lost their minister during the siege of the legations and had arrived too late to help relieve the legations. As negotiations dragged on in Peking between the foreign ministers and the Chinese plenipotentiaries, von Waldersee became impatient for more military action. The kaiser had given him a free hand to decide which punitive expeditions were necessary, and von Waldersee now conceived the idea of a major expedition to Shansi. This would presumably encourage the Chinese to come to a quick agreement in Peking. Failing that, it might precipitate the partition of China.[41] Von Waldersee's plan posed the gravest threat to Chinese sovereignty since the first contacts with European military power in the 1840s.

Von Waldersee was given his excuse for action in early February. The foreign ministers in Peking demanded, among other things, restoration of the good names of certain anti-Boxer officials who had been executed in 1900, the posthumous disgrace of some pro-Boxer officials (such as Li Ping-heng), and the execution of other pro-Boxer officials. When the court refused all of the ministers' demands, von Waldersee announced a six-day expedition westward to Shansi and possibly to Shensi. Because the Russians were preoccupied with seizing Manchuria and the Americans were involved with pacifying the Philippines, both powers opposed this expedition. The British, however, favored it so long as their own troops could stay in Chihli, and the French, not to be outdone by their European rivals, supported it and agreed to participate.[42] The prospects for European control over all of China had never been so real.

Once again the leading officials differed over how to deal with the foreigners' demands. Liu K'un-i, Sheng Hsüan-huai, and Li Hung-chang warned that the Allies were determined that all of their demands be met to the letter, thus implying that rigid diplomacy would lead to military disaster. Hsi-liang did not comment on the negotiations but ordered troops under Wan Pen-hua, the commander who had been transferred from Shantung during the Chiao-chou incident, to advance into Chihli to meet the German troops. On 20 February Wan's men met the Germans, stopped their advance, and managed to inflict some casualties on them while losing many of their own men.[43] The court continued to refuse many of the ministers' demands.[44] In the face of Hsi-liang's resistance and the court's intransigence, von Waldersee finally called off his expedition on 21 February, saving face by asserting falsely that all of the ministers' demands had been met.[45] Hsi-liang had supported the court in resisting the threats of the Allied commander who has since achieved high standing in the demonology of Chinese nationalism.[46] By so doing he not only helped save the reputation of such militant patriots as Li Ping-heng but also contributed directly to the defense of China's territorial integrity in its hour of greatest peril.

Dismissal from Shansi

During the spring of 1901 Hsi-liang's strategy toward the missionaries came under increasing pressure. At the request of missionaries who had lived in

Shansi, the Italian and American ministers in Peking demanded that Hsi-liang take better care of the several thousand Christians who were supposedly suffering under "deplorable conditions." [47] Hsi-liang replied that he had ordered local officials to supply relief to the converts and that six had already complied. The magistrate of Yang-ch'ü had granted tax immunity to the 6,000 converts of that district and was distributing grain and money to those suffering from the famine. [48] Hsi-liang established an office to handle missionary cases and then transformed it into a bureau of foreign affairs (yang-wu chü) patterned on one established in the 1880s by Chang Chih-tung. He appointed an official knowledgeable about the treaties to run it. [49] The converts of Shansi nonetheless continued to attack his policies and to call for foreign intervention. One wrote a letter to the foreign press charging that the governor's orders had no effect because "the people do not dread the threatened punishments." He concluded that "the ignorant people here can by no means be controlled" unless foreign troops came to the province. [50] In early March a Chinese-language newspaper in the treaty ports, which was run by a foreign missionary, planted the rumor that the ministers in Peking were secretly demanding the removal of Hsi-liang from Shansi. The foreign press eagerly picked up the rumor and spread it, hoping that it would come true. [51]

Hsi-liang's refusal to allow the Allies to invade Shansi also began to draw criticism. Li Hung-chang, who had previously used Hsi-liang's recalcitrance as an excuse for rebuffing the foreigners, interpreted the von Waldersee crisis as a near brush with disaster. He now began to transmit with approval German requests that Hsi-liang withdraw the forces (now numbering some 25,000) stationed in Chihli. Hsi-liang refused Li's suggestion and argued that the loss of Chihli simply had no place in his strategic plans. [52] This time Hsi-liang was unable to win the court to his view. The Grand Council at Sian agreed that the Allies were basically "inscrutable" in their aims but sided with Li by authorizing the withdrawal of all troops from northern Chihli. [53] Hsi-liang held out until the Germans promised not to take advantage of the withdrawal by penetrating Shansi, but he finally consented to withdraw troops across the border. When the French in southern Chihli insisted that the Chinese troops facing them also withdraw, Li Hung-chang bypassed Hsi-liang and instructed the local commanders to comply. When Hsi-liang countermanded Li's order, the conflict between the two officials became irreconcilable. It is possible that Li began to pressure the court to consider sanctions against Hsi-liang. [54]

Hsi-liang further jeopardized his position as governor by differing with the court over how to deal with officials who had previously favored the Boxer movement. The previous year the British minister, Ernest Satow, had demanded that the court decree the dismissal of thirteen such officials who were still serving in Shansi. [55] Hsi-liang had delayed any action on these men until he received an edict calling for their censure in January 1901. Even when court policy was made clear, he degraded only one official for believing in "the usefulness of bandits," while he dismissed scores for not resisting the Allied expeditions. In early March the court urged him to take further steps, and he impeached five officials for "poor management" of mission cases. Only one of these had appeared on the British minister's list, however, and the term "poor" was left discreetly undefined.[56] Hsi-liang's difference with the court on this matter came to a head when the court complied with British requests and ordered the arrest of an intendant who had been implicated in the killing of a British surveyor in 1900. Hsi-liang delayed a long time in carrying out the order and, once he had finally arrested the intendant, allowed him to escape. Amazed that Hsi-liang could be so openly contemptuous of a court order, the Grand Council instructed the Board of Civil Appointments to discuss his action and to find a fitting punishment.[57]

Hsi-liang's unwillingness to accede to foreign demands in the face of military threats played directly into the hands of his rival from Shantung days, Ts'en Ch'un-hsüan. Having rallied to the empress dowager early in July 1900, Ts'en had been rewarded with the governorship of Shensi, a post in which he enjoyed direct access to the throne at Sian. During the preceding six months, Ts'en had consistently opposed Hsi-liang's militant resistance against the missionaries and Allies, calling first for the disgrace of Yü-hsien and then for the punishment of Sheng-yün.[58] As the Allies advanced during February and early March, Ts'en repeatedly attended audiences with the empress dowager and suggested that Hsi-liang should "solve the mission cases so as not to allow [the Allies] a pretext for invading." [59] When the Board of Civil Appointments made its report concerning the escaped intendant, Tz'u-hsi reluctantly decided to remove Hsi-liang. On 13 March 1901, Hsi-liang was replaced by the more conciliatory Ts'en Ch'un-hsüan.[60] His persistence in resisting the foreigners had cost him his first major post with policy-making authority.

As governor of Shansi and coordinator of the imperial forces in North China, Hsi-liang had proved that he valued the defense of the country over the progress of his own career. Given the extent of foreign power in North China and the widespread feeling among many Chinese that resistance to it was futile, the length of Hsi-liang's Shansi tour was more surprising than its ultimate end. While he had retained the initiative in settling missionary cases and punishing subordinates, his successor was forced to concede missionary claims, which placed the province under strong foreign influence for the next forty-five years. He had limited the Allies' depredations in Chihli and kept them from Shansi, while his successor was tricked into allowing them to advance deep into Shansi, and they withdrew from that position only because of the wet weather of early summer.[61] Hsi-liang achieved these modest successes partly because his plea for a militant resistance struck a responsive chord among those at court who took pride in earlier efforts to resist the foreigners.[62] So energetically did he imbue his colleagues and subordinates with militancy that one general (ironically, a relative of Liu K'un-i) aspired to become a second Yüeh Fei, the heroic commander who had resisted the Jurched invaders during the Sung dynasty.[63] Hsi-liang vigorously protected such men when they were attacked by less stout-hearted rivals; he thus earned their personal devotion and encouraged them to act according to their principles.[64]

After his experience with the Reform and Boxer movements, Hsi-liang had developed his own view of militant resistance. He had defended the "imperial house" but also the "larger picture" and the "national prestige." Aware of the classical notions of military strategy, he frequently invoked the ancient concepts of the "lips" that protect the "teeth" and one province that "shields" another. He showed real concern with "binding up the minds of the people" and with giving direction to the people's "righteous wrath." He began to cooperate with "public-spirited and upright local elite" (*kung-cheng shen-ch'i*) in raising funds and creating militia to defend their homes and their country.[65] Having refined his own understanding of the national interest, he began to search for that popular support which was vital for translating his vision into reality.

3: INDEMNITIES AND CONCESSIONS IN HONAN

In his next major post as governor of Honan, Hsi-liang found that the Boxer indemnities were draining the treasury and causing suffering among the people. Foreigners had obtained large mining concessions in north Honan and were demanding others in the south. During his term at the provincial capital of K'ai-feng, he first showed his sympathy with Honanese agitation against the indemnities and then tried to get local support for reclaiming economic rights (*li-ch'üan*) in the province. In doing so, he became further involved in the politics of resistance.

Before receiving the Honan post, Hsi-liang had been named governor of Hupeh by the Grand Council, but the French and British ministers in Peking had intervened against him.[1] At the same time the empress dowager's favorite eunuch, Li Lien-ying, indulged in his usual practice of demanding bribes of new appointees and requested a "gift" from Hsi-liang. Hsi-liang had not pledged his loyalty to Tz'u-hsi in order to line the pockets of her favorites. He adamantly refused.[2] The influence of the foreigners and the eunuch resulted in withdrawal of the Hupeh appointment.

After Hsi-liang's integrity had lost him this post, his reputation for frugality won him another. The grand councillor, Lu Ch'uan-lin, who had become his main supporter at court, "energetically recommended" him to the empress dowager. In May 1901 Hsi-liang was named director-general of the Yellow River Conservancy with an office in K'ai-feng, Honan.[3] Once a key post for controlling the shipment of grain on the Grand Canal and for maintaining the Yellow River, the director-generalship had degenerated into a sinecure since the court had begun to transport grain by sea and the Yellow River had shifted its course to the north of Shantung. Earlier efforts to reform the office, including one in 1898, had failed because of opposition from certain boards in Peking and from the Honan governor, who feared that any change might bring him more work.[4]

Hsi-liang memorialized that the administration was permeated with corruption and waste. He argued that the court's recent commutation of grain tribute into silver had eliminated the last excuse for maintaining the director-generalship. To win the support of the incumbent Honan governor, Sung-shou, he explained that responsibility for supervising the work on the Yellow River had originally lain with the governor and that a reversion to this previous arrangement would not saddle him with so much extra work as to make him "bow under the burden." To persuade the boards that the time had come for reform, he spoke with the cautious spirit of reform that the empress dowager had begun to embrace since her journey through the country.

> I respectfully submit that normally when the dynasty established an office and divided up responsibility, each office had its special function; a combination of many policies and many efforts led to a great result.
>
> But when the winds of change are blowing, we must naturally act according to the times; often we must make reforms. . . . I therefore suggest that the director-general-ship of the Ho-tung River Conservancy be abolished according to the procedure in Shantung and that its functions be turned over to the concurrent management of the Honan governor.[5]

The boards and the newly created Bureau of Government Affairs (*Cheng-wu ch'u*) endorsed the proposal. They stated that Hsi-liang, as an "on-the-spot witness," doubtless knew the "real situation." [6]

In making this reform, Hsi-liang hoped to achieve both economy and efficiency. Since he was anxious to save funds, he carried out the cutback in administration almost immediately, providing a striking contrast with the notoriously corrupt director-general of grain transport, who took three years to carry out an order to abolish his post.[7] Then noting that his aim was "not only to save some salaries but also to obtain better administration," he combined the dismissal of dozens of officials, hundreds of officers, and a thousand soldiers with programs to improve the capacity of the officials and officers who remained.[8] He increased the salaries of officials responsible for dredging the river and repairing its banks and set up a special new office to "facilitate the travel of the merchants and to protect the fields of the people." [9] Perhaps Hsi-liang also hoped that by abolishing this irrelevant post he might obtain a more challenging position elsewhere.

Indemnities

When the empress dowager passed through Honan on her way back to Peking, she awarded Hsi-liang just such a position, naming him "concurrent" governor of Honan. In this post he was well placed to carry out his suggested reforms and to make sure that the reduction in personnel did not jeopardize supervision of the treacherous Yellow River. In March 1902 the court expressed its appreciation of his efforts by appointing him substantive governor of Honan. He was once more back in the thick of provincial administration.

Hsi-liang no sooner took office than he found that the accumulating indemnities had drained the provincial treasury of funds for administration. He discovered that funds previously earmarked for education were now going to help pay back the loans contracted to settle the Japanese indemnity of 1895.[10] He was able to found a provincial university (ta-hsüeh t'ang) to train primary and secondary school teachers, but he lacked the money to hire any foreign instructors to teach new subjects.[11] When he turned to the military, he learned that funds that formerly had gone to the army were being used to help pay off the 450 million tls. of the Boxer indemnity. Honan's annual share of the remittances was set at 900,000 tls. Hsi-liang planned to raise 120,000 tls. of this sum by eliminating ten of the thirty-nine battalions in Honan and another 180,000 tls. by terminating annual military assistance to Shantung.[12] When the court allowed the cutback in Honan but vetoed it in Shantung, he was unable to make reforms in the forces that remained. He could disburse only a pathetic 3,000 tls. to the provincial arsenal for the purchase of equipment in Shanghai.[13]

Hsi-liang also found that local, informal indemnities, imposed by missionaries on the spot, greatly increased the burden on the people. When the missionaries had returned to Honan in late 1901, they had availed themselves fully of official protection. One missionary said that he had made his "reoccupation of North Honan at the request of" Governor Sung-shou and had been given a reception by the magistrate that was "all we could ask." [14] Once returned, the missionaries had made clear that they expected compensation for the attacks against them during the Boxer movement. The Protestants in North Honan had claimed damages of 170,000 tls., and an intendant had already agreed to pay that sum. The French bishop of South Honan had demanded 200,000 tls. in reparations and the former governor had promised to pay it.[15] According to one foreign source, some missionaries compounded the burden by making "unnecessary exactions on both converts [and] nonconverts." [16]

The Honanese, who had a long tradition of opposition to oppression, reacted particularly vigorously against these indemnities. Honan had been the cultural and political center of China for the first three millennia of its history, and the Honanese were confident that they could tell a legitimate claim from an illegitimate one. During the last century they had formed associations of allied villages (lien-chuang she) to oppose tax extortion by local officials.[17] In 1901 local militia had been created to resist the Allied expeditions, and these militia still existed as well-armed and politically conscious units of local organization. Moreover, secret societies such as the Great Sword Society (Ta-tao-hui) had long been strong in the province; they now began training their adherents for military combat. The Honanese local elite, resentful that their examinations had been suspended as a condition of the Boxer settlement, sympathized with all groups that opposed the missionary indemnities.[18]

As the missionaries began to enforce their collection in late March, trouble broke out at Pi-yang district, which alone was paying some 10,000 tls.

According to Hsi-liang's report, a man named Chang Yün-ch'ing "opposed the payment of the indemnity for missionary cases and, when pointed out by the Christians for arrest, became filled with a bitter hatred." Chang and a local leader of the Ta-tao-hui, one Hsi Hsiao-fa, then joined in calling on the people of Kao-tien village to refuse to pay their allotted local indemnities. The villagers responded enthusiastically; they burned down a church, killed fourteen Christians, and set off for the district city. Clearly sympathetic to these people, Hsi-liang wired the court that they were "angry at being forced to pay indemnities for the churches." The court, less impressed by their sincerity, ordered him to give full justice to missionaries and converts, to arrest the leaders of the riot, and to remove the magistrate. Hsi-liang dutifully removed the magistrate and sent troops to suppress the insurgents, but by mid-April the disorders had spread through another district and were threatening three major towns in southern Honan.[19]

Hsi-liang's treatment of the rebels in April and May betrayed his continuing sympathy for them. In April his troops engaged them, but for some unexplained reason their leader, Chang Yün-ch'ing, "although injured, escaped." [20] During the next few weeks the court showed its alarm and concern by sending two more instructions for Hsi-liang to find Chang and arrest him immediately.[21] The bishop of southern Honan also submitted to Hsi-liang a list of rebel leaders that included Chang Yün-ch'ing. Still Hsi-liang seemed unconcerned. In early May his troops captured the secret society leader Hsi Hsiao-fa, but once again they allowed the popular Chang Yün-ch'ing to escape. When Hsi-liang memorialized asking for rewards for all those who had helped capture Hsi, the court retorted angrily that there would be time enough to discuss rewards once Chang was captured too.[22] Hsi-liang's reluctance to capture Chang contrasted sharply with the ruthless policies that his neighbors, Chihli Governor-General Yüan Shih-k'ai and Hu-kuang Governor-General Chang Chih-tung, adopted against similar rebels in their areas.[23]

At this point, however, Hsi-liang took two measures that greatly increased Honanese resentment of his administration. Showing the latent official mistrust of secret societies, he ordered that Hsi Hsiao-fa be publicly executed to serve as a warning to others. At the same time, Hsi-liang was also forced to impose new taxes on the people in order to pay for the central government's Boxer indemnity. During the previous months he had hoped to get along by increasing the price of salt and expanding the coverage of a mortgage tax, but in May he learned that the court would refuse his request to reduce Honan's quota from 900,000 tls. to 600,000. He therefore reluctantly approved Financial Commissioner Yen-chih's suggestion to "revert to an old statute" that provided for a hike in the land tax. He argued that "when divided up among the people the increase would be small, but when accumulated in the hands of the state it would be large." [24] This hackneyed justification could hardly mitigate the effects of one of the most unpopular measures the state could take. In the face of this increase, the Honanese may well have concluded that the Ch'ing had opted for the foreigners against the Chinese people.[25]

During May the insurrection spread, still under the leadership of Chang Yün-ch'ing, until it engulfed two prefectures. Apparently suspecting that Hsi-liang's sympathy with the rebels was keeping him from suppressing them with sufficient vigor, the court abruptly removed him from his post on 29 May without explanation.[26] For reasons that will become apparent below, Hsi-liang was kept in Honan for five months after the initial court order for him to leave the province. As if to bear out the court's suspicion, Hsi-liang still delayed capturing Chang Yün-ch'ing during this time. He finally arrested the Honanese insurrectionary only just before his departure.[27]

Meanwhile Hsi-liang had taken firm measures against other secret society rebels, capturing and executing numerous Ta-tao-hui leaders who had long been powerful in the province. He had also sought to mollify the foreigners by paying the missionaries 26,000 tls. to settle the Pi-yang incident. He had even bestowed an official rank on the French bishop to express appreciation for his "cooperative attitude" in negotiating the settlement.[28] Hsi-liang had undertaken these measures to restore state control and to prevent larger foreign claims. How surprised he must have been, especially in light of his leniency toward Chang Yün-ch'ing, when these measures brought him strong support from the missionaries. Hearing that Hsi-liang was going to be transferred, the bishop wired Chang Chih-tung asking him to intervene at court to have Hsi-liang kept in Honan.[29] Influenced by Chang's advice, the court delayed the transfer it had ordered in May.

In July Hsi-liang learned why he was being kept in Honan and sent a "secret report on self-government and sovereignty" directly to the empress dowager. He perhaps saw this as an opportunity to express resentment against the foreigners for having demanded his expulsion from Shantung and having blocked his appointment to Hupeh. Now that they were speaking on his behalf, he could openly express alarm that they were "intervening in domestic government, even grasping and manipulating the men of our administration." He argued that since "our China was the first independent country to appear, it has special independent authority." He alluded to the organic quality of the state and its hegemony over religious institutions to make his point.

> The governors-general and governors are the arms and legs of the emperor and are not for other men to slander lightly or to flatter by making comparisons among them. Bishops are of the same class as head Buddhist priests and are not wielders of the dynasty's authority. Nor should they [like certain Han dynasty officials] indulge in criticisms at the beginning of each month.[30]

Invoking for the first time foreign experiences, he exclaimed:

> Turkey is weak, but it does not take orders from Russia! The Transvaal is small, but it does not get instructions from England! How can it be that in our venerable China

provincial officials may be struck down or retained in office by foreign missionaries? [31]

Since the foreigners were actually intervening for him, he could argue convincingly that his protest was completely disinterested. "I only fear compliance with their demands because then a bishop could keep a governor [in office]; a priest, an intendant." Thereafter Chinese officials would be constantly "begging for help from abroad." [32]

Hsi-liang reminded the court that the local elite were forbidden by statute from interfering in court appointments; he implied that the foreigners should be even more completely excluded. If the dynasty failed to resist the foreigners' initiatives, he warned, it would lose prestige among the elite upon whose support it depended and would relinquish its legitimacy in the eyes of the people.

If the authority to govern ourselves is lost, how can we expect the local elite to remain obedient or the people compliant? How can we expect anyone to exert himself fully on behalf of the empress dowager and the emperor to save us from the present situation? Just in saying this I weep bitterly! [33]

After several wires to the throne in this vein, Hsi-liang finally won its consent to leave Honan as planned and to make his way to a less prestigious military post in Jehol. Once again he sacrificed his position to resist missionary interference—and this time it was interference which would have advanced his career.

Later in 1903, on his way from one post to another, Hsi-liang was asked to look into a dispute between the Honanese and local officials that had its origins in the period when he had served in the province. His successor in Honan, Governor Chang Jen-chün, had kept Financial Commissioner Yen-chih in office and had retained the land tax increase that Yen-chih had recommended. The Honanese had got an imperial censor to impeach Yen-chih for "oppression," and Chang had been forced to rescind the tax increase. He had refused to look into the charges against his loyal subordinate, however, and the court asked Hsi-liang to go to Honan to investigate. The charge against Yen-chih was that he had "oppressed the people" by "lightly changing the old statute on the land tax." [34] The censor referred unmistakably to the increase in the tax that Hsi-liang had approved, but Hsi-liang now shortened the charge to "changing an old statute," which deftly distinguished it from his characterization of his own policy as "reverting to an old statute." In addition to this sleight of hand, Hsi-liang lied, saying that Yen-chih had called for an increase in the land tax but that he, Hsi-liang, had vetoed it. He added that Yen-chih had surreptitiously increased the tax and that Chang Jen-chün had retained it to finance military reforms.[35] He thus sacrificed a loyal subordinate to mollify the court and the Honanese.

Hsi-liang's misrepresentation of the tax increase saved his own honor but caused his successor to lose face. Chang Jen-chün, who already resented Hsi-liang's policies on river conservancy and military reform, retaliated by impeaching him for "favoritism and nepotism." [36] These charges presumably referred to Hsi-liang's growing reliance on an intendant named Chao Erh-feng, who had served him earlier in Shansi, and to his failure to transfer his brother-in-law, Shan-ch'eng, who was prefect of Chang-te when Hsi-liang arrived in the province.[37] It was ironic that Chang should make these accusations since he had risen to power principally through contact with a powerful relative, Yüan Shih-k'ai.[38] In any case the charges had no visible effect on the progress of Hsi-liang's career. The court was aware that he was scarcely interested in creating a network of protégés within the bureaucracy.

Hsi-liang's interest lay instead in resisting the Boxer and missionary indemnities so as to restore the faith of the local elite in the Ch'ing. To the same end, he had delayed in executing court orders to arrest a rebel leader, had refused to profit from missionary intervention on his behalf, and had sacrificed a loyal subordinate.

Concessions

While serving in Honan, Hsi-liang also tried to resist the British mining concessions that had been imposed on the province in 1898. According to the original agreement, the British Peking Syndicate was to supply a Chinese firm, the Yü-feng Company, with capital while the firm was to supply the land and labor to open mines in Huai-ch'ing prefecture in northern Honan.[39] The two Chinese ex-officials who represented the Yü-feng Company had proved to be not only poor and incompetent but also corrupt and irresponsible. They had long since left Honan, along with all the funds that they had borrowed from the Peking Syndicate.[40] Neither officials nor Honanese had stepped in to take their place or to limit British claims to the conceded area.

Hsi-liang moved immediately to block the British engineers who were in Peking demanding permission to begin opening the mines in Huai-ch'ing. He was fortunate that the Ch'ing prince, I-k'uang, who headed the newly created Foreign Ministry (the Wai-wu-pu), was aware of his dilemma. I-k'uang memorialized that Hsi-liang should take steps to "open mines and railroads to preserve our rights." [41] I-k'uang suggested that he select "wealthy and upright local elite and merchants" and insist that they be allowed to manage the mines jointly with the British as had been stipulated in the original agreement. The Grand Council quickly approved I-k'uang's memorial and ordered Hsi-liang to "make preparations so that our rights do not fall by the wayside." [42] Hsi-liang replied that he would do his best to restrict the British activities in Honan.[43]

Hsi-liang's first tactic was delay. When the British Minister Satow requested a permit for the British engineers to begin work, Hsi-liang referred him to his predecessor, Sung-shou, who was in Peking. After gaining a month by this subterfuge, he sent an envoy in March to investigate the mine sites and kept him there for over two months. When the syndicate asked what he was doing, Hsi-liang suggested that it get in touch with another envoy in Peking. The syndicate looked for this envoy, only to find that he had already left for Honan. Satow first complained bitterly about these delays; then he exploded that Hsi-liang had wasted six months and was clearly trying to obstruct the project. In May 1902, Hsi-liang finally settled down to serious negotiations with the British.[44]

Hsi-liang next invoked article I of the 1898 agreement, which allowed the syndicate to open mines only after it had been shown that there were no "obstacles" in the area. He first cited a report from the prefect of Huai-ch'ing on conditions in Hsiu-wu district where the syndicate had proposed to begin work:

> The common people are themselves opening them up and are relying on coal mining as a business. If mines are opened [by the foreigners] they will harm the people's industry. Although many Honanese would [be employed in the foreign mines] and would receive salaries, [their income] would not be as great as that which they get now from their own industries. Moreover, there are many ancestral tombs in the area, so there are indeed "obstacles." [45]

To develop more sophisticated arguments, Hsi-liang appointed a man named Han Kuo-chün to be a new intendant of mining affairs for north Honan. Han, who had already served for a long time in various capacities in Honan, later recalled that he was chosen for this post because "the people . . . knew that I would not cheat them." [46] It was probably Han who wired the Wai-wu-pu that "the people are collecting capital to open mines; their capital is already great and their mining machinery good and fast. The people of the area can therefore be expected to obstruct [the Peking Syndicate's operations]." [47]

Meanwhile, Hsi-liang asserted close control over the Yü-feng Company in order to use it as a check on the syndicate. He announced that the previous Chinese managers had been removed and their loans from the syndicate nullified. He replaced them with two officials who received their salaries from the Honan government. He instructed the new appointees to watch carefully over the affairs of the company and to borrow no funds from the syndicate.[48] Where the corrupt ex-officials had failed, these upright officials might yet succeed.

Hsi-liang also asked Han Kuo-chün to encourage the people of Hsiu-wu to create their own mining firm to use new machinery. But the Wai-wu-pu felt that such activity went beyond merely "preserving our rights" and violated the understanding with the Peking Syndicate. Minister Satow, for his part, wisely ignored the question of popular opposition and simply stressed that the syndicate was ready to avoid grave sites or to pay adequate compensation for those which it had to disturb. In addition, the Honanese lacked the funds and organization to respond to Hsi-liang's call and undertake their own new mines at this time.[49] So the syndicate finally began work in Hsiu-wu.

But Hsi-liang had initiated a pattern of resistance that would eventually drive the foreign company from the area. By 1910 the people of Hsiu-wu would set up their own mines.[50] Although facing short-term failure, Hsi-liang had established a precedent for his successors, who would ultimately achieve a long-term success.

Hsi-liang also tried to resist the syndicate's plans to build a mining railway in north Honan. He seized on a set of mining regulations that Chang Chih-tung had memorialized to limit the Russians in Manchuria and, contrary to the original intent of the regulations, applied them to British activities in Honan.[51] In a report to the Wai-wu-pu, he argued that on the basis of these regulations the syndicate's proposed railway was "in conflict with our rights." He suggested that the line be shortened or rerouted to another destination altogether.[52]

Hoping to enlist the assistance of Sheng Hsüan-huai, who was director general of the Chinese Railway Company, Hsi-liang sent him a copy of his report and remarked that the syndicate's proposed line seemed "full of abuses." [53] But Sheng Hsüan-huai was more concerned with development than rights. He replied with a short lecture:

> . . . the mining railroads of all countries hook up to trunk lines [but] their seeking for extra profits is merely their way of avoiding capital losses. . . . The foreigners plot merely for profits; they certainly do not covet our land.[54]

Worried mainly about potential competition with the Peking-Hankow line, which was under his jurisdiction, Sheng asked the Wai-wu-pu to press for a regulation forbidding the Peking Syndicate line from carrying passengers.[55]

Unable to get the support of Sheng Hsüan-huai, Hsi-liang failed to enforce his interpretation of the court's regulations. The British minister, sensing dissension in the Chinese ranks, rejected not only Hsi-liang's proposed alternative route but also Sheng Hsüan-huai's proposed proscription of passengers.[56] The syndicate started work on the railway in 1902, obtained better terms from the government in 1905, and began running trains that carried passengers in 1907.[57] The syndicate railway affair showed the limits of what one official could accomplish in resisting strong foreign demands. Hsi-liang learned that without the cooperation of others he could not hope to resist the extension of foreign railways in China.

Hsi-liang next turned to keeping the British out of south Honan, where they had not yet obtained any concessions. In April 1902 he had rejected the demands of one foreign merchant to open mines in Yü-chou department, Nan-yang prefecture. Hoping to enlist the local population in the effort to resist further demands of this sort, he recommended that they create the

Yü-nan Mining Company "to open the mines ourselves." He soon announced the creation of an entirely Honanese company that would exclude the use of any foreign capital in opening new mines in south Honan. Since he regarded the managers as patriotic, he lent the company substantial state funds but still allowed it to be wholly run by "merchants." [58]

In establishing the Yü-nan Mining Company Hsi-liang expressed a view of the West that varied greatly from that of Sheng Hsüan-huai:

> The Occident's financial and legal systems are closely interrelated, and they help each other, especially in the fields of agriculture and mining. If a [business] starts to fail, those above and those below cooperate to increase their profits every day.[59]

This assessment may have been based more on Chinese traditions of business enterprise than on accurate knowledge of the West. But it may have come closer to the true nature of Western economic development than the Western notion of unbridled "free private enterprise." Whatever its accuracy, this judgment underlay Hsi-liang's strategy of cooperating with local society as a means of resisting Western economic encroachment.

By his politics of resistance, Hsi-liang had allied himself with the Honanese. On the indemnity issue he had clearly identified himself with the local population's anger at the missionary exactions. In the conflict over his removal, he had stated baldly that without independence there could be no self-government, and that without self-government, the people would not remain loyal to the state. In his effort to preserve the mining and railway rights of north Honan, Hsi-liang was unable to lead the people into an effective resistance. But he knew that the problem was more a lack of way than a lack of will. He remained convinced that cooperation between "those above and those below" could produce not only profits but also independence for China.

4: BANDITRY AND MINING IN JEHOL

Hsi-liang was next appointed military lieutenant-governor of Jehol, the portion of Chihli province north of the Great Wall and adjacent to inner Mongolia. Appointment to this post represented a step down because it was under the authority of the Chihli governor-general and because it was in a poor and marginal area. Yet Hsi-liang had been appointed to deal with a major problem, the banditry that had long threatened the summer palace in Ch'eng-te, the capital of Jehol. At the same time he assumed responsibility for preserving the rich gold and silver mines of the area from the numerous foreigners who coveted them. While in some senses a strange interlude between two important periods, the Jehol tour also had a significance of its own.

Banditry

Long known in the late Ch'ing as a "thicket of bandits," Jehol had deteriorated into utter chaos after the Boxer movement. Missionary reparations of 70,000 tls. had provoked the people of the area into a series of insurrections that had been far more violent than others in North China. Hsi-liang's predecessors had managed to capture the leaders of the uprisings, but they had done nothing to eliminate the causes of disorder. The court was particularly concerned because the Manchu Prince Tuan, who had been driven from power after the Boxer movement, was rumored to be massing a force of 50,000 Mongols in inner Mongolia in preparation for an attack on Peking to place his son on the throne.[1]

When Hsi-liang had passed through Peking on his way to Ch'eng-te, he had been instructed to "reorganize Jehol carefully and make changes in its system." He soon memorialized an eight-point program for putting the military district back in order. He sharply criticized "fat officials" as well as "ruthless bandits" in describing the chaos that had long prevailed:

> . . . during the last ten years, Boxer banditry and robbery cases multiplied by the day; the merchants were forced to flee; and the common people were scattered and

killed in countless numbers. Among those who remained, there was not a single village that was not robbed, not a household that was not ransomed. The people had nothing to live on; broken-hearted and weeping, their plight was extreme.[2]

He warned that while the worst was over, the "good people are still weak while the violent remain powerful." The political risks were obvious: "Jehol has long borders with Feng[tien] and Chih[li] and it protects the Sacred Capital [Peking]; it is thus of more than small importance." Safety lay in the restoration of good government: "If we want to eliminate the source of banditry, we must first clean up the administration; if we want to root out corruption, we must first be scrupulous ourselves." [3]

In addition to dismissing the incompetent and setting a personal example of probity, Hsi-liang increased the number of officials and intensified control of the countryside. His predecessors had had only six magistrates to govern a huge area that was only sparsely populated. Spread too thin, these officials had been unable to maintain order in their districts. Hsi-liang memorialized to create one new prefecture and three new districts to fill in the interstices among existing districts.[4] He thus cleared the way for the restoration of peace in the area.

To make this new structure work, Hsi-liang tried to reduce expenses and expand revenues. He avoided unnecessary new expenses by sending students to Pao-ting for military training rather than founding an academy in Jehol. He increased revenues by imposing new taxes on wine, salt, and opium. Since the treasury was still in debt, he looked around for other sources of revenue and came upon the imperial hunting preserve at Wei-ch'ang. Previous officials had received permission to open part of the preserve to Han Chinese colonization, but had not dared to proceed for fear of offending Manchu courtiers who still thought of themselves as hunters. Hsi-liang reassured the court by drawing up detailed regulations and boldly proposed opening 34,000 acres for settlement. To keep close control over the new settler population, he asked for the creation of yet another district. Because the main purpose was to raise money (not to settle new lands), he asked that the price for land set by his predecessors be raised.[5]

In suppressing banditry and instituting reforms, Hsi-liang showed some awareness of the needs of the frontier. He asked that qualified officials be allowed to serve longer in Jehol than the statutes allowed so as to improve the administration of this traditionally neglected area. He also manipulated stereotypes about the frontier to get court support in educational reforms. For example, he stated that the "culture of the people outside the Wall is simple and fierce" to persuade the ministries to disburse more funds for the old charity and new primary schools.[6] For the first time he began to develop a frontier policy.

Yet his frontier policy consisted primarily of carrying out the same measures

of efficient government that he had effected in the interior. When he found
that four tax collectors under the Mongolian Superintendency (Li-fan yüan)
were making extra exactions on the people, he dismissed them. He brushed
aside objections from the superintendency that only its officials could
administer the taxes fairly because only they knew Manchu and Mongol.
Hsi-liang apparently believed that honesty was more important than language
skills and that an upright Han Chinese could administer as well as an upright
Manchu or Mongol. He also implemented a strict extradition law, observing
that the Mongol chiefs in Jehol were notorious for "seizing property and
killing men without warning." As a Chinese official, Hsi-liang also opposed the
Mongol chiefs' practice of creating their own military forces to suppress
banditry. With obvious sarcasm he asked:

> Mongol princes and dukes of all banners train troops to protect themselves and to
> guard the border areas. Is this not very good? No one knows military matters better
> than these princes and dukes. Is that not right?[7]

Hsi-liang's answer to both questions was an emphatic "no," because the
Mongol chiefs often engaged freebooters from the interior who turned out to
be bandits. On the frontier or elsewhere, only legitimate authority should be
invoked to deal with banditry.

Mining

Hsi-liang continued his policy of resisting foreign efforts to exploit China's
mines. Since the rich gold and silver mines of Jehol had fallen into disrepair
during the previous decade, businessmen from several foreign countries had
signed agreements with Chinese merchants or Mongol princes to develop
them. Neither Hsi-liang's predecessors nor the Mongols themselves had
resisted this foreign encroachment.

Hsi-liang no sooner arrived in Ch'eng-te than he sought to undo past
agreements and to prevent new ones from being made. Since he had learned
how the court interpreted the 1902 regulations, he invoked the still broader
regulations of 1898 as grounds for resisting foreign claims. He appealed to
powerful court figures, such as a favorite of the empress dowager, Chang-i,
who had a personal stake in preserving the Jehol mines. He also argued that
the mines were a vital source of revenue in Jehol and could not lightly be
turned over to foreign control.[8]

Knowing that the court could be a weak reed to lean on, Hsi-liang also
moved directly to control the Mongol banner chiefs. A Han Chinese merchant
named Sun Shu-hsün, an agent for a German company, had signed a mining
contract with the chief of the Left Banner of the Kharach'in (Qaracin) tribe.
When Sun demanded that the state ratify the contract so that work could
begin, Hsi-liang found in his files a letter from the banner chief in 1900.
According to Hsi-liang, the chief had written:

I hear that in Peking there is a merchant named Sun who, in league with the foreigners, is amassing capital to open our banner's . . . gold mines. He seems to want to sell the banner to the foreigners. I beg that other Chinese shares [hua-ku] be called in and that foreign funds be excluded in order to halt rampant abuses.[9]

Hsi-liang argued that by this communiqué the chief had "strictly prohibited foreign capital shares in order to recover our rights." He rejected Sun's application for ratification of the contract. Under Hsi-liang's influence, another chief soon made "strong remonstrances" in Peking against foreign mining agreements and declared that he had "already begun mining operations with the ultimate intention of using modern machinery." [10]

Hsi-liang also tried to win back a chief who had become closely associated with Russian businessmen. The chief of the Middle Banner of the Kharach'in tribe had signed a contract with the Russian (Tao-sheng) Bank in Peking. When Hsi-liang appealed to him to let the contract lapse, the chief refused and instead asked him to ratify it so that work could begin. The chief wrote:

. . . I have discussed this with the Tao-sheng Bank and honor its wish to issue share capital, buy equipment and begin exploitation of gold mines. . . . Now we have signed a preliminary agreement . . . and given it the seal of approval of this banner. It is only because the foreign manager has not yet signed that I have not forwarded a copy.[11]

Seeing that this chief was intent on going ahead despite his opposition, Hsi-liang angrily denounced him for "monopolizing" the mines of his banner in the name of a foreign company.[12]

In his effort to protect the Mongols from the foreigners, Hsi-liang showed some sympathy for them. He noted:

In recent years the officials and people have been opening mines and the Mongol people have been getting a share of the mountains. They have not been reaping as great benefits as they could if they opened them themselves.[13]

But he went on to point out that the Mongols had only themselves to blame.

The banners do not understand where to open mines or how to raise capital. They are reckless in their search for large profits. They hastily make agreements opening all their banners to exploitation.

Recently [the foreigners] use fine phrases to lure them with the hope of profits. Soon the guest will usurp the place of the host, and the latter will have to withdraw without any rights. It is not by sitting on our hands that we will reap the benefits and avoid the dangers—this is obvious.[14]

In Hsi-liang's view, the officials had to lead the Mongols if they were to retain control over their mines.

To defend the Mongols who lacked the will or capacity to resist the foreigners, Hsi-lang resorted to strict and detailed regulations. He explained: "if we do not devise laws and establish regulations I fear that those above will have nothing to stand by and those below nothing to protect." He drew up a four-title, twenty-three-article mining code and created a special bureau to enforce it. The new code was designed in part to eliminate corruption in existing mines and to increase revenues. It forbade merchants to bribe clerks or to pay the salaries of mining officials, closed tax loopholes, improved tax collection procedures, and regulated the transfer of property. It provided for officials to manage certain mines on an experimental basis, with profits going to the state.[15] The code was thus part of the larger effort to reestablish good government in Jehol.

Other articles were aimed more explicitly at preventing foreign infiltration. One required foreign capitalists to make application through the new Jehol Mining Bureau and to meet detailed specifications before obtaining permits. Another took account of "conditions on the frontier" and sought to please the Mongols by specifying that the state should share any newly opened mines with them as it did with Han Chinese. The Mongols were given no special treatment, however, for it was twice stated in the code that "no matter whether [Han] people or Mongols, Chinese or foreigners, all must obey." [16] The regulations were designed to protect the frontier society in general, not just the Mongol tribesmen.

Hsi-liang was quite successful in reforming and regulating the mines of Jehol. He later reported that he had saved at least one mine from foundering in corruption and mismanagement. Under his successors the mining tax became the most important source of revenue. Hsi-liang also managed to resist most of the foreign encroachment. He isolated the Germans from the Mongol chiefs and so entangled the British in the regulations that they were unable to realize their concessions or begin work during the following decade. These successes became well known and seem to have influenced the policies of the court and of colleagues such as Yüan Shih-k'ai.[17]

Partially because of his high degree of Sinicization and his domestic orientation, however, Hsi-liang had difficulty in dealing with Mongols who had made contact with the Russians. The Mongol chief who had insisted on developing his mines with Russian assistance persevered in his plan and ultimately involved the Russians deeply in the work.[18] Hsi-liang's paternalistic attitude toward the Mongols no doubt had contributed to this failure. Despite his Mongol origins, he gave them little credit for intelligence or energy:

> The Mongol has a good but simple nature; he does not plan far or work carefully. He makes up stupid schemes and tries to take the easy way out; it is seldom that he is not cheated by others. This is pitiable! [19]

Faced with this kind of Chinese arrogance, the Mongols may well have preferred the Russians, who were at least pretending to respect Mongol culture and who had the funds and expertise to develop the mines.

After six months in Jehol, Hsi-liang seems to have longed for a better post.

His supporter at court, Lu Ch'uan-lin, had suggested that he be sent to Kwangsi to suppress banditry. At odds with his superior, Yüan Shih-k'ai, Hsi-liang must have jumped at the chance. Ironically it was his former acquaintance Jung-lu, who had once warned against Yüan's treachery, who now vetoed the transfer and thus kept him in Jehol under Yüan's authority.[20] Fortunately for Hsi-liang, Jung-lu soon died, and the court appointed him to the important post of governor-general of Fukien and Chekiang. Fragmentary evidence suggests that Chang Chih-tung, still governor-general of Hu-kuang, may have been behind this appointment. It was Chang who had impeached the incumbent governor-general in Fukien-Chekiang and Chang who enjoyed close relations with T'ieh-liang, the rising young Manchu who had first been appointed to fill the vacancy. Chang may have recommended T'ieh-liang for the post and, when he was vetoed for some reason, turned to Hsi-liang as second best. The story went that Chang met both T'ieh-liang and Hsi-liang for dinner in Peking at this time and made a pun on their names which suggested that T'ieh (iron) was better than Hsi (tin). Whatever the origins of this transfer, it too was not to be. The British and Japanese, who had extensive interests in Fukien and Chekiang, intervened at court and had the appointment withdrawn.[21]

Only in April 1903, did the court finally transfer Hsi-liang from Jehol to become governor-general of Szechwan. This transfer must have pleased Hsi-liang in several ways. It was a notable promotion from a post in the military hierarchy to one in the civil hierarchy. It was also a change from a poor and sparsely settled area to one of the wealthiest and most populous provinces in the country. Hsi-liang was replacing Ts'en Ch'un-hsüan, the official who had criticized his missionary and military policies and had helped ease him out of the Shansi governorship. Hsi-liang was so anxious to leave Jehol for Szechwan that he asked the court to relieve him of his duties even before his successor had arrived.[22]

Although only a brief moment in Hsi-liang's career, the Jehol stay revealed some interesting things about him. Remaining primarily the good administrator of domestic affairs, he merely modified his previous policies to take some account of the realities of the frontier. He appeared completely Chinese, both in his careful balancing of personal self-cultivation with administrative reorganization and in his paternalism toward his Mongol charges, an attitude that somewhat limited his effectiveness with them. Yet he also showed a flexibility that permitted him to learn from new experiences. Most important, he demonstrated the energy to carry out programs instead of just invoking clichés about the need for improvement. "It is not by sitting on our hands that we will reap the benefits and avoid the dangers." It was perhaps this kind of energy that landed him his next job, the most challenging of his career thus far.

Part 2: Expansion in Szechwan, 1903–1907

Although the strategy of resistance had had some striking successes, Hsi-liang seemed to realize that it alone would not save China from foreign encroachment. China had resisted the Allies only to be saddled with the Boxer indemnity. Hsi-liang had resisted the indemnities only to confront foreign mining concessions; he had resisted mining concessions only to see the Russians make gains among the Mongols. The time had come for a more positive approach.

As governor-general of Szechwan, Hsi-liang turned to the strategy of expansion to preempt several fields from the foreigners. With a territory the size of France and a population of 40 million, the western province offered the resources for undertaking large projects. Although long a part of China, it had been depopulated during the late Ming rebellions and had only recently been resettled with a vigorous and ambitious population. It was a strategic province, dominating the upper Yangtze and adjacent to Tibet, but it was far enough away from Western power to allow its officials to draft long-range plans.

While continuing some programs of simple resistance, Hsi-liang put most of his energy into expansion. He broadened his own world view beyond China, first to adopt some Western and Japanese techniques and then to assert the universal relevance of some Chinese ideas. Acting on his own view of political economy, he cooperated with the local elite in trying to create industrial enterprises and a railway. In reaction to British pressure, he formulated a Tibetan policy that eventually included both military campaigns and administrative expansion. By these various programs of expansion he sought to stem the tide of foreign influence in West China.

KANSU

SHENSI

TIBET

SZECHWAN

Pa-t'ang

Kham

Li-t'ang

Ta-chien-lu

□ Chengtu

K'uei-chou

HUPEH

Wan

I-ch'ang

Hankow

YANG-TZE

RIVER

Chungking

Ning-yüan

HUNAN

KWEICHOW

YUNNAN

Map 2. Szechwan

5: THE REFORM EFFORT

As one of the two dozen senior officials in the empire, Hsi-liang became one of the empress dowager's most effective provincial administrators. In undertaking reforms, he grew and changed. While remaining on guard against foreign domination, he modified his attitudes toward individual foreigners and even cooperated with some in carrying out his programs. He continued to obey court instructions whenever possible, but increasingly followed his own concept of the national interest in undertaking military reforms. In making educational changes, he drew on Western models and experience without neglecting China's own heritage. Indeed he decided that some aspects of Chinese culture had continuing value for the world outside China.

Foreigners

Hsi-liang had always expressed his xenophobia within the constraints of the treaty system. When the foreign press had berated him as a "notorious xenophobe," his superior, Chang Chih-tung, had defended him as "anxious to carry out treaty obligations." [1] Having become xenophobic because the foreigners had violated the treaties, he had more than once used the treaties to curtail their illegal excesses.[2] He rightly continued to suspect the foreigners of much "blind anti-Chinese feeling." [3]

As Hsi-liang came into personal contact with foreign consuls for the first time, he cultivated his reputation of xenophobia to throw them off balance. When he arrived in Chengtu, according to the French consul, "he displayed repugnance towards anything foreign, having European style carts taken from his presence, criticizing the clothing of the new policemen (modeled on that worn in the treaty ports), . . . and announcing that missionary questions would be surveyed closely." [4] After thus unsettling the consuls, he proceeded to harass them: he had a subordinate inform them that since they possessed only the rank of intendant they could not write directly to him or see him in person. The consuls argued heatedly that they were "guests," completely outside of the official hierarchy, and should have access to the governor-general. Hsi-liang allowed two weeks of acrimonious debate to go on before finally giving the consuls a "friendly reception" and ascribing the delay to a "misunderstanding" on the part of a subordinate.[5] By first distorting and then upholding the treaties, he hoped to impress the consuls with their utter dependence on them for their status in China.

After this initial warning, Hsi-liang continued to use the treaties to restrict the consuls. When the British consul-general tried to buy land in Chengtu, which was not a treaty port, he denounced the effort as a serious "breach of treaty." When the consul-general asked him to make an exception to relieve the "difficulty," he replied acidly: "The abolition of extraterritoriality would provide a solution to all such difficulties." [6] He could never have carried out this threat to abolish the treaties but he continually tried to enforce his own interpretations of them. According to the balanced judgment of another British consul-general, "if he did not actually dislike foreigners, he was prone to suspect them of evil intentions and he approached all international questions with a fixed determination to concede as little as possible on principle." [7]

He was equally firm in dealing with the missionary question. He admonished a consul that the use of gunboats on behalf of the missionaries would only "exasperate the people"; he told a missionary that he had "behaved foolishly in removing and destroying idols in a temple"; and he asserted authority over Chinese converts by requiring them to kneel when attending local courts.[8] Since violent opposition to conversion had been suppressed earlier, Hsi-liang found a new situation among the Christians of Szechwan.[9] The main conflict was no longer between the converts and the mass of the population but rather between the Catholics, who had long held a monopoly in the province, and the newly arrived Protestants. In 1903 Catholics who felt their privileged position threatened by Protestants banded together in Ning-yüan and killed a Protestant catechumen. Similar incidents occurred in Ya-chou in 1904 and elsewhere in 1905 and 1906.[10]

The foreign consuls were alienated by what one called "this religious war in China." The Frenchman, Bons d'Anty, wrote on separate occasions that there was "too much talk of persecution," that the "Christian would always be in a bad way vis-à-vis the people," and that the missions should cease calling for the use of gunboats on the Yangtze.[11] The British at different times deemed one missionary "not suitable," criticized another's "impulsive and hot-headed behavior," and expelled a third who had intervened in court cases on behalf of converts.[12] The consuls also criticized the missionaries' tendency to work in unsettled border areas. Bons d'Anty remarked that French missionaries exaggerated the antiforeign quality of banditry near Kweichow, and a British consul-general noted that brigandage there was "perennial . . . having no tie with political events." [13] Indeed, when some Catholic Lolo participated in raids on Protestant Han Chinese in that area, it was difficult to know whether the conflict was religious, regional, or racial.[14]

Hsi-liang took advantage of these fissures within the foreign and convert communities to keep both groups under control. He flattered the rather vain Bons d'Anty and persuaded him to remain aloof from Catholics who committed abuses. He appealed to the British consul-general for help in limiting Catholic influence in the province. With the consul neutralized and the consul-general sympathetic, he successfully prosecuted some powerful Catholic rowdies who had long been stirring up disorder in the province.[15] In another instance he took advantage of the consuls' indifference to expel a "high-handed priest" from the province. He repeatedly used unstable border conditions to justify harsh suppression of all troublesome parties, including converts.[16]

Since he felt less threatened by the foreigners, Hsi-liang showed vigor in protecting them from occasional outbursts of popular wrath. When a foreigner came under attack, he usually issued strict injunctions to prevent a recurrence, sent out well-armed troops, and summarily executed dozens of "bandit leaders." He rewarded subordinates who carried out these orders and defended one by arguing that his severity had prevented "foreign complications." He also took the initiative in reprimanding and transferring subordinates who did not deal firmly with antiforeign disturbances.[17] He thus won new praise from the consuls, one of whom deemed his attitude "completely satisfactory," and another of whom lauded his "exemplary vigor."[18] He entertained the foreign community on the empress dowager's seventieth birthday in 1905 and made a "very favorable impression on all the missionaries."[19]

Hsi-liang now saw his way clear to cooperating with certain foreigners on some reform projects. He issued a proclamation against footbinding to encourage the campaign that was already surging forward under the leadership of Societies for Natural Feet (t'ien-tsu-hui). In response to entreaties from Mrs. Archibald Little, the wife of a British businessman, he made further announcements against footbinding in colloquial Chinese and ordered local officials to have public criers spread the word. He also considered carrying the campaign to the local papers and schools.[20] He evinced keen interest in the missionaries' medical work and visited a mission hospital to celebrate the new year in 1907.[21] As a guest at the opening ceremonies of a missionary publishing house, he listened "graciously" to his host advocate Christianity on the Confucian grounds that "in education there are no distinctions among races."[22] As we shall see, Hsi-liang also drew on foreign experts in carrying out his military and educational reforms. He did not allow his residual resentment against the foreigners' abuses to keep him from enlisting their skills in realizing Chinese goals.

Military Reform

Like all governors-general, Hsi-liang was a civilian official with military responsibilities; like all Chinese, he was heir to a long tradition that stressed the harmony of civil and military pursuits.[23] In previous posts he had lacked not the motivation but the resources for building up a military establishment. Arriving in relatively prosperous Szechwan, he seems to have looked forward to expanding the military forces as the basis for national strength. In his own words, "during these critical times, with powerful neighbors closing in on all sides, the military is the foundation on which the country [*kuo*] must be maintained." [24]

Recognizing that "to become a strong country we must first train troops," Hsi-liang tried to build up the New Army (*hsin-chün*) that was being planned by the court.[25] He immediately faced unexpected financial difficulties. He found that his predecessor had taken four trained battalions with him to his new post, thus depriving Szechwan of a nucleus for the New Army while still draining provincial resources for their support. He asked the court for relief and was granted a 50 percent reduction in remittances to the four battalions.[26] He then recruited 1,700 Szechwanese in two months and began to train them. He used the new men to transform thirty-seven battalions of the old defense forces (*fang-ying*) into thirty battalions of the new reserves (*hsü-pei ying*).[27] He supplied Peking with 300,000 tls. to reform the Peiyang army. At the same time he added another battalion and a construction company to the Szechwan standing army and engaged a qualified officer to train them.[28]

In trying to improve his military forces, Hsi-liang faced a problem of priorities. Disturbances in Tibet made military reforms more urgent but also drained off the funds and troops necessary for effecting them. He was forced to get the court's permission to delay the training of a New Army. Although he developed two brigades of a land army (*lu-chün*), he proved unable to activate either of them by 1906.[29] He also found it difficult to reduce the decrepit main Chinese standing army, the Green Standard (*lü-ying*), since they might be needed at any moment to suppress an antiforeign uprising or a border feud. He warned, and the court agreed, that too rapid a reduction of the old troops would be contrary to the aim of "self-strengthening." [30]

Hsi-liang placed even greater emphasis on improving the provincial arsenal, which he considered to be one of the two most important projects of his administration.[31] Founded in 1877, the arsenal had actually deteriorated in the years just prior to his arrival in Szechwan. He immediately removed dishonest and incapable personnel and, according to a foreign observer, achieved a change "all around for the better." [32] Finding that the arsenal manufactured only 2,000 old large-bore Mauser rifles a year, he adopted the expedient of sending men to Wu-ch'ang, Shanghai, and Tokyo to purchase new arms. In the long run, however, he was convinced that this measure had serious limitations—purchasing arms from Wu-ch'ang and Shanghai risked serious delay in a crisis; getting them from Tokyo involved an unacceptable "loss of rights." He therefore began to plan an expansion of the Chengtu arsenal so that it could make the newest models of weaponry. He accepted the need for industrialization as the basis of military strength, memorializing: "Just as we must have new weapons to train new troops, so we must have new machinery to make new weapons." [33] Without waiting for the court's endorsement of his plan, he sent two agents to Europe to negotiate for this machinery.

In advocating the creation of a major arsenal in Szechwan, Hsi-liang knowingly entered a dangerous political thicket. For years powerful officials had struggled over whether to move the Kiangnan arsenal at Shanghai to a "safer" site further inland.[34] Hsi-liang carefully avoided citing a controversial memorial by Chang Chih-tung in favor of building arsenals in the interior and instead mentioned an earlier proposal by Jung-lu (now safely dead) to similar effect. In view of the current British invasion of Tibet and the Russo-Japanese war over Manchuria, he argued that it was imperative to build a large arsenal in the heart of China, secure from attack by the maritime powers and close to the western dependency. He showed that the expanded arsenal could actually serve three southwestern provinces: "although it certainly would benefit Szechwan, it would also benefit the larger picture." [35] This proposal, however, fell on deaf ears in Peking. The Commission for Army Reorganization (*lien-ping ch'u*), headed by Yüan Shih-k'ai and T'ieh-liang, reduced the suggestion to absurdity by pointing out that if every province developed its own arsenal it would hopelessly dissipate funds and disorganize production. The commission suggested that Chengtu's purchasing of arms from Wu-ch'ang would "mutually benefit" both Szechwan and Hupeh. It requested that there be "no more discussion of expanding the Szechwan arsenal" and received court approval to convey the order to Hsi-liang.[36]

Having already dispatched agents to Europe, Hsi-liang was probably shocked by this court veto of his plan. Previously he had delayed carrying out court orders that ran contrary to his own view of the "whole picture," but now he was confronted with a direct veto that he had either to obey or ignore. Since he was aware of the controversy over the Kiangnan arsenal, he probably realized that the court was more concerned with appeasing political cliques than with the merits of an inland arsenal. Whatever his reasoning, he quietly decided to ignore the court's veto and to proceed with the arsenal in line with his own view of the national interest. Thus, although he remained fiercely loyal to the court, he took a step that revealed the depth of his nationalist feeling. He was able to do this partly because he governed a large and self-sufficient province over 2,000 miles from Peking; he used his provincial or regional position to follow his own policy.[37] But his aim in doing so was not to build regional power but rather to strengthen a part of the nation located far from the Kiangnan arsenal up the treacherous Yangtze gorges. As if to prove that he was acting in good faith, he subsequently obeyed a court order to give funds intended for his arsenal to Peking to assist with central government military reforms.[38]

Overcoming formidable obstacles, Hsi-liang pushed ahead with his plan to build what one observer said was intended to be "one of the best and most complete arsenals whether in Europe or the Far East." [39] His agents in Europe contracted with a German firm for 500,000 tls. of machinery to make 18,000 new Mauser rifles and 9 million cartridges a year—nearly ten times the original capacity of the Chengtu arsenal.[40] He then persuaded the court to allow him to establish a lottery and a mint to meet these expenses. The mint was expected to produce profits of 20 to 30 percent, but it cost another 450,000 tls. to build. To pay for it he was forced to effect economies elsewhere, including, ironically, the arsenal, where he temporarily reduced the salaries of the personnel. While emphasizing the mint in the short run as a source of revenue, he kept his eye on the ultimate goal of a modern arsenal and hired three German engineers and an American chemist. They arrived along with the new machinery in 1907.[41] He had laid the foundations for an arsenal that would supply his successor with modern arms and that would last into the warlord era.[42]

Although some of Hsi-liang's military reforms merely followed the initiatives taken by the court and were modest when compared with those of Yüan Shih-k'ai and Chang Chih-tung, they nevertheless were a significant advance over those of his predecessor, the reformist Ts'en Ch'un-hsüan, and cleared the way for those of his successors Chao Erh-sun and Chao Erh-feng. More important, Hsi-liang had ignored court orders and had begun building an arsenal because he thought the national interest demanded one. He had placed devotion to the country ahead of loyalty to the dynasty and so showed the strength of his nationalist spirit.

Educational Reform

In the field of education, too, although he held fast to some Chinese values, Hsi-liang expanded his world view to take account of some Western ideas. In Honan in 1902, he had built some of the new schools and had supervised the first civil service examinations (*k'o-chü*) to include questions on contemporary world affairs.[43] In Szechwan he continued to value the examination system. When he presided over examinations in Chengtu, he felt that this duty took priority over seeing the consuls.[44] Hsi-liang apparently believed that the system should be expanded not just to include new subjects but also to take in a broader segment of the population. He asked for an increase in Szechwan's small quota, which had limited upward mobility in that rapidly growing province.[45] He seems to have agreed with his friend Lu Ch'uan-lin, who felt that abolishing the system as Yüan Shih-k'ai and Chang Chih-tung had proposed would be an extreme and unproductive measure.[46] In light of the social irresponsibility as well as social change that eventually followed abolition of the system, these reservations may have been well founded.

Hsi-liang tirelessly carried out reforms in other sectors, including military education. As a bannerman he used his prestige to throw open a banner academy (pa-ch'i shu-yüan) to all qualified Chinese. He then hired a Han Chinese teacher and created eight elementary schools to prepare prospective students.[47] Admiring the feats of Western medicine, he tripled the enrollment of the Military Medical School and engaged a French doctor to teach there.[48] Regarding sports as good preparation for combat, he encouraged students to hold competitions in Chengtu. According to one witness, he attended the meets with keen interest.[49]

Hsi-liang also improved the Military Preparatory School (wu-pei hsüeh-t'ang), which aimed to train scholars who "slight military affairs" and officers who "have little knowledge" of civil affairs. He established a special training army (wu-pei chün) to introduce students to combat conditions.[50] He willingly used Japanese instructors temporarily in the school, but replaced them with qualified Chinese as they returned from studying in Japan.[51] While encouraging the school to teach the Japanese curriculum of natural sciences, foreign languages, and the "arts of war," he put renewed emphasis on Chinese studies (Chung-wen), including the classics, history, geography, philosophy, and writing. He believed that certain Chinese cultural traditions contributed to military competence and vigor; as he put it, Chinese studies "convey the sages' teachings and relate to military affairs." [52] He so improved the quality of the school that the Commission of Military Affairs in Peking, composed largely of Hsi-ling's former antagonists, reclassified it as a secondary school rather than as a primary school as was provided by statute.[53]

Hsi-liang found precedents in Chinese history for the best in the West, including reforms in social control and welfare. Sidestepping the venerable pao-chia system of public security, he increased the Western-style police force by 2,000 men and extended it to twenty towns outside the capital. He built a new prison for 20,000 tls. and provided trained doctors to care for 600 inmates. Citing the Chinese ideal of "nourishing the people's livelihood to eliminate the source of disorder," he expanded a system of workhouses to sixty communities outside Chengtu. He argued the urgency of reforms on both Western and Chinese models:

> The floating population are really the source of banditry, and criminals left uneducated will not change. . . . The Chou dynasty achieved peace by putting these people in prison; the Han devised laws to change their characters by commuting their sentences to hard labor for many years. Recently all countries of East [Japan] and West have made exhaustive studies in prison administration and rehabilitation. . . . Now the Ministry of Justice has established a workhouse, imitating Europe and the West [Ou-hsi], drawing on the teachings of old, and making needed reforms, and this is all a critical necessity.[54]

In line with these ideas, he spent 15,000 tls. to build soup kitchens, workhouses, and handicraft schools for 1,200 beggars; and 5,000 tls. to construct homes for coolies, children, and old people. He soon achieved results that compared favorably with those of other reformers and that duly impressed the foreign consuls.[55]

Hsi-liang's attitude toward the West and Japan was reflected in his policies on study abroad.[56] In accord with court policy and the general trend, he expanded the number of fellowships available for study in Japan from 13 to 213.[57] At the same time privately supported students left in increasing numbers until there were 1,200 Szechwanese in Tokyo in 1905.[58] He also sent fifty-eight students on government fellowships to study technical subjects in Belgium.[59] To prepare students for study in Europe and to train interpreters for dealing with the consuls, he added courses in English and French to the Japanese language school (tung-wen hsüeh-t'ang) in Chengtu.[60] After engaging a Britisher to teach English, he sent his son, Pin-hsün, to study that language and, not surprisingly, started a trend that brought 1,000 students to study English by 1907.[61]

While encouraging study abroad, Hsi-liang seems to have shared the court's fear that the students might become alienated from their homeland. In 1906 the Ministry of Education attacked excessive Westernization and required students to prove proficiency in "Chinese learning" (Chung-hsüeh) before leaving to study abroad.[62] Fearing above all political alienation, the ministry adopted an argument strikingly similar to that of Japanese nationalists: that each country's educational system was unique and that China's should "respect the emperor as the basis of politics." [63] More concerned with cultural alienation, Hsi-liang stressed the Chinese cultural tradition:

> The regulations for schools say that we must choose among and understand the educational systems of other countries, and that in the middle and elementary schools attention may be paid to the reading of the classics. This is all very well. But given the rapid change in the spirit of the times, the young students have an insufficient foundation. They struggle to advance quickly. After they pick up one or two words of a foreign language they call it the "new learning," and they come to despise the classics and history.[64]

Since Hsi-liang believed in Chinese culture rather than in Japanese-style nationalism, he emphasized the universal significance of some Chinese values. He praised the five relationships, the doctrine of the mean, and later Confucian teachings, observing that

> the study of the way and virtue and the investigation of human nature—these were what held the people's minds together and what made our country's customs [kuo-su] so beautiful—these were praised throughout the world [huan-ch'iu] and never came under attack during a hundred generations.[65]

He admitted that any stodgy defense of "useless curios" and "ingrained habits" would only drive the young into "forming parties," but suggested selecting the relevant episodes of Chinese history as guides to "firming up the basis of the country."

> As for politics, nothing is [a] more detailed [guide] than history. If we now had to continue using only the devices of the past it would pose great obstacles—[this] cannot be overstressed. But the spirit of the provinces and the character of the people have been molded by several thousand years of established facts and precedents and by the writings of the first thinkers. Therefore, although we must choose from East and West, we must also pay attention to history as a reference tool.[66]

He urged, in sum, the need "to take up both Chinese and Western [studies] and prepare both from beginning to end."

Given limited resources, Hsi-liang accorded priority to Chinese over Western studies. He reoriented the preparation for students going abroad so as to stress Chinese subjects and used a variety of subterfuges to conceal his intention from the outspoken returned students.[67] He appealed to a group of students leaving for France not to imitate their predecessors who had brought back "dangerous ideas of a bad kind." [68] He also attacked the irresponsibility of students who did not return to help China. Reporting a shortage in teachers, he commented wryly that "although we sent students to Japan to study [to become teachers], they often had other plans after graduation." [69]

Hsi-liang also expanded the regular school system in Szechwan in several stages. At first, believing that "the expansion of education is the source of [improved] administration," he founded a college for officials with statecraft (ching-shih) as the trunk and internal administration and foreign affairs as the branches." [70] He next focused on teacher training, noting that if "education is the foundation for molding the people of the country, teacher training is the basis for expanding education." [71] He created a preparatory school for 160 students going to Japan to study the "methods of teaching," institutes for over 1,500 students who wished to become primary and secondary school teachers, and a provincial teacher's college for 500 students.[72] Toward the end of his term in Szechwan, he diverted funds and buildings formerly used for the examination system into new schools designed to achieve "universal education." By 1905 he could claim a provincial higher school, 8 middle schools, and over 4,000 elementary schools.[73] In 1907 the British consul-general reported that the higher school was nearly a university, the middle schools were flourishing, and the primary schools had appeared in every district—such had been the success of "almost feverish educational development on western lines." [74]

Hsi-liang also encouraged the press and used it to convey his own world view. In 1904, after excluding the *Pei-yang Official Gazette* from the province, he founded his own trimonthly, the *Szechwan Official Gazette*, to "explain court policies," publish "correct editorials," and translate "upright principles" from foreign books. He also started the *Chengtu Daily* "for the convenience of the merchants and the people." [75] In 1905 he created the *Szechwan Education Gazette* to "assist in the universalization of education." [76] Hsi-liang exerted strict control over the dissemination of information, sometimes as a result of foreign pressure. He dismissed the editor of his *Gazette* for offending the French consul and he destroyed copies of a book that annoyed the British consul-general.[77] His own ideas about authority could also lead to suppression. In 1905 the *Chungking Daily*, founded by colleagues of the anti-Manchu Sun Yat-sen and boasting a circulation of 3,000, published an article attacking the empress dowager. Hsi-liang's subordinates arrested the editor, imprisoned him without trial, and allowed him to die of mistreatment in prison.[78]

Hsi-liang took care to enlist the help of leading Szechwanese in carrying out his educational reforms. He found the local elite and students in Szechwan in near agreement with him about the superficiality of the education obtained by the students abroad and about their irresponsibility upon returning to China.[79] To get active assistance in implementing reforms in Szechwan, he resorted to both coercion and cajolery. He asserted state control over the private academies (*shu-yüan*) and thus brought them into the reform movement. He established special bureaus at the local level to popularize the "new learning" and convinced many leading scholars to support and expand the reforms.[80]

By a mixture of force and persuasion, Hsi-liang also managed to get the Buddhist monasteries to "volunteer" funds, buildings, and land for the new schools. He obliged peasants to pay taxes of 2 million tls. a year for educational reforms.[81] Although they were pressed into making contributions, these groups also benefited from the measures. Some monks went to Japan to deepen their religious understanding and some peasants took advantage of the movement toward universal education.[82] Just as all groups of Szechwanese— local elite, students, military officers, families, associations, and entrepreneurs —joined in creating more schools, so all groups benefited from the proliferation of many new kinds of schools—tuition schools and free schools, half-day schools and night schools, schools for girls and schools for the poor, schools to teach literacy and schools to teach manual labor in agriculture.[83]

Hsi-liang's military and educational reforms revealed much about his developing world view. He believed that the educated scholar should know about military affairs and the trained officer should know about civil matters. It was only during a period of great peril that the military became the "foundation on which the country must be maintained." The need for military security led not only to the training of troops in new ways but also to the purchase of machinery to make "new weapons." Yet even at the height of military expansion and reform, Hsi-liang's belief in the basically civil quality of true culture asserted itself. "Chinese studies" first conveyed the "sages' teachings" and then was relevant to "military affairs." Militarization without civilization was not national greatness but national decline.

Similarly in education, the reformer should "draw on the teachings of old" as well as "imitate Europe and the West" in order to arrive at the goal of self-strengthening. While hiring foreign teachers, sending students abroad, and expanding schools in Szechwan on foreign models, Hsi-liang was concerned that the new learning not be allowed to replace the classics and history. The "several thousand years of established facts and precedents" were not to be discounted; in the end, "nothing is a more detailed guide than history." Hsi-liang implied that the country's customs, which had developed continuously over so many centuries, could be shorn of their "useless curios" and be made relevant to the larger world outside China. If change without history would perforce be mindless, nationalism without culture would surely be soulless.

6: INDUSTRIAL DEVELOPMENT

Hsi-liang encouraged industrial development to prevent the foreigners from dominating Szechwan's economy. He appointed qualified subordinates to undertake a number of projects, but he relied principally on the local elite and students in planning a "self-managed" (*tzu-pan*) railway from Szechwan into Hupeh (the Ch'uan-Han line). He and the Szechwanese laid the foundations for "rights recovery" and for economic nationalism in the province.

Industrialization for Preservation

Hsi-liang's primary aim of defending Szechwan's resources from the foreigners appeared most clearly in the field of mining. He found that British, French, and German firms were trying to open the mines and exploit the oil deposits in several prefectures. As he had done previously in Honan, he skillfully invoked the terms of their contracts, the new regulations, and Chinese law to expel them one by one from the province.[1] Now more open toward foreigners, he did try to cooperate with the British businessman, Archibald Little, in developing the coal mines of Chiang-pei to the north of Chungking. But when Little violated his contract by establishing a covert relationship with a local merchant, Hsi-liang rallied public opinion throughout the province to support him in recovering the whole concession from the British.[2] He then encouraged the local elite of Chiang-pei to raise their own funds to open their mines and so prevent other foreigners from making claims on them.[3] In this and other cases, he successfully preempted the mines from the foreigners and made a small beginning toward developing them with Chinese capital and personnel.[4] While his achievement was still mainly in the realm of resistance, his aspirations had grown to encompass expansion.

Hsi-liang's first sustained effort at expansion came in other areas of the economy, such as minor industries and banks. In line with court regulations, he founded a Bureau to Encourage Manufacturing and appointed as head an intendant who had studied manufacturing techniques in Japan.[5] According to one observer, this intendant served as the "leading spirit in the attempt to develop industries on modern lines";[6] he sent twenty students to Japan to learn new methods and he founded handicraft schools and three "factories" in Szechwan. Hsi-liang appointed another experienced intendant to head a General Bureau of Commerce in Chungking to "protect, support and advocate" trade by encouraging "officials and merchants to manage together." [7] He instructed his financial commissioner, who had ties to the Shansi banks, to create an "official-merchant" banking system with headquarters in Chengtu and Chungking and branches in Hankow, Peking, Tientsin, and Shanghai.[8] A capable prefect whom he appointed to be an intendant to encourage industry carried out his duties imaginatively, even sponsoring an industrial fair that featured a model steam engine.[9]

Hsi-liang eagerly sought the cooperation of the local elite. A licentiate of Ho-chou had established a silk factory using "new methods" and had hired a Japanese expert, but he had fallen deeply in debt. Having appealed unsuccessfully to the local magistrate for assistance, he wrote to some fellow Szechwanese in Peking asking them to intercede. These Szechwanese officials, acting as leaders of the elite of their home province, wrote to Hsi-liang, explaining the case. Hsi-liang became personally interested in the factory. He ordered the magistrate to subsidize it with 10,000 tls., to turn it into an "official-merchant [jointly] managed company," and to classify it as a middle-level industrial school eligible for continuing assistance.[10] In another instance, the intendant to encourage industry had blocked a merchant-run factory in Lu-chou that competed with the state match monopoly. When informed of this conflict, Hsi-liang decided against the intendant and in favor of the Lu-chou merchants.[11]

In his campaign to preserve rights, Hsi-liang tried to use "native methods" so as to avoid buying machinery abroad.[12] Three of the six silk factories established under his aegis used only Chinese-built machinery, and the plans for a waterworks to be built with the help of the local elite of Chengtu expressly forbade the use of foreign machinery.[13] Hsi-liang differed with the official and entrepreneur Sheng Hsüan-huai by rejecting technological advances made at the cost of foreign control. He adopted a different approach from that of the scholar and industrialist Chang Chien by planning his industrial projects one at a time, with little interest in transforming the whole society in the industrial image.[14] He acted, in short, to preserve political sovereignty that was both pre- and postindustrial.

The Ch'uan-Han Railway

Hsi-liang wanted to build a railway from Szechwan to Hupeh primarily because foreign businessmen had expressed an interest in doing the same.[15] The British and French had long been searching for a way to penetrate Yunnan and Szechwan from their colonies of Burma and Indochina. The

Americans had sent a survey party to reconnoiter another route from Hupeh province into Szechwan.[16] By 1903 the British Peking Syndicate and the American China Investment and Construction Company had asked permission from the Wai-wu-pu to build a line from Hupeh to Szechwan, and French firms had expressed interest in the same line.[17]

Hsi-liang had become aware of these foreign plans even before taking up his post in Szechwan. When passing through Peking he had spoken with Chang Chih-tung about what Chang later called "spying foreigners and traitorous merchants plotting to monopolize the Ch'uan-Han railway." [18] He and Chang had discussed the strategic importance of a Szechwan line and had "heartily agreed" on the need to "raise funds and hurry to memorialize to build it ourselves to stop those outsiders who covet it." [19]

Rumors that the Chinese planned to build the railway whetted foreign appetites. According to British records, the businessman

> Townley, after much pressure, extracted a verbal promise from the [Ch'ing] Prince [I-k'uang] that, in case it should be decided later to construct the railway, and Chinese capital should not be available, priority will be given to British capital, American capital being also invited.[20]

The French entrepreneur de Marteau, not to be outdone, expected to get a part in financing the line by, according to him, "using the Empress's first eunuch, her doctor—our men—and Prince Ch'ing." [21] Thinking it of the "first importance" to get Hsi-liang's support, a representative of the Peking Syndicate had visited him in Peking. The French Minister had wined and dined Hsi-liang in such style that he had been left with a case of acute indigestion.[22]

On his way to Szechwan, Hsi-liang had worried that the court might sign some written agreement with the foreigners behind his back. He knew that Chang Chih-tung, as governor-general of Hu-Kuang, should be brought in on the planning of the Ch'uan-Han line at every step of the way. But he was aware that Chang believed that foreign assistance was absolutely necessary to build even self-managed railways quickly and profitably.[23] When Hsi-liang reached the town of Cheng-ting, Chihli, which Chang had counseled him to relinquish to the Allies in 1901, he decided to memorialize alone on his view of self-management and so present Chang with a *fait accompli*.

Hsi-liang's memorial of July 1903 provided the keystone for the rights recovery movement in Szechwan:

> A memorial to establish our own Ch'uan-Han Railway Company, to expand the sources of profits and to protect our sovereignty, humbly begging that it be approved by the Boards, and respectfully submitting it now for imperial perusal:
> I humbly submit that all countries are now struggling to be cock of the yard; wherever their railroads reach their power reaches too, and whenever we have allowed others to build we have automatically lost both profits and rights. China in

this situation must reform its laws and strengthen itself, and while there are many things to be done, railroads certainly cannot be delayed.

Szechwan is located in the remote interior of the empire; its production is abundant but transportation is poor, and it is difficult to get products in and out. The foreigners have long been watering at the mouth, scheming to undertake the construction of this road; moreover, Chinese have collected shares on pretexts while plotting with the foreigners to seize it by force; they have created an uproar on every side. If we do not immediately advocate that officials establish a company to collect Chinese shares to protect our rights, if the matter is allowed to drag along, we will not keep authority in our hands, and we will either have to borrow foreign funds or permit others to build it. We will end by seeing the guest take the place of the host and we will be forced to withdraw without any rights. I am particularly afraid that in this event all the countries would begin to fight among themselves and much wrangling would ensue.

This is all the more the case since Szechwan connects with Tibet on the west, Yunnan and Kweichow on the south, and is situated at the source of the Yangtze; if rail rights are in others' hands, the bamboo curtain will be withdrawn, and everything below the neck of the bottle,—all the provinces along the Yangtze—will lose their strategic significance. This shows that the Ch'uan-Han railway's importance for Szechwan is small while for the whole situation it is great, and if we do not decide to do it ourselves today we will not be able to succeed [tomorrow].

Although I am exceedingly ignorant, local officials have responsibilities which they cannot pass to others, and I do not dare not concern myself with this with all my energy. After thinking it over carefully, I suggest that we act according to the statutes of the Peking-Kalgan railway, having Szechwan establish a Ch'uan-Han Railroad Company, first collecting only Chinese shares on a trial basis, without allowing speculators to join the company, and then engaging engineers and personnel to undertake a survey and construct both trunk and branch lines according to the statutes. All countries which are peaceful and friendly look at China's self-strengthening and are uniformly sympathetic. As for the details of management, I will memorialize concerning them after I arrive at my post and I will ask for a rescript to act accordingly.[24]

Hsi-liang's proposal to manage without any foreign assistance stood out against the trend of the times.[25] A Chinese contemporary commented accurately that "self-management began with the Ch'uan-Han railroad." [26] The planned railway would be by far the largest of its kind, stretching some 1,200 miles, or thirty times further than the self-managed Swatow-Ch'ao-chou line planned at the same time.[27] It would be more completely self-managed than its prototype, the Peking-Kalgan line, which received substantial financial support from a Sino-foreign railway company.[28] The very proposal of such a daring project had far-reaching consequences even before the work began. It stimulated the rights recovery movement in other provinces, including Hupeh, Shansi, and Yunnan, and set a precedent for twelve other self-managed railways during the following decade.[29]

Hsi-liang showed clearly that he understood the need for both haste and care in undertaking this large project. As soon as the Wai-wu-pu approved his proposal in July 1903 and the Grand Council created a Ministry of Commerce in Peking to oversee self-managed lines in December, he memorialized in January 1904 for the establishment of a Ch'uan-Han Railway Company.[30] In his memorial he urged that work on the line begin immediately.[31] At the same time he recognized the need for thorough preparations:

> The road bed of the Ch'uan-Han will wind around many obstacles and through perilous mountains; everyone knows that it will be far more difficult [to build] than the Lu-Han [Peking-Hankow] line. I know the difficulties of getting funds and the dangers of construction. . . . If we do not plan carefully we may advance quickly at first but have to slow down later, and then we would be sorry without having any remedy for it.[32]

To plan the work, Hsi-liang established a committee of talented officials and secretaries. As official manager (tu-pan) he named the judicial commissioner, Feng-hsü, who had exhibited "unswerving integrity and complete incorruptibility." [33] He appointed the intendant, Shen Ping-k'un, who had studied in Japan, as assistant manager (hui-pan) to handle the technical aspects.[34] He used his financial commissioner, Hsü Han-tu, who had banking connections, as official co-manager and assigned intendants familiar with the treaties and with the press as his assistants.[35] He engaged as secretary a clerk named Lo Tu, who had long resided in the province and was regarded by the Szechwanese as an upright official.[36] He told his personal secretary and financial expert, Chou Hsün, who was another "first-generation Szechwanese," to give absolute priority to the railway.[37]

Hsi-liang continued to resist British and French pressure to participate in the project. The British businessman Townley, "using his own methods," had drawn Prince I-k'uang into a correspondence that the British minister fallaciously claimed confirmed British rights to participate if China failed to raise the funds.[38] When the British consul-general in Chengtu tried to use this correspondence to force Hsi-liang to admit the British to the project, Hsi-liang adamantly refused and declared: "I have some authority and . . . I intend to exercise it." [39] In fact, he had delegated authority over the line to Official Manager Feng-hsü, who, despite his honesty, tended to run the company without consulting the other officials and even without keeping in touch with Hsi-liang. Inexperienced in diplomacy, Feng-hsü got involved in a correspondence with the French consul, Bons d'Anty, at the end of which the consul claimed that "the Railway Company is tied to the French." [40] Learning of this, Hsi-liang ordered Feng-hsü to disavow whatever he had promised the French consul. The consul then angrily demanded of Hsi-liang: "Is the Railway Company under your control? Or in the hands of the Company?" Hsi-liang shot back: "So-called 'self-management' means that Szechwan will manage Szechwan's affairs; it cannot mean that the company will act by itself without reporting to the governor-general first." [41] Hsi-liang saved the situation, but, having lost confidence in Feng-hsü, he removed him from his post at the company and eventually sent him out of the province.[42]

This incident confirmed Hsi-liang in his determination to use only Chinese engineers to survey the route. He now rejected Feng-hsü's original plan to hire French engineers and made clear, as he wrote in one wire, that he wanted "only Chinese." [43] He wired Sheng Hsüan-huai in Shanghai to ask that the Chinese engineer Chan T'ien-yu, who was planning the Peking-Kalgan line, or some qualified returned student be sent to Szechwan. Sheng replied that Chan was busy and the students abroad not yet ready to return.[44] Under constant foreign pressure to engage foreign engineers, Hsi-liang in desperation finally sent his English interpreter, who knew nothing about surveying, to do a "preliminary survey" of the route.[45] This gesture earned Hsi-liang the contempt of the foreign consuls but achieved its aim of holding them at bay until some qualified Chinese engineers became available to do the work.[46]

Hsi-liang next tackled the formidable task of raising the estimated 50 million tls. needed for the line. Since the regular provincial revenues were already allocated, some officials in the company proposed raising the land tax which, at 600,000 tls. a year, was considered to be among the lightest in the empire. Because of his experience with the political consequences of such increases, Hsi-liang quickly vetoed this suggestion.[47] Instead he ordered that shares be sold to officials, local elite, and merchants in Szechwan and throughout the empire on a voluntary basis.[48] He set an example by using 2,000 of his 39,000 tls. annual income to purchase twenty shares and ordered his subordinates to buy amounts in similar proportion to their salaries.[49] He exhorted the local elite and merchants to participate, offering official ranks in return for contributions. Most Szechwanese had greeted the railway plan enthusiastically. One of them wrote that "the iron road will enable our good people of Szechwan to transport themselves easily in and out of the province, thus benefiting commerce." [50] Yet during the first year the Szechwanese purchased only 800,000 tls. of shares, and Chinese outside the province purchased even less.[51] The financial expert, Chou Hsün, sadly concluded that only 3 million tls. of the 50 million could be raised voluntarily.[52]

As Hsi-liang pondered this dilemma, he received assistance from an unexpected source—the Szechwanese students in Japan. During the Feng-hsü–Bons d'Anty affair the students in Japan had accused him of "selling Szechwan to France" and had founded a provincial association to defend Szechwan's right to build its own railway.[53] After he removed Feng-hsü and appointed Chao Erh-feng in his place, the students submitted a petition in a very different tone:

> Hearing this from afar we were first moved to weeping and then we jumped for joy!
> . . . How fortunate we are that Heaven looks on, showing concern for us

Szechwanese through the governor-general in this difficult situation, bringing the province to life just when it is on the brink of death.[54]

Praising Hsi-liang's "high character and clear intelligence," the students worried only about Szechwan's response:

> If, while the governor-general advocates and plans self-management, we are unable to realize his goal, then it will take a long time to collect capital and begin construction. While the governor-general will not have failed the Szechwanese, the Szechwanese will have failed him.[55]

The students purchased 60,000 tls. of shares, spoke for 300,000 more, and sent an impassioned twelve-page appeal to the local elite to invest.[56]

Realizing that voluntary contributions would never suffice, the students recommended "grain contributions." Their petition continued:

> Szechwan's departments and districts have for long had regulations on the collection of grain for undertaking important local matters. There is no doubt about this nor is there any aspect [of it] that would excite popular criticism as would an addition to taxes. . . . [If current abuses are eliminated], local officials could devise ways of encouraging people who grow grain to speak for shares on the basis of how much land they rent out—with small households . . . being exempted to avoid trouble. We ask that his Excellency investigate and devise ways [of doing this].[57]

The students also stressed that these mandatory contributions would "absolutely not be an increase in taxes." [58]

Hsi-liang seized on this suggestion as a means of stirring the Szechwanese upper class into action. Within two weeks he ordered Chao Erh-feng to call together 700 prominent residents of Chengtu "to consider ways and means for the raising of funds to construct a railway in Szechwan with native money alone." The general consensus at the meeting was "that the required funds could easily be raised by landholders, who should apportion a certain percentage of the rentals each year for a stated period." [59] With students, local elite, and merchants behind him, Hsi-liang memorialized in January 1905 to collect 3 percent of all rent income above ten piculs (1 picul = 110 pounds) of grain annually. The funds would be placed in rent shares (*tsu-ku*), which would earn interest for the contributors.[60] He drew up regulations that gave the local elite great control over the process of collection and spread the burden to all parts of the province where land was rented.[61] Since tenancy was especially widespread in Szechwan and since more land was rented out than was actually taxed, he and his experts expected to raise from 2 million to 4 million tls. a year by this method.[62]

Hsi-liang also found other sources of revenue. He donated 280,000 tls. originally designated for the mint and promised that he would turn over some profits from the mint once it began to function.[63] He imposed a heavy new tax on opium shops and "encouraged" the wealthy salt and tea merchants to buy shares according to their capacity.[64] Using all these methods he expected to raise nearly 20 million tls. by 1910.[65] To quiet the fears of Szechwanese about mismanagement, he pledged that any funds put into the company could not be withdrawn and that "no matter what crises may come up in the future, they [the funds] will absolutely not be used for any other purpose." [66] In February 1905 his plan was approved by the appropriate ministries, which noted with awe that he and the Szechwanese were apparently "willing to assume responsibility for the difficulties involved." [67]

Hsi-liang next had to decide where to begin work on the line, which, when completed, would run between Chengtu and Hankow.[68] The British and Feng-hsü had recognized that the stretch between Chengtu and Chungking would present fewer difficulties and promise a larger market; they had recommended beginning work on that part.[69] Hsi-liang and the Szechwanese, however, wished to build the more difficult section first and hoped to preempt the interprovincial stretch from foreign penetration. They advocated beginning work on the I-ch'ang-Wan-hsien (I-Wan) section, which would parallel the Yangtze gorges and tie the two provinces together.[70] In January 1905 Hsi-liang received a wire from Chang Chih-tung, whom the court had placed in charge of all railways in Hupeh. Chang also recommended beginning work on the I-wan section in order, he said, to skirt the rapids, make profits, and prevent foreigners from "getting their hands on the rest of the line." [71] Having regretted his early impetuousness in memorializing without consulting Chang, Hsi-liang concurred in his recommendations.[72] He soon memorialized to start work at I-ch'ang to "avoid the perils of the . . . gorges, . . . move products quickly, and transport materials easily." [73]

To oppose Chang's unstated plan to borrow abroad, Hsi-liang enlisted the support of the Szechwanese. Promising that he would never allow the foreigners to "get mixed up in" the line, he appealed to the Szechwanese to invest in it without fear.[74] In his appeal he came close to defining self-management as Szechwanese management:

> . . . all intelligent men regard construction of the Szechwan-Hankow railway as the most pressing need of Szechwan at the present time. Immediately upon entering the province last year, I memorialized the throne to assign the construction . . . to the province of Szechwan itself, and recently gentry and literati, natives of Szechwan, merchants from other provinces resident here, have all united in urging this course.[75]

He argued that since the Szechwanese were building the line and needed the I-Wan section as an "exit," they should have control over how it (as well as the rest of the line) was to be built.

Chang Chih-tung, however, still embraced his own notion of self-management and refused to give Szechwan authority over the I-Wan section since it lay largely within Hupeh.[76] At the same time Shen Ping-k'un, who would accept a foreign loan, succeeded Chao Erh-feng at the head of the company in

Chengtu.[77] To check Chang and Shen, Hsi-liang appointed a famous Szechwanese Hanlin compiler, Hu Chün, who opposed a loan, as general director (*tsung-tung*) of the company. After secret discussions, he sent Hu to Wu-ch'ang to negotiate with Chang.[78] To tighten control further over the company and to quell talk of a loan, Hsi-liang assumed the post of official manager and appointed another Szechwanese, Ch'iao Shu-nan, who also opposed a loan, as local elite business manager.[79]

Called upon to support Hsi-liang against Chang Chih-tung, the Szechwanese local elite felt entitled to offer some advice on the management of the Ch'uan-Han Company. Several of them petitioned Peking that they were "of one mind" with Hsi-liang in fearing foreign penetration of the company. They asked the court to guarantee that no loan would be made and, if necessary, to "assist the people in their efforts" to build the line by providing funds.[80] Another petitioner praised Hsi-liang's "official supervision and popular management" in Szechwan and asked that a compromise be reached with Hupeh as soon as possible.[81] Many Szechwanese recommended that the court appoint a special "general supervisor" to oversee the construction of the railway in both provinces and prevent further discord.[82] Thus, far from being merely "provincial" in their aims, the Szechwanese wanted to build the road as quickly as possible, prevent foreign intervention, and cooperate with Hupeh.

In September the court ordered Hsi-liang and Chang to discuss the proposed general supervisor.[83] Jolted by this threat of central control, Hu Chün and Chang got down to serious bargaining. They first discussed a proposal that Szechwan build the I-wan section and leave rights over it under the control of Hupeh. Hu might have accepted this idea if Chang had not wired Peking asking permission to borrow from England to build the section.[84] Hu's worst fears confirmed, he held out against this and two further proposals. Finally he and Chang decided that Szechwan would build the section in its own way (without a foreign loan) and would restore control over it to Hupeh in twenty-five years.[85] Hsi-liang and Chang then formally agreed on this formula and memorialized the throne for its approval.[86] Hsi-liang also wired the throne that there had been no disagreements "based on boundaries," which was true.[87] The fundamental difference had been over whether to take a foreign loan, and Hsi-liang, by his maneuvering, had won a decision against it.

Hsi-liang also differed with Chang over the hiring of foreign engineers. He had early decided that he would appoint a Chinese chief engineer who would then be given full authority both to hire and to supervise foreigners.[88] He nonetheless found this issue "troublesome" because neither the company official Shen Ping-k'un nor some of the Szechwanese local elite fully shared his suspicions regarding foreign engineers.[89] In order to persuade Chinese engineering students abroad to return to help, he wired London, Paris, and Berlin offering them salaries equal to those paid foreign engineers. In the meantime he sent three more men to do another "survey" and created a

Railway School in Chengtu for forty students.[90] When the British and French consuls insisted that he hire their nationals to survey the line, he told the Britisher "never to bring up the topic again" and warned the Frenchman: "If a foreigner offers us assistance . . . , we have the liberty to accept or refuse; who can stop us?" [91] When Chang Chih-tung informed him that he had hired two "first class" Japanese surveyors who would not be allowed to interfere in administration, Hsi-liang refused to share the expenses or heed their advice. He instead sent Hu Chün abroad to engage two Chinese engineers.[92] He later compromised by allowing the Japanese to survey the line, sending his own team of returned Chinese students to survey it again, and comparing the results.[93] He finally appointed one Hu Tung-chao as chief engineer and approved the hiring of foreign experts to work under him.[94]

Hsi-liang next turned to his relations with the Szechwanese. He had previously brushed off rumors spread by Szechwanese officials in Peking that the company was run by a "dictatorship of officials and clerks," but he now took notice when a censor impeached the secretary, Lo Tu, for bribery.[95] He examined the charges and found that while Lo Tu had taken advantage of his secretarial post to become wealthy, he had contributed some of his wealth to the company and he had not accepted bribes as had been charged. Hsi-liang managed to convince the court and the Szechwanese that Lo Tu was honest and worth keeping in the company.[96] Another Szechwanese accused Shen Ping-k'un of diverting company funds for his own use but could offer no proof for his charge. Hsi-liang found that Shen indeed favored wealth and power over honesty and probity, but he responded to the "solicitations of notables" to keep this capable official in his post.[97]

Some Szechwanese also began to charge that the rent levy was oppressive. An official in Peking, Tu Te-yü, first tried to get the levy repealed and then wrote to Hsi-liang asking that landlords receiving up to 100 piculs of rent be exempted.[98] Hsi-liang replied:

> If we could collect shares without relying on official power or computing people's rents, how could we not want to do this very much? But most shares so far have been sold only by means of official and local elite persuasion. Even these cannot compare with the amounts raised by the levy on rent.[99]

Students in Tokyo, led by P'u Tien-chün, who had first proposed the rent levy, now asked for exemptions for those who received up to fifty piculs of rent and a time limit on the collection of the levy.[100] Some Szechwanese in Peking rallied to Hsi-liang's defense, however, and characterized Tu's criticism as "excessive." The local elite within the province generally accepted the new levy.[101] Hsi-liang therefore maintained the exemption at ten piculs; but he increased interest to 6 percent, promised that income from rents would not exceed 40 percent of the total, and pledged that the levy would be suspended as soon as voluntary contributions increased sufficiently.[102] By these concessions and some subsequent propaganda, he persuaded most Szechwanese that the rent levy was the necessary foundation for self-management.[103]

Rumors spread also that company funds had been diverted to other projects. The students in Tokyo charged that 3 million tls. had been used on the mint and demanded that the funds be returned to the company.[104] Although it is unlikely that such a large diversion took place, it was said that the company promised the students to pay back any such loans within seven years.[105] Some members of the local elite in Szechwan related the rumor that 700,000 tls. had been diverted to a military campaign in Tibet. Hsi-liang became "violently angry" at this accusation, but the company seemed to confirm its validity by responding that if such diversions had been made, they had been repaid "long ago." [106] Perhaps suspicious of the conduct of his subordinates, Hsi-liang ordered them to publish the company accounts. They showed that the company had received 4.5 million tls. and spent 200,000 tls.[107] Since the financial records appeared accurate, Hsi-liang was able to regain the confidence of a majority of the Szechwanese and to neutralize the cries of anti-Manchu revolutionaries who were beginning to use the charges to discredit the dynasty.[108]

These struggles over corruption, oppression, and diversion of funds led some Szechwanese to demand that the Ch'uan-Han Company be transformed into a "merchant-managed" concern.[109] Hsi-liang had eliminated "official practices" (such as rake-offs) and used members of the local elite (such as Hu Chün and Ch'iao Shu-nan), but since he had created the company as an official enterprise, he had never adopted the regulations for merchant management. In late 1906 Szechwanese in Peking founded an association dedicated to turning "the conduct of the railway over to the local elite and merchants." [110] They were supported by students in Japan who took foreign practices as their example and by local elite in Szechwan who called for a "new and cultured merchant" company.[111] Hsi-liang responded by calling a meeting of the shareholders and adopting a compromise "to gain the confidence of the public." [112] He declared the company merchant-managed, but kept Hu and Ch'iao as president and vice-president responsible to the governor-general. He allowed a Shareholders Association to elect directors and accountants, but forbade them from "interfering with the authority of the president and vice-president." [113] He thereby won the support of the Szechwanese for the project that was of the greatest importance to him on the very day before being removed from his post.

Aftermath and Legacy

Hsi-liang had provided a crucial link between the Ch'ing and the Szechwanese and his removal eventually led to a national crisis. His successors, preoccupied with other issues, paid scant attention to the railway and allowed work on it to stall.[114] Moreover, in the absence of leadership, the state and local society became estranged over two issues related to the railway. When expert surveys showed that it would be more practical to build the Chengtu-Chungking section first, many Szechwanese favored changing the original plan, but the governor-general insisted on beginning with the I-Wan section.[115] When the Ch'uan-Han Company lost 3 million tls. in the Shanghai stock market crash of 1910, some Szechwanese blamed "official corruption," while the state replied that the company was largely in Szechwanese hands.[116] Taking advantage of these controversies, the president of the Ministry of Posts and Communications, Sheng Hsüan-huai, who had always favored centralization of all railway lines, nationalized the Ch'uan-Han line in 1911. This measure touched off active opposition from the badly compensated Szechwanese shareholders.[117]

In Hsi-liang's absence, the effort to exclude foreign capital from the line also flagged. Some officials and Szechwanese who saw the benefits of a foreign loan now began assuming leadership in the province and in the company.[118] Chang Chih-tung obtained permission to discuss a loan with the British and in 1909 concluded an agreement with the British, French, Germans, and Americans to build the Hupeh section of the line.[119] In 1911 Sheng Hsüan-huai, who had consistently advocated foreign loans for railways, signed a final agreement with the four powers, giving America control over the I-Wan section.[120] Claiming that the court was "selling the province to the foreigners," Szechwanese of all groups and classes flocked to a "railway protection movement" that fatally weakened the Ch'ing.[121]

Despite this disappointing aftermath, Hsi-liang's cooperation with the Szechwanese on the Ch'uan-Han line left an important legacy for later patriots. The company collected 16 million tls. by 1910, an amount greater than that raised by any other self-managed company and sufficient to begin work on the line.[122] Sixty miles of track had been built by 1911.[123] Construction progressed slowly partly because of the emphasis on independent effort. As one of Hsi-liang's subordinates remarked, "if the railway could not be built with Chinese capital and Chinese engineers, it would be better not to build it at all." [124] Another reason was Hsi-liang's concern that proper surveys be done before extensive work began.[125] Just as later expert surveys were advising beginning with the Chengtu-Chungking section, better technology permitted steamship transport through the Yangtze rapids to Chungking, so reducing the need for the I-Wan section.[126] When Hsi-liang's vision of a self-managed railway was realized fifty years after the fall of the Ch'ing, the Chinese-built line would run from Chengtu to Chungking.[127]

Hsi-liang's projects in industrial development aimed not only at "expanding the sources of profit" in a rich province with poor communications but also at "protecting our sovereignty" in a remote area that elicited intense foreign interest. So intense was that interest that Hsi-liang balked at hiring foreign advisers and insisted on using "native methods" so far as possible to achieve self-management. Since Hsi-liang provided the leadership and the Szechwan-ese the resources, self-management meant that "Szechwan will manage Szechwan's affairs." But in the larger sense, it meant that China would manage China's affairs so that the guest would not take the place of the host, and the Chinese would not have to withdraw without any rights.

Despite considerable initial success, Hsi-liang saw his plans dissolve in political controversy. Yet even this result revealed something important about Chinese attitudes toward industrialism and capitalism. Hsi-liang's reluctance to plan for the total transformation of China into an industrial society modeled on the West, with one project linked to another, was echoed in Szechwanese criticism of using railway funds to build the mint that was later to help pay for the railway. Hsi-liang's refusal to turn the railway over to pure "merchant management" reflected the same distrust of the profit motive that later led the Szechwanese to castigate company representatives for losing millions of taels in the 1910 stock market crash. Hsi-liang and the Szechwan-ese were more devoted to cooperation and solidarity than to mechanization and accumulation. He granted the local elite control over the collection of the rent shares, and they praised him for "official supervision and popular management." He answered their charges of corruption, diversions, and oppression; and they announced that they were "of one mind" with him. United in their daring to undertake the huge project and in their determina-tion to overcome all difficulties, they struggled not for technological change, which so intrigued the West, but for political dignity, which the West seemed intent on denying to them.

7: TIBETAN POLICY

Just as Hsi-liang enlarged his world view and worked to develop the provincial economy, so too he expanded Ch'ing control over the western dependency of Tibet. He acted partially to accommodate demands by foreigners in Szechwan but primarily to resist the British who invaded Tibet from India in 1904. After an initial reluctance to act, Hsi-liang was forced to undertake three phases of frontier policy. In the first he implemented some reforms to keep open the road to Lhasa; in the second he directed a military campaign in Kham (inner Tibet); in the third and final phase he extended administration to areas that previously had not been governed by the Chinese. He pointed the way to a full forward policy that brought all of Tibet under direct Chinese rule for the first time.

Noninvolvement

Hsi-liang at first ignored the expeditionary force that the British sent under Colonel Francis Younghusband to force Tibet to open its doors further to British trade and influence.[1] He had not mentioned it during his audience with the empress dowager or during his discussions with Chang Chih-tung in Peking. Nor had he discussed it in his first memorial after arriving in Chengtu.[2] He had already decided to focus on domestic reforms and did not want this frontier crisis to divert resources from the main task at hand.

By virtue of his post, however, he was drawn into the gathering crisis. The governor-general of Szechwan had long played a prominent role in formulating policy and in supplying troops to Tibet. Moreover, after centuries of increasing influence, China now faced a major turning point in its relations with the dependency. Would it, as it had in the early Ch'ing, be able to defend Tibet from a foreign invasion and so expand Chinese control?[3] Or would it, as had been the case more recently, fall back before the foreigners and suffer a loss of influence in Lhasa?[4] The question was all the more pressing because the young and vigorous dalai lama was expressing interest in a kind of autonomy that might lead to Tibet's falling out of the Chinese orbit and into the Western "international" system.[5]

Soon after Hsi-liang arrived in Chengtu, the newly appointed resident in Lhasa, Yu-t'ai, and his assistant, Kuei-lin, passed through the capital on the way to their posts. Hsi-liang complied with a court order to "discuss" the crisis with them.[6] But he informed them frankly that he "knew nothing about Tibet" and would gladly leave negotiations with the British about the withdrawal of the Younghusband expedition to the residents, who were experienced in such matters.[7] He was not to evade his responsibilities so easily, however, for he soon received an explicit court order to "assist" the residents in persuading the Tibetans to come to terms with the British.[8]

Resident Yu-t'ai, recalling that his predecessor had been dismissed for failing to get the Tibetans to deal with the British, realized that he was undertaking a delicate mission.[9] On the political plane, he had to persuade the Tibetans to negotiate without seeming to give Chinese consent to British claims. On the military plane, he needed to display enough force to awe the Tibetans into discussions but not so much as to appear to the British to be in control of the situation and thus responsible for the Tibetans' lingering recalcitrance. To facilitate his task in Lhasa, Yu-t'ai asked Hsi-liang for a military escort.[10] Since Hsi-liang had just begun his military reforms, he had no troops to spare and gave him a mere forty men.[11] Yu-t'ai later picked up several hundred more troops at Ta-chien-lu (Tar-tsen-do), but they were neither well armed nor well trained.[12]

The assistant resident, Kuei-lin, had the equally difficult assignment of maintaining peace in Kham, or inner Tibet, known for its valiant warriors. His problem was to guarantee the safety of the foreigners living there without appearing to the Tibetans to condone their activities. When he was asked by some missionaries to maintain strong garrisons in the area, he agreed and suggested to the court that these garrisons actually be expanded. He also asked that his post be moved from its traditional location in Lhasa to a new site in Ch'a-mu-to (Chamdo), a town in the heart of Kham. Finally he asked permission to strengthen his forces by increasing pay, improving organization, training officers, and creating a special battalion of 500 men on the model of the Hunanese militia that had reduced the Taiping Rebellion.[13] Hsi-liang approved the relocation of the assistant resident's post in Ch'a-mu-to and authorized him to reform and strengthen his military forces. But he questioned the possibility of raising militia on the frontier and opposed any military expansion on the grounds that it would "demand supplies that we do not have." [14]

Hsi-liang also doubted the feasibility of other changes suggested for Kham. A Szechwanese official in Peking memorialized for the appointment of a general supervisor who would expand the salt and cotton trade and tax the tea trade between Szechwan and Tibet. The income from these measures would support the development of gold mines in Li-t'ang (Lethang) and the expansion of colonization in Pa-t'ang (Pa). Hsi-liang responded that these proposals cost too much and ignored the realities of the Tibetan frontier. The Tibetans would not buy more salt because they already had plenty or more cotton goods because they did not wear cotton clothing. They would buy less of the more highly taxed tea and get it instead from India.[15] The Szechwan government had earlier invested in the mines at Pa-ti and Pa-wang (Cyarong) but with little result because the Tibetans opposed Western methods and became "difficult to manage." Since Tibetans already cultivated most of the arable land in Tibet, Han Chinese colonization was both unnecessary and risky. In sum, "the critical state of affairs in Tibet is not going to be solved by commerce, mining, and colonization." [16]

Under pressure from others, Hsi-liang did authorize a few modest changes. After reading a memorandum by Sir Robert Hart, supervisor of the Chinese Imperial Customs Service, he agreed "in principle" to stationing a battalion at Ch'a-mu-to. Learning that British and French businessmen intended to demand concessions in the mines of Kham, he instructed subordinates to preempt them by opening mines in Pa-ti, Pa-wang, Ta-chien-lu, and Li-t'ang.[17] Urged by the court to consider colonization, he ordered the Commissary of Pa-t'ang to survey lands available for colonization and reported that 200 Han Chinese families were opening 200 mow (1 mow = .16 acres) of new lands.[18] To avoid difficulties with the missionaries who feared the Tibetans, he raised the rank of the official at Ta-chien-lu from subprefect to independent subprefect and granted him more funds with which to handle "diplomacy concerning churches outside the pass." [19]

Hsi-liang still refused to become actively involved in outer Tibet, and the result was catastrophic. He rejected another appeal from Yu-t'ai for 4,000 troops and thus crippled the resident's efforts to press the dalai lama to negotiate with Younghusband.[20] Unwilling to make concessions to the British, the dalai lama instead asked the resident to protect his kingdom from them.[21] Hsi-liang also refused Yu-t'ai's request for 40,000 tls. and so deprived him of the funds necessary to influence the development of the situation. The dalai lama then purged the Tibetan peace party, sent troops to resist the British, and attacked Yu-t'ai's own garrison for being in league with the foreigners.[22] Yu-t'ai could begin to reestablish his influence only after the dalai lama fled, leaving behind his rival, the panchen lama, and a regent to negotiate with Younghusband. But the resident was still so weak that he had to agree to a convention with the British that imposed a large indemnity on Tibet, opened two more Tibetan towns to trade, and gave the British the right to send a representative to Lhasa at will. On instructions from Peking, Yu-t'ai later refused to sign this convention which would have made Tibet as much a part of the British empire as of the Chinese.[23]

Reform

Hsi-liang reacted to this humiliation by taking more interest in the affairs of Tibet. He recognized that his refusal to support Yu-t'ai had contributed to the resident's impotence during the maneuvering and negotiations in Lhasa. He therefore agreed to disburse 10,000 tls. more a year so that the resident could maintain himself with dignity.[24] Realizing the need for good communications with outer Tibet, he embarked on a series of reforms in inner Tibet to keep the road open to Lhasa.

His first reform in Kham involved the five states of Hor, to the north of Ta-chien-lu. These states had fallen under the control of the state of Nyarong (San-chan or Chan-tui) in the 1860s and thus indirectly under the influence of the Tibetan hierarchy in Lhasa.[25] Hsi-liang now memorialized that these states lay along the strategic northern route into Tibet and that their governments were "insufficiently organized for the long run." He was obviously concerned that they might be used by the dalai lama, who was agitating against the foreigners and against the Ch'ing. Hsi-liang therefore reduced the annual taxes that Szechwan normally imposed on the states and sent some Chinese military officers to "assist" the chiefs in their administration. As if to emphasize his concern with the crisis in outer Tibet, he refrained from instituting such reforms in neighboring states that did not lie along a route into Tibet.[26]

Hsi-liang next developed the gold mines of T'ai-ning (Gata Gomba), a military camp between Nyarong and the state of Ming-cheng (Chala).[27] The chief of Ming-cheng, a young and vigorous man, had long been trying to open these mines but had been continually opposed by the lamas of T'ai-ning and the Lhasa-appointed governor of Nyarong.[28] To obtain support against the lamas and the governor, the chief had cultivated ties with foreigners living in Ta-chien-lu and had become a "blood brother" of a missionary of the China Inland Mission. As he drew closer to the foreigners he became further estranged from the lamas, the governor, and the dalai lama.[29] In order to support the chief against the lamas and wean him from the foreigners, Hsi-liang sent out a special envoy with 10,000 tls. to help open the mines. Whether by design or error, the agent subsequently entrusted the funds to three Chinese converts of the China Inland Mission.[30]

Hsi-liang still resisted pressure to undertake a military build-up in Kham. He refused the request of the assistant resident, Kuei-lin, for a full battalion to escort him to his post at Ch'a-mu-to. Aware of the danger of traveling in Kham without troops, Kuei-lin begged to be relieved of his assignment on the grounds that he was going blind.[31] Hsi-liang appointed in his place another Manchu bannerman named Feng-ch'üan, who had served many years in Szechwan as a local official and who was reputedly "upright and fearless," or, in less complimentary terms, "arrogant and harsh." [32] He again refused entreaties to supply Feng-ch'üan with a large force and instead sent him on his way with only 150 policemen.[33] The new appointee was "reluctant" to go without troops but had a reputation of bravery to uphold and soon left Chengtu on the 1,100-mile trip to Ch'a-mu-to.

Even with the limited forces available to him, Feng-ch'üan dealt severely with the Tibetan people along his route. Because he had long enjoyed good relations with the French in Szechwan, he took a personal interest in capturing Tibetans who allegedly had robbed a Catholic priest in Li-t'ang. He jailed one man suspected of the crime, executed two others, and demanded 1,500 tls. in indemnity from a nearby lamasery that he held responsible for the antiforeign atmosphere in the area. He refused to listen to an envoy from Nyarong who arrived to claim that the men were innocent residents of his state.[34] In Pa-t'ang he punished other alleged robbers and demanded that the local chief, Lo Chin-pao, doff his hat as a sign of respect. He ordered land reclamation and colonization there expanded from 200 mow to over 50,000 mow, so threatening the lamas of the nearby Ting-ling lamasery who owned nearly one-half of the land in Pa-t'ang. He added insult to injury by turning over some of the new lands to the Catholic missionaries of Pa-t'ang. He also recruited 200 Tibetan soldiers for his forces and trained them in the Western style.[35]

Feng-ch'üan took two other highhanded measures that were unauthorized by Hsi-liang. Earlier Yu-t'ai had reported that the "power of the lamas [in Pa-t'ang] is greater than the power of the officials" and had suggested that the lamas be reduced in number and authority.[36] Hsi-liang had quietly shelved this proposal, which ran contrary to traditional Ch'ing policy of patronizing the lamas to control Tibet. But Feng-ch'üan no sooner arrived in Pa-t'ang than he wholeheartedly endorsed Yu-t'ai's proposal, memorializing that the number of lamas should be reduced from 1,500 to 300 and that no young men should join a lamasery for twenty years.[37] Another official, perhaps in Peking, had suggested that the state of Nyarong "should be brought back to our possession again." [38] Without waiting for Hsi-liang to consider this extremely delicate issue, Feng-ch'üan memorialized that the "return" of Nyarong was "crucial to the frontier." He boldly suggested that the Ch'ing order the Lhasa-appointed governor to withdraw from the state or face an invasion and reorganization.[39]

The harsh implementation of reforms without adequate military support yielded bitter fruit both in T'ai-ning and Pa-t'ang. In T'ai-ning the lamas decided that Hsi-liang's mining envoy was associated with the Protestant converts, and they protested strongly against a "Sino-foreign plot" on their mines. Hsi-liang responded by instructing the Ming-cheng chief to expand his military forces. He also sent out his own task force to overawe the lamas. When the Chinese force advanced on T'ai-ning and asked the lamas to acquiesce in the reforms, it was attacked and several of its members, including an officer, were killed.[40]

The situation at Pa-t'ang deteriorated even further. The lamas of Ting-ling regarded Feng-ch'üan's arbitrary changes as an attack on their economy, religion, society, and culture. Asked to turn over some Tibetan refugees from Ch'ing justice, they flatly refused. When Feng-ch'üan dispatched some policemen to the lamasery, the lamas forbade them to enter; conflict ensued and a lama was killed. The enraged lamas immediately led a large group of

Tibetans to surround Feng-ch'üan's headquarters and cut off his water supply. They accused the assistant resident of trying to bribe them and of staying illegally in Pa-t'ang when his post was supposed to be at Ch'a-mu-to. They charged that he was a veritable "foreign official" (yang-kuan) who protected the missionaries and trained troops in the Western style. When Feng-ch'üan sent out his police to break the siege, the Tibetans killed twenty of them. Feng-ch'üan's Tibetan recruits then mutinied. When the crowd surged forward, Feng-ch'üan escaped out a back door, scattering rubies in his wake. He fled to the office of the Pa-t'ang chief, Lo Chin-pao, who agreed to quiet the mob in return for Feng-ch'üan's promise to return immediately to Ta-chien-lu.[41]

The lamas were still not satisfied that they had foiled the Sino-foreign assault on their rule in Tibet. They led angry crowds to attack one Catholic mission near Pa-t'ang and another further south near the Yunnan border. They killed dozens of converts and two French priests. Moreover, after Feng-ch'üan left Pa-t'ang, he was ambushed as he crossed a narrow ledge along a sheer cliff. Seventy of his men were killed along with him. Only the Pa-t'ang commissary, who had treated the Tibetans more respectfully, was spared. This suggested that the lamas hated Feng-ch'üan and the foreigners more than they did the Ch'ing or the Chinese.

Military Suppression

Hsi-liang immediately memorialized in favor of suppressing the T'ai-ning lamas with military force:

> The lamas oppose officials and kill officers—their wildness is extreme. If they are not brought to heel, mining will be set back and frontier affairs will become impossible to manage. . . . If the lamas are once stupid like this, they will eventually try to get those near and far into league with them.[42]

He ordered the Ming-cheng chief to send 2,000 men to the lamasery and instructed the provincial commander-in-chief, Ma Wei-ch'i, a veteran Muslim general, to lead a well-armed battalion of reserves against the rebels.[43] According to foreign records, the lamas tried to forestall an invasion by announcing that "if the Emperor really wants to open gold mines at T'ai-ning and refrains from using force . . . , [we] will allow it and pray for his Majesty in the monasteries as before." [44] The Ming-cheng chief and the provincial commander-in-chief rejected this peace offer and invaded T'ai-ning. Their troops plundered and laid waste to the lamasery.[45] One officer who stole 2,000 items, including bronze Buddhas, gold saddles, jade scepters, and spiritual scrolls from the lamasery later was banished to Sinkiang for life. Hsi-liang nonetheless rewarded the chief and Ma Wei-ch'i for the firm suppression campaign.[46]

When he reported Feng-ch'üan's assassination to Peking, Hsi-liang advocated an expansion of military control and thus of the military forces:

> By burning churches and killing officials, the lamas have committed great crimes.
> . . . We must extend the command of Heaven in order to suppress the rebellion and
> restore order. . . . The finances of Szechwan are in bad straits, but we must increase
> our troops in order to maintain control. We must have rations for several soldiers in
> order to sustain one soldier on the frontier. We must have several piculs of grain in
> order to transport one picul to its destination.[47]

To finance this military expansion, he sold more ranks, diverted more funds to the military, and curtailed expenditures for all troops not directly involved in Tibet.[48] Placing the Tibetan crisis nearly on a par with the Ch'uan-Han railway, he ordered two railway officials to lead battalions into inner Tibet and told his private secretary to become an expert in Tibetan affairs.[49]

While preparing for a campaign, Hsi-liang still hoped to avoid unnecessary force. He argued that "to govern the barbarians, we must first conquer their hearts." [50] He tried to placate the aroused people of Kham by instructing the new assistant resident, Lien-yü, to pass by Ch'a-mu-to and go right on to Lhasa. Because he recognized that it would be difficult to conduct military operations in a rugged terrain among a hostile population, he announced that he would authorize a full-scale campaign only if the lamas failed to punish those responsible for Feng-ch'üan's assassination.[51] The lamas too tried to combine threats with reason. They held the commissary and the chief hostage, and they warned that they could count on the support of Nyarong in resisting any military attack. But they also admitted that the murder of Feng-ch'üan was inexcusable, and they beheaded eight men accused of the crime.[52]

Although the lamas had met his primary condition, Hsi-liang found it increasingly difficult to halt preparations for a campaign against Pa-t'ang. The provincial commander-in-chief, Ma Wei-ch'i, naturally favored a military solution. The court ordered Hsi-liang to take "all necessary measures" to protect the remaining missionaries on the frontier.[53] The French consul characterized Hsi-liang's reluctance to use force as "moderation bordering on weakness" and urged him to take stronger measures.[54] The Protestants favored a military campaign after which they hoped to "become actors in the drama of teaching and encouraging industrial work." [55] The Catholics, hoping to expand their missions further into the Buddhist kingdom, openly called for the "destruction of the Ting-ling lamasery." [56] Sensitive to missionary claims arising from the killings of the two priests, Hsi-liang was drawn into elaborating plans for an invasion.[57] He asked Yu-t'ai in Lhasa to help keep Nyarong from assisting Pa-t'ang. Then he ordered Ma Wei-ch'i to lead 4,000 men to Pa-t'ang to "get all of the principal criminals." [58] On his way to Pa-t'ang, Ma refused to deal with envoys of the lamas, who arrived bearing the heads of Feng-ch'üan's supposed murderers. In a phrase reminiscent of that of the Catholic missionaries, Ma announced that the Ting-ling lamasery would "have to be destroyed." [59]

Having rejected all compromise, Ma and his five battalions encountered fierce opposition from the Tibetans. He fell into repeated ambushes and suffered numerous casualties before reaching Pa-t'ang. But he took the town, captured the chief, Lo Chin-pao, and sent him off to Chengtu for punishment. He and his men then marched to the lamasery, killed many of the lamas, watched others commit suicide, and drove the rest off into the hills. Hsi-liang was surprised that Ma had acted so harshly and had refused to take prisoners. He immediately recalled him to Chengtu on the grounds that he was in bad health.[60] Despite obvious reservations about Ma's methods, Hsi-liang praised him for his martial skills and awarded him the high military honor of a Yellow Riding Jacket.[61] When Hsi-liang later decided to grant amnesty to Lo Chin-pao, who had tried to mediate the conflict with the lamas, Ma opposed the decision and demanded the death penalty for Lo. So strongly did Ma feel that he even sent troops to attack Hsi-liang's bodyguards.[62]

The pressure on Hsi-liang to take more decisive action on the frontier continued to mount. The court directed him to make far-reaching plans to maintain order in Kham for all time. Hsi-liang complied by proposing to move two high provincial officials to Ta-chien-lu and to station large garrisons in Li-t'ang and Pa-t'ang.[63] An official elsewhere in the empire memorialized that Hsi-liang should eliminate the remaining "trouble makers" in Pa-t'ang and "proclaim the laws" in that frontier town.[64] Hsi-liang therefore approved the plan of the new commander, Chao Erh-feng, to lead 2,000 men armed with Mausers and foreign cannon to "clean out" the remaining resistance. Chao led his army to Pa-t'ang, executed more lamas, and pacified the surrounding countryside.[65] He then advocated a campaign against the neighboring lamasery of Sang-p'i in the state of Hsiang-ch'eng (Chantreng) on the grounds that it had assisted the Pa-t'ang lamas in their resistance.[66]

Hsi-liang knew that the Sang-p'i lamas had supported the Pa-t'ang resistance and had also attacked a Catholic mission. Still he opened communications with them and tried to entice them into a compromise to satisfy Chao without a further campaign. This effort failed, however, and the Catholic archbishop of Ta-chien-lu pressed Hsi-liang to keep Chao in Kham and, implicitly, to follow his advice. Hsi-liang finally approved Chao's expedition because, as he later rationalized, if Sang-p'i "had not been punished, Pa and Li would sooner or later have fallen from our grasp." [67]

The military suppression campaign reached its height with the attack on Sang-p'i. According to Hsi-liang, Chao laid siege to the formidable stone lamasery for six months with "battles every day" and "some of the fiercest fighting in several decades." Adopting a typically Tibetan strategy, he cut off the source of the lamasery's water supply. Once the lamas had been weakened, he stormed the barricades in June 1906.[68] Under Chao's attack, many lamas were killed or committed suicide. Others burned the lamasery and fled into the hills. Chao's bloody suppression campaign may have been the origin of his later reputation as a "butcher." Yet once victorious, he put out the fire, proscribed looting, and spared those who had surrendered.[69] The Tibetans naturally resented this campaign, but the hierarchy in Lhasa refrained from protesting because Sang-p'i was clearly within China's traditional sphere of control.[70] With this campaign, Hsi-liang finally acknowledged the necessity of using force to control Tibet. He memorialized that "The policy of managing barbarians by humbling one's self to conquer their hearts only nourishes an abscess and encourages rebellion." [71] To celebrate the fall of Sang-p'i he held a "grand theatrical entertainment" in Chengtu.[72]

Administrative Expansion

Hsi-liang now expanded the regular administration of districts and officials to areas that had joined in the rebellion. He abolished the Pa-t'ang chiefdom and replaced it with a Chinese magistrate; he reduced the number of lamas in the lamaseries; he reformed the tax, legal, and land systems; and he planned the construction of schools, roads, a telegraph, and a railway.[73] In 1907 he memorialized in favor of developing mining in Li-t'ang, greatly expanding colonization in Pa-t'ang, and forming a special frontier brigade to keep order throughout Kham.[74]

Hsi-liang also worked to expand Ch'ing control to the state of Nyarong, which had fallen under Lhasa's influence in the 1860s. He reviewed his predecessors' efforts to recover that state in order to learn from their mistakes. He found that Governor-General Lu Ch'uan-lin had conquered Nyarong in the 1890s but had subsequently lost it to Lhasa when his subordinates intrigued with the dalai lama and when he failed to transform the state into a district with a Chinese magistrate.[75] Hsi-liang carefully consulted with key subordinates and undertook a new initiative to recover the state.[76] He memorialized: "When the dalai lama has fled and the Tibetans are in an urgently repentant mood, . . . we can get twice as much accomplished with half the effort. This is clearly the time to act." [77]

Despite such aggressively expansionary statements, Hsi-liang proposed to recover Nyarong through diplomacy rather than force. He rejected the counsel of some of his generals who assured him that "we could exterminate such a small state in the wink of an eye." He argued:

> We can, of course, level the hills, clear the land, and establish military colonies, but it would appear that this would not be consistent with the court's desire to be "gracious to those from afar and kind to the weak and the young." [78]

On the other hand, he differed with those who suggested that he could regain control of Nyarong simply by urging Lhasa to withdraw its governor. "I fear that they will act like the lamas of T'ai-ning—as sheep and dogs—and will merely try to undermine our authority." He proposed instead that the Ch'ing take advantage of Lhasa's earlier proposal to return Nyarong if Szechwan paid the costs of Lhasa's past military expeditions to pacify the state.[79]

The court quickly approved Hsi-liang's proposal and ordered all officials concerned with it to help him carry it out.[80] This plan probably would have resulted in the peaceful incorporation of Nyarong into the Chinese state as a new district governed by a magistrate. By 1907, however, Hsi-liang had not yet taken the necessary steps to implement his policy. The initiative in frontier policy was already passing out of his hands and into those of Chao Erh-feng.

Chao Erh-feng, who was Hsi-liang's favorite subordinate, was rewarded for his success in the Pa-t'ang campaign by being named to the newly created post of frontier commissioner of Szechwan and Yunnan. Chao received the right to memorialize the throne directly and soon began to advocate a more expansionary program than Hsi-liang's. Hsi-liang held that China's authority extended only as far as it had in mid-Ch'ing times, to the area of Pa-t'ang.[81] Chao assumed responsibility for protecting a Catholic mission that the French insisted on reestablishing west of Pa-t'ang in Markham Gartok (Chiang-ch'ia), a state that had never been under China's control.[82] Hsi-liang had spent only 1 million tls. in four years on the frontier, but Chao proposed an initial outlay of 2 million tls. plus an annual expenditure of 3 million tls.[83] Hsi-liang remained generally skeptical of the need and wisdom of colonization; Chao encouraged it to strengthen the frontier and popularized it as a means of relieving population pressure in Szechwan.[84]

Chao's greater expansionary thrust carried over into the cultural and administrative fields. Hsi-liang founded a school for Tibetan studies to train 120 Chinese administrators in Tibetan, arguing that the "important thing in frontier matters is to understand the native's mentality and this can be done only through his written and spoken language." Chao concentrated instead on founding Chinese schools to teach Mandarin to the Tibetans.[85] While Hsi-liang showed reluctance to extend the regular district form of government to Li-t'ang, which had not participated in the rebellion or fallen under Lhasa's control, Chao favored the establishment of districts at Li-t'ang and throughout Kham.[86] Chao was more aware than Hsi-liang of foreign encroachment in Manchuria and Mongolia as well as in Tibet, and he advocated a forward policy to protect all of those frontier areas.[87]

A more active frontier policy was advocated also by the Chinese trade commissioner, Chang Yin-t'ang, who was negotiating the final commercial agreement to open Tibet to the British. Coming from a background of international affairs and diplomacy, Chang criticized the resident, Yu-t'ai, for weakness in dealing with the British in 1904 and for laxness in permitting a British expeditionary force to kidnap the panchen lama and take him to India in 1905. In alarmist tones, Chang warned the throne that the panchen lama planned to invite British protection and to declare Tibet independent (*tu-li*) of China.[88] Chang therefore proposed to follow the example of the British in India by establishing a garrison of 20,000 troops in Tibet and bringing that dependency under full administrative control.[89] In late 1906 the court signaled its interest in this plan by removing Yu-t'ai from his post and appointing Chang to take his place.

In May 1907 Hsi-liang was removed from his post in Szechwan. One reason may have been his refusal to make presents to the right people in Peking.[90] Yet he had long refused to make such gifts, and there is evidence that he became more flexible about this issue in Szechwan. According to his private secretary, Chou Hsün, he was prevailed upon by advisers to give 200 tls. in gold to each of the grand councillors at New Year's. Rumor had it that one surprised grand councillor said to another: "200 in gold from Hsi-liang is equal to 2,000 in gold from anyone else." [91] The main reason for his removal was probably that the court had decided to favor the more aggressive Tibetan policy of Chao Erh-feng and Chang Yin-t'ang.

Once installed as acting governor-general of Szechwan, Chao Erh-feng allowed foreign missionaries to penetrate further into Kham; engaged Chinese and foreign advisers to develop the schools, mines, and agriculture; and established district magistrates in Li-t'ang, Hsiang-ch'eng, and other states previously under local chiefs. Appointed imperial commissioner for Tibet, he cooperated with his brother, Chao Erh-sun, who succeeded him in Szechwan, to seize the state of Dege (Te-ko) and reorganize it into a district. The Chaos then conquered and reorganized other states, such as Markham Gartok, which had formerly owed allegiance only to Lhasa. In 1910 Chao Erh-feng led 2,000 troops to Lhasa, causing the dalai lama to flee to India, and bringing all of Tibet under direct Chinese control for the first time. He reorganized Nyarong into a district and Kham into a province just as the Ch'ing fell in 1911.[92]

This late Ch'ing expansion into Tibet enjoyed the support of the politically active public in China. The Szechwanese supported both Hsi-liang's effort to cooperate with the chiefs in Kham and Chao's more ambitious program of replacing them with Chinese magistrates.[93] As Hsi-liang expected, the Szechwanese did not respond enthusiastically to pleas to migrate to Kham, but, as Chao hoped, they approved of Han intermarriage with Tibetans to create a new and solid frontier society.[94] They concurred in Hsi-liang's determination to give priority to the Ch'uan-Han line, but they strongly backed Chao's Tibetan campaigns as well.[95] The press throughout the empire, representing all political persuasions, supported the Ch'ing expansion into Tibet, suggesting that it was part of the larger nationalist movement of the time.[96] Hsi-liang and the Chaos thus converted the British invasion of Tibet into a Chinese nationalist triumph.[97]

During his years in Szechwan, Hsi-liang moved from a preoccupation with domestic affairs to a direct concern with frontier matters. From his earlier experience in Jehol, he had become convinced that honest administration would suffice to control the frontier; no special knowledge of the frontier peoples was needed. Then the British invasion of Tibet and pressure from other foreigners who wished to exploit opportunities in Kham forced Hsi-liang to realize that he must act to forestall increased foreign intervention in the dependency. Once he recognized that some of the states of Kham were "insufficiently organized for the long run," he and his subordinates instituted reforms that angered the Tibetans and led them to rebel against Chinese rule. The rebellion had to be suppressed if frontier affairs were not to become "impossible to manage," and the suppression campaign was later justified by a variant of the domino theory: "If Sang-p'i had not been punished, Pa and Li would sooner or later have fallen from our grasp." Under great pressure to quell the disorder, Hsi-liang shifted in a matter of months from saying that "to govern the barbarians, we must first conquer their hearts," to asserting that "the policy of managing barbarians by humbling oneself to conquer their hearts only nourishes an abscess and encourages rebellion." Hsi-liang was even willing to take advantage of the Tibetans' plight under the British heel to "get twice as much accomplished with half the effort." Still his policies seemed moderate when compared with Chao Erh-feng's determination to turn Tibet into another Manchuria in order to defend it from the British and with Chang Yin-t'ang's desire to make it into another India to prevent it from becoming "independent." Hsi-liang went far along the road to frontier expansion but not so far as some colleagues who were more affected by the Western threat and model.

Almost buried beneath the strident rhetoric of expansion but present from the beginning to the end of Hsi-liang's term was another theme that promised further change in his frontier and minority policies. This theme of "conquering the hearts" of the barbarians appeared first in the strategy of deploying military forces in inner Tibet according to the terrain and local population and culminated in the rejection of the facile military argument that "such a small state" as Nyarong could be "exterminated in the wink of an eye." The ideal of being "gracious to those from afar and kind to the weak and the young" obviously was related to such projects as establishing a school to teach Chinese administrators the Tibetan language so that they could understand the "native's mentality." In another time and place, this theme would lead to frontier and minority policies different from the expansionary ones adopted by necessity in Szechwan.

Part 3: Radicalism in Yunnan, 1907–1909

As Hsi-liang left Szechwan, he seems to have reflected that he had defended the province at the cost of imitating foreign countries. He had taught their values, adopted their techniques, and accommodated many of their activities and thereby risked losing the students to another way of life, pressing the landlords into opposition, and driving minorities into revolt. He apparently concluded that further expansion might undermine the culture, disrupt society, and weaken the empire.

Hsi-liang was now transferred to Yunnan where he faced the dilemma in much starker terms. With a small population and infertile lands, Yunnan ranked as one of the poorest provinces in the empire. Located on the southwestern frontier, it was at the very periphery of Ch'ing control. Its Han Chinese population was at odds both with the Manchu overlords and with local ethnic minorities. The province had recently been chosen by anti-Manchu radicals as the chief target of a campaign to create a revolutionary base in South China.

As governor-general of Yunnan-Kweichow, Hsi-liang concentrated on Yunnan, where he displayed a radicalism that drew on some fundamental Chinese traditions concerning the good society. Perhaps unconsciously he adopted a style of government that showed the influence of certain Legalist, Confucian, and even Taoist teachings concerning the state, society, and the empire. He drew selectively on a statist tradition to run the administration, reform the military forces, and attack the opium problem; on a populist tradition to appeal for support from such groups as the peasantry, workers, and students; and on a quietest tradition to deal with the ethnic minorities. By this means he hoped not just to preserve their loyalty to the Ch'ing but also to get their support in the larger national revolution.

Map 3. Yunnan

8: MANAGING THE STATE

From the time Hsi-liang arrived in Yunnanfu (or K'un-ming) in May 1907 until he left a year and a half later, he administered the province without calling upon foreign experts, purged the old military forces to organize the new, and mounted an offensive against poppy cultivation and opium smoking. In the true statist fashion, he used authoritarian methods to implement his concept of the common good.

Administrative Antiforeignism

Hsi-liang continued to dislike the foreigners and to express his feelings within the constraints of the treaties, which had the force of Chinese law. In some cases he held the foreigners to the law to restrict their activities. When a British businessman instructed a Chinese agent to buy land outside of Meng-tzu, Hsi-liang had the agent arrested, tried, and convicted of illegally purchasing land outside a treaty port.[1] In other cases he invoked the treaties to restrain Chinese from illegal acts against the foreigners. When the Triad Secret Society (San-tien-hui) in Ssu-mao planned an assault on missionaries, Hsi-liang sent troops to intervene and later rewarded the officers who had captured the leaders.[2] Thus his preoccupation in Yunnan with administrative control merely reinforced his earlier tendency to be antiforeign within the law.

Hsi-liang was determined that the state monopolize the expression of the antiforeign impulse. He once invited a prefect named Ch'in Shu-sheng, a favorite of the empress dowager who had written a book attacking missionaries, to join him at dinner with the British consul-general. Ch'in refused the invitation in order to avoid eating with a foreigner. Hsi-liang was so impressed with his strength of character that he promoted him to be intendant at T'eng-yüeh, in western Yunnan, to deal with the British in Burma.[3] After arrival in T'eng-yüeh, Ch'in endorsed a pledge by local notables to prevent a missionary from buying land and building a chapel. Ch'in told the local elite: "missionary propaganda is the curse of the place; if you are unanimous you can prevent the lease of the house and the sale of the land. Officials dare not."

When Hsi-liang learned of Ch'in's action, he wired him that the missionaries had a right by treaty to buy land in T'eng-yüeh and that Ch'in should issue a proclamation to that effect to inform all those who might be "ignorant." [4] Hsi-liang obviously resented Ch'in's implication that the officials were too weak to do their duty and should therefore yield leadership to the local elite.

Hsi-liang's concern for administrative autonomy led him to conduct the affairs of state without foreign aid. Having arrived in Yunnan during a great famine, he immediately wired Peking for assistance. The court promised him 40,000 bags of flour from the missionaries on condition that the donors take part in distributing it. Hsi-liang refused the offer on the pretext that it would be impractical to ship the donated grain all the way from North China. In reality, he was reluctant to share his administrative authority with the missionaries even on such a worthy project as famine relief. Instead he instructed his subordinates to face up to the problem and to enlist the local elite in dealing with it.[5] In this way he retained official control over relief and ensured that the state received the chief credit for it.

In Yunnan Hsi-liang lacked the resources to hire foreign advisers. Even had the funds been available, he seems increasingly to have shared a growing Chinese feeling that the acceptance of foreign advisers on foreign terms would be, in the words of a recent study, "a form of submission." [6] A foreign journalist who traveled through Yunnan at this time noted that "with the exception of two or more Japanese, . . . there are . . . no foreign teachers in any of the schools or colleges in Yunnan." [7] Even more important, in contrast to his practice in Szechwan, Hsi-liang proceeded to carry out his military reforms without any foreign advisers. Although much of our information about his antiopium campaign comes from sympathetic missionaries, he conducted that campaign too without any direct foreign assistance. His determination to do without foreign help was merely the other side of his radical effort to draw on Chinese traditions and resources to effect great changes in the current situation in the province.

Military Reorganization

Even before his arrival in Yunnan, Hsi-liang had heard about the sad state of military affairs in the province. On his way to his post he had secretly memorialized to impeach his predecessor, the lackluster Ting Chen-to, for incompetence and corruption.[8] He had moved in secret because Ting, widely known as incapable, was a fellow provincial and protégé of the powerful Yüan Shih-k'ai.[9] As much as Hsi-liang wanted to discredit Ting, he did not want to alienate Yüan, whose attitude would affect any future effort at military reform in Yunnan. In addition to holding his predecessor strictly accountable for the lack of reform, Hsi-liang explained to the court that thereafter the state would have to assume full responsibility for improving the military forces and could not rely on the Yunnanese to do it.[10] He believed that a strong state was also a responsible one.

During his first two months in Yunnan, Hsi-liang investigated the military forces. He then memorialized that "what I have seen is no different from what I had heard."

> To begin with, the types of troops are often mixed up and the weapons are not ready for use. In the capital are stationed [three battalions] of infantry and one of artillery. These battalions are spread all over in offices, lookout towers, and temples because they have no barracks. The troops walk around the streets at night, entering and leaving without restrictions, and they have even less discipline than do the little-organized braves [yung-ying]. If they are unaware of the regulations, how can we begin to speak about training them?
>
> Moreover, the officer's school has no one who has had any previous training in military studies [lu-chün hsüeh-shu], so there is no one to train them. In name we have an artillery, but in fact there are few who know anything about rifles; new kinds of cannon have not been purchased; the old kinds which exist can hardly be moved; and there is no one who is familiar with using them. [Two battalions] have no trained troops in them whatsoever, and they patrol the . . . railway, spread over a huge area in a helter-skelter fashion; what is more, we have just investigated and found that there are abuses such as deficiencies in the quotas. . . . Because the province has suffered from a lack of supplies, it has sent out the old army under the name of the new army; since it has lacked men, it has had a new army in name but no new army in fact.[11]

He thus proposed to enforce the regulations and pursue a "rectification of names," the age-old goal of reforming institutions to make them correspond to the ideal.

The court was obviously shocked at this picture of corruption and chaos beneath a façade of reform and reorganization. It immediately turned the incompetent Ting over to the Ministry of Civil Appointments for punishment and instructed Hsi-liang to discipline all lower officials in Yunnan who had been responsible for the situation.[12] The court appreciated Hsi-liang's sharp distinction between the name and the reality. In another edict to leading reform officials, including Yüan Shih-k'ai, Chang Chih-tung, and Tuan-fang, the court pointed to Hsi-liang as a model for guarding the "national essence" and heeding the "larger picture." It warned them not to rest on their laurels and concluded: "You must all work together to cut out the evils of drift and to establish the foundations of wealth and power." [13] Reaching the height of its reform effort, the court under the empress dowager strongly favored officials such as Hsi-liang who conscientiously applied the regulations on the local level.

Having obtained this enthusiastic support from Peking, Hsi-liang moved quickly to "cut out the evils" of the local military establishment. He memorialized first on the need for a ruthless campaign against the dishonest, arguing that "in order to raise the morale of our weary troops, we must first punish all the corrupt officers." [14] Long a model of official probity, he believed that rampant corruption was a major obstacle to efficiency. He sent special deputies to investigate the forces scattered around the province and soon reported to the throne that many "battalion commanders wallow in corruption." [15] The worst offenders included two lieutenant-colonels who commanded troops along the French railway from Laokay in Indochina to Meng-tzu in Yunnan. These officers had allowed their forces to fall 20 percent below the legal quota but had continued to draw the statutory pay and to pocket the difference. Outraged by their lack of self-respect and dedication, Hsi-liang "invited" them to Yunnanfu. Meanwhile he obtained a secret rescript from Peking authorizing strict punishment. As soon as they arrived, he had them arrested and executed.[16]

Although these two officers and others yet to be purged were Chinese Muslims, Hsi-liang acted against them because of their corrupt behavior, not because of their minority religion. A large number of the accused were Muslim because many Muslims had risen to prominence in the Yunnan officer corps during the suppression of the southwestern Muslim uprising in the nineteenth century.[17] Although demonstrating loyalty to the Ch'ing and bravery in combat, they often had lacked the education and training that would have led them to restrain their greed or to welcome reforms. The officers removed at this time had violated the Ch'ing military statutes for the regular Green Standard forces as well as those for the New Army. The penal code stipulated execution for the two lieutenant-colonels because their ranks were relatively low and their crimes blatant. But high-ranking Han Chinese officers who committed similar offenses were also severely punished at this time. One brigade commander was transferred to a hardship post and three junior officers were banished to hard labor in Sinkiang.[18] The Muslim religion of many of those punished had more to do with the consequences of the campaign than with its motivation.

Hsi-liang next moved against another Muslim, a colonel named Ma Tien-hsüan, who commanded the key portion of the Green Standard forces along the railway. Ma had reported more men than he actually commanded and had appropriated the additional salaries. Hsi-liang noted that Ma had been in a good position to set an example for the whole province. Decrying Ma's falsification of reports and theft of funds, he memorialized for permission to fine him 10,000 tls. and to banish him to hard labor in Sinkiang for the rest of his life.[19] When Ma was arrested and held in Yunnanfu pending a decision, some of his Muslim troops tried to break in to free him, but they failed to get support from others who remained loyal to the governor-general. Ma then appealed to the French consul to intervene on his behalf, but the consul expressed distaste for Ma's well-known "malversations" and flatly refused assistance.[20] At that point, the provincial commander-in-chief, who was close to Ma and at odds with Hsi-liang, urged that the fine or the banishment be dropped, but Hsi-liang insisted on imposing the full penalty. Finally two prominent Yunnanese appealed for suspension of the sentence because of Ma's past loyalty to the dynasty. Always sensitive to the sentiments of local leaders, Hsi-liang finally consented to Ma's staying in Yunnan to "care for his aged mother." [21]

Hsi-liang's campaign reached its peak in a secret attack against the brigade commander, Pai Chin-chu, another Muslim stationed at K'ai-hua in southeastern Yunnan.[22] Without even reporting his plans to the throne, he quietly "invited" Pai to Yunnanfu to "explain" why his forces were undermanned by 50 percent. Guessing what was in store for him, Pai put his largely Muslim forces on alert and refused to go. He boldly wired Hsi-liang that "one man in my army is worth two in any other." When Hsi-liang inquired: "What experience have you had to justify this boast?" Pai replied: "Why don't you try me and see?" [23] After Hsi-liang again ordered him to Yunnanfu, Pai made arrangements to surround the provincial capital with his own troops to ensure his safety. When Hsi-liang led 200 carefully picked men out of the city toward K'ai-hua to prevent this, Pai threatened to destroy a station on the railway to embroil Hsi-liang with the French.[24] At that point a censor in Peking, perhaps having heard of this "secret" confrontation in Yunnan, impeached Hsi-liang for "incompetence" and a rumor spread that he would soon be replaced as governor-general by T'ieh-liang.[25]

Facing a tough commander and under pressure from Peking, Hsi-liang was forced to compromise. Eager as he was to improve the officer corps, he would not do it at the cost of armed conflict with the powerful Muslims or at the risk of his post as governor-general. He therefore got Pai to promise that he would improve and expand his troops to protect the frontier, and in return he permitted him to stay at his post. Because he had operated in ostensible secrecy from the beginning, Hsi-liang could now drop his charges without losing too much face. Indeed he even tried to appease Pai by recommending him to the throne as "energetic and sincere" and worthy of promotion.[26] If Hsi-liang hoped that such a promotion would result in Pai's transfer out of the province, he was disappointed; the court did not oblige him. His relations with Pai continued to be stormy: the wily general even opened secret negotiations with the anti-Manchu movement outside China. Only later would Hsi-liang learn whether or not his compromise in halting the campaign against corruption had earned him continuing Muslim support.

In the effort to root out the corrupt officers, Hsi-liang had used capable and upright officials with long civil and military experience in Yunnan.[27] He replaced those removed with other qualified men who had long served with distinction in the province.[28] He thus revitalized the old army by installing new men whose primary loyalties were to the dynasty and to the reforms.

When Hsi-liang began to organize the New Army, however, he found a dearth of well-educated officers in Yunnan. He was forced to turn to teachers and students whom he had trained in Szechwan, men who displayed experience, knowledge and probity, as well as loyalty to Hsi-liang.[29] Shen Ping-k'un, who had gained both financial and military experience in Szechwan, became the new financial commissioner and director of the Militia Bureau.[30] Ch'en I, formerly assistant director of the Szechwan military preparatory school, assumed the key post of general commander (*t'ung-ling*) of the land army.[31] One graduate of the Szechwan preparatory school served as commander of the First Regiment and another as director of the army elementary school in Yunnanfu.[32] Another loyal official, who had served Hsi-liang in the past and had since distinguished himself as the "most capable" intendant in Yunnan, took over as police intendant.[33] Other protégés appeared as commander of the railway patrol and defense forces and as director of the provincial arsenal.[34] Together these men supplied a base on which to build the rest of the military establishment.

Hsi-liang now carried out the reforms that previously had taken place in name only. He retained just 10 percent of the existing Green Standard forces, selected the best from the rest for special training, and sent the vast majority to their homes to resume farming.[35] He used one battalion from Szechwan and another from Kwangtung as nuclei of the new land army and added seven more battalions, thus attaining three-quarters of his goal of a full division.[36] He reorganized thirty-nine motley battalions of "braves" into forty-seven battalions of the new railway patrol and defense forces.[37] He instructed the provincial arsenal to pursue the modest goal of producing ammunition for existing rifles and sent agents to Hankow, Shanghai, and Tientsin to purchase new arms and ammunition.[38] He established an officer school (*chiang-wu-t'ang*), which began to train a new generation of Yunnanese military students, and he directed even the provincial college to focus on military studies.[39] He reformed the police force and reorganized the militia into defense corps (*pao-wei-tui*). In addition to constructing new barracks, improving troop pay, and forbidding corporal punishment, he personally inspected military installations and occasionally supervised drill and target practice.[40] He generated 1.3 million tls. locally and pried 540,000 tls. out of Peking to lay the foundations for a military establishment that impressed foreign contemporaries and historians alike.[41]

In carrying out these military reforms in Yunnan, Hsi-liang served primarily the centralized state that was for him still the symbol of the nation. He enforced court regulations concerning the old and new army, even against officers such as Ma and Pai who enjoyed considerable provincial standing. He recruited Yunnanese soldiers and at least one Yunnanese officer for each of the new battalions in accordance with the court's statutes on the New Army, while still drawing the bulk of his officer corps from outside the province.[42] In his view, his duty was to plan the reforms; the court's duty was to support him.

According to the memoirs of an official who served in Peking at that time, "with tears in his eyes, [Hsi-liang] would often beg us to send down as much help as possible on the reforms." [43] If the court should assist the reforms, it should also have the authority to direct them. When the court appointed one Ts'ui Hsiang-k'uei as division commander in early 1909, Hsi-liang willingly turned over "sole authority" to him. Ts'ui arrived in Yunnan with "ten foreign-trained officers and one hundred sergeants and corporals selected from the Peiyang army." Hsi-liang doubtless respected him because, as the British noted, Ts'ui had served for fifteen years in military schools in Peking, Tientsin, and Tokyo and was "crafty, antiforeign, able, energetic and good in his technical knowledge." [44] By carrying out court regulations to improve the officer corps and to organize the New Army, Hsi-liang succeeded in radically transforming the quality of the military forces in the province and in increasing the prestige of the dynasty in the eyes of local society. A Yunnanese military student in Japan, Li Ken-yüan, who was later to become an important provincial leader, praised Hsi-liang as one of the two good officials of the last six to serve in Yunnan.[45]

The Opium Suppression Campaign

Hsi-liang adopted equally authoritarian methods in leading the campaign to suppress opium in Yunnan, part of a larger late Ch'ing reform that has been called the "most vigorous effort in world history to stamp out an established social evil." [46] The Chinese had known the poppy since the seventh century and had smoked opium since the seventeenth century, but trade and consumption had become a problem only in the eighteenth century.[47] At that time, the Ch'ing had prohibited the sale and consumption of the drug and had tried repeatedly to enforce the laws.[48] It had been unable to halt the trade, however, because the British had become dependent on it to pay for purchases in China. It had failed to stop consumption, perhaps in part because the Han Chinese elite, frustrated under Manchu rule, turned increasingly to it for escape.[49] Unprecedented wealth also permitted indulgence, and peace, broken only by frontier skirmishes, may have left the various elites bored and prone to experiment with drugs.

During the nineteenth century the opium problem worsened. The British, increasingly dependent on the income from opium to finance their trade with China and their administration of India, forced the Ch'ing to legalize the opium trade.[50] At the same time the Han Chinese, despairing of serving a Manchu elite that was itself being humiliated by the foreign powers, took increasingly to the drug.[51] Annual imports quadrupled between 1840 and 1870, and consumption spread downward from the elite to 25 percent of the townspeople and 2 percent of the country residents. The Chinese began growing the poppy to compete with foreign imports, thus swelling the total

amount of opium available in China. In the 1880s, the Ch'ing state, both in
Peking and in the provinces, became dependent on the likin tax on the opium
traffic for much of its revenue. With the state increasingly interested in opium
for revenue, many observers concluded that "the only solution . . . lay in the
development of a real sentiment against the drug among the Chinese
people." [52]

But some statesmen such as Chang Chih-tung had taken the lead in
attacking opium. As governor of Shansi in 1881, Chang had written a friend:
"The real calamity in Shansi is . . . the opium. Sixty percent of the country
folk, 90 percent of the city dwellers, and 100 percent of the officials, clerks, and
troops are addicts." [53] While perhaps exaggerating the extent of addiction,
Chang drew a convincing picture of the consequences: "The people are thin
and poor, everyone rises late. . . . It is a veritable ghostland. How can we
speak of rousing ourselves to action when, with this endless decline, we cannot
even talk about a country." [54] He warned that "to shake off the poverty and
weakness of China, we must make the suppression of opium a large part of our
program," and he called for an end to the cultivation, sale, and consumption
of the drug in Shansi within one year.[55] The court approved Chang's proposal,
and local officials in Shansi, such as Hsi-liang, were ordered to "enforce the
prohibition . . . by publicizing the attendant dangers." [56] In this campaign
Hsi-liang had "managed according to the law" and had received a promotion
for his efforts. Apparently he had been greatly impressed by Chang's call for
official leadership and for an imminent deadline and by his reference to the
need to "incur pain to rout out a chronic habit and benefit the common
people." [57]

Chang and Hsi-liang had continued their opposition to opium during the
next two decades. Chang, in his "Exhortation to Study," had cried out that
"unless something is soon done to arrest this awful scourge in its devastating
march, the Chinese people will be transformed into satyrs and devils." [58]
Hsi-liang, as financial commissioner in Hunan, had helped to impose a stiff
consolidated tax on opium dens to discourage consumption of the drug in that
province.[59] Later both Chang and Hsi-liang had taxed opium more to get
revenue than to suppress the drug, but in 1905 the public in China and abroad
had begun to rise in outrage against the vice.[60] Chinese students abroad,
embarrassed at China's reputation for opium addiction, had agitated for
reforms, and their call had been taken up by reformers at home. Models for
action had been provided by the Japanese, who had stamped out opium in
Taiwan, and the Americans, who had moved against it in the Philippines.
Most important, British public opinion, fired by letters from indignant
missionaries who had always opposed the drug, now pressed the British
government to help end the trade.[61] In late 1906 the Ch'ing persuaded the
British to join in a coordinated ten-year program for the suppression of the
trade and use of opium in China. At the same time the court decreed strict

regulations to stamp out cultivation of the poppy, which had grown to such an extent that China produced three times as much opium as it imported from abroad.[62]

Just before leaving the leading opium-producing province of Szechwan in March 1907, Hsi-liang had memorialized, calling for a strict suppression campaign. He opposed opium not because of China's image abroad and not because foreign countries were attacking it in their colonies, but rather because of its effects on Chinese society:

> In my humble opinion it is disaster greater than flood and fire, and limited to a single area; its damage is more pitiful than that of war, and it is visited on one place. The tuber of aconite is harmful and the secretary bird is poisonous, but the danger in those cases is visible; people see it and know enough to escape. But the evil from opium flows everywhere, to the most remote places, and its harm spreads until it affects the whole body. Although the calamity of it is unparalleled, at the outset it seems to give pleasure. Up to the local elite and down to the lowly servant, it grips not only the worthless coward but the worthy brave. The reason why the country has been getting weaker and foreign affronts more severe over the last several decades is that the people's spirit has not been aroused; and the reason why the people's spirit and the people's power have fallen into weakness like this is simple: opium. If the little people do not break the habit, how can we expect to develop agriculture, industry and commerce? If the officials and scholars do not put away the vice, how can we advance the level of the administration, military, and education? This time the proclamation has been crystal clear; the people have been greatly moved, and even the foreigners are unanimous in their praise.
>
> Opium suppression is the foundation on which China is seeking wealth and power, and everyone, including officials, local elite, and the masses must know this; going forward with their full strength and determination, they will be able to achieve it.[63]

Thus Hsi-liang had initiated a campaign in Szechwan that his successors carried on with equal vigor.[64]

Yunnan was second only to Szechwan in opium production. Its 60,000 piculs a year (one-third of national production) was of the best quality and so brought a consistently high price.[65] In many respects, Hsi-liang faced a situation that was the most challenging in all of China. Yunnan's opium each year sold for 8 million tls., comprising by far the largest single slice of the provincial economy.[66] The annual export of opium to Indochina equaled 70 percent of the total provincial exports and brought in some 1.7 million tls. of foreign exchange.[67] The tax on opium each year provided the provincial government with 500,000 tls., or enough to supply one-half of the military expenditures.[68] Many Yunnanese, including the minorities on the frontier, cultivated the poppies and sold the harvest for cash income.[69] Most ominous, so many Yunnanese had become addicted to smoking that the British expert who had earlier visited the province, Sir Alexander Hosie, had described a "whole province given over to its abuse." Hosie had concluded: "I was quite able to realize that anyone who had seen the wild abuse of opium in Yunnan would have a wild abhorrence of it." [70]

Undaunted by the enormity of the problem, Hsi-liang launched his campaign with zest. He started from scratch in enforcing the court's regulations by dismissing all officials in his office who smoked. After creating an opium suppression bureau in Yunnanfu, he closed eighty opium dens in the capital district and confiscated their pipes and lamps. He ordered officials in K'un-ming district to register the number of people who smoked and the number of acres under cultivation. He also drafted provincial regulations more draconian than those of the court. The court had allowed persons over sixty to continue smoking indefinitely and others to continue for five years, but Hsi-liang instructed officials of all ages in Yunnan to quit immediately or face dismissal. This order represented a serious threat to the many addicts who would find it difficult to quit at once. He also ordered all those who were not officials to quit within one year or face prosecution by the state. The court had refrained from establishing a monopoly over the opium trade to avoid angering the foreigners, but Hsi-liang established a de facto monopoly by decreeing the end to all private trade within one year. While the court regulations stipulated a grace period of ten years for ending cultivation of the poppy, he cited a regulation encouraging a shorter reprieve and cut the period to three years. He posted these regulations in Yunnanfu with the warning that "the first year will be one for exhortation; the second for zealous prohibition; and the third for recourse to force." [71]

As the first year began, foreigners in Yunnan noted that Hsi-liang was more in earnest than his predecessor, but they gave him little chance for success. Contrasting American vigor in the Philippines with Chinese lassitude in Yunnan, the British consul at T'eng-yüeh stated that "the American official has moral courage, energy and resource, qualities which are not part of the Chinese nature." He concluded: "I cannot imagine any measure by which the Chinese can suppress the cultivation." [72] The British consul-general in Yunnanfu remarked that Hsi-liang's subordinates looked upon his regulations with "positive dismay," and added: "I venture to think that the task is beyond his powers." [73] Thus the campaign was to test not only the viability of the Ch'ing in the eyes of the Han Chinese but the vitality of the Chinese people in the eyes of the foreigners.

Pushing the campaign outside of Yunnanfu, Hsi-liang ordered every local official to post the regulations along with appeals written in both classical and colloquial style calling for the end to smoking and cultivation.[74] He instructed policemen to register smokers in the cities and militiamen to register acres under cultivation in the countryside.[75] He encouraged the organization of antiopium associations (chin-yen-hui), published articles in the Yunnan Gazette (Tien-nan ch'ao-pao), and distributed illustrated leaflets in the colloquial language to bring the message to the poorly educated. To shame smokers into reform, he publicized their names and made notorious offenders wear red garb inscribed with the words: "Opium Convict." [76] Hsi-liang recognized that such propaganda must be supported by careful rehabilitation. He advertised thirty-seven different kinds of medicines (some of which he had brought with him from Szechwan), opened five dispensaries to care for addicts, and encouraged the local elite to open others.[77] He became personally active in the campaign, planting trees where poppies had grown and visiting at least one village near the capital to "exhort the people." [78]

In reporting on his campaign, Hsi-liang mentioned modestly and vaguely that his exhortations were eliciting an "enthusiastic response" in Yunnanfu.[79] Fortunately we have a more detailed report from the British consul-general to confirm his appraisal:

> The Gentry are reported to be pleased at the movement and the Magistrate is said to have broken off the habit. A large number of the officials, gentry and people have given it up. Over 3,000 are taking medicines at the Dispensaries. Money is being subscribed by the gentry and others to purchase medicines for sale at less than cost price or to be given away. . . . Practically all the ground is now planted with other crops. . . . All the opium dens in the city are closed and nearly all in the villages.[80]

In the capital city, where Hsi-liang had direct administrative control, he was able to make striking progress through threats and exhortation.

Missionary reports show that progress elsewhere depended on his influence in each area. In Ch'ü-ching, in eastern Yunnan, where there had previously been complete official "indifference," the new regulations and proclamations finally appeared. But since the prefect continued to smoke, few of the local elite gave up the habit, opium dens flourished, and no attempt was made to limit cultivation of the poppy.[81] In Ta-li, in western Yunnan, where officials had not been "keen" on suppression, there was a more distinct change for the better. Because the newly appointed brigade general, "being a special friend of the new Viceroy," was serious, the local elite were "more in earnest than formerly," cultivators were beginning to register their lands, and the "people themselves" were "taking action" to create an antiopium association.[82] The British consul in T'eng-yüeh reported that "the Gentry and officials seem now to be more in earnest since the new Viceroy has begun to make things move." [83] The consul-general in Yunnanfu agreed that the campaign would continue throughout the province "only so long as Hsi [-liang] continues to ply the bellows." [84]

As the second year, the one for "zealous prohibition," began, Hsi-liang redoubled his efforts. He ordered the magistrate of the capital district of K'un-ming to "encourage" the people to "pull up all the poppies found growing there" and soon reported to the throne that "the people volunteered to pull out their own poppies in order to grow beans." [85] To prepare the way for stricter measures, he informed the British consul-general that more vigorous action would benefit the common people. In words reminiscent of those of Chang Chih-tung, he declared that it was the "comparatively few middlemen who reaped the profits of opium cultivation and not the peasants who would be better off with bean and wheat crops." [86] The missionaries agreed with this judgment.

Hsi-liang soon memorialized calling for a one-year limit on cultivation and smoking in Yunnan. He stressed the need for bold state action to help the people root out their baser impulses:

> . . . I enquired into public opinion and found that everyone thinks the present deadline is too lenient and will only complicate the matter. . . . The T'ang official Han Hung said: "If the Emperor is virtuous and the officials respectful, then they can do things." Otherwise the lower ranks of common people will follow their old habits and continue to smoke on the pretext of a longer deadline. In order to reduce the amount of land under cultivation, we will have to make up registers every year by household; this will be a lot of unnecessary bother. . . . If we continue to allow them to go to the deadline [of three years], it will be a self-reinforcing trend. I am afraid that the brave will withdraw and the serious will fall idle; in the end there will be no definite deadline at all.
>
> Looking at conditions and assessing the realities, I suggest that we take advantage of the current enthusiasm of the people to reduce the deadline. All smokers and cultivators should desist completely by the end of this year [January 1909]. The fat merchants . . . who have the product on hand must sell it by the end of this year and change their businesses. . . . The military and civil officials should act as leaders of the people, and if they go beyond their own limit of six months they will be punished. Where the body is weak and the craving strong, the prohibition of opium may be painful, but still we must not have pity and must help cut off the fixation with selfish desires. With the direct interdiction, there will be no place to sell opium and [sales] will be cut short even without prohibiting them.
>
> The ancients said: "With the coming of the fierce tiger even the weak can jump a broad gorge; before the powerful T'ai Shan, even the strong jump up and rush away in retreat." In the affairs of the empire, a firm spirit can accomplish much. With regard to the people and what they are looking for, what could be better than using our authority to lead them and to mold their attitudes?[87]

Cloaking his Legalism in Confucian garb, Hsi-liang moved decisively against the cultivation, smoking, and, by extension, the trade in opium.

Without waiting for court approval (which apparently was never explicitly given), Hsi-liang declared that he would enforce the new one-year deadline in Yunnan.[88] His increased zeal was received in the province with a mixture of awe and alarm. The missionaries agreed with Hsi-liang that public opinion generally supported a quick, complete, and absolute prohibition and that such a program would be far easier to administer than a more gradual one.[89] Many Yunnanese responded favorably: addicts voluntarily gave up their pipes while peasants dug up their poppy fields. The foreign consuls, however, now criticized Hsi-liang for "impatience," "authoritarianism," and "autocracy." [90]

Certain powerful interest groups in Yunnanese society condemned the deadline as "hasty, rash, and ill-advised." [91] Local elite petitioned for a more gradual prohibition on cultivation, and merchants propagandized openly against the deadline on trade.[92]

Hsi-liang took advantage of the support of enlightened opinion to press his deadline against the recalcitrants. Finding that local officials were dragging their feet, he dispatched "secret emissaries" to investigate conditions at the local level and report directly to him.[93] He sent one such investigator to Ch'ü-ching to warn the prefect to set a better example for his subjects and another to Lo-p'ing to threaten the magistrate with dismissal if he failed to limit cultivation on schedule.[94] Moreover, Hsi-liang brooked no inefficiency on the part of these secret agents whom the foreigners deemed crucial to his whole campaign. When one of them submitted a confused report on conditions in western Yunnan, Hsi-liang flew into a rage and threatened to have him executed.[95] According to foreign observers, the police avoided outright "brutality," but executed their functions so vigorously that some addicts gave up the drug too abruptly. A few died as a result.[96]

Hsi-liang likewise imposed strict controls on Chinese subjects to choke off the opium trade. He abolished the likin tax on opium and instructed local officials to burn all opium left in the warehouses of Chinese merchants. Having enforced these severe measures on the Chinese, he pleasantly informed the French that they could buy as much opium as they could find in the province.[97] When he could not avoid a direct confrontation with the foreigners, he dealt with them carefully but firmly. After the intendant at Meng-tzu confiscated 264 cases of opium from a French firm that had refused to pay taxes, the French delegate demanded the return of the cases and payment for damages. Hsi-liang ordered the opium returned to the French but collected the back taxes and refused to pay any damages.[98] The French were aware of the growing sentiment against the trade throughout China and dared not press their claims further.

Hsi-liang realized that he could not rid Yunnan of opium so long as other provinces continued to grow it and send it across the borders into the province. He also feared that some Yunnanese would oppose complete abolition unless other provinces enforced the same regulations. He was aware that the British had agreed to reduce their exports to China only on condition that China make substantial progress toward total suppression by 1911. He had learned in Shansi that a one-year deadline was necessary in order to succeed within three years. For all of these reasons, he soon memorialized that "we cannot plan for Yunnan without planning for the whole picture." He suggested that a one-year deadline be imposed by the court uniformly throughout the country.[99] Impressed with Hsi-liang's argument, the empress dowager upbraided the opium commissioners in Peking for laxity and goaded the Grand Council to decree that "cultivation would be prohibited within the next year." [100] But the empress dowager died in November 1908, before the order was issued, and she took with her the driving force behind a more immediate deadline. The Bureau of Government Affairs later rejected Hsi-liang's suggestion, arguing that deadlines would continue to differ in each province because conditions differed. [101] This argument neglected the fact that no province faced greater obstacles to rapid reform than Yunnan, but it reflected the court's understandable concern that local officials find alternative sources of revenue before eliminating opium. [102] The court did praise Yunnan as a model province, and some other provinces voluntarily followed its example by reducing their deadlines. [103]

Meanwhile Hsi-liang was having considerable success in Yunnan with his policy of "zealous prohibition." He eliminated smoking and cultivation in K'un-ming, and his agents did the same in several other districts. Under continual pressure, many local officials fell into line. The magistrate of Fu-min district, for example, persuaded local smokers to surrender their pipes and sent six mule carts full of them to Yunnanfu. He personally supervised the plowing up of all the remaining poppy fields. [104] By such means as these, the provincial administration reduced the export trade to a trickle. The French even became alarmed that Yunnan would have no foreign exchange with which to pay for imports from Indochina. [105]

As the second year of the campaign came to a close, however, there were still certain areas that had not suppressed opium completely. One British observer estimated that there were still some 4,000 acres under cultivation. [106] Peasants in these areas let it be known that they would "oppose with force any attempt to prevent the cultivation of the poppy"; missionaries reported that there would be a "storm" of protest if the administration made good on its threat to resort to force. [107] Aware of this situation, Hsi-liang resisted the counsel of subordinates who wished to use force immediately. The intendant of I-tung asked permission to send troops to Ch'ü-ching to prevent the people from planting a new crop of poppies, but Hsi-liang refused, trusting to his own prestige to awe the recalcitrants into obedience. In this case he succeeded. A missionary reported that "the people have . . . come to the conclusion that the poppy is banned and have resigned themselves to the inevitable." Indeed, they had pulled up all their plants. [108] The intendant of I-hsi suggested using troops to destroy crops in the hills along the Burmese frontier, but, again, Hsi-liang demurred for fear of sparking a conflict with the Kachin tribesmen. [109] In this case involving the highly autonomous frontier minority, he was less successful in imposing change through pressure and persuasion.

In early 1909, Hsi-liang was forced to make good on his declaration that "since the evil of opium is bottomless, no measure to suppress it could be too severe." [110] Finding that the prefecture of Ch'u-hsiung, in western Yunnan, still had a strip of poppy fields ninety miles long, he sent one of his special agents to prod the magistrate of Chen-an department into action. The magistrate duly visited a village that was still cultivating the poppy but was driven off by a crowd of angry peasant women. He fled back to Chen-an pursued by 2,000 peasants armed with sticks. The gateman panicked and allowed the mob to enter the town. The peasants chased the officials from their offices and released all inmates from the jail. Finally the magistrate found a way to wire Yunnanfu for assistance. Hsi-liang at first was so alarmed that he prepared to lead troops there in person, but he was soon persuaded that it was unnecessary. Instead he sent a well-armed force of 200 men who retook the town, killed 118 of the insurgent villagers and destroyed all remaining poppy fields in the department.[111] He removed the timid magistrate from office to set an example for the rest of the provincial officials.[112]

Hsi-liang's use of force brought the opium suppression campaign in Yunnan to its height just before he was transferred from the province. He fell short of complete success because he had made allowances for the autonomous Kachins on the western frontier. His successors, anxious to be assured of a substitute source of wealth before eliminating opium, compromised with both Chinese and foreign opium merchants.[113] Nevertheless, the late Ch'ing effort stands out in comparison with those of subsequent administrations. While the Ch'ing was unswerving in its attempt to eradicate the abuse, later governments until 1949 gave only lip service to the goal. They ended by profiting from the drug rather than suppressing it.[114]

Hsi-liang succeeded in eliminating 80 percent of the smoking, cultivation, and trafficking in opium by 1909.[115] The campaign, of course, had been initiated by the court and was the "most successful of the Manchu reforms." [116] Enlightened Yunnanese, such as Li Ken-yüan, supported the effort and applauded the thousands of opium pipes that hung on the walls of Yunnanfu as trophies of the campaign.[117] Yet Hsi-liang may claim the greatest credit for the success of the campaign in Yunnan. The court noted that Yunnan had become a model for other provinces, and a Yunnanese historian wrote that "Hsi-liang suppressed opium with thunderous vigor, and it was said that it would soon be completely eliminated." [118] The British opium expert Hosie, after another trip through Yunnan in 1910, reported that "To his Excellency Hsi-liang . . . belongs the chief credit for the present great reduction in the cultivation of opium in Yunnan." [119]

Hsi-liang's strictness in his military and opium reforms owed something to the severity of the Ch'ing statutes and to the example of Chang Chih-tung. But it seems to have resulted even more from the overwhelming nature of the problems before him and the statist tradition on which he drew in dealing with them. He had showed concern for laws and regulations before, but he showed new determination in making realities correspond to names, punishing severely all offenders of the law, making proclamations crystal clear, and even resorting to force when necessary. All of these efforts were highly Legalist in inspiration. One might well trace his frame of mind to more recent thinkers than those of the third century B.C. Yet it is important to understand that Hsi-liang seems to have fallen back on the most fundamental authoritarian methods in Chinese political theory in order to deal with the rampant abuses he found in Yunnan. It was with such methods that he was able to restore some sense of efficiency to the government in the province. Since effectiveness is one of the prime requirements for public faith in government, it was perhaps not surprising that his measures—however strict—restored some of the Ch'ing's prestige in the eyes of the Yunnanese.

Hsi-liang was equally determined to restore the Chinese people to a sense of self-confidence and vigor. That was apparent in his constant effort to keep the Legalist fist in the Confucian glove. Among the Confucian—perhaps even Mencian—strains in his reports was his appeal to "public opinion," the "people's enthusiasm," and the peasants' "volunteering" to pull up poppy plants. Hsi-liang carefully blended the Legalist stress on authority with the Confucian emphasis on persuasion: "With regard to the people and what they are looking for, what could be better than using our authority to lead them and to mold their attitudes?" He tried to mold attitudes by his programs of propaganda among the general populace and by programs of rehabilitation among the addicts. He remained convinced that a firm spirit could accomplish much, and, perhaps drawing on the subitist strain in Chinese thought, he argued that the sooner things were done the better. Only by a vigorous effort from the top down could the finer yearnings of the Chinese people be realized.

9: LEADING SOCIETY

Hsi-liang also worked hard to reestablish Ch'ing leadership over the Yunnanese by involving them in the rights recovery movement. He continued to cooperate with the local elite but focused new attention on other groups including the workers, peasants, and young intellectuals. In the true populist fashion, he hoped that by appealing to the minds of the people he might retain their support for the dynasty.

The Ko-chiu Tin Workers

Yunnan had long been an important mining province, producing primarily copper and tin. One mine in the Ko-chiu hills, Meng-tzu district, Lin-an prefecture, produced most of the tin in China.[1] Some years earlier this mine had had a foreman who was famous for his solidarity with his workers. He had shared his wealth with them, protected them from disorders, and even sought their counsel in making decisions.[2] No senior official in Yunnan could ignore the productivity of the Ko-chiu mine or the welfare of its workers.

Angered by the decline in the world price of tin and by French prospecting outside the treaty port of Meng-tzu, the Ko-chiu workers had become the most violently antiforeign group in the province. In 1899 two Ko-chiu leaders had organized a band of workers to attack Meng-tzu. They burned down the foreign-staffed imperial customs office and killed two Chinese functionaries before being driven back to the Ko-chiu hills by provincial forces.[3] Then the Ch'ing had joined the French in founding the Lung-Hsing Company (the Syndicat du Yunnan) to open all mines "discovered by the syndicate." In reaction, a man named Chou Yün-hsiang had organized an Association to Protect Yunnan (Pao-Tien-hui). In 1903 he had led thousands of Ko-chiu workers to take both Meng-tzu and the prefectural city of Lin-an before being driven off and forced back into the mountains.[4] The provincial officials, fearing Chou's popularity among the workers, neglected to press the military campaign. Chou was still in the hills with his intrepid band when Hsi-liang took up his post.

Hsi-liang had arrived to find the court and the French pushing ahead with plans for beginning work in southern Yunnan. After years of delay due to the disturbances in Yunnan and the "ill-health" of its staff, the syndicate had joined with some Yunnanese to petition the court to form a subsidiary Lin-an Mining Company to exploit the mines of the prefecture.[5] The court approved the petition without scrutinizing the Yunnanese participants. Only afterward did it instruct Hsi-liang to investigate to ensure that no abuses arose.[6] The court's offhand manner in dealing with the syndicate resulted from the fact that it was more interested in developing the copper mines elsewhere in the province than in protecting the tin mines of Lin-an.[7] By way of contrast, Hsi-liang was acutely aware of the situation in Ko-chiu and from the beginning concentrated his attention on dealing effectively with it.

Hsi-liang had the intendant at Meng-tzu, Wei Ching-t'ung, direct the effort to protect Ko-chiu and contain the French. Hearing that the syndicate had sent a surveyor named Collins to the village of Ku-shan, at the base of the Ko-chiu mountains, to discuss plans with one Min Li-sung, Wei sent police to arrest Min and his son and imprison them at Meng-tzu. He charged that Collins had gone to Ku-shan without notifying the proper officials, had discussed buying lands without authorization, and had ignored the presence of graves on the lands. One week later Wei elicited a petition from Min Li-sung's clan elders who alleged that the lands belonged not to Min Li-sung but to the clan as a whole. Wei concluded that Min Li-sung and his son had violated the Lin-an mining contract and had "forgotten the public interest in searching only for private gain." [8]

The French responded vigorously. The consul at Meng-tzu admitted privately that Wei had acted according to the terms of the contract, but he asked the minister in Peking to rebut Wei's arguments.[9] He claimed that the local magistrate had given Collins authority to go to Ku-shan and had provided him with a military escort, that Collins had discussed only the rental of Min's lands, that the lands had no graves on them, and that they were clearly owned by Min Li-sung since he had rented them before to a Chinese entrepreneur. He requested that the Mins be released, that a proclamation be issued setting the record straight, and that Wei be dismissed from his post for having "obstructed" French enterprise. The minister transmitted these demands to the Wai-wu-pu and demanded that the provincial authorities thereafter "assist" the Lin-an Company in "developing profits." [10]

Hsi-liang was instructed by the court to handle this case so as to "avoid a lot of diplomacy." He discovered that several of Wei's charges were questionable and consented to his removal from Meng-tzu. He made clear his own feelings, however, by promoting him to the high post of judical commissioner and by demoting the magistrate who had supplied Collins with an escort. He declared that Wei had acted according to the contract that required foreign agents to get permission from high authorities before contacting private landowners. He released Min Li-sung when he publicly "admitted his errors," but he continued to hold the son, who refused to repent.[11] He thus warned landowners in the Ko-chiu area not to deal with the French.

Hsi-liang continued in other cases to outmaneuver the foreigners who wanted to exploit the Lin-an mines. As soon as he heard of the syndicate's intention to investigate a mine, he would send special official-merchant entrepreneurs to open it.[12] His strategy was opposed by certain wealthy Yunnanese merchants of Meng-tzu who, according to the French, "consider their interests to be one with ours."[13] Some landlords ventured to protest to Peking that Hsi-liang's policies would deprive them of their personal profits.[14] But most Yunnanese enthusiastically followed Hsi-liang's leadership in protecting their lands. One landowner, who had previously contracted with the French to clear off his lands, now withdrew from the agreement, justifying the move as an effort "not to provoke the authorities." The French consul underestimated popular opposition to foreigners, but correctly assessed the importance of Hsi-liang's role when he said that "none of the people will deal with the company out of fear of reprisals."[15] Thus was initiated the movement to save the lands, reclaim the concessions, and develop the mines of Yunnan with Chinese capital.[16]

Hsi-liang regarded rights recovery not just as an end in itself but also as a means of retaining the loyalty of the Ko-chiu mine workers. He had justified Wei's strong action against the Mins by asserting that if they were allowed to sell their lands to the foreigners "the people will become insubordinate and will create even greater complications."[17] His successor later stated that he had been worried primarily about the Ko-chiu mines: "last year Hsi-liang forbade Min Li-sung from selling his land because it was near the crucial Ko-chiu mining area."[18] Against the background of uprisings in 1899 and 1903, Hsi-liang was able to invest the old clichés of "popular opposition" and "complications" with real meaning and to use them effectively against the French. At the same time he knew it was in his interest and that of the dynasty to keep the tin workers happy.

Hsi-liang later became even more explicit about the need to protect the Ko-chiu workers. Unable to open its own mines, the syndicate had decided that the next best course was to purchase ore directly from the Ko-chiu mine. Hsi-liang regarded this plan as even more threatening to the peace. He reported that foreign agents had gone to the mine to negotiate and he underlined his reasons for anxiety:

If we allow them to buy the products of the mine and introduce Western methods [to process them], they are bound to be better than our methods. As a result, several tens of thousands of brazier families will have their livelihood harmed; and they may well create incidents. Therefore we must energetically defend [against this intrusion]. . . .

The original agreement . . . envisioned using Western methods to open and exploit abandoned or new mines in order to expand the sources of profit. Ko-chiu has been opened a long time and the braziers and miners have lived in peace. However, they depend on this for their livelihood. If we allow the syndicate to buy ore, the benefit to the miners will be slight and the harm to the braziers great.[19]

Using such arguments, Hsi-liang moved quickly and effectively to keep the French from buying the ore and throwing the Ko-chiu braziers out of work. It remained to be seen if he had succeeded in retaining their loyalty to his administration.

The Tax-Paying Peasantry

Hsi-liang's concern about peasant support was revealed in the way in which he went about trying to recover the railway concessions in Yunnan. The British, pushing eastward from their colony in Burma, asserted an "interest" in building a railway from T'eng-yüeh to Yunnanfu (the T'eng-yüeh line) and from Yunnanfu north to Szechwan (the Tien-Shu line). The French, advancing from their colony in Vietnam, also claimed a right to construct the latter line. They had already obtained a concession and built fifty miles of a line from Laokay north toward Yunnanfu (the Tien-Yüeh line).[20] Hsi-liang's predecessor had founded a Yunnan-Szechwan and T'eng-yüeh Railway Company in cooperation with the Yunnanese, but by the time Hsi-liang arrived in the province it had raised only 123,000 tls. of the millions needed to reclaim and build these lines.[21] The railway recovery movement modeled on that in Szechwan had made little headway.

Hoping to spare the Yunnanese the burden of financing these lines, Hsi-liang first memorialized asking for court assistance.

. . . the people of this area have long been exhausted and, in a poor frontier region, such matters [as railways] always depend on official guidance. The state must provide the leadership in raising funds. May Heaven favor the court so that it may remember that railways in Yunnan are closely tied in with the security of the whole situation and are not simply for transportation. I must ask the Grand Council to order the Ministry of Posts and Communications to draft careful and complete plans and to disburse additional funds with which to carry them out. If it can set aside a certain percentage of the profits of the Chin-Yü [Tientsin-Pukow] and Lu-Han lines each year, we would soon be able to undertake this project. Moreover, in the future, the finished Yunnan line, as the virtual progeny of the Chin and Lu lines, would let the foreigners know that we are steadfast and united, not divided off by provincial boundaries. While the Chin-Yü and Lu-Han can continue to specialize in realizing profits, Yunnan, Szechwan, and Tibet will enjoy peace. This plan will benefit both Yunnan and the larger picture.[22]

Assistance from the central government was so much out of the question that the court did not even bother to reply to this plea.

Forced to turn to the Yunnanese, Hsi-liang tried to apportion the burden according to ability to pay. He set to work on the director of the railway company, Wang Hung-t'u, a wealthy former official who owned the largest bank in the province.[23] On paper Wang had been contributing tens of thousands of taels to the company, but actually he had been placing these funds—and all others contributed to the company—in his own bank and lending them out for interest.[24] Under cover of prolonged "preparations for beginning work," Wang had stalled all construction to avoid spending the funds that he was using so profitably in his bank.[25] Angry at this magnate's irresponsibility, Hsi-liang issued a proclamation criticizing the company's inaction. He concluded:

> Be it therefore notified to officials, local elite and people throughout the province that henceforth if the governor-general and director do not make plans for these lines to the utmost of their ability for their speedy completion, then the governor-general and the director have wronged Yunnan and blame rests with them.[26]

He retained Wang as nominal director of the Company, but never referred to him as such in his memorials. He set an example by contributing part of his salary to the company and forced Wang to follow suit, causing tens of thousands of taels to flow into the company coffers for the first time.[27]

Hsi-liang outflanked Wang by making another well-to-do Yunnanese ex-official, Ch'en Jung-ch'ang, co-director with full substantive authority over the company.[28] He worked with Ch'en to elicit the following petition from the other Yunnanese who were running the company:

> There are many officials and local elite from Yunnan in the various provinces. Several times already the company has written them, exhorting them to subscribe, but, looking on us as virtual strangers, they have not answered. Since the inhabitants of Yunnan are poor and burdened, they hope that their compatriots who live elsewhere would do their duty in aiding the community. It would be completely unjust for the whole cost of buying back [the railroads] to fall on the inhabitants of Yunnan and for those born here and exercising public functions elsewhere to take no interest at all in their home province. We beg you to telegraph immediately all provinces asking them to search out and press officials from Yunnan, both active and designate, to subscribe immediately.[29]

Hsi-liang immediately enclosed this petition in a wire to fellow officials throughout the country:

> I am convinced that Yunnan is now in a more perilous situation than a house on fire or a man who is drowning; it can be saved only by the united efforts of all the people. Knowing how much you take an interest in the fate of our country and take to heart all that concerns it, I send you this telegram to ask you to order your subordinates in the most pressing manner to subscribe. Those who persist in refusing are men without patriotism, objects of the reprobation of their compatriots, and whom you should consider unworthy of your favor. Men who are educated and trusted with public office could not sink so low.
>
> I am full of hope; I ask you to give the order and send me the money that you collect to save us from peril.[30]

He hoped that by giving state leadership to provincial feelings he might persuade the wealthiest Yunnanese to contribute generously to a patriotic project.

He next put pressure on the rich merchants and local elite in Yunnan. He demanded 700,000 tls. in "contributions" from the leading merchants of Yunnanfu, to be apportioned among them according to ability to pay. When he asked two extremely wealthy businessmen to meet their quotas, they refused and fled the province to Burma. He instructed the intendant at T'eng-yüeh to raise 20,000 tls. from the wealthy merchants there.[31] He then appealed directly to the local elite to make "graduated contributions":

> Wealthy families will subscribe to the major shares, middle families to the medium shares, and poor families to minor shares. The office for calling for subscriptions will strenuously invite and explain, and will settle the respective allotments so that a body of some tens of millions of men may subscribe some tens of millions of taels. . . . Many scraps of fur together will make a robe, many silk threads a lifesaving cable. Whether for peace or peril, the whole community is affected, and wealth hangs on this one scheme.[32]

He divided the province into four areas and sent a special envoy to ask each to subscribe 5 million tls. over a ten-year period. He demanded so much of the local elite that some of them petitioned Peking to complain about his excessive zeal.[33]

Hsi-liang found that even these vigorous measures were insufficient to raise the needed funds. He explained to the court why he was unable to use the rent-share scheme that he had adopted in Szechwan.

> Since Yunnan is a poor province there are few rich families and wealthy merchants; most of the wealth comes from trade in agricultural produce. Although the peasants are gradually becoming aware and many are becoming zealously devoted to the public interest, their intentions are still greater than their capacities and it is therefore very difficult to get funds.[34]

No alternative remained but to raise the land tax, a measure Hsi-liang had resorted to only once before in his career. He first added five taels to each picul of tax collected in K'un-ming and, when no opposition developed, extended the increase to the rest of the province. He noted the disadvantages of raising taxes but pointed out that "this particular matter pertains to the public interest of the whole province, and all the people are in agreement [on this]. . . . Moreover, given the extraordinary danger on the frontier, we cannot afford not to raise these funds." He hoped to raise 1 million tls. a year from this increase.[35]

As Hsi-liang undoubtedly foresaw, the tax increase was, in the words of the British consul-general, "most unpopular." [36] He therefore tried to make it palatable to the peasantry who stood to suffer the most from it. He extended the increase to lands held by the Christian churches, thus appealing to the antiforeign feeling that was strong among the peasantry. He instructed subordinates to show "proper sympathy" to the people, and tried to turn the cliché into reality by emphasizing the availability of tax relief during a famine. He also suspended the increase in some particularly sensitive areas. Finally, he announced that all proceeds of the new tax would go into a bond issue guaranteed by the state—a measure that Chinese students had long been urging on Ch'ing officials so that the state could earn the trust of the people.[37]

As the funds began to come in, Hsi-liang tried to retain this trust by conserving the money with the utmost care. While others in the province and outside argued that Yunnan should buy back all foreign concessions in order to save the T'eng-yüeh line, Hsi-liang relied instead on skillful but inexpensive diplomacy.[38] He informed the British that their interest in the line was based on a simple communication and not on a treaty. In any case, "the Yunnanese had . . . the special privilege of constructing the T'eng-yüeh railway." [39] He advanced these arguments so adamantly that the British consul-general reported privately that "Nothing I can say or do here would dislodge him from this position." Under Hsi-liang's diplomatic barrage, the British representative later recognized privately that "the clear language of . . . the Burma-Chinese convention is altogether against us." [40] Hsi-liang held off the British without spending a tael of company funds.

In planning a line north of Yunnanfu Hsi-liang was more willing to envision large expenditures in the future but equally careful about spending company funds in the present. He advocated a route northeast into Kweichow that would be long, expensive, and would fall one-third outside of Yunnan, while the nominal company director, Wang Hung-t'u, favored a line north to Szechwan that would be shorter, cheaper, and would fall wholly within Yunnan.[41] While the Yunnanese may have liked Wang's plan because it was in the provincial interest, they probably admired Hsi-liang's plan because it would be more effective in strengthening the frontier.[42] In any case, Hsi-liang must have had full provincial support when he moved to block another of Wang Hung-t'u's plans—to hire French engineers for the supposedly Chinese line. Hsi-liang had appointed the antiforeign Ch'en Jung-ch'ang expressly to meet this eventuality, and he now appealed to Peking to send a Chinese engineer to do the job. He also established a railway school to train eighty students in engineering and appointed a Chinese surveyor to make a preliminary survey to keep the foreigners at bay.[43] He spent some company funds for these activities, but they were a small price to pay for keeping the potentially lucrative and strategic Tien-Shu line out of foreign hands.

Much as Hsi-liang would have liked to repurchase the French Tien-Yüeh line, which was already partially completed, he showed the greatest caution in using company funds for this purpose. The French Société de Construction had so bungled this line that the French consul in Yunnan called it a "disastrous affair" and advocated reselling it to the Chinese. When the Société went bankrupt in 1907, it began to consider selling the line. Fearing that an open offer to sell would be a "confession of impotence," however, it refused to discuss price until the Chinese had made a bid.[44] The Yunnanese regarded the railway as a badge of servitude to the colonial masters of neighboring Vietnam; they became increasingly eager to repurchase the line. Hsi-liang knew that the cost was estimated at 80 million tls., far beyond the means of the whole country let alone of a single province.[45] He was initially cool to the idea of repurchase and warmed to it only after the Société went bankrupt. For a brief time he saw it as a means of encouraging the Yunnanese to support their own railway company. In the end, however, he returned to his original view that repurchase was just too expensive to be considered.[46] When the French government bailed out the Société in 1908 in the name of French grandeur and civilization, Hsi-liang told the French representative that the line was not worth buying even if the French decided later to sell it.[47] By recognizing that railway concessions made by treaty were still beyond the reach of the revolution, Hsi-liang saved the company's funds for more realistic efforts.

It was difficult to foresee the impact of these railway policies on the peasantry. On the one hand, Hsi-liang had tried to apportion the cost according to ability to pay and had spent the funds economically in the fight to recover the Tien-Shu line. On the other hand, he ultimately had been forced to increase the land tax, which fell squarely on the peasantry, and he had not been able to wrest the Tien-Yüeh line from the French. To make its sentiments known, the peasantry would need the leadership of another group of Yunnanese.

The Young Intellectuals

Most critical to the success of Hsi-liang's effort to lead local society was his relationship to the increasingly radical young intellectuals. During the administration of his predecessor Ting Chen-to, Yunnanese students had begun to organize to save the province from foreign encroachment and official mismanagement. Some had joined Sun Yat-sen's newly formed Revolutionary Alliance (*T'ung-meng-hui*) in Tokyo. Others, such as Li Ken-yüan, had founded an Association for Yunnanese in Japan, which published a monthly journal called *Yunnan Miscellany* (*Yün-nan tsa-chih*).[48] Yunnanese students in Vietnam had also joined Sun's Alliance. One of them, Hsü Lien, had returned to Yunnan to found an Association for Lectures on Culture to inform the Yunnanese of "the illegitimacy of the Ch'ing government and the danger of powerful neighbors pressing in." The scholar Li Po-tung had established a clandestine press in Yunnanfu. He published two books advocating rights recovery at any cost, including, if necessary, a provincial declaration of independence from the Ch'ing.[49] The students also organized Dare to Die Associations (*kan-ssu-hui*) to defend the province from foreign intervention and Manchu misrule.

Empress Dowager Tz'u-hsi

Hsi-liang in 1908

Huang Hsing

Ting had allowed these young intellectuals to infiltrate the provincial educational system. There were nine members of the Alliance in the university, four in the school of law and administration, two in the police school, two in the Japanese language school, and one in the normal school. They coordinated their activities through an underground provincial student association.[50] Considering Ting "too lax in military affairs," they demanded that he hire a foreign-trained expert to reform the military system. The man they proposed was Yang Chen-hung, who had worked in the provincial treasury in the 1890s until an accusation of forgery had forced him to flee to Japan. He had studied there for a few years and had just been named by Sun Yat-sen as leader of the Yunnan branch of the Revolutionary Alliance.[51] Ting had been aware of Yang's shady past, but perhaps was ignorant of his more recent activities or afraid to refuse the demands of the radical intellectuals. He engaged him to teach a special course in gymnastics and to "inspect" the Ch'ing forces stationed along the frontier. Other Alliance conspirators had complemented Yang's activities by organizing Public Education Associations (kung-hsüeh-hui) throughout the province. They later recorded that their aim was "nominally to study science but actually to plot revolution." A student named Kao Yen had created one such association in Lin-an prefecture and had established contact with over sixty other branches elsewhere in the province.[52]

Ting had permitted the intellectuals to gain so much influence that when he failed to please them by carrying out extensive reforms they threatened to have him removed. He had retaliated by transferring Yang Chen-hung to a minor military post on the western frontier and by jailing a large number of dissident students. The students, however, had already wired Peking, asking the court to remove Ting. At this point a student illegally entered a government telegraph office in Yunnanfu and was injured while being arrested. His friends, including one Yang Ta-chu, demonstrated against this arrest and so abused one clerk of the telegraph office that he died. After this clear proof of Ting's failing grip on the administration, the court agreed to transfer him from the province. Feeling their strength, the young intellectuals then drafted ten demands that they expected Ting's successor to meet.[53]

Hsi-liang proved to be considerably harder to manipulate than Ting. He met immediately with the educational commissioner, Yeh Erh-k'ai, who was known to be a very strict official, and discussed the whole educational system. He then memorialized to express his concern:

> In a distant place like Yunnan, without schools how can the minds of the people be enlightened? In a poor place like Yunnan, without education how can the people's industry be expanded or their livelihood ensured? Now in the provincial capital there are already a dozen schools, including the university, the elementary school, and the industrial schools; but they are in name only, not in fact: the classes offered are not complete, the various grades are confused, and nothing is according to the regulations. So how can anything be gained from the schools? Outside the capital

they are either not established or are established in name only. . . . This is all due to the lack of funds and to the ignorance of the officials and local elite. But the contentiousness of the educated elite and the rambunctiousness of the students surpass that of the provinces of the interior. If things continue as they have in the past, how will the educated ranks be filled and where will talent be formed? . . . I am very worried about all of this.[54]

Hsi-liang clearly intended to reassert leadership over the educational system.

Hsi-liang and Yeh Erh-k'ai first restored discipline among the students. They ordered the arrest of Yang Ta-chu and the others who had demonstrated at the telegraph office. They later released them and allowed them to return to their homes, but terminated their state scholarships and dashed their hopes for careers. Yeh adopted similar policies toward other students who were innocent of involvement with the Revolutionary Alliance. He demanded that a student who had dropped out of school after a semester pay a full year's tuition. When the student refused, Yeh had him imprisoned. The intellectuals charged the new administration with oppression. One student recorded that the anti-Manchu "revolution stopped temporarily, for it was very easy to arouse suspicions in the capital city." [55] This repression was not wholly effective, however, for the intellectuals who fled to Japan rushed to join the Revolutionary Alliance. Those who stayed behind, such as Hsü Lien, Li Po-tung, and Kao Yen, redoubled their efforts against the Ch'ing in the hinterlands.

Yeh next tried to reestablish control over the schools and the newspapers. He reduced the number of students in the schools to have an excuse to exclude the uncooperative. He abolished the special course on gymnastics that had disseminated anti-Manchu propaganda and created an office of education to supervise the courses, teachers, and students in schools throughout the province. He tried to compete with the Alliance and association press by founding an *Official Education Gazette* (*Chiao-yü kuan-pao*), which carried approved information on educational reform. He sent out secret agents to investigate developments in the countryside and soon became known as the best informed official on student agitation.[56]

Yeh saw no conflict between restoring Chinese learning to a place of honor in the schools and making reforms that would improve the quality of education. He refused to send more students to study in British Burma, arguing that most were not well enough prepared to study abroad, and he declined to hire foreign advisers in the schools in Yunnan, preferring to rely on Chinese educated abroad. He stressed instead the need to reform the educational system in Yunnan by reintroducing the reading of the classics and requiring participation in manual labor in the secondary schools. He thus drew on two rather different but equally ancient and important Chinese conceptions of the proper role for the scholar in society. In addition he saw the need to learn, as he wrote, "from Eastern and Western ways" of education, and he added new courses in English and French to the Japanese-inspired basic curriculum. On the practical level, he constructed what one foreigner called "fine new buildings," founded elementary normal institutes, and developed a new college for women. The ethos of Yeh's reforms was perhaps best illustrated by the fact that the women who came to teach in the women's college all had natural feet.[57] This radical departure was in one way merely a return to the situation which had existed prior to the decline in the status of women in the tenth century A.D. The spirit of quiet reform spread outside the capital to influence the policies of magistrates in the outlying districts.[58] Although some of the young intellectuals charged that Yeh wished to "repeal the reforms," it would appear that he instead effected changes that had previously existed only on paper.

Hsi-liang meanwhile appealed to the intellectuals for support by seizing the initiative in the rights recovery projects dear to their hearts. In some cases he had begun to reform the military, recover the mines, and preserve the railways even before the students became actively concerned about these issues. We shall see later that he also adopted policies regarding the frontier and minorities that commanded the students' respect. Under Hsi-liang's aegis, the anti-Manchu revolution slowed temporarily because the more fundamental anti-imperialist revolution gathered steam.

At the head of the movement for rights recovery, Hsi-liang actually protected some radical institutions and apparently had indirect contacts with a few radical students. When he was asked by the British and French consuls to suppress the *Yunnan Miscellany* for its "hysterical" attacks on imperialism, he staunchly refused, even though the newspaper was also anti-Manchu. Indeed, he not only tolerated the paper but praised one of its founders, the scholar Wu K'un, as "educated and upright," and even invited him back to Yunnan from Japan to assist with educational reforms.[59] Hsi-liang had shown great confidence in the intendant, Ch'in Shu-sheng, who had earlier supervised a school in which Hsü Lien had been allowed to propagate his ideas. He also favored another intendant, Wei Ching-t'ung, who had so sympathized with Yang Ta-chu's demonstration at the telegraph office that he had helped him escape from his home town and flee to Japan.[60]

Whereas Yeh Erh-k'ai remained the epitome of the official concerned primarily with quelling disorder, Hsi-liang was becoming something of a radical leader, willing to cooperate even with anti-Manchu agitators against foreign encroachment. The intellectuals themselves had occasion to recognize this difference. According to an Alliance historian, Tsou Lu, one military student during this period "did not guard his words and was jailed." Yeh recommended that he be executed, but Hsi-liang refused, saying: "By executing one man we would incur the wrath of many."[61] The student was later released unharmed. This shrewd gesture, designed to maintain control over the young intellectuals, was also a radical act, corresponding to the highest ideals of the scholar elite. Whether such an exercise in Mencian benevolence could retain the loyalty of the intellectual community would soon be tested in the crucible of rebellion.

Hsi-liang's cautious populism had grown out of practical politics. He did not want the brazier families disturbed because they might "create incidents"; he showed "sympathy" to the peasantry because he feared they might resist his tax increases; he declined to alienate the students because they were particularly "rambunctious" in Yunnan. Yet this populism was more than opportunistic: it rested on his earlier concern about the minds of the people, which had shown through even authoritarian policies toward the military and opium. It was based on the classics and history, particularly on the ideas that the people are the most important root of government and that popular support is the most necessary asset of revolutionaries. It was not a populism from outside the tradition or even of the "little traditions" against the "great tradition." It was rather the populism that lay at the heart of all Chinese theories of government and that was particularly important in the Mencian variety of the Confucian school.

One may doubt whether Hsi-liang cared very much if the brazier families had their "livelihood harmed" or insisted very often that the students "participate in manual labor," yet he was certainly sincere when he argued that Yunnan could be saved only by the "united efforts of all the people." He proved his commitment to this idea when he publicly suggested that the wealthiest banker had "wronged Yunnan" and when he called upon prosperous Yunnanese serving elsewhere to assume responsibility for saving their home province. His belief in equity led him to decree that the burden of building the railways should be rationally apportioned among the various classes, with "wealthy families subscribing to the major shares, middle families to the medium shares and poor families to minor shares." This concept of social equity had a long tradition in Chinese thought and was only beginning to gain widespread acceptance in the West. Thus it was radical in the sense that it represented a return to fundamentals in the Chinese context and in the sense that it was a harbinger of the future on the global scene.

10: SUPPRESSING REBELLION

As a radical leader, Hsi-liang was forced to compete with other radicals, including Sun Yat-sen, for the support of the Yunnanese. While Hsi-liang's authoritarianism had created a number of enemies, his populism had made him a number of friends. Yet to be determined were the attitudes of the ethnic minorities who constituted a large portion of the population and were located along the strategic western and southern frontiers. To gain their support, Hsi-liang shifted to a radical minority policy. He broke with the current trend toward extending bureaucratic control over the minority states and reaffirmed the older ideal of respecting their political integrity and cultural autonomy. The effectiveness of this quietist minority policy was to be severely tested in a series of conspiracies and a revolt.

The T'eng-yüeh Conspiracies

Even before Hsi-liang arrived in Yunnan, the young agitator Yang Chen-hung had begun planning the first of several conspiracies that would develop in the western city of T'eng-yüeh during 1907 and 1908. After Yang had returned from Japan as head of the Yunnan branch of the Revolutionary Alliance and had clashed with Ting Chen-to, he had been sent to the minor post of battalion commander in T'eng-yüeh. Having symbolically cut his queue and adopted Western dress, Yang had decided to work actively for the overthrow of the dynasty that had ruined his career and, he thought, betrayed the country. He persuaded his superiors to allow him to found a school for "physical education" similar to the one he had run in Yunnanfu. Again he used it as a cover for lecturing against the dynasty and the foreigners. He founded study associations that secretly organized against the Ch'ing and publicly opposed British plans to build a T'eng-yüeh railway. He had made contact with several chiefs of the autonomous Shan states along the Burmese frontier, hoping to move them to act against the Ch'ing. He had blundered by insulting one of the claimants to the throne of Chan-ta, however, and the claimant had complained to his superiors, who had then informed the British of Yang's activities. Although the British consul called for Yang's dismissal, Ting Chen-to had told him to take no notice of Yang's growing influence.[1]

Hsi-liang no sooner took command than he dismissed Yang from his post and ordered him to Yunnanfu to stand trial on the old charge of forgery that had first caused him to flee Yunnan and join the anti-Manchu movement. Perhaps feeling that he could win Hsi-liang with his antiforeignism, Yang dutifully set out for the capital. But en route he received a letter from his brother warning him that he would certainly be imprisoned and would probably be executed if he proceeded to Yunnanfu. Yang considered leading a lightning revolt on the spot but was dissuaded by calmer associates. Instead he retraced his steps and slipped across the frontier into Burma. After meeting with another claimant to the throne of Chan-ta and with members of the Alliance branch in Rangoon, he sailed for Japan.[2]

Annoyed that Yang had escaped, Hsi-liang put a price of 50,000 tls. on his head and urged the British to detain him in Burma. He also sought permission to establish a consulate in Rangoon, ostensibly to assist Chinese merchants. The British considered Yang a political refugee and refused to hold him. They also denied permission for a consulate, which they surmised would be designed to keep watch on Chinese agitators. Although unable to capture Yang, Hsi-liang had driven him from Yunnan to Burma and from there to Japan. He had cut short the first T'eng-yüeh conspiracy and, according to one of Yang's comrades, administered a setback to the anti-Manchu movement.[3]

Hsi-liang moved quickly to assume the anti-imperialist mantle that Yang had so proudly worn in T'eng-yüeh. By undertaking to protect the T'eng-yüeh railway from the British, he deprived the conspirators of that issue. After announcing that his predecessor's weak frontier policies toward the British were to be "completely reversed," he removed the officials who favored the British and retained only those who opposed them.[4] He cashiered the intendant, even though he had adequately reported Yang's anti-Manchu activities, because he was a "flaccid dummy," "unequal to frontier requirements." [5] He added two battalions to the garrison and made plans for adding three more. He instructed the officers to prepare for a possible British invasion by raising pay, drilling continually, and building two new camps.[6] He also supported his new antiforeign intendant, Ch'in Shu-sheng, who rejected all British frontier claims, including some concerning the Kachin tribesmen of Yunnan who raided into Burma.[7]

This firm frontier policy at first entailed some administrative expansion over the Shan minority people of western Yunnan. An agricultural people inhabiting low, malarial valleys, the Shan spoke a Thai dialect and believed in Buddhism. They lived in autonomous states including Chan-ta, Chen-k'ang, and Kan-ai.[8] Ch'in Shu-sheng discovered that a succession dispute in Chen-k'ang had long threatened to bring British intervention there. Arguing the need to strengthen the frontier, Hsi-liang memorialized in favor of reorganizing the state:

> These cunning and crafty people have all assisted their own factions, spread rumors and indulged in open agitation. As a result the whole frontier has been stirred up. . . . These tribes have constantly schemed to appropriate more and more; their disorders have lasted for years. Not only is there at this time no legitimate heir or even means by which to force a compromise, but also close and distant relatives are raising the rabble to revolt. [If things continue this way] I think that it will take a long time to reestablish peace.
>
> This is a case where we must remove the chief and replace him with a regularly appointed official [kai-t'u kuei-liu] and reorganize the state in order to bring an end to restlessness. The headmen [t'u-mu] and people, having suffered under the harsh rule of the chief and having witnessed a long period without a rightful successor, ardently wish to be directly under the rule of a Han Chinese official. They have all indicated this same feeling.[9]

The invocation of the conflict between the Shan people and their chiefs could not hide the fact that this proposal embodied an assault on the autonomy of the Shan states.

Indeed the plan for the reorganization of Chen-k'ang so alarmed the Shan chiefs that it spurred plans for a second conspiracy.[10] The acknowledged leader among the chiefs had long been Tiao An-jen, head of the wealthiest state of Kan-ai, whose family had been ruling since Ming times. Tiao had achieved renown while still a young man by killing a tiger at twenty paces. He had further demonstrated his bravery against the British in the 1890s. After unsuccessfully begging Ch'ing officials to resist the British who were pressing in from Burma, Tiao had led his own men into battle and had suffered severe casualties. In the ensuing settlement, which the Ch'ing signed, Tiao's state of Kan-ai lost sixty square miles of land to the British. The officials still refused to create larger garrisons to prevent further disasters, so Tiao had concluded that the dynasty was "incapable of acting" and had gone to Japan to find ways of "helping his own country." [11] Thereafter he had made contact with the veteran anti-Manchu conspirator, Ch'in Li-shan, and had agreed to turn Kan-ai into a revolutionary base in return for military assistance.[12] He had also joined Sun Yat-sen's Revolutionary Alliance, obtained a military commission, and used Alliance funds to hire Japanese advisers to develop Kan-ai.[13]

Hsi-liang's reorganization of Chen-k'ang rekindled Tiao's active hostility to the Ch'ing. Tiao was related by marriage to the chief of Chen-k'ang and resented any attack on his authority. He also feared that the policy might be applied to other states, including his own. He and several other Shan chiefs issued a manifesto declaring that they would resist "with force" any extension of the policy beyond Chen-k'ang.[14] After learning about this manifesto, Hsi-liang ordered an investigation of the chiefs. He discovered that Tiao had long been critical of the Ch'ing, close to the Alliance, and bold enough to employ Japanese advisers without authorization from the provincial government. He may also have discovered that Tiao had imported 2,000 rifles from Burma.[15] He concluded that the Shan chief was not merely resisting the new policy of reorganization but was seriously plotting against the state.

Hsi-liang took immediate steps to avert any dangerous developments. He instructed Ch'in Shu-sheng to watch Tiao carefully, "expose his errors, and discipline him, not allowing him to give only the appearance of obedience while actually carrying out a rebellion." [16] In fact Tiao had been using Ch'in Li-shan and Sun Yat-sen more successfully than they had been using him. The Japanese advisers paid for by Alliance funds were helping him to cultivate mulberries, breed silkworms, construct silk and match factories, and improve the mines and schools. A British visitor later reported that they were "engaged in legitimate work and showed some enthusiasm for their experiments." [17] After a detailed investigation, Hsi-liang came to a similar conclusion. He reported that when he had called Tiao to account for using the advisers the chief had "wept bitterly and promised to mend his ways." He then granted Tiao permission to keep the advisers for another year.[18] At the same time he did not relax his guard because, as he reported, the Shan leader was "at heart still unreconstructed." [19] By keeping close watch, he allowed Tiao no opportunity for carrying further any plans against the Ch'ing.

As Hsi-liang was considering whether to reorganize other Shan states, he received strangely contradictory advice from his favorite intendant, Ch'in Shu-sheng. Secretly Ch'in urged Hsi-liang to depose all of the Shan chiefs and to reorganize their states into districts; publicly Ch'in accepted a petition from the chiefs against reorganization and forwarded it to Hsi-liang with his own stamp of approval.[20] While Hsi-liang might have been won to the first recommendation out of a concern for a strong frontier or to the second out of a desire to retain the allegiance of the chiefs, he naturally became suspicious of Ch'in's simultaneous advocacy of both policies. Although he had previously placed great trust in the antiforeign intendant, he now delayed a decision on reorganization and investigated Ch'in's background and motives.

Hsi-liang may have found that Ch'in himself was plotting against the dynasty. Ch'in had earlier expressed his sympathy for the anti-Manchu movement by permitting public demonstrations in his prefecture in support of the assassination of the Manchu governor of Anhui.[21] After being transferred by Hsi-liang to the T'eng-yüeh intendancy, he had further shown hostility to the Ch'ing by appointing three of Yang Chen-hung's accomplices to high civil and military posts.[22] This fragmentary evidence suggested that Ch'in may have publicly approved the chiefs' petition in order to win their support while secretly recommending reorganization in order to lead the Ch'ing into a ruinous confrontation with them. Hsi-liang found the evidence alarming enough to remove Ch'in and send him from the province.[23]

By the time Hsi-liang resumed consideration of how to deal with the chiefs, he had received an edict from Peking in support of reorganization. Yunnanese officials at court, speaking on behalf of the "elders and people" of Yunnan, had petitioned the Censorate, pointing out that the "chiefs are cruel and oppressive," and asking that they be "replaced by regularly appointed officials to save the [Shan] people's livelihood." This petition was well received at court because it accorded with the general policy of expanding administrative control over autonomous areas in order to strengthen their ties to China. The Grand Council's edict, enclosing the petition, ordered Hsi-liang "to investigate the frontier situation accordingly and manage satisfactorily." [24] Hsi-liang's loyalty to the court and his sensitivity to Yunnanese opinion pushed him toward reorganization.

Despite this pressure, Hsi-liang finally recommended against reorganizing the other states. He naturally shared the court's anxiety that chronic disorder might invite foreign intervention; he had been moved by this consideration to reorganize Chen-k'ang. He also joined the Yunnanese elders in criticizing the chiefs, claiming that they were all "stupid—the people hate them and are exasperated with their rule." His experience with Chen-k'ang nonetheless had taught him the risks involved in trying to extend direct control over the minority states. He memorialized that while there had been

> no resistance from the people, the chiefs had spread rumors with the intention of duping them. From the perspective of wanting lasting peace on the frontier, there is of course nothing to do except to replace the chiefs with regularly appointed officials.
>
> But replacing the chiefs with such officials is meant to benefit the people; it is clearly never the wish of the chiefs. If there is resistance at every turn, then I fear that they will only be encouraged in their tendency to look outward and will only rush to advance their plans for causing trouble.[25]

The "tendency to look outward" may have referred both to pretenders who fled to Burma for support and to chiefs who used foreign advisers. The "plans for causing trouble" probably alluded to the chiefs' long-standing resistance to Ch'ing interference as well as to their recent contact with anti-Manchu conspirators.

Hsi-liang's major point was that while reorganization was "not really wrong," he could not support it in a memorial to the throne because it entailed too many "difficulties." After noting that he would need an army to deter Shan resistance and money to pay new Han officials, he demanded: "where can we get this military and financial strength?" He observed that he would need talented men to fill the new offices and wondered: "how can we get good officials" to serve in "malarial areas"? Rather than reorganize the states, he proposed allowing the Shan chiefs to continue to rule and he advocated making reforms in the local Chinese bureaucracy that oversaw them. He recommended the reduction of customary fees, which officials were allowed to demand of the chiefs, in order to eliminate the chiefs' main excuse for exploiting their own people. He also proposed the immediate settlement of all outstanding succession disputes in the Shan states.[26] These reforms and the justifications for them were cautiously stated, but their eventual significance was quite radical. By departing from the trend toward reorganization and by lightening the burden on the chiefs, Hsi-liang was pointing the way to winning the allegiance of the minorities by suasion rather than force.

Perhaps partly because it was couched in such conventional terms, Hsi-liang's counterproposal was well received in Peking. The Grand Council issued a circumspect but favorable rescript: "your way of handling this matter is quite appropriate; carry it out carefully so as to obtain good results." [27] Hsi-liang instructed his new intendant to investigate and decide all succession disputes immediately.[28] He also gave Tiao An-jen increasing latitude and even informed the British that he was, after all, "a good-hearted man whose head had been turned by meddlesome advisers." [29] Hsi-liang thus reached out to retain the friendship of the chiefs and to invite their cooperation in resisting both the rebels and the foreigners.

By adopting this radical minority policy, Hsi-liang—perhaps unwittingly— dealt a blow to a new conspiracy by the persistent Yang Chen-hung. Upon his return from Japan to Burma in the fall of 1908, Yang had heard about the reorganization controversy and had regarded it as an excellent "pretext for overthrowing the Ch'ing." [30] He had sneaked back into T'eng-yüeh and had begun plotting with the chiefs of Chan-ta and Kan-ai, who agreed to accept arms from his organization in Burma. But his carefully laid plans were disrupted when Hsi-liang vetoed reorganization. The chiefs, whose positions were now confirmed, were no longer in the mood to organize a rebellion against the Ch'ing. They chose Hsi-liang and his radical minority policy over Yang Chen-hung and his effort to lead a rebellion against the Manchus.[31]

Failing in his effort to enlist the Shan chiefs, Yang turned to other dissatisfied Yunnanese for support. When the empress dowager and emperor died in November 1908, he appealed to the local elite to join a kind of Han Chinese dynastic revolt that he expected to lead from T'eng-yüeh north to Peking. He was again blocked when Hsi-liang managed to persuade the local elite that Tz'u-hsi's death would not weaken the movements for reform and rights recovery.[32] Yang next appealed for support among the peasantry, who were just then beginning to feel the effects of Hsi-liang's land tax increase. He managed to win over several military officers and to organize some peasants into Dare to Die Associations. He then led several hundred men to attack the prefectural city of Yung-ch'ang. But he was unable to turn latent resentment against the tax increase into open defiance of the Ch'ing. He ultimately failed to take Yung-ch'ang or to light the fires of rebellion in the countryside. Forced into retreat by advancing provincial forces, he was wounded in the fighting and died before he could reach the Burma border.[33]

Thus ended the last T'eng-yüeh conspiracy.[34] To some extent the plotters had failed because of their own weaknesses, but they had also faced stiff competition from a tough opponent. On balance it had been Hsi-liang's radical minority policies that had retained the loyalty of the national minorities and so isolated the conspirators.

The Ho-k'ou Revolt

Hsi-liang meanwhile had faced an even more serious and dramatic revolt on the southern frontier at Ho-k'ou. The Revolutionary Alliance had founded a branch in Vietnam in early 1907 to encourage revolts by the Triad Society in southern China. During 1907 the Alliance and the Triads had joined in three uprisings in Kwangtung and Kwangsi, each one stronger than the last.[35] In December of that year, Hsi-liang learned of a fourth revolt on the Kwangsi-Vietnam frontier. Three Triad leaders, Huang Ming-t'ang, Wang Ho-shun, and Kuan Jen-fu, had led one hundred men against the mountain town of Chen-nan-kuan, and had been joined there by the three principal Alliance leaders, Sun Yat-sen, Hu Han-min, and Huang Hsing.[36] The Alliance leaders had considered further advance too risky and had returned to Vietnam, leaving the Triads to fend for themselves. Soon afterwards the Triads had been expelled from Kwangsi and Sun from Vietnam. Hu had settled in Hanoi to plan future attacks; Huang Hsing had gone briefly to Kwangtung before returning to Vietnam to prepare for a revolt in Yunnan.[37]

During the Chen-nan-kuan revolt, Hsi-liang realized that the rebels depended on French sympathy in Vietnam. To be sure, some of the French positions were prescribed by international law: they could refuse to extradite fleeing rebels because they were political refugees.[38] But the French also introduced their own interpretations of the law by refusing to extradite common criminals because they might be tried for political rather than for civil offenses.[39] They refused legitimate Ch'ing requests to open a consulate in Hanoi and even tried to use the issue to enlarge their own concessions in Yunnan.[40] So intent were the local French administrators on favoring the rebels that they departed from their own stated policies. Although they promised to intern all agitators or expel them from the colony, they actually interned only the most minor and expelled only the most famous. Middle-level leaders such as Hu Han-min and Huang Hsing continued to pass as Cantonese merchants and journalists. According to Alliance records, the French recognized the rebels as "belligerents" in their "war" against the Ch'ing.[41]

Having discovered that the rebels planned to attack Yunnan, Hsi-liang moved to end private French support for their cause. He suspected that French firms based in Vietnam had helped the rebels smuggle 15,000 rifles and 5,000 revolvers into Yunnan in early 1908. He ordered a local official to search the warehouses of the Union Commerciale Indo-chinoise in Yunnanfu.[42] It is not known whether any arms were found, but the British confirmed that French firms were involved in the trade. The French delegate was incensed at the search, which he regarded as a serious breach of the treaties. He wrote to Peking demanding an indemnity of 10,000 tls. and the removal of Hsi-liang from Yunnan.[43] The court rejected both demands and encouraged Hsi-liang to continue his precautions against a rebellion. The incident nonetheless increased French hostility, which made Hsi-liang's task all the more difficult.

Hsi-liang next urged the French authorities to arrest the Triad leaders, including Kuan Jen-fu, who were hiding in Vietnam. He wrote the French that several "live at 15 rue Neuve, Hanoi, have more than 2,000 rifles, and intend to make trouble in Yunnan." His subordinates flattered the French by arguing that they should be able to track down such rebels in their "well-governed" colony. And they threatened them by warning that they would take no responsibility for damage to French property if the rebels invaded Yunnan.[44] Under such pressure the French detained Kuan and seven others on the charge of lacking identity cards. They claimed, however, that there were no other rebels in Vietnam and refused to arrest those roaming near the Yunnan border. After examining the detainees' proforeign propaganda, moreover, the French expressed admiration for their "civilized" attitudes and decided that they were less of a threat to French interests in Yunnan than was Hsi-liang. In late April 1908, as the scheduled date for the uprising approached, the French wardens reportedly made a toast to its success and released the Triad leaders from jail.[45]

Afraid that Hsi-liang was on the point of discovering his exact plans, the chief Alliance coordinator in Hanoi, Hu Han-min, decided to advance the date of the attack to 1 May. He had earlier chosen the frontier town of Ho-k'ou as the target, both because it was a strategic garrison town and because it was on the French Tien-Yüeh railway, which stretched north toward Yunnanfu. On 29 April Huang Ming-t'ang, Wang Ho-shun, and Kuan Jen-fu led 150 armed men past both French and Chinese guards across the Namti River bridge into Yunnan. They enlisted the support of a full battalion of sympathetic Ch'ing forces and set out for Ho-k'ou. As they launched their attack on Ho-k'ou early the next morning, they were joined by the chief of police and a battalion commander who honored an earlier promise to defect with all of their men. Two more Ch'ing battalions followed, and a fourth disintegrated on the field.[46] When the garrison commander, Wang Chen-pang, gathered 150 men around him and continued to resist, the rebels asked the French resident at Laokay to grant him asylum in Vietnam. When offered asylum, Wang asked the resident instead for a "few soldiers" to strengthen his resistance. After this was refused, he declared that he "could not now give up the traditions of his past life but preferred to stay there and die." [47] The rebels then overwhelmed the resisters, forced Wang to commit suicide, cut off his head and hung it in a public place. They took control of the rest of the town and cut the telegraph lines to Yunnanfu. Since Wang had failed to wire news of the uprising, the rebels were able to advance northward with the element of surprise still in their favor.

The rebels immediately sought to transform foreign sympathy into foreign assistance. On 1 May Huang Ming-t'ang issued the following proclamation, which was soon translated and sent to several foreign newspapers:

> The Government of the Chinese National Army [*Chung-hua kuo-min-chün cheng-fu*] announces to all the countries of the world: this military government has today raised a national army to overthrow the Ch'ing government and establish a socialist democratic nation [*she-hui chu-i chih min-chu kuo-chia*]; at the same time it wants to be kind toward friendly countries in order to preserve the peace of the world and advance the happiness of mankind. The following proclamation is for such friendly countries:
>
> 1. Wherever the military government extends its control, foreign persons and property will be protected.
> 2. Wherever the government is established, all rights already obtained by the foreigners through treaties will continue to be effective.
> 3. The government will not recognize what the Ch'ing government has previously given the foreigners in the way of rights for which no treaty has been signed.
> 4. If foreigners help the Ch'ing or harm the National Army, they will be considered as enemies.
> 5. If foreigners supply the Ch'ing with arms they will immediately be seized.
>
> In the year 4,606 of the founding of China[48]

The rebels' explicit recognition of the treaties and weak commitment to rights recovery suggested that they were appealing more to the foreigners than to the Yunnanese.

In line with this manifesto, the rebels granted safe passage to the French consul, who happened to be traveling through Ho-k'ou. They promised that they would scrupulously protect the Tien-Yüeh railway so long as the Ch'ing did not use it against them. They also decreed that any of their followers who created disturbances or burned churches would be executed on the spot. They exhorted the people to remain calm and to return to their normal occupations.[49] These measures probably cooled the enthusiasm of the antiforeign Yunnanese, even as they made a good impression in powerful foreign circles. The French Société de Construction and the Banque d'Annam applauded what they called a "peaceful 1789." They promised substantial financial assistance as soon as the rebels proved themselves by taking the city of Meng-tzu.[50]

With Hsi-liang and the court still unaware of developments, the rebels secured their base at Ho-k'ou with the help of the 3,000 Ch'ing turncoats armed with 1,000 Mauser rifles and 200,000 rounds of ammunition. After winning over another Ch'ing commander stationed along the Tien-Yüeh railway and thus gaining several hundred more troops, 200 rifles, and 30,000 rounds of ammunition, they set off in three columns toward the north.[51] Observers abroad pronounced the revolt the greatest threat to the dynasty since the Taiping Rebellion. An authoritative historian of the Alliance has written that "There had never been a brighter moment; it appeared that all of Yunnan province could be taken as a revolutionary base." [52]

When the court finally learned of the uprising through the Imperial Customs Service, the Wai-wu-pu frantically wired Hsi-liang:

> Is this true? What rebel party is it? How did this happen? We hope that you report in detail by wire. If it is true, you must send out troops to suppress it without delay. This is important.[53]

Hsi-liang had long been concerned about rebel infiltration across the southern frontier and had taken diplomatic measures to prevent it. But he was shocked at the sudden loss of Ho-k'ou. As he later recalled: "At that time the influence of the bandits was on the increase, the people were terrified, and the whole province was shaken." [54]

As the rebels advanced, Hsi-liang wired the Grand Council, taking full responsibility:

> Ho-k'ou is the southern door into Yunnan. Although I took precautions to defend it, it was finally lost. This is my responsibility. I must ask you to order the ministries to discuss a severe punishment to make an example for all of the officers on the frontier.[55]

The council wired back, ignoring the plea for punishment but reprimanding him for unpreparedness and holding him responsible for any foreign intervention that might result. It ordered him to raise the funds and troops necessary to throw back the rebels and concluded:

> You have received much imperial favor and cannot pass responsibility to someone else; you must rouse your own spirits to undertake these various operations satisfactorily, meeting the emergency and suppressing the rebellion, thus satisfying the concern of the dynasty for the pacification of the south.[56]

During the first week of May, Hsi-liang deployed his troops in three columns to deal with the rebels as they advanced northward. He obeyed court instructions to appoint the Muslim Pai Chin-chu commander-in-chief. Apparently aware of the disgruntled commander's previous contacts with the Alliance, however, Hsi-liang also adopted several measures to ensure that he would have no opportunity to join the revolt.[57] He restricted Pai's authority to the eastern and middle routes, instructed him to discuss all strategy with the intendant of K'ai-kuang, and asked him to cooperate with a nearby trustworthy prefect. As a further check on Pai, he asked the court to instruct General Lung Yü-kuang, a Yunnanese on duty in Kwangsi, to return home to raise militia against the invasion from the south. He chose the capable and loyal General Tseng-hou to command the best forces located in Meng-tzu and another officer to command troops on the western route toward Man-hao.[58]

In his reports, Hsi-liang exaggerated French assistance to the rebels, perhaps partly out of genuine ignorance and perhaps partly to justify his own failure to prevent the fall of Ho-k'ou. In several wires to Peking he charged that the French had allowed a thousand rebels to cross the Laokay bridge, had formally urged Wang Chen-pang to seek asylum in Indochina, had directly encouraged the rebels at Ho-k'ou, and had permitted them to use the Tien-Yüeh railway to transport matériel. He demanded that the French be required to pay an indemnity to cover the damage wrought by the rebels. The Wai-wu-pu accordingly instructed the Chinese minister in Paris to request that the governor-general of Indochina strengthen the frontier garrison, punish the guards who had permitted the rebels to pass, prevent any others from passing, and intern or expel all agitators. The Wai-wu-pu threatened to demand an indemnity unless these minimal steps were taken, and it announced that it would take no responsibility for French losses during the disorders.[59]

During the second week of May, Hsi-liang faced important contests on each of the three military routes. On the eastern route toward K'ai-hua the rebel leader Wang Ho-shun, who had already obtained the defection of two Ch'ing battalions, advanced on the expectation that Commander Pai Chin-chu would honor his earlier promise to defect.[60] The wisdom of Hsi-liang's previous efforts to reward and restrict the intrepid commander now became apparent. On 6 May Pai ended his vacillation and promised Hsi-liang that he would soon launch an offensive against the rebels.[61] When Pai refused to join the rebellion, Wang Ho-shun halted his advance.

On the central route, Hsi-liang prepared to defend the strategic treaty port of Meng-tzu. Huang Ming-t'ang had led a rebel column along the Tien-Yüeh railway straight toward Meng-tzu with the express hope of taking that city and obtaining modern arms and foreign support.[62] Hsi-liang's capable intendant, Tseng-hou, took command of the New Army forces located there and prepared for an all-out battle to defend the city. Huang, who was under strict Alliance orders not to damage foreign property, realized that the assault necessary to take Meng-tzu would very likely result in some loss to French property and would jeopardize French support. He therefore reconsidered his strategy and halted his advance.[63]

It was along the western route that Hsi-liang faced the most dangerous situation. The Triad leader Kuan Jen-fu had led a column toward Man-hao adjacent to the Ko-chiu hills in order to join up with Chou Yün-hsiang and the mine workers.[64] The Ch'ing commander at Man-hao convinced Kuan to accept a temporary cease-fire in return for control over part of the town. Kuan therefore halted before ever reaching Ko-chiu. In addition, he hesitated to appeal directly to Chou Yün-hsiang for support apparently because, as the British surmised, he was "afraid that the miners would be more than he could control." [65] Hsi-liang's earlier attempt to win over the antiforeign Ko-chiu workers now had its effect. They not only refused to join the Ho-k'ou revolt but actually enlisted in the Ch'ing army that was on its way to crush it.[66]

With the revolt faltering, the French began to modify their policies. The governor-general of Indochina informed the Wai-wu-pu that "friendship" for the Ch'ing compelled him to begin interning all rebels and expelling all Chinese merchants who assisted them. He would also send two additional companies to Laokay to enforce a stricter surveillance of all persons crossing the frontier.[67] He agreed that the Ch'ing had a right to protect the railway and promised to ask the Société de Construction to arrange for joint Sino-French inspection of all railroad cars.[68] In Paris the Ministry of Foreign Affairs decided that the governor-general of Indochina could extradite common-law Chinese criminals even though they might later be tried for political offenses.[69] These measures were in part positive responses to Hsi-liang's diplomacy. They also reflected French anxiety about the effect on their interests should they continue to support the rebels in what looked increasingly like a doomed effort. When the rebels failed to take Meng-tzu, Alliance records state that in response to the rebels' requests for aid, the Société de Construction and the Banque d'Annam gave them "only their laughter." [70]

At this point, the Alliance leader Huang Hsing tried to take direction of the rebel movement and to lead another offensive. Huang Ming-t'ang had refused to advance again from Ho-k'ou, complaining about a lack of arms, while Hu Han-min had ordered such an advance as a precondition for the supply of any more arms.[71] Huang Hsing went from Hanoi to Ho-k'ou to urge another attack on Meng-tzu. When he failed in this mission, he returned to Vietnam to recruit a band of troops loyal to him alone. He then attempted to re-enter Yunnan, but was arrested by the newly vigilant frontier patrols. He tried to pass himself off as a Cantonese, but apparently spoke the dialect so badly that he was mistaken for a Japanese. He was immediately expelled from the colony. Whether or not "the loss of Huang Hsing was disastrous for the Hokow campaign," it was clearly a sign of its declining fortunes.[72]

At this time, Hsi-liang left Yunnanfu and went south to the departmental town of T'ung-hai, nearer to Meng-tzu and the front lines. He was anxious to rouse the spirits of his troops and to assure them of his personal commitment to their struggle. He may also have wished to keep a close eye on Pai Chin-chu, who had just exerted his influence in Peking to get one of his former patrons appointed coordinator of the whole campaign in Yunnan. As the Alliance press noted drily, Hsi-liang went to T'ung-hai to "coerce his more intimate enemies." [73] Perhaps seeing the ambivalence of Hsi-liang's motives, the Grand Council wired:

> Your courage is very moving, but you should not advance too close to the front; if you do, you will have to transfer troops to protect yourself, thus detracting from the fighting forces and interfering with the campaign.[74]

To prove his caution, Hsi-liang purchased a fast horse that he planned to ride to safety if the occasion demanded it. At the same time, he insisted on demonstrating his dedication to the defense of Meng-tzu by staying in T'ung-hai throughout the rest of the campaign.

By the third week, Hsi-liang had stopped the rebels' advance, but he lacked the military superiority to drive them back to Ho-k'ou and out of the province. He had mobilized 5,000 troops, only slightly more than the rebels had. The New Army at Meng-tzu was better armed than the rebels, but the other provincial forces carried old-style Mausers that often failed to fire. Additional troops and arms promised by other provinces would arrive too late to be of use.[75] Hsi-liang's main superiority was in money. He had persuaded the court to disburse 500,000 tls., far more than the Alliance could raise among the overseas Chinese. But it was difficult to translate these funds into actual power in the immediate conflict.[76] He could not count on military or financial superiority to bring the rebellion to an end.

Hsi-liang relied instead on political support, which he sought first among the Yunnanese local elite. He had already urged them to raise militia to defend their homes against the "outsiders," and, according to Ch'ing records, they had responded well by assuming the brunt of the burden in defending K'ai-hua. Other members of the local elite, including Lung Yü-kuang, also raised militia, which operated with increasing success throughout the southern portion of the province.[77] The Triad leaders, who were Kwangsi men, ignored Yunnanese sentiment and appealed instead to the floating population of the Namti valley, much of which had come from Kwangsi. This group, although mobile and discontented, was hardly the key to power in Yunnan. In a broader sense, Hsi-liang's earlier leadership of the movement to save Yunnan's mines for the Yunnanese had appealed to the patriotism and provincialism of many local elite. The rebels made no apparent effort to tap these sentiments. Sun Yat-sen, operating from Singapore, was so insensitive to the prevailing climate of opinion that he offered an overseas Chinese full "rights" to all the mines of Yunnan in return for 100,000 tls.[78] This policy of promising Yunnanese property as political rewards to outsiders must have done little to win the local elite to the rebel standard.

Hsi-liang also vied with the rebels for the allegiance of the few young agitators who had remained in the hinterlands. Kao Yen was running a Public Education Association near Man-hao, Hsü Lien was leading a Dare to Die Association near Yunnanfu, and Li Po-tung was teaching in a school near Meng-tzu. All of these young intellectuals had indicated that they favored rebellion, but none of them joined this revolt. Contrary to Alliance explanations, they did have plenty of time in which to rally: their ultimate inaction resulted primarily from their reservations about the rebels' means and goals. Kao Yen, who had strongly favored enlisting the Ko-chiu workers, probably decided not to join Kuan Jen-fu when Kuan failed to appeal to the workers for support. Hsü Lin, who bitterly opposed French colonialism in Vietnam, may well have disdained supporting a movement that depended on French sympathy. Li Po-tung, long violently hostile to foreigners, very likely called off his plan to attack Meng-tzu when Huang Ming-t'ang announced that foreign interests in the city were to be preserved at all costs.[79] The young agitators chose Hsi-liang's antiforeign radicalism over the rebels' anti-Manchu radicalism.

The Chinese press, too, had little enthusiasm for the rebels' combination of opposition to the dynasty and assurances to the foreigners. The newspapers had refrained from taking a strong stand either for or against the revolt so long as it had appeared that neither the Alliance nor the Ch'ing was seeking foreign assistance. It was only during the third week of the revolt that Chinese students in Europe wired the *Yunnan Miscellany* in Japan to report that the Ch'ing had requested the active assistance of French troops in defeating the rebels.[80] This misstatement, perhaps an exaggeration of Wang Chen-pang's request for a few French troops or of the Wai-wu-pu's demand for French surveillance of the frontier, immediately aroused the press into a fury against the Ch'ing. To combat this rumor the officially inspired press in the treaty ports churned out another: that the French had offered aid but the Ch'ing had refused it.[81] This was an equally wild distortion, either of Wang's refusal to seek asylum or of the court's warning to Hsi-liang against foreign intervention. It nonetheless helped to restore Ch'ing prestige in the eyes of many Chinese.

The anti-Manchu students in Japan seized on the first rumor as a means of discrediting the Ch'ing and appealing to the Yunnanese. The ubiquitous Yang Chen-hung and the determined Yang Ta-chu called a meeting of 2,000 students in Tokyo and persuaded the majority to endorse a declaration of Yunnanese independence. Their impassioned manifest declared:

> Yunnan! Yunnan! . . . What shall we say? . . . Yunnan belongs not only to the Yunnanese but to the Han race and to China. . . . Yunnan has decided not to accept the orders of the Ch'ing and not to allow the intervention of foreigners. . . . When at the end of the Ming the country died, Yunnan died last; but after this, if China is again lost, Yunnan will be lost first. . . . The independence of Yunnan is the foundation for the independence of China.[82]

In addition to demonstrating loyalty to their province and opposition to the dynasty, the students were determined to save China from the foreigners. Unlike the rebels, who had promised to respect foreign interests, the students repudiated the treaties and called for complete rights recovery.[83] Thus it was only after the threat of French intervention against the Ho-k'ou revolt in the third week of May that the students in Japan roused themselves to pledge assistance to the rebel cause.[84] They had ignored Sun Yat-sen's earlier appeal for funds but they quickly responded to Yang Chen-hung's call to form a provincial association and they soon raised 1,000 tls. for the defense of their province from foreign rule.[85] Significantly, even this money came too late to assist the Ho-k'ou rebels.

As the revolt moved into its fourth week, Hsi-liang competed with the rebels for the allegiance of the minority peoples. The Shan leader Tiao An-jen was in the midst of his campaign against reorganization. Earlier he had been appointed commander of the revolutionary army of Kan-ai. Now he received instructions from Sun Yat-sen to send troops and arms to Ho-k'ou. He delayed as long as he could, then responded that the arms ordered from Burma had not yet arrived.[86] He obviously did not wish to sacrifice his state on the altar of a faltering rebellion, and he may have resented the Alliance's cooperation with the foreigners, especially with the British in Singapore. He probably still hoped that Hsi-liang would not extend direct Ch'ing control over his state, and he may have suspected that, in any case, the Shan would fare little better under a militant Han Chinese republic.[87] He ultimately was of no help to the rebels.

Hsi-liang faced greater difficulties in retaining the loyalty of the Miao chiefs. A few months earlier he had decided to reorganize the Miao state of Pei-sheng, in the northeast, in order to tighten control over the population and to prevent further antiforeign incidents. Recalling the precedent set by O-erh-t'ai, the great eighteenth-century governor-general who had first brought the Miao under Ch'ing authority, he had argued: "Abolishing the harsh rule of the present chief and appointing an official would bring the Miao together, promote development, clean out the bandits, and firm up border defenses." [88] The court had agreed that firmness was the essence of good government and had authorized complete reorganization "without delay." News of this reorganization had undoubtedly reached all of the Miao chiefs in the province, causing uneasiness similar to that among the Shan.

The Wai-wu-pu had recently urged Hsi-liang to extend the reorganization to the southern Miao. These peoples, living on the frontier next to Vietnam, were thought to be even more unruly and susceptible to foreign influence than those in the northeast.[89] But Hsi-liang again ignored the court's suggestion and followed his own minority policy. In this case he was moved by a concern that the Miao chiefs might assist the Ho-k'ou rebels as they retreated south. This fear was almost realized when the Triad leader Wang Ho-shun and his men drew back into the San-Meng Miao states south of Man-hao. Having ruled out reorganization, Hsi-liang was able to instruct the local Ch'ing commander to cooperate with the chiefs against the rebels.[90] The effects of this effort at cooperation were enhanced by the rebel Wang's long-standing inability to get along with ethnic minorities. To ensure the isolation of the rebels from the southern Miao, Hsi-liang also transferred two loyal Miao commanders from Kweichow to assist in suppressing the revolt.[91] He thus won the competition for Miao support.

Hsi-liang's final contest with the rebels involved the Triads indigenous to

Yunnan. He had earlier suppressed the Triads of Ssu-mao and executed their most important leaders for planning attacks on the foreigners. While he had severely weakened the organization, he had also given it good reason to hate his administration. Sun Yat-sen's call for support from the secret societies of Yunnan should have fallen on receptive ears in Ssu-mao.[92] But the Alliance leaders Hu Han-min and Huang Hsing had become involved in a bitter debate with the Triad leaders Huang Ming-t'ang and Wang Ho-shun over arms supplies, and this debate had postponed crucial decisions on strategy.[93] It was not until the fourth week of May that Huang and Wang began to woo their fellow Triads in Ssu-mao. By this time the Ssu-mao Triads, as opportunistic as most secret-society members, probably sensed defeat. Moreover, as renowned antiforeignists, they may have mistrusted the Ho-k'ou leadership.[94] They still might have rallied, but Huang and Wang mixed up their signals and finally did not even carry the campaign to Ssu-mao to encourage them to revolt.[95] The rebels thus squandered their last chance for political support in Yunnan.

During the last week of May, Hsi-liang's three columns pushed south on a wave of political support with almost no opposition. They retook Ho-k'ou on 26 May after the rebels had abandoned it and had fled across the frontier into Vietnam. Hsi-liang's victory, which was Sun's "eighth failure," reestablished Ch'ing control in the province and ended the Alliance strategy of seizing a southern province as a revolutionary base.

Hsi-liang's victory over the rebels had sprung in part from his established position in the province and from his military and financial superiority. But it owed even more to his consummate skill in winning the acquiescence—in some cases the support—of the population under his command. By checking dissident generals, placating antiforeign mineworkers, appealing to the local elite, inspiring the students, respecting the minorities, and managing the secret societies, he was able to neutralize his enemies and to enlist his friends in a gradual campaign to isolate the rebels and throw them back to Vietnam. Based on his other broader policies toward the Yunnanese, this success tended to confirm that he was in closer touch with Yunnanese aspirations than were his adversaries. Since these aspirations were in some ways quite radical, Hsi-liang emerged from his Yunnan experience as perhaps a more authentic Chinese radical than his opponents in the Alliance leadership. His record should cause us to question, at least, whether the Alliance really had a monopoly on the radicalism of the period.

Hsi-liang was successful in part, of course, because he was better placed than Sun Yat-sen to force subordinates to carry his ideas into actual policies. In the crucial matter of minority policy, for example, Sun had claimed to lead a movement against racial oppression, but his agents Yang Chen-hung and Wang Ho-shun (who were in other ways more radical than Sun) betrayed their Han chauvinism by insulting the minority chiefs of Yunnan. Even more important was Hsi-liang's own understanding of the minorities' sensibilities and his flexibility in dealing with the chiefs. While Sun had appealed to the minorities primarily by reiterating his call for an anti-Manchu revolution, Hsi-liang had responded to the minorities' own concerns and reversed the policy of reorganization that had nearly driven them into revolt. This shift permitted him to cooperate with the chiefs in isolating the conspirators and rebels and driving them from the province.

Indeed, Hsi-liang and Sun Yat-sen seem to have differed significantly and fundamentally in their conceptions of Chinese nationalism. It had been primarily for tactical reasons that Sun had adopted a highly racial definition of nationalism, but he had become wedded to and limited by that definition in his longer-range strategy. Hsi-liang had based his policies on a broader definition of nationalism, one that took account of all the minority ethnic groups in China. His shift in minority policy was partly a response to immediate circumstances, and he remained silent on the larger philosophical considerations behind it. But he may well have been influenced by fundamental Chinese notions of interstate relations, including some which appeared as early as the first millennium B.C. The idea of China as the "central kingdom" that attracted all minority states to its brilliant civilization arose with the earliest culture, but it was the Taoists who spelled out the belief that a large state should always attempt to attract the smaller state rather than try to dominate it. This notion had a profound influence on all subsequent Chinese theory concerning minority and frontier peoples; it may well have had some effect on Hsi-liang's own minority policies. Whatever its origins, Hsi-liang's recognition of the need to respect the political structures of the minority states was his first step toward a truly radical minority policy, one based on the assumption that China was the model for the eventual establishment of a global community of harmonious nation states.

The Phalong Incident

Hsi-liang's gradual reconquest of Ho-k'ou went counter to the advice of the Grand Council, which had urged a major assault directly on the town to cut off the rebels before they could escape across the frontier. Hsi-liang had opposed such an assault, which was also recommended by his commander, Tseng-hou, because it entailed too many risks while his "rear area" was not secure.[96] He knew—but naturally did not tell the court—that his own strategy would save the Commander Pai Chin-chu from having to choose between fighting the rebels or joining them. It would allow the Ch'ing to marshal public support and to isolate the rebels without incurring many casualties. Neither the Ch'ing nor the rebels lost more than several dozen men during the campaign.[97] It had been civilized warfare at its best.

Although politically wise, Hsi-liang's strategy for retaking Ho-k'ou proved diplomatically embarrassing. The flight of several hundred rebels across the international frontier had created a disturbance. The pursuing Ch'ing forces, imbued with Hsi-liang's propaganda against the French, raised the tension still further. On 7 June a Ch'ing patrol chased some rebels across the border near the village of Phalong, Vietnam. At the same time, a column of French troops advanced northward toward the fleeing rebels. The Ch'ing patrol opened fire on the rebels and in the process hit the French, killing a Vietnamese private and a French lieutenant. Partly because of the difficulty of determining the motives on both sides, the Phalong incident led to a great diplomatic controversy.

Hsi-liang handled his first major diplomatic crisis with modesty and skill. He first blamed the incident on the rebels, claiming that they had fired on the French troops. When a preliminary investigation proved this untrue, he abruptly changed his stand. In an anguished note to the French delegate in Yunnanfu, he wrote:

> We, the governor-general, in hearing of this have felt profound horror and sincere regret.
>
> If the Chinese soldiers have really acted in this manner, they have outraged not only the sentiments of the governor-general of Indochina but also the laws of our empire, and certainly it would be for us to accept the blame.[98]

Hsi-liang distinguished sharply between propaganda against the French in China and an attack on French forces outside China. He ordered a complete investigation into the origins of the incident. He also instructed his commissioner of foreign affairs, a qualified diplomat who spoke some French, to open negotiations with the French.[99] Deeply chagrined, he repeatedly begged permission to resign but was consistently refused by the court.[100]

Long irritated at Hsi-liang, the French seized on this incident to discredit him. On 9 June Premier Georges Clemenceau convened the Council of Ministers in Paris to decide what claims to make. The French Ministry of Foreign Affairs soon wired Peking, revealing the degree of its anger by the enormity of its claims: dismissal and punishment of all responsible officers and privates in the Ch'ing army; reparations of 250,000 tls. for the families of the two victims; and removal of Hsi-liang from the province with the promise that he never return. The ministry charged that he

> is the real author of the atmosphere from which we are suffering in Yunnan [and] of which we have just had another deplorable proof. . . . The disgrace of Hsi-liang would complete the renewal of the administration in Yunnan by purging it of this hostile and Gallophobic character who represents a danger to our good neighbor relationship and [who acts] contrary to the concessions obtained for mines as well as for . . . the railway.[101]

In addition, French firms were to be allowed to open mines in Yunnan without official or popular opposition and to build a railway from T'ai-yüan in Shansi to Sian in Shensi.[102]

If Hsi-liang had badly miscalculated the risks of baiting the French, the French had grossly underestimated the changing temper of public opinion in China. The court naturally agreed to punish the responsible officers and to compensate the families of the dead men. But it refused to transfer Hsi-liang from his post. Members of the Grand Council, such as Prince I-k'uang, and members of the Wai-wu-pu, such as Yüan Shih-k'ai, defended Hsi-liang, saying that "the removal of officials is a matter of internal administration." [103] The Chinese press, such as the *Peking Daily*, begged the court not to give in:

> France is trying to abuse her power because she thinks that China is still a weak country, but today the Chinese are conscious of their power. Even if the government were to give in to France, the people would not allow this behavior. Let the French be careful! [104]

Yunnanese officials in Peking and local elite in the province petitioned the court demanding that it resist the French demands. Merchants in Canton threatened to boycott the Indochina trade, and students in Japan wired urging them to make good on their threat.[105] This sustained outcry from all groups of Chinese, from Manchu grand councillors to Yunnanese student agitators, confirmed the court in its refusal to transfer Hsi-liang.

Hsi-liang took advantage of this extended crisis to sharpen his diplomatic awareness. At the local level he supported his skilled negotiator and helped him to reject the French demands concerning the mines in Yunnan. At the national level he watched the court use the international balance of power to resist French demands on the T'ai-yüan-Sian railway. The court obtained the diplomatic support of the British and Japanese, who regarded the French claims as an unfortunate reversion to "earlier practices." It received even stronger verbal support from the Americans, who considered them an infringement of the Open Door.[106] After several weeks of sparring, the Wai-wu-pu forced the French to drop their "demand" for the line and to rephrase their claim into a request for a "favor" that would speed the Phalong settlement. Then, sensing victory, it refused to entertain this request. Finally, months later, it forced the French to drop the issue altogether.[107] The *North China Herald* pointed out with its usual hyperbole: "For the first time, perhaps, in Chinese diplomatic history, the demands of a powerful European country have been boldly rejected by the Peking government without consideration or hesitation!" [108]

During his term in Yunnan, Hsi-liang had returned to the fundamental ideals of the Legalist, Confucian, and Taoist schools to deal with domestic problems, political unrest, and relations with minority states. These ideals had been shared by the Yunnanese, at least to the extent of allowing Hsi-liang to retain control of the province and to lead it forward in some radical reforms. The Phalong incident, during which the Chinese showed themselves "conscious of their power," was a fitting climax to Hsi-liang's term. It underlined the importance of political leadership according to high ideals if the Chinese people were to have faith in themselves and to present a solid front against the foreigners. The incident also confronted Hsi-liang for the first time with the complexities of direct relations with the foreign powers. In this sense it was a good introduction to the diplomatic tangle awaiting him in his next post.

Part 4: Disintegration and Collapse in the
Northeast, 1909–1912

As Hsi-liang looked back on the past decade, he saw the parts of a national revolution without the whole. He saw resistance without the elimination of foreign control, expansion without the full development of China's capacities, and radicalism without the complete realization of fundamental ideals. The time had come for greater efforts in all directions.

Such efforts were especially necessary in the Northeast where Hsi-liang served next. Manchuria covered a huge area, the size of France and Germany combined, but was thinly populated with only some 15 million people. It had long since succumbed to intensive foreign influence and was increasingly plagued by internal divisions. Jehol was strategically located but poor in resources.

In the Northeast, Hsi-liang combined the three approaches of resistance, expansion, and radicalism. As governor-general of Manchuria, he paid closest attention to foreign affairs and adopted several complex policies to deal with them. He also addressed himself to domestic affairs and became more involved in politics than ever before. As military lieutenant-governor of Jehol, he proposed his own strategy for solving critical dilemmas facing the dynasty. His efforts marked the climax of his career—his accomplishments were its denouement.

RUSSIA

Aigun

AMUR RIVER

Hulun Buir

HEILUNGKIANG

• Tsitsihar

Chinese Eastern Railway

T'ao-nan •

Harbin

KIRIN

South Manchurian Railway

Ch'ang-ch'un

□ Kirin

FENGTIEN

Vladivostok

JEHOL

Chang-wu

Fakumen

Ch'ang-pai-shan

Hsinmintun

• Fu-shun

Railway

Sheng-ching (Mukden)

SEA

Chin-chou

• Pen-hsi-hu

OF

Ching-feng

Antung Railway

YALU RIVER

JAPAN

Hu-lu-tao

An-tung

Kwantung

KOREA

Dairen (Ta-lien-wan)
Port Arthur (Lü-shun)

Map 4. Manchuria

Gulf of Chihli

11: FOREIGN DISASTER

As governor-general of Manchuria (the Three Eastern Provinces of Fengtien, Kirin, and Heilungkiang), Hsi-liang dealt first with matters of policy raised by the Japanese, Americans, and Russians. He tried to resist the Japanese, who were operating from their stronghold in the Kwantung peninsula, by rejecting their diplomatic claims and obstructing their frontier activities. He sought to cooperate with the Americans, who were advocating the Open Door, by expanding the economy and preempting it from more powerful neighbors. He worked to restrict the Russians, who were conspiring with the Mongols, by adopting a radical minority policy toward the chiefs.

In early 1909 the Ch'un Prince Tsai-feng, regent to the infant Emperor P'u-yi, had removed from power many followers of Yüan Shih-k'ai, including the governors-general of Chihli and Manchuria. Greatly impressed with Hsi-liang's handling of the Phalong incident, Tsai-feng had first considered appointing him to the metropolitan province of Chihli, but had finally decided instead to send him to the frontier of Manchuria.[1] Holding Hsi-liang in "high favor," Tsai-feng also appointed him an imperial commissioner, thus enhancing his status and potential influence.[2] Apparently greatly pleased with this challenging new assignment, Hsi-liang rushed off to Peking to meet with the regent and discuss the Manchurian situation.[3]

In preparing for these consultations, Hsi-liang might have reviewed recommendations he had made concerning Manchuria five years earlier. At that time the Russo-Japanese War was drawing to a close, and the court had asked leading officials to make suggestions on how to deal with the growing crisis in the Northeast. Hsi-liang had memorialized that "the nation cannot have long-term plans without self-strengthening" and had sent 300,000 tls. to Peking to be used to improve the imperial armies of Manchuria.[4] He had also recommended some short-range diplomatic policies to meet the "emergency of the moment." The first of these had been to restrain the enemy nations, including Japan and the Western powers, by gathering intelligence about the domestic conditions in each country and using this knowledge to influence the public opinion in each in China's favor. While appropriate at the time, this policy had since become obsolete because China fully understood the motives of the powers and had little hope of stirring up opposition within the countries to their aggressive actions in Manchuria.

Hsi-liang's two other recommendations, however, revealed his fundamental approach to foreign affairs and remained relevant to the situation in 1909:

> *Choosing among policies.* The Japanese claim preeminence in martial skills and ostentatiously parade their virtuous intentions; indeed, they may not in the end refuse to return our lands to us. Yet they also say that as our military forces are unreliable they will have to keep their forces stationed in Manchuria. They say that as our policies are not good enough they will have to think about intervention. This is leaving Manchuria in name while staying in fact. How does it differ from the Russian occupation itself? Up to this time we have relied on their word that they are not occupying the area or harming our sovereignty [*chu-ch'üan*]. . . . But, in fact, the Japanese have poured out their treasure, braved many battles and left many bones to whiten the battlefield to obtain their goals and we have calmly accepted this. All of which is to ask: How will the Japanese be able to forget all this? . . . We cannot give up our lands nor can we sacrifice our sovereignty. When the time comes that we cannot save them through mere discussions, we must handle the situation according to the lesser of two evils. We have not yet reached this predicament, but when we do, the imperial persons should decide according to the relative powers at play at the time.
>
> *Resistance.* Now when the countries have not yet opened their conference we should take the opportunity to look at the powers' malicious intent masked under their pleasant countenance . . . , because after they halt the fighting between Japan and Russia and finish the peace discussions, they will combine to plot against us. Although it is true that all countries are out for their private gain and benefit, yet in bringing harm to East Asia they are all together. Now they are going to try to bring harm to China in order to limit Japan's activities. The Japanese currently fear that with China weak and Russia strong they will have nothing with which to build themselves up. . . . Even more, if Europe and America are going to try to run things in East Asia, Japan will not be able to bow her head to follow them. Thus we must prepare a policy of resistance. If we do not ally with Japan [*lien-Jih*], we will be unable to accomplish any kind of resistance. The situation changes all the time, but, in the short-term, in order to put up a resistance, we must first have a good policy for dealing with Japan. Only then will we be able to rely on Japan without any fear.[5]

In sum, China should protect her own sovereignty by military force and should cooperate most cautiously with self-styled altruistic powers against the more predatory.

Resisting the Japanese

By 1909 the Japanese had become by far the most threatening of the foreign powers involved in Manchuria. Their influence had grown during the preceding five years as they had imposed their own interpretations of the Portsmouth Treaty and the Sino-Japanese Agreement of 1905.[6] The military governor of Fengtien, Chao Erh-sun, had been unable to resist them and had asked to be removed from his post.[7] The governor-general, Hsü Shih-ch'ang, had compromised with them only to come under mounting attack from public opinion, the local elite, and censors for an "appeasement" that "lost the country's rights." [8] Rising Japanese influence was the most important issue faced by the governor-general of Manchuria.

In Peking, Hsi-liang learned that the Japanese refused to withdraw the troops left over from the Russo-Japanese War until several disputes were settled to their satisfaction. The first and most important was the improvement of a light, narrow-gauge military railway that they had built during the war from An-tung, on the Yalu River, northwest to Mukden, the capital of Fengtien (the An-feng line). The accords of 1905 had allowed them to improve the railway within three years for commercial use, and a subsequent agreement of 1907 had permitted them to make slight alterations in the route as they changed the tracks to standard gauge.[9] Since the details had been left for discussion with the Chinese government, the Japanese were now demanding that a final agreement be reached so that they could begin work. In order to force the Ch'ing into negotiations they were sending surveyors along the line and protecting them with policemen and troops.

Ordered by the court to handle the An-feng negotiations, Hsi-liang hurried to Mukden and prepared some guidelines for the forthcoming talks. In a wire to the Wai-wu-pu, he argued that the Japanese threatened China's national security because they had two intentions that were "favorable to them and unfavorable to us." First, they planned to broaden the gauge and to connect the line with a railway bridge that they were building (without China's authorization) across the Yalu River. This would provide them with a second route—in addition to their South Manchurian railway (the SMR)—for sending troops into Manchuria. Second, they planned to change the routing of the An-feng to connect its northern end with the SMR, thus integrating further their railways in Manchuria. Hsi-liang proposed to block their plans by insisting on a literal reading of the accords, which stipulated only the improvement (kai-liang)—and not the reconstruction (kai-tsao)—of the line. He also suggested insisting on the withdrawal of all troops and police that infringed on Chinese sovereignty along the line.[10] He hoped thereby to rectify the concessions made by his predecessor and to enforce his own interpretation of the 1905 accords.

The Wai-wu-pu immediately approved Hsi-liang's guidelines and authorized him to begin negotiations with the Japanese consul-general in Mukden. The consul-general, however, refused even to open discussions until the term "improvement" was dropped. He also argued that the demand for troop and police withdrawals was "irrelevant" to the An-feng issue. When Hsi-liang insisted on negotiating all of his proposals or none, the consul-general referred the matter to the Japanese minister in Peking. On 1 August, amid charges and countercharges of delay, Hsi-liang consented to discuss questions of gauge and routing last if the consul-general would discuss the other points first.[11] This concession still failed to move the negotiations forward.

The Japanese had already exceeded the three-year limit stipulated in the 1905 accords for beginning work on the An-feng line. They probably knew a good deal about Hsi-liang's past success in invoking the terms of Sino-foreign contracts to resist foreign enterprise in China. Seeing that he was now using the same tactic of legalistic delay, they tried to shock him into cooperation by accusing him of seeking to destroy a railway project granted by treaty. When they still failed to cow Hsi-liang, they decided to proceed with the work on the line without any accord. On 6 August they informed the Wai-wu-pu of their decision to act unilaterally and underlined their determination by announcing it to the foreign ministers and press in Peking.[12]

The Wai-wu-pu had always given the An-feng line low priority and had urged Hsi-liang to conclude discussions quickly. It had emphasized instead its own discussions with the Japanese over the status of Korean immigrants in Yen-chi. The Ch'ing had long permitted the Koreans to cross the Yalu River and work lands on the Chinese side. Since they had originally posed no threat to China they had been allowed virtual autonomy and self-government. As the Japanese consolidated their grip on Korea, however, they began to assert their authority over the Koreans living in Manchuria as well. The Ch'ing had become concerned that the Koreans would act as a fifth column for Japanese aggression, and in August 1909 Chinese troops clashed with Japanese policemen in a continuing struggle over the authority to rule the Koreans in Yen-chi. The court, afraid of aggravating the Yen-chi controversy, then ordered Hsi-liang not to press the Japanese too hard on the An-feng question. When the Japanese announced that they would begin work on the An-feng without an agreement, the Wai-wu-pu consented just so long as China could have its way in Yen-chi. The Wai-wu-pu then wired Hsi-liang that there would be no danger of the Japanese using the An-feng line to transport troops since it was clearly stated to be a commercial railway. It instructed him to permit the broadening of the gauge and altering of the route, to postpone questions concerning troops and policemen, and to ignore the Yalu River bridge and planned construction of a connection with the SMR.[13]

Abandoned by the Wai-wu-pu, Hsi-liang was forced to come to terms with the consul-general. He could take some comfort in a minor Japanese concession regarding the routing of the line near Mukden, but he had to surrender his explicit demand for the withdrawal of Japanese troops and policemen and his implicit effort to prevent the connection of the An-feng with the Yalu bridge and with the SMR.[14] When Hsi-liang signed the An-feng agreement with the Japanese consul-general on 9 August, he knew that he was participating in a major diplomatic disaster.

Hsi-liang differed with the Wai-wu-pu not merely over priorities but also

Hsi-liang in 1910

The Ch'ing Prince I-k'uang

Sun Yat-sen

over the fundamental problem of how to deal with the Japanese. He denied that Chinese troops had been to blame for the clash in Yen-chi and demanded an indemnity from the Japanese to cover damages. After he investigated Japanese claims to sovereignty over the Koreans, he argued that there was "iron proof" that the Koreans were subject only to Chinese authority. Thus he was doubly frustrated when the Wai-wu-pu settled even this supposedly highest-priority issue to Japan's satisfaction. The court also permitted the Japanese to build a railway from Kirin to Ch'ang-ch'un (the Chi-ch'ang line) and then to continue it south to Hui-ning (the Chi-hui line) on the Korean border. It not only yielded authority over the Koreans but allowed the Japanese to open yet another route for a possible invasion of Manchuria.[15]

Angered that the court had not supported him, Hsi-liang demanded of the Grand Council: "How do these concessions differ from those made by treaty after defeat in a war?" [16] The prince regent responded by blaming Hsi-liang for "breaking off the negotiations." Prince I-k'uang accused him of being "unfamiliar with the details" of the An-feng question.[17] Hsi-liang counterattacked privately. According to an acquaintance, he "vigorously upbraided" the senior vice-president of the Wai-wu-pu, Na-t'ung, who had wielded his great influence on behalf of concessions to the Japanese.[18] When the chief counsellor of the Wai-wu-pu, Ts'ao Ju-lin, was traveling in Manchuria, Hsi-liang pointedly neglected to offer him any hospitality, probably because Ts'ao openly favored the recognition of Japanese claims in Manchuria.[19] Unlike these men, Hsi-liang no longer saw any congruence between Chinese and Japanese interests in Manchuria.

The Manchurians, who also hoped to resist the Japanese, were disappointed at the settlement. The people of Kirin had agitated since 1902 for their own Chi-ch'ang line and had recently formed a People's Association to Protect the Railway (kung-min pao-lu-hui) to raise 1.7 million tls.[20] Manchurian students in Tokyo had wired the Wai-wu-pu to "devise stratagems" to save the An-feng line.[21] Hsi-liang had tried to use this public sentiment by warning the Japanese against "agitating the people" and by asking the court to permit public discussion of the issues. But the court, wedded to secrecy, had refused.[22] After the Chi-ch'ang and An-feng were lost, the Manchurians tried to save the Chi-hui; after the Chi-hui was conceded, they demanded that the court annul the whole settlement and permit them to build the lines.[23]

When the court refused to reconsider, Manchurian students in Japan proposed an empire-wide boycott against Japanese products. Some 5,000 students then demonstrated in Mukden, picketed Chinese firms dealing in Japanese goods, and wired student organizations throughout the empire to join the boycott. Soon the boycott spread to Peking, Tientsin, Shanghai, Fukien, and Hong Kong, causing a national uproar and reducing Japanese exports to China over the next weeks by 8 million yüan.[24] Under heavy Japanese pressure, the court and Wai-wu-pu intervened to crush the boycott in

Peking, Tientsin, and Shanghai, and they issued strict orders for local officials
to suppress it elsewhere throughout the empire. Hsi-liang defied these orders
and instead protected the boycotters and their supporters. When the newly
established provincial assembly (tzu-i-chü) prepared to discuss the boycott and
the Japanese consul-general demanded intervention to stop the debate,
Hsi-liang refused on the grounds that he had no authority to act.[25]

As a result of this whole matter, Hsi-liang lost whatever faith he might
originally have had in Japanese good intentions in Manchuria. In October he
met for two and one-half hours with the Japanese elder statesman, Itō
Hirobumi, to discuss the affairs of the three provinces. When Itō issued his
usual warning to China to reform itself so as to be able to "preserve the peace
of East Asia," Hsi-liang agreed on the necessity for self-strengthening and
promised to persevere with reforms. Hsi-liang then mentioned that despite the
recent settlement the Japanese army continued to retain all authority in the
"occupied areas" and refused to settle outstanding questions. He asked Itō if
he had "any suggestions on how to manage this." Itō replied by contrasting
the current situation in Manchuria with that prior to the Russo-Japanese War
during which, he said, Japan had devoted resources and lives to "get it back"
from Russia. Itō said that minor disputes between China and Japan should not
be allowed to affect the "larger picture." [26]

Hsi-liang then replied heatedly:

> In this world [t'ien-hsia], continual misunderstandings over little matters can cause
> large matters to arise. Your country originally threw in money and contributed lives
> because Russian power in East Asia was too great; it was for this that you undertook
> a righteous campaign. I am sure that your country was not treading the old path
> taken by the Russians. Your country never approved of what the Russians did. Yet
> during the period since the end of the war, the administrative authority within the
> occupied territory has not been returned to our government. Although I am clearly
> aware that this matter must be subject to compromises, the common people [yü-min]
> do not know this and their sentiments are easily aroused.
>
> In the midst of all of this, the [Japanese] consul's authority is too small and
> incomplete. The police, troops, railways, and businesses are all outside the limits of
> his jurisdiction. [Yet] I can negotiate only with the consul. For example, during this
> recent An-feng railway affair, I originally explained my proposed ten points to the
> consul, saying that what had to be refused could be refused, and what could be
> discussed would be discussed. Then, when I had already granted a change in the
> railway gauge and was in the midst of discussing other points, there was
> unexpectedly this business of "taking unilateral action." When one is discussing the
> facts of a case, one ought not to make such a move even though it is easy to execute.
> Your country did not know that this matter would give rise to this movement which
> is now harming the sentiments between China and Japan; if it had, your country
> would have realized that its actions were not worth it.
>
> I really think that in this case your country turned a small matter into a great deal
> of trouble, and this was really a shame.[27]

Itō warned that one "cannot simply take public opinion as a guide; in fact, when public opinion becomes an obstacle, the government should suppress it." [28] He did promise to take up Hsi-liang's complaints after returning to Japan; but he was unable to do so because three days later he was assassinated by a Korean at the Harbin railway station.

Hsi-liang continued to resist the Japanese throughout his term but he was repeatedly undercut by the court. He tried to restrict their purchase of new lands for the An-feng line and to block their construction of the Yalu River bridge only to see the ministries yield on both issues.[29] He sought to limit their influence over the Koreans in Yen-chi but found that the court settlement allowed Japanese influence to grow in proportion to the increasing numbers of Koreans immigrating to the area.[30] He strenuously defended a Chinese merchant who had owned the large Fu-shun coal mine, but saw the Wai-wu-pu consent to Japanese demands that he be held responsible for all his past debts.[31] He resisted Japanese demands on the Pen-hsi-hu mine but in 1910 could get little beyond back taxes in payment for it.[32] He tried to protect the woodlands along the Yalu River from Japanese lumber companies but again received no support from the Wai-wu-pu.[33]

Nor was Hsi-liang able to get financial support for frontier reforms despite Manchuria's inflexible revenues of only 15 million tls. a year and its annual 50 percent deficit.[34] With such limited funds, he could establish only a few new administrative units along the Korean frontier.[35] He asked the court for 600,000 tls. to improve the military forces in the area but received only half that amount.[36] He got nothing at all when he asked for 1 million tls. to reform the police, expand schools, and establish industries along the frontier.[37] When he tried to follow court suggestions to colonize the frontier, he could not get enough funds to promote colonization even in the strategic area adjacent to the Korean and Russian borders.[38] In seeking to resist overwhelming Japanese pressure, Hsi-liang marshaled great personal energy and understanding but could not muster the crucial support of the court.

Using the Americans

Unable to resist the Japanese, Hsi-liang tried to expand the Manchurian economy to save it from their grasp. When he had passed through Peking he had discussed railways with the former military governor, Ch'eng Te-ch'üan, who had earlier proposed building a wholly Chinese trunk line on a north to south axis to unite the three provinces of Manchuria.[39] Realizing that Manchuria itself could not finance such a large project, Hsi-liang had secretly memorialized for the court to invest a "massive amount of funds" and the "strength of the whole nation" in the railway.[40] He had asked the Ministry of Posts and Communications to "devise ways" of surveying a line from Chin-chou in southern Fengtien to Aigun in northern Heilungkiang (the

Chin-ai line) and had even ordered a preliminary survey of his own.[41] But the court had failed to offer any political or financial support.

Hsi-liang soon wired another secret memorial, noting that foreign troops were only hours from Mukden by rail:

> If one morning something happens and the Japanese suddenly move in, Kirin and Fengtien will be in their sack. If the Russians then spit on their hands and take Heilungkiang, we will be able to do nothing about it.[42]

Appealing directly to the dynasty, he asked the throne if, in the words of Sung T'ai-tsu, it wanted "someone sleeping next to its bed." He concluded by pleading once again for the court to put "the strength of the whole empire" into a Chinese railway in Manchuria.

During the Sino-Japanese negotiations in August, perhaps to placate Hsi-liang for the concessions on the An-feng line, the court finally responded to his pleas. But it did so in a way which Hsi-liang had not expected. Instead of approving a massive national effort to supply him with funds, it authorized him to "secure foreign funds . . . to equalize the influence of the various countries and to increase the prosperity of the interior." [43] Hsi-liang's predecessor, Hsü Shih-ch'ang, had earlier tried this same approach for a similar line in Manchuria and had failed, partly because of Japanese pressure. Hsü nonetheless had continued to favor it as the only way to get sufficient funds to build the long line quickly. When Hsü had left Manchuria he had memorialized secretly in favor of a large railway loan from America. He had continued to push his plans in his subsequent role as head of the Ministry of Posts and Communications.[44]

In the absence of a national commitment to build the line, Hsi-liang acquiesced in the plan to contract a foreign loan for it. He took this about-face from his earlier position in Szechwan because he recognized that the problems in Manchuria were far more critical and the time left for resolving them far shorter. The political will and financial resources that had permitted self-management in Szechwan were more limited in Manchuria.[45] Hsi-liang, like his predecessors, preferred to borrow from the Americans not because he believed naïvely in their altruistic protestations (as has sometimes been suggested) but rather because they were weaker than the other foreigners in Manchuria and therefore less of a threat and easier to manipulate to China's advantage. Moreover Hsi-liang may have looked fondly on the Americans for having recently come to his defense during the Phalong incident. In the midst of that controversy Hsi-liang had sent a wire to the admiral of the American fleet visiting China expressing hope for friendship between the two countries.[46]

Once persuaded of the necessity of a loan, Hsi-liang became an eager and tenacious advocate of obtaining one as quickly as possible. In early September he chided the court for failing to act on his railway proposal and implied that it ought to adopt a more serious attitude in its negotiations with the

Americans.[47] At the time the former American consul to Mukden, Willard Straight, was in Peking representing the American Group of bankers interested in Manchuria. In late September Hsi-liang persuaded the court to send Straight to Mukden to discuss a loan directly with him. When Straight arrived in Mukden, Hsi-liang negotiated a draft agreement with him for the Chin-ai railway. As soon as the draft was done, on 2 October, he pressed Straight to sign it immediately to prevent any misunderstanding. Straight wanted to delay until he received authorization from his superiors and until his British colleague could arrive in Mukden. Hsi-liang then became "very angry" and explained that he needed Straight's signature to win the consent of the ministries to the project. When Straight still refused to sign, he wired Peking and lied that Straight had already signed. He then told Straight what he had done. Outmaneuvered and anxious not to offend Hsi-liang, Straight finally signed without the authorization of his superior or the concurrence of his colleague. Hsi-liang then wired the signed draft to Peking before the court could make a decision on the project.[48]

Hsi-liang's memorial enclosing the draft agreement justified a foreign loan by referring to the extraordinary circumstances in Manchuria:

> In my humble opinion, the situation in Manchuria after the Russo-Japanese War was one of mutual competition and a division between north and south. The Japanese had Lü-shun [Port Arthur] and Ta-lien [Dairen] as naval bases; their railway went from I-chou in Korea across the Yalu [sic] to An-tung and on to Fengtien [Mukden], and then from Fengtien north to Ch'ang-ch'un and south to Lü-shun. Recently they were admitted to joint management of the Hui-ning railway from the Chi-ch'ang to Korea, and thus all of the troops of the country [Japan] could arrive here in less than a day. The Russians had Vladivostock as a naval base, their railway ran from Moscow into Heilungkiang, followed along the river, and passed through Poli to Vladivostock. Recently they have been reconstructing the railway by Lake Baikal, using double tracking, and all of their troops are able to reach here in less than a day. The very life of the Eastern Provinces therefore lies in the hands of the Japanese and the Russians; this is obvious—there is no use trying to deny it.
>
> But the disaster does not end there. The Japanese are black hawks and dangerous wolves, the Russians are high-handed aggressors, their collected ambitions are not small, their deep plots and secret plans are known to everyone. Their delay [in moving against us] was simply a matter of waiting, a result of the mutual contentiousness after the war when they did not dare to create an incident lightly. Then we could take our ease from morning to night, but a few years later this is impossible. Now we are in the midst of an almost irretrievable situation. If we wish to think about saving it, we will not be able to avoid disaster unless we build another railway besides those of these two countries. [Manchuria is like] the human body; when its veins are cut, it can continue to exist but it cannot live.
>
> But in making plans for the Eastern Provinces, the routes are long and the funds needed are great. Not only are the ministries unwilling to raise and expend the funds but also the other provinces are unwilling to help. In this situation, if we try to use

the strength of the whole country to plan it and that strength gives out before the railway is finished, then it will lead to danger. How much more if we discuss doing it ourselves [tzu-hsiu]; if we are not blocked by Japan we will be blocked by Russia; no matter which road, they will never let us build it and our hands will be tied as we wait for our death—surely a pitiable state.

We have worried about this and discussed it thoroughly; if we do not borrow the funds of the foreigners we will not be able to administer the Eastern Provinces; and if we do not borrow the strength of the foreigners, we will not be able to resist Japan and Russia.[49]

The throne immediately issued a rescript ordering the relevant ministries to confer together and memorialize.

Eager to force the pace of negotiations, Hsi-liang had taken a number of steps that would alienate the court. He had exceeded his instructions of 19 August, which had specified that he was merely to "discuss" a foreign loan. He had dared report to the court that he had offered to "take the loan and pay it back" without even consulting Peking and had been dissuaded from this only by Willard Straight. He had ignored an earlier warning from the Wai-wu-pu to move "cautiously" in light of past Japanese objections and had merely cited Straight's casual remark: "Don't worry about Russian or Japanese intervention." [50] He had placed the central government on the spot by specifying in the draft agreement that no other nation should "have a voice in the management or control of the company without the full permission of the imperial Chinese government." While promising that further negotiations could be conducted so as "not to lose any sovereignty," he had granted the Americans control over the company and a generous 10 percent of the profits of the line.[51] His position was all the more precarious because the prince regent and I-k'uang had already criticized his stand on the An-feng line; Chang Chih-tung and Lu Ch'uan-lin, who might have been expected to support him, were both sick and the Grand Council was in the hands of the hostile Na-t'ung.[52]

Of the three ministries that debated the draft agreement, the most important was the Foreign Affairs Ministry, dominated by its senior vice-president, Na-t'ung. Having originally delayed negotiations and sent Straight to Manchuria, Na-t'ung now memorialized, asking the throne to annul the contract pending reconsideration by the central government.[53] He also exerted his influence over the acting president of the ministry, Liang Tun-yen, who otherwise might have favored the contract since he had told the Americans he "would prefer to see American capital act independently in China." [54] Liang's chief counsellor, Ts'ao Ju-lin, also opposed the Chin-ai line because he feared Japanese and Russian reactions to it. When Ts'ao submitted a list of ten projects recommended for Manchuria later in the year, he pointedly omitted all mention of the Chin-ai proposal.[55]

The president of the Ministry of Finance, Duke Tsai-tse, also strongly opposed the draft agreement. A member of the Empress Dowager Lung-yü's party, he automatically opposed members of the prince regent's party, including Hsü Shih-ch'ang who had originally proposed the Chin-ai loan.[56] He also hoped to build a branch of his own Ta-Ch'ing Bank in Manchuria and had expected to finance it through a broader development loan from the American Group. Acting on the basis of these private objections, he publicly charged that the generous terms of the agreement undermined China's sovereign rights. This charge was effective but did not reflect the duke's true feelings. He favored a similar loan for his own ministry at this time and would later favor a larger loan for a central government currency reform. Of these proposals, two vice-presidents of the ministry opposed only the plan to borrow funds for the Manchurian line.[57]

The Ministry of Posts and Communications was divided over the desirability of the draft agreement for a Chin-ai loan. The president, Hsü Shih-ch'ang, who had first proposed the loan, defended it by arguing that self-management was impossible and borrowed funds better than none at all. Hsü, however, was more concerned about court politics than about Manchurian development and allowed direction within the ministry to pass to his senior counsellor.[58] The Counsellor, Liang Shih-i, who was capable but corrupt, controlled many railways, including the Peking-Mukden (the Ching-feng line) with which the Chin-ai might compete by providing an alternative route to the sea.[59] He had earlier visited Manchuria and met with Hsi-liang. He so differed with him in style that he tried to discredit him in Peking by saying that he had panicked after the assassination of Itō Hirobumi in Harbin. Although he made plans for all kinds of railways all over North China, Liang did not even mention the Chin-ai project in his diary.[60]

In late November the three ministries memorialized their opposition to the Chin-ai loan. In the memorial each ministry put forward its most respectable arguments. Na-t'ung warned against the Americans by stating that "it is not only the Japanese and the Russians but the whole world who are competing [for Manchuria]." Tsai-tse pointed out that a bank would be needed to pay back the loan, that broad economic development should precede railway expansion, and that the provision for profits was "harmful to our rights." Liang Shih-i demanded "a comprehensive economic development plan" that would help provide traffic for his existing lines as well as for any new ones. The ministries demanded that Hsi-liang thereafter consult with them before taking initiatives so that "inside and outside can plan together." Impressed by these arguments, the throne issued the simple rescript: "As discussed." This killed the draft agreement for the moment.[61]

Perceiving the nature of the opposition, Hsi-liang immediately addressed himself to overcoming it. He instructed a subordinate who was personally close to Tsai-tse to write him a letter explaining the need for a loan in Manchuria.[62] He showed the depth of his feeling by memorializing an argument that previously he had always hesitated to use, the contention that

China should follow the example of certain other strong and wealthy nations. He suggested that China should imitate America, which had built railways to serve as the foundation for economic expansion. He assured the ministries that they could revise the terms on profits when negotiating the final agreement. He submitted another memorial explaining that he had set aside a development loan temporarily because it would slow down the negotiations for a railway loan and would jeopardize China's rights. He promised that the Chin-ai and Ching-feng would benefit one another and proceeded with his plans to open up a port at Hu-lu-tao, which was intended to serve as a terminus for the Chin-ai.[63] While adopting this reasonable approach to Tsai-tse and Liang Shih-i, he apparently had little hope of winning over Na-t'ung with mere arguments. He therefore urged the Americans to put pressure on him, or, as Straight expressed it with characteristic grossness and exaggeration, "to rant a bit and kick Na in the stomach." [64]

In yet another (this time secret) memorial, Hsi-liang tried to turn talk from profits and development to politics and diplomacy. He repeated that all countries, including America, were to be distrusted because they all "hover like hawks and stare like tigers," waiting for the Japanese and Russians to clash "in order to realize their own schemes." He argued in favor of "moving together with the Americans to put resources behind our own plans" before they got angry and demanded greater concessions or, alternatively, lost heart and sold out their rights to the much more dangerous Russians. He continued:

> Although this is called a commercial railway, in fact it embodies a policy of politics and diplomacy. It is not so much a question of our not having funds at this time. Even if we had a surplus of funds and our country's strength still remained deficient, how could we be sure that they [the Americans] would not intervene? Or, if they did not intervene, how could we guarantee that they would never join with others in encroaching on us? I am afraid that, in that case, even the mines and forests would eventually no longer be ours.
>
> In borrowing their money, therefore, we will also be borrowing their influence; they will exchange their influence for our rights and we will use their influence to strengthen our frontier. When I talked with the agent of that country, Straight, he granted that this loan, unlike those made to the provinces in the interior, had the greatest relevance to foreign relations. [The Americans] understand that large amounts of capital are needed to assert their influence so that later they can resist both Japan and Russia, and the Eastern Provinces will have the means to keep themselves alive. Our respective secret feelings, therefore, have already been uncovered and are known. To my mind, all of this discussion about the Chin-ai railway is aimed at saving us from disaster, not simply at increasing profits.[65]

Hsi-liang's repeated appeals plus the Americans' stated intentions finally won court support of the plan. The Grand Council promised that Hsi-liang would be backed in "all his difficulties," and Lu Ch'uan-lin called for more airing of views on Manchuria. Tsai-tse offered to resign and, when refused permission, gradually acquiesced in a loan provided it covered the Ta-Ch'ing Bank and colonization on the frontier. Hsü Shih-ch'ang endorsed the loan on the grounds that the Chin-ai was a strategic rather than a commercial railway, and Liang Shih-i consented on condition that the Ching-feng be fully protected from competition. Liang Tun-yen argued that the Americans could be trusted because they had virtually committed themselves to seeing the project through despite Russian and Japanese objections. In mid-January 1910 the ministries jointly memorialized to proceed with the negotiation of a detailed contract. The prince regent issued a rescript on 20 January: "As discussed." [66]

Hsi-liang now turned to the reactions of the British, Japanese, and Russians. Even before he negotiated the draft in October, he had known that the British tended to support the Japanese, who opposed any line parallel to the SMR and that the Russians objected to the extension of any Chinese line to Aigun.[67] Since then he had listened to the Japanese quietly seeking "participation" without formally approaching Peking, and to the Russians making an "inquiry" and being rebuffed by the Wai-wu-pu. Even the court was staunchly resisting the two powers by arguing that the line was an internal matter.[68] Once the agreement became formal and public in January 1910, the British urged Peking to heed the Japanese and Russian demands for "consultation." But these powers were not very confident about their legal grounds for objecting to the line. The Japanese merely asked to "participate" in its construction and eventually to connect it to the SMR. The Russians avoided taking a stand by proposing joint construction of an alternative railway further west from Kalgan to Kiakhta (the Chang-ch'ia line).[69]

Hsi-liang counted partly on American assistance to overcome these pressures. From the beginning he and Straight had agreed on the absolute priority of the Chin-ai and on the need to use the British to resist the Japanese and Russians. Straight, however, was not only a strategist but also a financial agent and an American diplomat. He was intensely interested in reaping a profit from the railway and in obtaining the acquiescence of other powers in the line. He had asked the Russians to participate financially to ensure the line's feasibility and had become enthusiastic about "internationalizing" the line to include perhaps even the Japanese. Even more damaging, American diplomats in Mukden and Peking did not consider the Chin-ai a priority item. They actually damaged its chances of success by alienating the Japanese over duty evasion in Dairen and the Russians over administrative control in Harbin, matters that they judged to be more crucial.[70]

Hsi-liang also counted on the court to approve his course as he sent agents to Tientsin to negotiate the final agreement with Straight. When the Wai-wu-pu advised him to delay lest the Americans later intervene on behalf of their supposed rights, he wired that he had to fulfill a promise to Straight and that the court should assist him by taking a strong stand against Japanese and Russian opposition:

> I of course expected Japanese and Russian verbal opposition; but this line is absolutely not parallel or even related to theirs. The two powers have consistently tried to prevent us, squeezed nearly breathless as we are between them, from building a new life line, as though our smallest plan for survival would be an obstacle in their throats. If we always let them have what they want, how can we bear to think of the larger picture? They are always talking about the opening of Manchuria; why are they now going back on their word? [71]

In late April a final agreement was concluded in Tientsin and sent to Peking for approval. When Straight left for Russia with the promise to return soon to begin work, Hsi-liang wired the court urging immediate approval to avoid complications. But once again the court lost its nerve. It ordered Hsi-liang not to proceed with construction of the line until the Russians and the Japanese dropped their objections.[72]

Hsi-liang's Chin-ai project received the final blow in July 1910 when the Russians and Japanese, each fearing that the other might join the Chinese in building the line, signed a convention to preclude the possibility. They publicly prohibited any change in the status quo in Manchuria, except for the improvement of their own lines. They secretly agreed to use military force to defend their mutual interests in Manchuria.[73] The two powers soon succeeded in their principal aim of destroying the Chin-ai project by frightening the Americans and the court away from it. The State Department tried to put the best face on events by wiring Tokyo that the Russo-Japanese agreement seemed to be in line with its proclaimed policy of the Open Door. The Wai-wu-pu embraced the same convenient myth by wiring the Japanese that the agreement did not appear to infringe on Chinese sovereignty in Manchuria.[74] The Wall Street bankers in the American Group withdrew hastily from the project with the explanation that "their business was to make money." [75] Hsi-liang made one last plea, asking the court to transfer funds it had received for the Hu-kuang lines or to borrow new funds from the Belgians and Germans to build the Chin-ai and Chang-ch'ia lines. But his suggestion went unheeded in Peking.[76] The Chin-ai project was dead.

Thwarted in his attempt to get funds for a railway, Hsi-liang tried to get them for other development projects. In mid-August he memorialized secretly to persuade the court to negotiate a foreign loan for 20 million tls.—half of which was earmarked for a development bank and the other half for colonization and mining.[77] When the court did not respond, he memorialized again in September with the governor-general of Hu-kuang, Jui-cheng. He argued that America was forced to lend massive sums abroad because of rising labor costs at home, and he pleaded with the court to borrow this money before it was absorbed by some other capital-poor country. He again showed the expansionary nature of his aims by invoking the model of the United States, which had used railways to integrate a whole continent. He also suggested that China could use railways to unify the country, thus bringing the people together in one polity and facilitating the preparation of a constitution. In any case, whatever the future of railways, China would have to borrow massive sums simply in order to survive:

> How can one consider borrowing funds as losing the country, bringing up Egypt and Turkey as examples? Your officials agree that Egypt and Turkey certainly died through borrowing funds, but our country is going to die from not borrowing funds and present plans will take us there quickly. If we lose this opportunity through delay, then in several years we fear that we shall want to borrow and others will not allow us to. This is why your officials say that borrowing funds . . . is the first policy for saving the country.[78]

This memorial marked the peak of Hsi-liang's drive for foreign assistance to expand China's economy on the model of a great power.

Moved by Hsi-liang's appeals, the prince regent directed the Grand Council to inquire into the possibility of a "large national loan" to carry out a reform of the currency. Hsi-liang quickly acted to force the court to include Manchuria in its plans by opening secret negotiations with the British Hong Kong and Shanghai Banking Corporation for a development loan of 20 million tls. The court learned of these talks, however; and, preferring to deal with the Americans, it ordered the new president of the Ministry of Posts and Communications, Sheng Hsüan-huai, to negotiate an American loan of 50 million tls., half of which would be for Manchuria. Hsi-liang next tried to pressure the American Group into an early response by opening negotiations with the Mukden consul, F. D. Cloud, who represented a rival American firm, for a loan of 5 million tls. This maneuver, which Straight called "pretty sharp practice," succeeded in its aim of hastening the negotiations, driving Straight and the court to conclude an agreement for 50 million tls. (including funds for Manchuria) by the end of October.[79]

Hsi-liang and his successor, however, were again unable to keep the court and the Americans behind the strategy of development. The court tried to tailor the loan to avoid alienating either Russia or Japan, and the Americans tried to balance off these two powers by bringing in the French and Germans. Agreements were signed in April 1911 for both the currency and development projects, but the Russians and Japanese later successfully combined forces to exclude funds from their "spheres of influence" in Manchuria.[80]

Hsi-liang finally tried to use American assistance in developing some mines in Fengtien. He had noticed that the Americans had protested Japanese claims to the T'ien-pao-shan mines, even though they had admitted privately that their own claim was "very weak." Their protest had failed to prevent the court from granting the Japanese rights to joint management of the mine.[81] Then

Chinese merchants representing American capital in Shanghai inquired about the possibility of developing gold mines in Hai-lung. Hsi-liang jumped at the suggestion, granted them excellent terms, and wired the court to approve the proposal quickly. He hoped by this means to preempt the mines from the Japanese and Russians. This time the court approved, but the American-backed merchants failed to take advantage of the concession. A year later they still had not begun work.[82] Hsi-liang was thus frustrated in his third and final effort to use the Americans to develop Manchuria.

Managing the Mongols

Meanwhile Hsi-liang had been trying to deal with the Mongols in order to contain the Russians. The some 1 million Mongols of western Manchuria were less Sinicized than the Mongols of Jehol and were under far more direct Russian influence.[83] Hsi-liang's predecessor, Hsü Shih-ch'ang, had adopted an expansionary policy, including the establishment of fifteen units of local government and the promotion of railways. Both measures were designed to encourage Han Chinese colonization of the area.[84] In areas where Han settlers outnumbered the Mongols, Hsi-liang continued this policy by creating three more units of administration.[85] But elsewhere he adopted a quite different policy of relying on the Mongol chiefs to restrict Russian penetration of their banners.

Hsi-liang showed considerable respect for the culture and the language of the Mongol people. He was, of course, a bannerman who still spoke and understood Mongol. Now he also became something of a Mongol specialist for the Manchu court, at one point interpreting for it some old agreements written in Mongol script.[86] He acted principally, however, as a Chinese statesman concerned about Russian penetration of the Mongol areas. He urged the court to recognize the Mongol language for use in the schools. Stressing that the Russians had mastered the language and used it to increase their influence in the banners, he suggested that Chinese officials would be well advised to do the same. He argued:

> if the languages are not mutually comprehensible, it is difficult to force the civilizations to be the same. . . . Recently Mongol writings have been dying out, Buddhist texts alone are cited by the priests, and the common language falls into an incomprehensible slang. We must immediately plan for the preservation of the Mongol language. To strengthen the frontier we must expand education; to expand education we must translate books.[87]

He arranged for the translation into Mongol of works approved by the Ministry of Education and later reported that six volumes had been completed and were contributing to the "enlightenment of the Mongols." At another point he took the position that languages were the unalterable foundations of culture and concluded: "since languages cannot be made the same, it is difficult to merge civilizations into one." [88]

He also encouraged the Mongols to reform their institutions in a way that would build a sense of Mongol patriotism. The Pin-t'u Prince of the Left Wing Forward Banner of the Khorch'in (Qorčin) tribe submitted a petition on the question of Buddhism. He noted that Mongols had been Buddhists for over 600 years and that "religious liberty is embedded in the laws of all countries, no matter what their culture." But, he continued,

> as time went along superstition became ever more rampant and students followed one another in reading and reciting the classics without ever looking at anything else. They never wrote anything themselves and got more stupid and vile every day. Since we want to plan to become strong, we must move to control our religion.[89]

The prince requested Manchu and Mongol teachers "familiar with current events" who could teach the Mongols about "plots of the foreign countries to encroach on them" and could "help the Mongol people give birth to a love of country which would ensure the preservation of the race." Hsi-liang observed that this proposal was "most correct" and forwarded it to the throne for approval.[90]

Hsi-liang also accorded the Mongols political status by referring to them as a "country" (kuo). In warning the court of the need to understand the Mongols and to unite with them to ward off the Russians, he drew on the metaphor of the Warring States period:

> [unless we understand the Mongols] some morning there will be an incident, [the Russians] will be familiar with the situation, and Chin [Russia] will be able to use the talent of Ch'u [Mongolia] for its own purposes; we will be cut off and will experience the evil of Cheng [Mongolia] calling for help and Sung [China] not hearing.[91]

He showed that his concern was more than rhetorical by approving a petition from the Pin-t'u Prince for a Mongol army, although this proposal was similar to one he had mocked seven years earlier:

> The Mongols are very brave, fierce and well qualified to serve as troops. Since we want to guard against disaster on the frontier, we must make use of their military prowess. I suggest that we . . . train an army and establish it on the frontier of outer Mongolia to prevent unpleasant surprises.
>
> . . . The Mongol people are accustomed to shooting from horseback, bearing up under the cold weather, and fighting according to the terrain. With a little training they could become crack troops. Some say that the area is distant and provisioning difficult, but in the whole world [t'ien-hsia] there is not a country [kuo] without troops. The Mongol frontier is immense; we cannot be lax in its defense.[92]

He later carried out this proposal by creating a Mongol army.[93]

Hsi-liang regarded the Mongols as distinct but not necessarily inferior. He dismissed the proposal that Mongols be allowed to rule in areas inhabited by Han Chinese. His reasoning was the same as that which he used to oppose the extension of Han Chinese rule over the Mongols. He argued that the Mongols did not know the language well enough to administer the Chinese. He pointed out incidentally that some of them were lax in governing their own areas and continued to need supervision in collecting taxes, taking the census, and suppressing opium. He objected to the proposal that "authority be divided between different kinds of government and not between Mongols and Han." He pointed out that the Kharach'in chiefs of Jehol, where such a plan had been instituted, were far more Sinicized than the Cherim League chiefs of Manchuria. Above all he appealed to the teachings of Chinese history and rejected the current tendency to follow foreign models of imperial control:

> Although our dynasty brought the Mongol frontier under control and obtained the Mongols' great respect, it has never imposed the same system there as it has in the interior. Moreover, we should remember that there are differences among the various countries East and West in the ways that they administer dependencies and we must not try to force them all into the same mold.[94]

Instead he wished to maintain the distinctiveness of Mongolia so as "to strengthen the protective fence [fan-li] and bring peace to the frontier."

Hsi-liang's attitude toward the Mongol chiefs was nowhere better illustrated than in his handling of their financial problems. The Chen-kuo Duke of the Forward Banner of the Ghorlos tribe near Ch'ang-ch'un, who was also president of the Cherim League, had gone into debt to Chinese merchants during military campaigns in the T'ung-chih period. To prevent him from borrowing from foreigners to pay off these debts, Hsü Shih-ch'ang had established a special military unit to supervise the duke's banner. Finding that the duke had continued to become indebted to Chinese merchants, Hsi-liang supported his request for a state loan:

> the foreigners seek to take advantage of the situation . . . [and so] naturally we must extend the loan with the intention of making it possible for the whole nation to lead the dependencies and to firm up the loyalty of the Mongol banners.[95]

The court approved the loan of 150,000 tls.; the duke thereafter strongly supported the dynasty.

Hsi-liang was more interested in winning over the chiefs than in profiting from colonization. The Ta-erh-han Prince of the Middle Banner of the Right Wing of the Khorch'in tribe controlled the largest banner in the Cherim League. This banner was strategically located on the borders of Fengtien, Kirin, Jehol, and Chahar. The prince had long owed over 350,000 tls. to Chinese merchants but had refused Hsü Shih-ch'ang's orders to open 200 square miles of land to colonists to pay his debts. He had also permitted what the Chinese called "Mongol bandits" to harass any Chinese who tried to move into the area. Hsi-liang found that even if the prince opened the lands he would still not obtain enough to pay his debts because the statutory price for the land had been set too low. He memorialized that in view of the "larger picture" it was "impossible to be restricted to the regulations" and asked that the price be raised so that "the Mongol bannermen and the [Han] people will be treated on an equal basis." [96] The court approved this proposal, and Hsi-liang persuaded the prince to open his lands in 1910.

Hsi-liang next dealt with the so-called Mongol bandits, who had been attacking the colonists and threatening to cause international difficulties. The most important of them was T'ao-k'o-t'ao, who had been born a noble in the Ghorlos Front Banner but had left in 1905 after failing to persuade his prince not to sell his lands to colonists. He had moved south to the Cherim League where he had attracted a band of followers from among discontented Mongol herdsmen. He and his men had burned a colonization bureau, killed some Japanese surveyors, and clashed over 100 times with provincial forces, but they had always escaped to the hills to take refuge in the banners of sympathetic chiefs.[97]

Hsi-liang at first hoped to win over the Mongols by dismissing two officials whose exactions had forced the herders into rebellion. When T'ao-k'o-t'ao continued his activities and nearly precipitated an international incident by robbing some Russian merchants, Hsi-liang decided to take bolder action to suppress his movement. With the help of the newly cooperative Chen-kuo Duke and Ta-erh-han Prince, his subordinates located the "bandit" leader and led forces against him. They succeeded in driving him first out of the Cherim League and then out of Manchuria altogether.[98] Late in 1910 Hsi-liang learned that the Mongol was in Russia near Lake Baikal organizing Russian Cossacks and Buriat Mongols in preparation for a campaign into Manchuria. T'ao-k'o-t'ao reportedly hoped to lead disaffected Barga Mongols as well as the Cherim League in revolt against the provincial administration.[99] Hsi-liang had driven him from Manchuria only to see him become one of the leaders of the movement for Mongolian independence.

Hsi-liang's encounter with T'ao-k'o-t'ao showed that although he had managed to deal with the Mongol chiefs, represented by the duke and the prince, he had not won the Mongol people, whose cause was defended by the "bandit." The chiefs, who had always profited from colonization, had consented to more of it once Hsi-liang had arranged for them to obtain higher profits.[100] The ordinary herders, who had always suffered from colonization, continued to resent the transfer of their pasture lands to the Chinese peasant settlers.[101] So long as the chiefs and the herders were divided, an outside suzerain could rule them, but the day was approaching when they would unite against Chinese colonization.

Hsi-liang found it all the more difficult to satisfy the commoners because he came under increasing pressure to promote colonization. Many other officials, both in the provinces and in Peking, regarded colonization as the best way to strengthen the frontier. Hsi-liang's responsiveness to their views appeared most clearly in his handling of the Barga Mongols of Hulun Buir in western

Heilungkiang. At first he had respected the Bargas' opposition to colonization and had discontinued his predecessor's policy of promoting Chinese emigration to that area. During 1909, however, the Ministry President Tai Hung-tz'u, soon to become a grand councillor, memorialized in favor of promoting colonization in all sparsely settled areas of Manchuria. The court implicitly approved this recommendation by urging Hsi-liang to "develop" the frontier.[102] In 1910, fearful that his own policies might be inadequate to hold the frontier, Hsi-liang quietly reduced the price of land in Hulun Buir in order to "settle more people and strengthen the frontier." [103] He managed to pacify the Bargas in the short run but lived to see them declare their independence from China.

Colonization was advocated also by many members of the Manchurian local elite, some of whom profited greatly by speculating in land on the frontier. Hsi-liang at first resisted this interest group; he refused the plea of a local notable to open pasture land to farming and argued that herding was as noble an occupation as sedentary agriculture. Soon, however, he yielded to the request of another Manchurian to encourage colonization in an area inhabited by Mongol herdsmen. In a third instance, a member of the local elite of Chang-wu district petitioned for a reduction in the price of land held by the Pin-t'u Prince. Despite his close ties with the prince, Hsi-liang accepted the petition and ordered his subordinates to make preparations for carrying it out. He managed to keep the peace between the Mongols and the Han during his administration, but it was the Mongols of Chang-wu who later led an important revolt against the Ch'ing.[104]

Hsi-liang was forced into favoring colonization, finally, as a means of dealing quickly with Russian influence among the banners. The Wu-t'ai Prince of the Right Wing Forward Banner of the Khorch'in tribe, for example, had long been in debt to Russian merchants. He had consistently refused Hsü Shih-ch'ang's orders to open his lands for settlement as a means of paying his debts. Hsi-liang offered to increase the size of the prince's banner in return for a pledge to open more lands to cultivation but the prince again refused, arguing the need to protect the common herders. Hsi-liang then offered to give the prince the state's usual portion of the income and rent from the new lands. Hsi-liang reported that he still had to "encourage [the prince] repeatedly until my tongue hurt" before he finally agreed to open some lands in July 1910. Although the prince's decision to open lands to colonization gave some promise that he would have revenues in the future with which to pay his debts to the Russian merchants, Hsi-liang still worried that the Russians might exert unwarranted influence in his banner in the meantime. He therefore soon took the rather contradictory step of lowering the price of land in part of the prince's banner in order to accelerate colonization and "strengthen the frontier." He was able to deal successfully with this chief as with the others during his term, but he later watched from afar as Wu-t'ai led the Mongols of Manchuria against the provincial administration.[105]

In Manchuria, Hsi-liang had drafted policies when the "very life" of the area lay "in the hands of the foreign powers." He had devoted his main efforts to reviving a "body" whose "hands were tied" and whose "veins were in danger of being cut." The foreigners had regarded his "plans for survival" as "bones in their throats"; he had viewed the foreigners as "wolves," "tigers," and "hawks." He had based his resistance to Japan on the principle that "we cannot give up our lands, nor can we sacrifice our sovereignty." When the court had denied him the support necessary to uphold this principle, he had sought to expand the economy, first by calling on the "strength of the whole nation," and then by moving "together with the Americans to put resources behind our own plans." He had advocated building railways to serve as the foundation for economic development, invoking the United States as a model. Yet he did not wish China to become like America in all respects, and he continued to insist that "although this is called a commercial railway, in fact it embodies a policy of politics and diplomacy." His final strategy was to respect the military, linguistic, political, and cultural autonomy of the Mongols in order to attract them to China and protect them from the Russians. This strategy showed both the growth in his understanding of the ethnic minorities and his firm determination to base policy on China's own view of interstate relations and the world order.

12: DOMESTIC CALAMITY

While governor-general of Manchuria, Hsi-liang also served as governor of Fengtien, which was troubled by severe divisions along political and social lines. He resisted the extremists, including corrupt Manchu princes who tried to centralize the administration and violent Alliance agitators who attempted to overthrow the dynasty. He sought to broaden the dynasty's base of support there by reforming the army, banners, and administration and by cooperating with the upper class in other reforms. He developed into both a political radical who advocated the acceleration of constitutional reforms and a social radical who was responsive to the needs and even to the demands of the lower class.

Resisting the Extremists

The regency of the infant emperor, P'u-yi, which had taken power in 1908, showed little of the determination and direction that had characterized the government of the empress dowager in its last years. The Ch'un Prince Tsai-feng, brother of the hapless Kuang-hsü Emperor, was dominated by his wife, the daughter of Jung-lu and the mother of P'u-yi. Although lacking ambition himself, he had been driven by his wife into a power struggle with his sister-in-law, the Empress Dowager Lung-yü, who had been appointed co-regent. Incapable of fulfilling the barest duties of his position, Tsai-feng was hardly able to assume the grand role of autocrat that his wife and others tried to thrust on him. He wrote inappropriate endorsements on memorials, and he often had nothing to say in audiences with the highest officials. Soon he became the butt of jokes even among his close relatives, who depended on his position and favored his policies.[1] He had, however, appointed Hsi-liang to the post in Manchuria and initially expressed interest in his plans there. For this reason and perhaps also because Tsai-feng was more pitiful than obnoxious, Hsi-liang at first spared him any criticism. Instead he tried to persuade the prince to move against the more reprehensible members of what was coming to be known as the "dictatorship of the princes."

Hsi-liang first took issue with the Ch'ing Prince I-k'uang, who had used his broad experience in public affairs to increase his power under the regency. Hsi-liang had occasionally cooperated with I-k'uang on public matters, but he now grew increasingly critical of his private conduct. Hsi-liang's friend at court, Lu Ch'uan-lin, had failed to persuade I-k'uang to award offices according to the merit of the candidate rather than the size of the gifts he offered. By 1910 the prince was said to possess 90 million mow of land, 20 million tls. of movable property, and 13 million tls. of credit with foreign banks.[2] Realizing that Tsai-feng was too weak to curb I-k'uang's excesses and that a public attack on the powerful prince might backfire, Hsi-liang waited to confront him face to face. According to the well-informed Fei Hsing-chien, Hsi-liang met I-k'uang in Peking and "criticized his corruption to his face as damaging to the country."[3] This reprimand evidently had no effect on the prince's behavior and merely diminished Hsi-liang's influence at court.

Hsi-liang's next target was the regent's younger brother, Tsai-hsün, who had been appointed commissioner of the navy in one of a series of moves to concentrate power in the regent's own family. Tsai-hsün earned Hsi-liang's contempt by his inexperience and incompetence: he had misunderstood the strategic requirements of a continental empire and had persuaded the regency to instruct the provinces to raise 13 million tls. a year for a large navy. Hsi-liang responded by sending 100,000 tls. from Manchuria, enough to prove his obedience but only one-fifth of what the court had expected.[4] Hsi-liang's reservations about Tsai-hsün's competence were soon matched by outrage at his corruption. When the prince passed through Manchuria in 1910 he tried to force Hsi-liang to make him a personal gift of another 100,000 tls. According to a reliable source, Hsi-liang "angrily refused him."[5] This action showed that he did not fear extending his struggle against incompetence and corruption to the regent's own family.

Hsi-liang also appealed directly to Tsai-feng to curb the activities of his other younger brother, Tsai-t'ao, who had been made commissioner of the army. Tsai-t'ao was honest but woefully immature and naïvely enthusiastic about the West. In his effort to discover the source of "progress," he had taken numerous "inspection trips" abroad, including one in 1910 that cost an estimated 250,000 tls. On these tours, the young prince would often express unrestrained admiration for foreign ways of doing things; when visiting Japan, he eulogized the Japanese navy.[6] When Hsi-liang heard about this, he secretly memorialized the regent outlining his objections.

> Before 1894 the atmosphere was closed; there were few who went abroad to study and those who did were for the most part poor and hardworking scholars. In the past several years the emphasis has shifted to groups of officials and imperial nobles; there is nothing they have not investigated and no country that has not welcomed them. Looking at what they have learned as recorded by their followers, there is nothing of practical use; and those who have welcomed them have been simply the

powers which have been trying their best to use them out of ulterior motives; it has all been a case of wasting money on the pretext of paying for inspections. To imitate others' good points in order to make up for our shortcomings, what is wrong with this? But [those going abroad] must, like those sent by Peter the Great of Russia and Bismarck of Germany, go right into the factories and be willing to serve in the armies, thereafter bringing back what they have learned for the use of the country. By staying only a few days and looking around according to their whim, how can they grasp the important things?

Thus, for example, the prince of the third degree, Tsai-t'ao, recently went to Japan; the Japanese took advantage of his status to open direct communication between the imperial families in order to press their schemes [on him] and get him into their clutches. Recently I have heard rumors that the English are talking about not even entertaining him. If this be true, what a shame it is for our country! Your official's crude opinion is that in the future we must choose the most enlightened and hardworking among the princes and send them to study in foreign schools for several years; then they will obtain useful knowledge. If they only travel and observe as a mere formality, then their trips abroad are but grand tours, of no benefit to the country.[7]

Despite its boldness, this memorial failed to keep the regency from sending Tsai-t'ao abroad again or from rewarding him handsomely when he returned.[8]

Hsi-liang next confronted the regency's effort to centralize military and financial authority in the hands of the court in Peking. Just as Prince Tsai-feng hoped to enhance his control by having Tsai-hsün and Tsai-t'ao develop the navy and army on the model of the German Reich, so the Empress Dowager Lung-yü tried to increase the power of her faction by having Prince Tsai-tse, the minister of finances, centralize finances on the model of other "modern" states.[9] Tsai-tse, who was at least honest, capable, and sincerely desirous of reforms, first imposed a new stamp tax on the provinces. Hsi-liang recognized Peking's need for more revenue and so dutifully overrode local opposition to collect the new tax.[10] But when Tsai-tse tried to assert central control over the salt administration, Hsi-liang moved quickly to protect what had become the chief source of revenue for the Manchurian military. In addition to sending wires himself, he got other provincial officials to join him in protests to the throne. As a result, the salt plan was modified, but its imposition on the provinces was merely delayed.[11] The trend toward financial centralization continued.

Hsi-liang opposed the regency's effort at centralization because it was excessive and counterproductive. To be sure, the post of governor-general of Manchuria had been modeled on the powerful governor-generalships of Tseng Kuo-fan and Hu Lin-i, who had used their autonomy to suppress the Taiping Rebellion. Some scholars have described the Manchurian post as an example of the regionalism that weakened the Ch'ing in the nineteenth century and led to warlordism in the twentieth.[12] Yet both regionalism and warlordism were different from the decentralization involved in the Manchurian administration. Hsü Shih-ch'ang had proposed a strong governor-generalship precisely in order to defend the Manchurian frontier from encroachment, and the court had approved it for the same reason. Moreover, when Hsü had held the post, he had dedicated himself to defending the frontier, not merely to strengthening a regional power base.[13] Hsi-liang likewise favored a decentralization that would place decision making at the lowest possible level and thus ease quick responses to foreign threats on the frontier. His sincerity in this matter was confirmed when he also proposed the decentralization of authority within Manchuria. He kept Fengtien in his own hands, but granted the governors of Kirin and Heilungkiang the right to memorialize the throne directly.[14]

In April 1910, Hsi-liang memorialized secretly to explain that he opposed excessive centralization on the grounds of both history and reason.

Today the saddest thing is the business about the centralization of authority. Its advocates say that they have heard the foreigners criticizing our twenty-two provinces as twenty-two small countries, and they want to reorganize them into one whole. Their intentions are not bad. They do not realize, however, that in the light of China's history and geography, it is very difficult to impose [such centralization] completely; even some Westerners have said this. The Han set up feudal princes over the masses and survived while the Sung eliminated the frontier garrisons and grew weaker; if we stress the inner and shirk the outer, strengthen the trunk and weaken the branches, we have only to look at the centuries to see what happens. Speaking of our dynasty, at the time of the Taiping and Nien uprisings the former governors-general and governors such as Tseng Kuo-fan and Hu Lin-i devised policies and accomplished the work of the restoration. During the Boxer bandit calamity, Kiangsu, Anhui, Hunan, and Hupeh all made an agreement to defend their territory; fortunately there were the former governors-general Liu K'un-i and Chang Chih-tung to support them and no harm came to the gods of the soil and grain. Moreover, in the case of Szechwan, Shensi, Yunnan, and Kweichow, all separated off by several thousand li, if everything had to be done according to the will and direction of the ministries it would necessarily result in cramps and paralysis; opportunities would be missed. Even if the ministry officials knew everything and had complete plans, still it would be difficult to run things from a distance. How much more is this the case with the two or three new arrivals who presume on their prejudiced views to influence the authorities, saying that so long as they speak within the gates of the country they can urge on from afar and get results. . . .

In general, then, the court shares its authority with the governors-general and the governors while these latter share their authority with the departmental and district magistrates. Without the departmental and district magistrates, even if there were governors-general and governors, they could not govern a province; without governors-general and governors although there were ministry officials they could not rule the country. Governors-general and governors without authority would be the same as not having them at all. The laws of our dynasty are good; our emperor has authority to degrade inefficient officials. If some evil arises, a rescript can be sent in the morning and the official obliged to take off his hat in the evening; so what is the problem? If it is desired to have the several officials of the ministries use only their thinking and talent to run the twenty-two provinces, then the provincial officials will become redundant. [In that case,] with respect to providing leadership in the localities, the local officials will be divided; if there is some crisis, the ears and eyes of the center will not perceive it; if the outer provinces then prove incapable of handling it, the calamity will be great.[15]

Despite its eloquence, this memorial failed to dissuade the Manchu princes from continuing to gather power into their own hands.

Hsi-liang also stalwartly resisted the other extreme, the anti-Manchu agitators who belonged to Sun Yat-sen's Revolutionary Alliance. In 1909 the Alliance had sent a former military officer and veteran rebel named Hsiung Ch'eng-chi to Kirin to plan a rebellion. Hsiung had first founded a newspaper to campaign for rights recovery and then slipped off to Japan to join the Alliance. There he had stolen some secret documents from the Japanese military command. He had then returned to Kirin planning to sell them to the Russians and so spark a military conflict from which the Alliance might benefit.[16] When this plan failed, he had tried to mobilize the famous Manchurian secret society of Red Beards (Hung-hu-tzu) to join a revolt against the state. Hsi-liang heard about this plot and moved quickly to end the threat.[17] When Hsiung visited the railway station in Harbin during Tsai-hsün's tour, he was arrested and charged with plotting to assassinate the Manchu prince. Hsiung protested that he was planning not a racial revolt against the dynasty but a political campaign against corruption.[18] Hsi-liang may have been moved by this shrewd appeal, but he could not forgive Hsiung for his alliance with the Red Beards, whom officials called "Mounted Bandits." He joined the Kirin governor in memorializing in favor of the death penalty. The court approved, and Hsiung was executed in Kirin in late February 1910.[19]

Up to this point, Hsi-liang had enjoyed the support of the brigade commander of the Sixth Division in Manchuria, Wu Lu-chen. Wu, who had been educated in Hupeh and Japan, was the most illustrious of those late Ch'ing military officers who served in the New Army but had close ties with the anti-Manchu movement.[20] He formally joined the Alliance but continued to alternate his support between it and the Ch'ing, depending on which was resisting imperialism more actively. He had so disdained Hsü Shih-ch'ang that he once refused to dine with him, but he had come to respect Hsi-liang for his resistance to the Japanese and he had served him loyally and capably as frontier commissioner.[21] When other Alliance members had proposed joining the Red Beards in revolt, Wu had opposed it, saying that only "pure patriots" should be enlisted in the revolution.[22] He had proved his loyalty to Hsi-liang in an even more dramatic way. The Yunnanese military student, Li Ken-yüan, had come to Mukden to see Wu and to offer his services in the New Army. When Li was unable to get an interview immediately with Hsi-liang, he fell to brooding about the Yunnanese who had died during Hsi-liang's suppression of the Ho-k'ou revolt. He finally decided to "do something to move the whole country"—that is, to assassinate Hsi-liang. When he learned about the plot, Wu had been horrified that one patriot should kill another. He had persuaded Li to abandon the plan and to leave Fengtien.[23]

Beginning in late 1909, however, Hsi-liang began to lose influence over Wu Lu-chen. He had not been able to persuade the court to disburse funds necessary for frontier defense and had finally been forced to abolish Wu's post as frontier commissioner. His decision to call for the execution of Hsiung Ch'eng-chi further alienated Wu, perhaps leaving him with the same feelings of bitterness that had affected Li Ken-yüan only a short time before. Wu now agreed with other Alliance members to create some kind of an incident to embroil Hsi-liang in difficulties.[24] He sought the cooperation of the commander of the Second Mixed Brigade near Mukden, Lan T'ien-wei, who shared his background and outlook. But Lan hesitated to join because, he said, key troops continued to be loyal to Hsi-liang and to the Ch'ing. The other officers ended by dropping the plan.[25] Hsi-liang was either completely ignorant of the plot or very cool in dealing with it. He continued to show confidence in the plotters by asking Wu to become his personal secretary and by praising Lan for his exemplary behavior.[26]

Hsi-liang managed to limit the importance of the anti-Manchu parties by keeping firm control over the military forces. He did this by choosing officers on the basis of their professional competence and loyalty to the dynasty irrespective of their personal ties to him or to the Peiyang (North China) clique of his predecessor. He kept the relatively capable Peiyang commander, Ts'ao K'un, in charge of the Third Division in Ch'ang-ch'un, but impeached the Peiyang brigadier-general, Chang Hsün, who had left his post in charge of the Fengtien and Huai units and showed himself derelict in his duties. He replaced Chang with a politically astute Peiyang officer, Chang Hsi-luan, who had previously won over some Red Beard leaders to the government. When Wu Lu-chen finally left Manchuria in 1910, Hsi-liang replaced him with yet another Peiyang officer who had carried out reforms in both the old and new armies. He called in his own military protégé, Ch'en I, from Yunnan, less to extend personal control over the Manchurian forces than to expand them and to deal with frontier problems.[27] Ironically, it was the expansion of the New Army that eventually gave Wu Lu-chen and Lan T'ien-wei a base from which to deal the Ch'ing a mortal blow.

Expanding the Political Base

Hsi-liang meanwhile worked hard to expand the political base for carrying out domestic reforms in Fengtien. Long before Itō Hirobumi reminded him, he had recognized that domestic reforms were the indispensable foundation for a strong foreign policy. In his words,

> In the Eastern Provinces, diplomatic difficulties always obstruct domestic administration. At the same time, however, we must improve domestic administration if we expect to make any progress in foreign affairs.[28]

In the secret memorial of May 1909, he had promised to take full responsibility for carrying out military and economic reforms in order to strengthen the province against external enemies and internal dissidents.

Hsi-liang first tried to reform the military forces so that indigenous troops could take over as the Peiyang units were gradually withdrawn. He and the governors of Kirin and Heilungkiang reorganized scattered battalions of the antiquated patrol and defense forces into three divisions of the New Army, with one division stationed in each province. He and Commander Ch'en I selected several battalions of the Peiyang Sixth Division and recruited new men to form a wholly new Twentieth Division, led by well-trained officers such as Wu Lu-chen and Lan T'ien-wei. Hsi-liang spent 3 million tls. a year, or nearly 60 percent of the provincial budget, on the military.[29] He exercised strict supervision over his officers, once warning one to maintain discipline among the troops so that they did not harass the population or damage property.[30] He also spent 2 million tls., or 20 percent of an enlarged budget, to train a police force that could maintain public order and national sovereignty in competition with the Japanese police. He left his successor with the core of an impressive military establishment.[31]

He next expanded the Manchu banner forces that had once played a particularly important role in Manchuria. He and the head of the Banner Affairs Bureau, the Manchu scholar Chin-liang, launched a five-year program of banner development, which included the creation of new posts for qualified bannermen, the establishment of a development bank, and the organization of an industrial school for bannerwomen. They sent certain families of bannermen to Yen-chi where they could raise their own food, open new lands, and strengthen the frontier. Hsi-liang, who was particularly concerned about the frontier menace, organized 300 of the colonists into military units to defend their lands from the foreigners. Chin-liang, who was especially interested in strengthening the dynasty, created a Manchu army to "protect the imperial tombs" near Mukden.[32] They thus revitalized the nearly defunct banners and enlisted their help in strengthening the country.

To help finance the expansion, Hsi-liang cut out corruption and cut back the administration. He impeached corrupt officials and officers and replaced them with men of known probity. He dismissed several personal secretaries (mu-yu) who had obtained their positions through friends and relatives and hired instead men who had proved themselves in regular civil posts. He retained the most qualified among his higher-ranking subordinates and replaced the less competent with men who had studied abroad or who had obtained the higher civil service degrees.[33] He slashed expenditures on buildings to a fraction of the previous 2 million tls. a year and eliminated expensive posts, including the governorship and right and left councillorships in Fengtien. He reportedly continued his earlier practice of rising at five each morning and working until midnight; he was so diligent that his subordinates began to fear that he would soon abolish the weekend in the interests of economy and efficiency.[34] Through these measures he saved over 400,000 tls. for more meaningful expenditures.

Hsi-liang devoted part of these savings to educational, agricultural, and industrial reforms. He maintained the already established secondary and technical schools and placed new emphasis on the development of primary schools to achieve "universal education." He hired foreign experts and Chinese returned students to improve and expand the experimental agricultural stations. With the help of Han Kuo-chün, who had served with distinction in Honan and studied industry in Japan, he developed officially run companies based on European, Japanese, and American models. During his term he tripled annual expenditures on education and increased expenditures on agriculture and industry by 20 percent, thus placing the state in the vanguard of cultural and economic expansion.[35]

As part of his effort to expand the political base, Hsi-liang tried to cooperate with the representatives of the upper class, who were meeting for the first time in the newly established provincial assembly (*tzu-i-chü*). He wrote that "what the state cannot do" in such fields as education and the economy, "I have advocated that the people manage in the hope of making a beginning at least." [36] The assemblymen responded by assuming some responsibility for education, increasing their contribution to building schools, and helping to boost the number of literacy schools from 3 to 260. They agreed to encourage Manchurian farmers to raise more wheat to compete with imports from abroad and more mulberry bushes to supply the domestic silk industry. They predicted success so long as the officials continued to cooperate with the people; and foreign observers soon noted a marked increase in the agricultural production of the province.[37] Hsi-liang and the assemblymen also established some commercial research associations and encouraged the local elite and merchants to found machine shops and silk filatures, a textile factory producing "patriotic cloth," and a 1 million tls. electric power plant. By 1911 officials and merchants together ran nine factories in the province.[38]

Hsi-liang did encounter some difficulties in cooperating with the assembly on certain economic reforms. When he asked help in distributing a new breed of sheep to the countryside, the assemblymen refused on the grounds that this was an "official responsibility." He proposed the reactivation of a company designed to protect Chinese fishermen from foreign competitors, but the assemblymen merely seized the occasion to criticize earlier mismanagement of the company. He suggested reviving an old jointly managed shipping company on the Liao River, but the assemblymen again refused because the previous effort had failed.[39] A legacy of mistrust and past failures complicated his effort to cooperate with the assembly to expand the economy.

The greatest obstacles to Chinese economic development, however, were Japanese competition and control. The Chinese set up eleven bean and bread companies but the Japanese retained control of the markets for both commodities. The Chinese founded sixteen factories between 1905 and 1911, but the Japanese created fifty-seven in the same period. The Chinese increased their exports from Fengtien sixfold, but the foreigners—principally the Japanese—increased their exports to Fengtien eightfold.[40] The Japanese also held the most promising sources of wealth within the province. Through the accords of 1909, they had strengthened control over the three largest mines in the province: the Fu-shun, which produced 2,000 tons of coal a day, and the Yen-t'ai and Pen-hsi-hu, which together turned out 150 tons a day. Since the best mines were under foreign control, Hsi-liang and the assembly could only establish an association to preserve the remaining mines. They also encouraged investments by overseas Chinese in the mines, but, given Hsi-liang's experience in trying to entice Chinese capitalists from Shanghai to develop the gold mines, it seems likely that they had little success.[41] Since the Chinese lacked abundant capital for investment, they were reluctant to invest what little they had in the less promising mines of the province.

Hsi-liang made significant progress in expanding the political base with respect to the army, banners, administration, and assembly. He achieved less in expanding the economy, partly because of differences with the assembly but largely because of the overwhelming presence of the Japanese. Indeed the Japanese threat to Fengtien grew so great that it drove Hsi-liang to take a quite different approach in his efforts to save the country.

Radicalism in Politics and Society

To bridge the gap between the court and the people and to defend against the Japanese, Hsi-liang assumed radical positions. He advocated an acceleration of the introduction of constitutional government and an increase in state concern for the lower class. Although he adopted these positions in response to the current situation, he justified them by appealing to fundamental Chinese ideals concerning the good state and the just society. By this time keenly aware of the world outside of Manchuria, he nonetheless adopted measures that were characteristically Chinese in origin and conception.

Hsi-liang's new attitude toward institutional reforms became apparent as soon as he arrived in Fengtien. Earlier he had opposed such reforms as the creation of representative councils (i-shih-hui) on the grounds that the local elite already participated sufficiently in government.[42] But in Fengtien he enthusiastically fulfilled his predecessor's promise to set up a consultative council (hsing-cheng hui-i-ch'u) which brought the local elite formally into the government. He successfully supervised what he called the "thorniest task to date"—the unprecedented provincial elections of 1909 in which 52,000 members of the upper class chose electors who selected fifty members of the provincial assembly. He oversaw the establishment of new organs of local government, including the town councils (*i-shih-hui*) and executive boards (*tung-shih-hui*), which strengthened state ties with local society. He also saw to the creation of the independent courts (*shen-p'an-t'ing*), which were designed to recover Chinese sovereignty in the treaty ports by separating justice from administration.[43]

Hsi-liang showed great skill in dealing with the newly created provincial assembly. During its first session in 1909, he handled all differences with it so carefully that it did not exercise its privilege of referring disputes to the national assembly (*tzu-cheng-yüan*) soon to convene in Peking. At the closing meeting of the session, the assembly president, Wu Ching-lien, expressed the hope that the "officials and people" would continue to "work together." Hsi-liang responded by summarizing the spirit that had developed:

> during this session of the provincial assembly, superior and inferior have been of one mind. Officials and local elite have followed the laws and shared both trust and sincerity, without any misunderstandings. In these troubled times this has been a rich experience, far surpassing that of any other province.[44]

During the 1910 session the assembly did refer one dispute to Peking, but it was minor compared with those occurring at the same time in other provinces.[45]

Hsi-liang became more radical during the course of an extended debate over central government constitutional reforms. The regency was committed to establishing a national assembly, which would meet in late 1910, and a parliament (*kuo-hui*), scheduled to convene in 1917. Although half of the members of the national assembly would be appointed and half would be elected indirectly, all members of the parliament would be elected, presumably by direct vote. The national assembly would have merely consultative functions, but the parliament would have legislative—and perhaps even constituent—powers. This plan for the gradual introduction of constitutional government had been drafted explicitly on the model of Meiji constitutional reform by men who had been educated in Japan.[46]

As the Japanese consolidated their hold on Manchuria in October 1909, provincial assemblies throughout the empire began to protest. The president of the Kiangsu Provincial Assembly, the noted scholar-reformer Chang Chien, concluded that the court would have to accelerate the introduction of constitutional government if it was to keep the support of the people and resist the foreign powers.[47] Chang called a meeting in Shanghai of delegates from sixteen provincial assemblies (including two men from Fengtien) to found a Constitutional Preparatory Association (*yü-pei li-hsien kung-hui*) to petition the court for the early convening of parliament.[48] In January 1910 they submitted their first petition, signed by 200,000 men, requesting the establishment of parliament within a year to deal with foreign encroachment, financial disorder, and official irresponsibility. The Grand Council rejected the petition, arguing that such a move would "hinder the success of constitutional government in its early stages." [49]

Hsi-liang's past experience had prepared him to join this radical movement. He, like Chang Chien, had been deeply affected by the defeat in 1895. He had shared with Chang admiration for Fan Tang-shih, the poet who had withdrawn from public life in anguish over China's growing predicament. Hsi-liang, as an official, and Chang, as a scholar, had long stressed the need for close cooperation between the state and society. When faced with the crisis of expanding Japanese control, Hsi-liang had urged the provincial assembly to discuss the issue. Hsi-liang placed great trust in his subordinate Cheng Hsiao-hsü, who had edited the *Constitutional Magazine* and had been active in Shanghai politics.[50]

In April 1910 Hsi-liang secretly memorialized the throne, giving his own arguments for accelerated reform:

> As the deadline approaches for completing preparations for the constitution, salvation from the present dangers really depends on thorough change. The capital [Peking] must prepare the cabinet [*nei-ko*], which is still not responsible, and the banner system, which is still not reformed. The scholar-officials are accustomed to extravagance and waste; there are few of them who honestly fulfill their duties. Those at court and those outside often speak of civilization, but many have the habit of climbing by using connections. Like dogs and flies, they completely lack a sense of shame; like fish in pots or swallows in nests they daily pursue their own pleasure. Thus in every province in matters of education, police, self-government, opium suppression, financial reforms and independent courts, there is either negligence or oppressive exaction, or the name without the reality or the semblance of something without its actuality. Comparing the present with the past ten years, has there been any progress? Or has there simply been decadence? Our finances are destitute, the people are all excited, things are neither new nor old; not only is this the occasion for the countries of East and West to laugh loudly at us, but also I fear difficulties between superior and inferior and an eventual slide into collapse—even to think of it makes my blood run cold.
>
> In my crude opinion we must realize the constitution, so that there will be no nobles or base persons, no higher or lower, and all will have to accept administration according to the laws, rooting out their private selfishness. If there is ruinous corruption in the laws and a rejection of common rights, if the government grows daily more lax and the people's hearts flow away, then although we may finally have a constitution in nine years, still we shall end by following the example of Persia, Turkey, Vietnam, and Korea. How could this be a cause for rejoicing? [51]

While not yet daring to press specifically for an early convening of parliament, he moved far ahead of the court in advocating "thorough change" toward a "responsible cabinet."

During the summer of 1910, as the situation deteriorated with the Russo-Japanese agreement, Manchurian delegates became some of the most ardent advocates of further petitions for faster reform to save their provinces.

They helped to transform the association into a more permanent organization, the Delegation to Petition for a Parliament (*kuo-hui ch'ing-yüan tai-piao-t'uan*), which drew up a second (and stronger) petition. In June they submitted it to the Censorate with 300,000 signatures. Again the court rejected it, saying that "undue haste would lead to repentance," and this time ordered the petitioning to cease. Undaunted, representatives from Manchuria persuaded the Delegation to announce that the Manchurian crisis, which was "related to China's survival," could be solved only by the immediate convening of parliament. It drafted a third petition to that effect, claimed to obtain an astronomical 25 million signatures, and submitted it directly to the prince regent on 3 October. Representatives from Fengtien wrote letters in blood to the Delegation, demanding that it persevere this time until complete success. They also staged a sit-in at the office of the prince regent, vowing to stay until he decreed an early parliament. A few even mutilated themselves to dramatize their selfless determination.[52]

As the court considered the latest petition, Hsi-liang again spoke out, this time publicly, in behalf of faster reform. He drafted a strong memorial and obtained the signatures of seventeen other governors-general and governors before sending it to the Grand Council on 25 October. The first part of the memorial was an extended apologetic for a responsible cabinet and an early parliament. To win over the prince regent, he remained vague about whether the cabinet would be responsible to the throne or to the parliament. He asserted that the cabinet, headed by a "responsible" man, would not encroach on imperial authority, that the throne would still retain control over the military and finances, and that the court system would be independent of the cabinet. To reassure those who liked to cite the gradualist model of Japan, he argued that the parliament would not become disorderly, that it would merely air differences which would be better discussed than ignored, and that it would assist the court in expanding its revenues to run the empire and effect other reforms.[53] In sum, accelerated reform would diminish neither the authority of the prince regent nor the possibility of learning from the Japanese.

Hsi-liang continued that the situation in Manchuria and in the country as a whole simply would not permit the dynasty to go on without accepting "responsibility" for its policies.

> Now, in the wake of the Russo-Japanese agreement, Korea has died and the powers' policy of equalizing their influence has changed; the situation is very dangerous, already far worse than that prevailing in Te-tsung's time. We cannot delay, we cannot wait; we must fix a date for the establishment of a cabinet and parliament so that state and society can combine their energies; this is much better than fearing what will happen afterwards. How can the emperor allow conflicts over a few short years to keep him from making a decision?
> Hsi-liang and the rest of us are again annoyingly persistent, but it is only with awe of the emperor in our hearts. In the end there was no way to save the Ming house,

and all of its officials were representatives of a dead state; and how could it have been otherwise? There was no responsibility! Thus when the polity is not good, the officials and people of the empire have no one to take responsibility. When there are only the gods of land and grain to obey, what kind of an impression does this make? The warning of Yin is not distant, so how can we be without fear? If Hsi-liang and the rest of us knew this and did not speak out, we could not face our present emperor, much less our former sovereign.

We beg your august person to come to a decision, to depute an official to organize a cabinet, and to issue a clear order for the opening of a parliament next year. You should instruct the Committee for Preparing the Constitution to submit ways of selecting the members and to carry out the imperial orders. This will greatly benefit the imperial clan; it will also greatly assist the people's livelihood.[54]

Hsi-liang's wire, combined with those from other provincial officials, forced the regency to face the division between two factions at court. Prince I-k'uang, who had much to lose in a responsible cabinet and much influence over the scheduled date for a parliament, headed the antireform faction, which also included Grand Councillors Na-t'ung and Shih-hsü. Prince Tsai-tse, who had called for a parliament since 1909, led the reform faction, which included Princes Tsai-hsün and Tsai-t'ao and Grand Councillors Yü-lang and Hsü Shih-ch'ang. According to a rumor, when the Empress Dowager Lung-yü heard about the Manchurian agitation for accelerated reform, she came out of self-imposed isolation to demand that the Prince Regent Tsai-feng explain what he was doing to save Manchuria and satisfy the petitioners. Tsai-feng reportedly replied that he would take steps to save the Manchu homeland and to compromise on the pace of reform. When the National Assembly demanded the immediate creation of a cabinet responsible to a parliament, Tsai-feng used this extreme demand to force the antireform faction to accept a compromise.[55]

In early November, the court announced a new position, which had been designed largely by I-k'uang. First, the Grand Council, which I-k'uang headed, would transform itself immediately into the "new responsible cabinet." Thus I-k'uang would retain his position, the Grand Council would keep its authority, and the new cabinet would be "responsible" only to the throne. Second, parliament could be convened earlier than expected but not as early as the petitioners wished.

We are desirous of meeting the wishes of our subjects. But it must be understood that before the summoning of a parliament a great deal of time is required in order to have the necessary preparations duly perfected; this cannot be done in a year or two. We now command that the period elapsing before the opening of a parliament be shortened to the fifth year of Hsüan-t'ung and that tentative regulations prescribing official duties shall be drawn up.[56]

By creating a cabinet responsible to the throne and granting the early convening of parliament for 1913, the wily I-k'uang conceded something in name but yielded nothing in fact. Sensing a tactical victory, he persuaded the regency to order all petitioners to "return to their homes and await quietly the issuance of further decrees." [57]

Hsi-liang refused to accept the court's new plan and pushed doggedly ahead in his attempts to persuade the prince regent to make meaningful concessions. He realized that his previous ambiguity concerning the cabinet's responsibility had provided a loophole through which I-k'uang had slipped. Now he sought to correct the error by stressing the need for the "simultaneous" creation of the cabinet and parliament in 1911. With an obvious reference to the corrupt and inflexible I-k'uang, he begged the throne to make the cabinet really responsible. This would keep "high officials" from using their public offices for private benefit and from adopting policies which would drive the people into forming "parties." At first it appeared that this plea had touched the prince regent; it was rumored that Hsi-liang would soon be transferred to become a member of the Grand Council (or cabinet). But I-k'uang naturally expressed "displeasure" at the tone of Hsi-liang's memorial and intervened successfully against his appointment to the council. Because he had already exhausted what little influence he had in order to obtain a compromise, Tsai-feng increasingly became a captive of the antireform faction.[58]

In the face of the court's intransigence, Hsi-liang began to cooperate more closely with the Manchurians. One of the two representatives he had appointed to the National Assembly now rose in a meeting of that body to warn that Manchuria would suffer most in the absence of an immediate parliament and to inquire how the Grand Council proposed to defend the frontier. This challenge elicited no response from the court. The members of the Delegation who had returned to Fengtien after the dissolution of their organization now persuaded the provincial assembly to ask Hsi-liang to memorialize again for an earlier parliament. When Hsi-liang duly complied and met with another rebuff, a rumor circulated in Mukden that the court would "prefer to have a Boxer movement rather than to open the parliament." [59] Although it might have been an exaggeration, this rumor further angered the people of Mukden.

As official and Delegation efforts failed, the movement took to the streets of Mukden. On 4 December, some students followed Hsi-liang's carriage through the streets of the capital shouting: "Please open the parliament!" On the fifth they demanded an audience with him but were refused by an aide, and on the sixth they met at the assembly to organize a protest. They were joined by scholars and merchants; representatives from educational, agricultural, and newspaper associations; delegates from the assembly, prefectures, and subprefectures; and envoys from minority groups such as the Muslims of Harbin. The protesters made a banner inscribed with the words: "The whole population of Fengtien province demands the prompt opening of a parliament." They then set out for the office of the governor-general. By the time they reached their destination they were 10,000 strong.[60]

Hsi-liang at first tried to persuade the demonstrators to disperse, citing the imperial edicts proscribing any further petitions. He soon yielded to sympathy for the crowd, however, and agreed to receive a small delegation headed by the president of the assembly, Wu Ching-lien. Wu submitted the following petition, signed by 11,000 people.

> The situation in the Eastern Provinces now is even more critical than that obtaining when the three petitions [of the Delegation] were submitted. The Russo-Japanese treaty and Japan's absorption of Korea do not permit the least delay. The Japanese are working nights to broaden the base of the An-feng railway and it is rumored that they will complete the work next year; their immigrants along the track increase daily and they stir up the Red Beards to intimidate our outer areas. The Russians encroach on our frontiers with their policies of expanding transportation; their plots to move in settlers are even worse than those of the Japanese; not only do they craftily demand navigation rights without precedent, but they also plot to seduce our frontier people as tools for sneaking into Mongolia and this situation is so hazardous that we may not finish the day. If we really have to wait until 1913, there is no way of knowing whether by that time this land will still be ours.
>
> At the present time, at court and outside, above and below, there is not a person who does not publicly recognize that a parliament is good medicine for saving our life. If we do not have this medicine, then it is all over; if we have it, then the quicker we swallow it the sooner we will be saved from disaster. If we wait, it will mean that the medicine will not be able to take effect, and the loss of the Three Provinces will drag down the whole country; this is what burns our hearts and boils our blood. We must personally demand again that the period be shortened. How much more in the case of planning for the official system, the cabinet, the members, the election laws, and the constitution. If they are planned slowly, then even in three years they will not be finished; but if they are planned in a hurry, in a few months they will be complete. We must beg that you memorialize asking that a parliament be called during the eighth and ninth months of next year [September-November], to unify the people's minds and protect the larger picture.[61]

Deeply moved by the "prostration and weeping," Hsi-liang accepted the petition and agreed to memorialize "on behalf of the people."

In his memorial of December 1910, Hsi-liang sided with the people against the regency. He warned the regency not to underestimate the high purpose and sincerity of the petitioners. "When over 10,000 men prostrate themselves, lament, and beat their brows until blood flows, the din that they make with their exertions does not come from mere self-interest." Rather it came from the purest kind of "nationalism."

> In my opinion, after 1894 and 1904, stirred up by powerful neighbors, there was a birth of nationalist thinking [*sheng kuo-chia chih ssu-hsiang*]; the people knew that if they did not mass together they would not be able to defend even their own lives. When they saw the sad case of the extinction of Korea as a country they greatly

feared that the map of the Three Provinces would also fall to strange countries, and that they would not be able to recover from the calamities which would ensue. The pain of their worries was great. As their situation is particularly dangerous when compared with that of the other provinces, it is natural that they should have special demands. When I came east, I investigated the situation and looked for ways to prevent the death of the Three Provinces; although there was not one method that worked, yet the minds of the dependable people did not die and they continued to be obedient to the court. For a long time now this huge area has been slowly eaten up and is now already partially lost; and yet for 300 years the people have been loyal. If, in the twinkling of an eye, we hand it over to others, will this not be just a repetition of Korea? In general, then, the situation is critical—a great calamity to the people and a great source of sadness for the dynasty. So why must we be so loath to give up this little period of two years which would give the masses a new beginning? [62]

He urged the court either to grant the petitioners' request for a parliament in 1911 or to permit him to resign his post. He cleared the court's way to dismissing him by requesting a sick leave to care for an "old ailment." [63]

The prince regent ignored Hsi-liang's challenge to dismiss him but granted him the sick leave and issued a long rescript refusing to call a parliament in 1911.

The issue of advancing the deadline for the parliament was previously discussed in detail by the court, decided satisfactorily and made known in a clear rescript; there was no need for another memorial. The Three Eastern Provinces are important; the governor-general has a responsibility to govern and pacify the people. When matters become difficult it is especially important that he take full responsibility for them, without making excuses and shirking his duty, so as to fulfill the functions of his office.[64]

The regent also gave free rein to I-k'uang who advocated forceful suppression of the remaining petitioners and agitators. Under his influence, the Ministry of the Interior ordered the expulsion of everyone who had come to Peking from Fengtien to support Hsi-liang's memorial. Eighteen consented to leave under armed guard but four refused; of these, three were imprisoned and the fourth was killed as he jumped from the wagon taking him to jail. The court instructed Hsi-liang to keep close watch on the agitators who were returning to prevent them from "creating another incident." [65]

The court's expulsion of the Fengtien demonstrators wiped out what little good will had been engendered by the creation of a cabinet and the promise of an early parliament. It drove those reformers who had temporarily accepted the compromise into renewed opposition to the regency. It also touched off a cycle of repression and protest that involved larger and larger numbers of people. To show their support of the expelled petitioners, the students of Mukden boycotted their classes, leading students elsewhere in the empire to follow their example. The regency responded in January 1911 by ordering Hsi-liang and other officials to compel the students to return to school on pain of severe punishment.[66] Instead of isolating the radicals, the regency's actions increasingly radicalized the whole of the Chinese upper class. It thus contributed to the very political disintegration that it sought to prevent.

Hsi-liang's period of leadership of the movement for a responsible cabinet and an early parliament—now drawing to a close—should not be interpreted as an effort to ally with the upper class in political reforms in order to isolate the lower class, which wanted social reforms.[67] Rather his aim had been to gain the support of all classes, to rally them against the imperialists, and to unite them in a political revolution that would isolate the extremists. Furthermore, as we shall see, he firmly believed that fundamental Chinese notions of social equity should be realized and extended downward to include the lower class.

During the first session of the provincial assembly, Hsi-liang showed more concern for social welfare than did the representatives of the upper class in the assembly. In one case he asked them to help pay for some prison reforms, which had been highly praised by independent observers, but they refused on the grounds that prison reform was the state's responsibility.[68] In another case he wanted the assemblymen to build workhouses (hsi-i-so) for the poor in addition to one that he had already built. He acknowledged that China had evolved its own peculiar social structure which could not be easily compared with those of Japan and the West. Social inequality nonetheless had also appeared in China and should be reduced in accord with the ancient ideal of "neither noble nor base persons." He told the assemblymen:

> In general, whenever the rich and poor classes are very unlike one another, the theory of socialism [she-hui chu-i] cannot be realized. Thus the government must pay close attention to welfare.[69]

Far from trying to prevent a real social revolution, he was urging the upper class to carry out a revolution toward an egalitarian society. The indignant assemblymen replied that the state should run the welfare system and the paupers should learn to support themselves.[70]

Hsi-liang also encouraged the assemblymen to help make other members of the upper class more responsible to the people. He asked the representatives, few of whom were merchants, to assist with the registration of all merchants so that they would not become "traitorously" involved with foreign businessmen and create "complications" in foreign affairs. The assemblymen, whose cultural superiority to the "money-making merchants" exceeded their class solidarity with them, readily complied.[71] Hsi-liang also asked the assembly to encourage the students being taught in the "new schools," most of whom were from the upper class, to give up their dreams of bureaucratic power and commercial wealth and to return to their villages to help educate their families and neighbors. The assemblymen, who in any case could look out for the interests of their own sons, cooperated with this measure, which was designed to achieve "universal education." [72]

In other ways Hsi-liang showed sympathy for the peasant majority, who bore the brunt of the financial burden of reforms. In one case, when 10,000 villagers marched on a district city near Mukden to protest new taxes to pay for reforms, he immediately agreed to negotiate with the leaders and ended by granting many of their demands.[73] In another instance, an "allied village association" of 1,000 peasants attacked a district city near Chin-chou to "expel the police and abolish the schools." The local magistrate adopted a conciliatory posture. He first tried to negotiate, then sent troops, and, when some of the troops defected to the insurgents, agreed to turn the new institutions over to "local control." When some of the peasants still held out for repeal of the new taxes, the magistrate agreed to find other ways to pay for the new institutions.[74] The administration thus retained the reforms while reducing their burden on the lower classes.

Hsi-liang's administration also attempted to protect the peasantry from exploitation by foreign businessmen. Many of the peasants who sold grain to the foreigners would contract to sell a whole year's crop in advance in order to obtain the funds needed to buy seeds and equipment. At harvest time they would often find that they had not been able to produce as much as they had agreed to provide to the foreign (usually Japanese) merchants. To cover their defaults, more and more farmers in Fengtien were forced to mortgage their lands to the Japanese. In a message to the assembly, Hsi-liang noted that this was the way India had succumbed to British control. He prohibited the peasants from making sales in advance and organized an official company to purchase their grain to sell to the foreigners. When some Fengtien merchants attacked the official company for interfering with their own private enterprise, Hsi-liang emphasized that the company was designed merely to protect the peasantry. He offered to abolish it as soon as some patriotic merchants set up a company of their own to serve the same function.[75]

Hsi-liang's most radical decision came when members of the lower class rioted against the upper class in 1910. Early in the year he had prohibited the export of all food grains because a famine had been predicted for the fall. When merchants in An-tung nonetheless continued to sell grain to the foreigners, a man named Li Sheng led several hundred poor peasants from three nearby villages to An-tung to protest. They marched on the merchants' shops and demanded that they divide the grain among the starving poor instead of exporting it. The wealthy merchants not only refused but organized an armed militia and called on a member of the district council to intervene. When the magistrate of An-tung reviewed the case, he admonished the councilman for misconduct, charged the merchants with being "rich but valueless outlaws," and ordered all those with surpluses to "contribute" them to the poor. Fortified by official sympathy, Li Sheng and his followers raised their demands from temporary relief to "equal grain" for the whole winter. As Hsi-liang's magistrates observed without intervening, the "grain riots" spread from An-tung to another district and to two other subprefectures, affecting many villages and towns. In the end the officials even required the merchants to institutionalize their "contributions," forcing them to borrow from banks whenever necessary to pay their fair share.[76] Thus Hsi-liang and his subordinates permitted the lower class to force the upper class to pay attention to the needs of the poor.

As a political and social radical, Hsi-liang found little room for maneuver under the regency. He soon renewed his request to retire. After the end of his first "rest cure" in December 1910, he memorialized, frankly outlining his political reasons for wanting to retire:

> I have already been in office for almost two years and have been unable to complete a single task. Above I cannot face my sovereign; below I cannot face the people. I have been ungrateful for favors shown me and neglectful of my duties, both crimes that I cannot run away from. I must therefore respectfully ask for heavenly favor to allow me to leave my post, and to send another capable official to take over so as to give due importance to the frontier. I am overcome in imploring this! [77]

Granted another brief rest cure, he took it and then memorialized again, arguing that both health and politics were forcing him to withdraw.[78] He was granted another rest that might have developed into full retirement had not another crisis loomed unexpectedly. In late 1910 and early 1911 Hsi-liang was called upon to fight a virulent pneumonic plague that spread through Manchuria into Chihli, taking thousands of lives, occasioning further foreign intervention, and symbolizing the inability of even the best administrators to deal with the problems of the time.[79]

As soon as the plague had ended in April 1911, Hsi-liang was granted permission to leave his post and to "return to his banner for a cure." As he left Manchuria to his successor, Chao Erh-sun, in May, the court was forming the famous "Manchu cabinet" responsible only to the emperor, and representatives from Fengtien were organizing a secret political party that envisioned ultimate provincial independence from the Ch'ing.[80] He could console himself that he had done everything possible to save the tie between the regency and the Manchurians, but he clearly feared that the continuing disintegration would lead to complete collapse. He could not foresee that the collapse was imminent or that it would bring him back briefly to the councils of state.

In the face of enormous domestic and foreign pressures, Hsi-liang had managed to retain control over the political process and to devise a complex strategy for dealing with his political rivals. He had directed a courageous campaign against the Manchu princes, criticizing one for "corruption damaging to the country," another for taking "grand tours," and the rest for trying to "use only their own thinking and talent to run the twenty-two provinces." He had led both subordinates and local elite in reforms to broaden the base of support of the dynasty, realizing that the "improvement of domestic administration" was the key to internal order as well as to respect on the world scene. Finally he had become radically concerned with the sentiments of the people under his control: "As their situation is particularly dangerous when compared with that of other provinces, it is natural that they should have special demands." Believing that "salvation from present dangers really depends on thorough change," he had worked for a responsible cabinet and an early parliament so as to make a "new beginning." Breaking with members of his own class, some of whom he characterized as "rich but valueless outlaws," he had sought to "pay attention to welfare" and had sympathized with the peasant masses in their struggle for equal grain. He had apparently hoped to stem the tide of disintegration and to lead a kind of revolution from above. Largely unable to realize this goal, he left Manchuria in 1910 a considerably older and greyer man, but he was not yet ready to retreat into total cynicism or despair.

13: COLLAPSE

Hsi-liang rested for five months in his banner before he was urgently recalled to Peking in October 1911. Faced with the collapse of the dynasty, he recommended resistance, including the use of military force against army mutineers and the use of political persuasion against republican rebels. To deal with the collapse of the empire, he proposed the strategy of expansion, including the extension of state power to the local elite and the strengthening of the throne by removing it from politics. Confronted with the collapse of a world order, he chose the path of radicalism, withdrawing completely from public life and ordering his son to do the same. The retirement he chose and the alternatives he rejected revealed the priorities of his patriotism.

Resistance for the Dynasty

When the regency learned about an uprising led by army conspirators at Wu-ch'ang on 10 October 1911, it became painfully aware of the critical need for capable provincial leadership. It knew that the revolt had succeeded partly because the governor-general of Hu-kuang, Jui-cheng, had fled his post at the first sign of trouble.[1] The regency therefore immediately sought the support of outstanding provincial officials in retirement, including Ts'en Ch'un-hsüan, Yüan Shih-k'ai, and Hsi-liang.[2] Ts'en, who had a provincial base in Kwangtung, refused to serve; Yüan, who had support in the Peiyang army, posed numerous conditions. Hsi-liang, who stood on his record as one of the most capable and devoted governors-general of the previous decade, was the only one of the three to rally to the court without reservations. He left his banner immediately and arrived in Peking on 14 October.[3] This response showed him to be a model loyalist but decisively undercut his political leverage at court. Instead of being rewarded with the key provincial post of Hu-kuang governor-general, he saw it go to the more circumspect Yüan Shih-k'ai. Rather than obtaining another provincial post, for which he was suited by experience, he was forced to stay in the capital in an atmosphere of intrigue for which he had little taste. Still, he was so intent on defending the dynasty that his friend Chin-liang found him "very excited" and engrossed in "devising plans." [4]

Hsi-liang's first plan was to deal with officers of the New Army who mutinied in North China. During the last week of October the court transferred Commander Chang Chao-tseng, at the head of the Twentieth Division, and Commander Lan T'ien-wei, at the head of the Second Brigade, south from Manchuria to Chihli. On the twenty-ninth Chang and Lan mutinied at Luan-chou and threatened to march on Peking unless the regency established a cabinet responsible to an elected parliament with full authority.[5] Despite his past role in creating the Twentieth Division and in sponsoring constitutional reform, Hsi-liang seems to have felt that this mutiny portended unwarranted military encroachment on civilian government. He begged the court to allow him to "take important troops to garrison Luan[-chou] and protect the capital." [6] But the court actually had few such "important troops" to send. In the Han Chinese Eastern Army, the nominally loyal Third Division was actually under the control of Ts'ao K'un, who was following his own line between the court and Yüan Shih-k'ai at this time. In the Manchu Western Army, the best troops were under Prince Tsai-t'ao, the reformist younger brother of the regent, who was privy to the Luan-chou plot. The regent realistically decided against military resistance and on the thirtieth granted in principle most of the mutineers' demands.[7]

Hsi-liang next offered a plan for dealing with Shansi, which had followed Hupeh, Hunan, and Shensi in declaring its independence of the Ch'ing on the twenty-ninth. The court had not known that Wu Lu-chen was in touch with the Luan-chou mutineers and sympathetic to the Shansi rebels when it appointed him in early November to lead his crack Sixth Division west to Shansi. On 4 November Wu issued his own manifesto demanding reforms similar to those already requested and refusing to advance on Shansi until they were met. The Ch'ing Prince I-k'uang, who increasingly dominated the court, moved quickly and ruthlessly to have Wu assassinated.[8] The court then called in Hsi-liang, who had already offered his services as governor of Shansi. In an audience on 10 November the regent instructed him to "lead troops," presumably westward to pacify Shansi.[9] Hsi-liang had long differed with I-k'uang and respected Wu Lu-chen; he may well have hesitated to undertake this mission in the wake of I-k'uang's brutal assassination of Wu. When he went to see the grand councillors to confirm his appointment, moreover, they reportedly demanded a gift of 80,000 tls. According to Chin-liang, Hsi-liang "changed color" and declared: "In all my life I have never paid a cent for an office. How much less should I do so in these times!" He ignored friends who urged him to compromise just this once to save the dynasty. Once Hsi-liang had alienated the greedy I-k'uang, the prince overruled the regent and withdrew the appointment. Hsi-liang's former military subordinates, Sheng-yün and Chang Hsi-luan, who were less fastidious about gifts, obtained the Shensi and Shansi posts.[10]

Hsi-liang meanwhile advocated another kind of resistance against the republican uprisings at Wu-han and Nanking. Under the court's policy of harsh military suppression, the commander of the Eastern Army, Feng Kuo-chang, attacked the three cities of Wu-han and burned down a third of Hankow before retaking it from the rebels. The Manchu Liang-kiang general-in-chief, T'ieh-liang, vetoed the Liang-kiang governor-general's efforts to compromise with the Nanking Provincial Assembly, headed by Chang Chien, and threatened total annihilation of all who had any dealings with the republicans.[11] Hsi-liang was appalled that commanders showing such ruthlessness and insensitivity should continue to be used by the regency. During his audience on 10 November, he exclaimed:

> as the situation is already acute and as it has been aggravated by the evil-doing of Feng Kuo-chang and T'ieh-liang, [I] would request the issue of a decree emphasizing the throne's decision to pardon no one who should manifest anti-[Han] Chinese feelings.[12]

I-k'uang reportedly greeted this outburst with stony silence, but the Regent Tsai-feng understood the gravity of the appeal. He told Hsi-liang: "The court has never been partial toward Manchu or Han, military or civilian, and you must lead troops to make this known." [13] As we have seen, Hsi-liang never got the troops; even if he had got them, he would never have been able to undo the damage already wrought by the regency. For the regency had already precipitated the collapse of the Ch'ing dynasty.

Expansion for the Empire

Hsi-liang now turned his attention to saving the throne as the focus of the empire. His first strategy was to extend state authority down to the local elite, an action that had been repeatedly promised by the regency. He agreed with the National Assembly, meeting in Peking, which announced on 3 November that "if a short scheme of the constitution be first of all proclaimed to the people, . . . [it] will do more good than a million soldiers." [14] Within a few days he was discussed in the assembly as one of seven men capable of serving as prime minister. In the audience on the tenth he pressed the court to make further concessions to the local elite, who had now declared thirteen provinces independent. His position seems to have influenced an edict that appeared four days later and called for measures to save the "whole nation" from "collapse." According to this edict, all senior provincial officers should

> instruct the scholars and gentry of the provinces concerned, to nominate quickly for each province three to five persons who are well known and respected, conversant with politics and rich in experience, competent to represent the whole province, to

come to Peking as soon as possible for the holding of a public conference to decide the nation's policy and to tranquillize the people's minds.[15]

These "representatives" were to "air the desires of the low," while specially appointed "condolence commissioners" were to "proclaim the virtues of the high."

Hsi-liang's effort to save the throne by extending political authority to the local elite did not gain widespread support. Under the aegis of I-k'uang the court turned away from compromise with the local elite and toward reliance on the Peiyang army to control the situation. It eschewed popular feeling against the foreigners and openly sought the support of the foreign powers.[16] On the other side, members of the local elite, such as Chang Chien of Kiangsu, attacked the court for its harsh suppression campaigns in Wu-han and Nanking. Chang refused to serve as "condolence" or any other kind of "commissioner" for the throne.[17] On 15 November the court named Yüan Shih-k'ai prime minister to carry out its policies concerning the rebels and the foreigners.

On the same day the court named Hsi-liang to his old post of military lieutenant-governor of Jehol. In one sense this appointment was a demotion, for Hsi-liang had served in far more important posts in the past. His friends labeled it a "disaster," and the press speculated that he would not even accept it.[18] In another sense the appointment was an honor. The court, which had fled to Jehol in 1860 to avoid an Anglo-French expedition, was now planning to make a similar "imperial progress" or "hunting expedition" to the summer palace to avoid Chinese rebels and opportunists. On 17 November Hsi-liang accepted the appointment. He may also have joined an association of officials who wanted the throne to grant an immediate armistice to the rebels, to call a conference to discuss the merits of monarchy and republic, and to retire to Jehol to await its outcome.[19] Yüan Shih-k'ai soon arranged a truce with the rebels at Wu-ch'ang and opened talks with the rebels at Nanking concerning the future form of government. But Yüan wished to retain some military control over the court and so adamantly opposed its withdrawal to Jehol.[20]

Hsi-liang arrived in Jehol on 19 December and immediately began planning for the arrival of the court. He asked that the imperial hunting grounds at Wei-ch'ang, which were currently under the authority of the governor-general of Chihli, who was a protégé of I-k'uang, revert to the authority of the Jehol military lieutenant-governor. He ordered the construction of a large moat around the hunting grounds to serve as a last line of defense.[21] When it became apparent that the court had decided against coming to Jehol, he continued to make recommendations to strengthen its prestige. He memorialized strong support for the National Assembly, which had again called for the immediate creation of a constituent assembly. He also rewarded a Mongol lama of Jehol who had contributed to the education of his fellow Mongols and thus showed his "enthusiasm for the public good." [22] He still hoped to preserve and reform the throne, which could serve as a focus of the loyalties of all political and racial groups.

During January 1912 Hsi-liang proposed other measures to save the throne. Hearing that Yüan Shih-k'ai would join Sun Yat-sen in demanding the abdication of P'u-yi, he wired the Grand Council to permit the transport of modern arms from Han-yang to Jehol. When he learned that I-k'uang favored a voluntary abdication to get "favorable terms" for the throne, he angrily wired the Grand Council for 80,000 tls. to create four new battalions in Jehol. He justified this request as necessary to deal with local "banditry," but his real motive was to save the throne from its most ardent "defenders" in Peking. It was perhaps more than coincidence that he demanded 80,000 tls., the exact amount which I-k'uang had asked in bribes when Hsi-liang had been appointed governor of Shansi.[23] If I-k'uang could be so determined when his own financial interest was at stake, Hsi-liang seemed to ask, why could he not be equally firm when the imperial throne was in the balance?

Although never cited as a member of the Imperial Clan party (tsung-she-tang), Hsi-liang probably agreed with the princes of inner Mongolia who opposed an abject abdication. These princes now sent a message to the court negotiators in Peking:

> Is the republic for China proper or for the whole empire? If it is for the latter, Mongolia and Tibet, which form a large part of it, are not only still destitute of republican conceptions, but are strongly promonarchical. They firmly oppose the adoption of a republic. They will sever from the empire when the old government is gone, and this will mean the dismemberment of China.[24]

Such pressure forced the Empress Dowager Lung-yü, who had assumed increased importance at court since 1911, to warn the republicans that any abdication would depend on a promise of favorable treatment to national minorities. On 6 February the republicans promised that the five races would enjoy "equal rights" under the new government. The throne could retain its titles, palaces, lands, and tombs as well as receive 4 million tls. annually for its maintenance.[25]

With the symbol of the throne thus protected, Hsi-liang relaxed his opposition to abdication and made plans to retire. Already on 4 February he had asked that an "assistant" be sent to help him in Jehol. On the ninth he asked the court for permission to retire so that he could return home to treat his "old illness." On the twelfth his request was granted and the infant Emperor P'u-yi abdicated the throne.[26] The 2,000-year-old imperial institution and Hsi-liang's thirty-seven-year career came to a close on the same day.

Radicalism for a World Order

After retiring in 1912, Hsi-liang lived quietly at a health resort in Ta-ku, on the coast of Chihli.[27] He explained his decision to withdraw from public office, referring to an illness that had plagued him for several years. Indeed, the illness may have worsened as he now reached his sixties. Yet he had overcome bad health and fatigue to take office in 1911, and he might well have done so again had he deemed the effort worthwhile. Another possible explanation for his retirement was that he believed in the neo-Confucian ideal of serving only one dynasty and wished to remain a pure Ch'ing loyalist (*i-lao*). But perhaps the most important reason for his withdrawal was his belief that the governments which arose in the wake of the Ch'ing did not meet basic Confucian standards of legitimacy.[28] They lacked the cultural vitality, political cohesion, and domestic order that were the hallmarks of good government. He apparently decided not to serve again until a good government was reestablished.

Once retired, Hsi-liang explicitly refused Yüan Shih-k'ai's call to "participate" in the new republican government.[29] His motives may have been in part personal. He had learned early of Yüan's political ambitions, chafed under his official supervision, differed with him over military strategy, and probably resented his recent cooperation with I-k'uang to ease the infant emperor out of power. But his main differences with Yüan ran deeper. Hsi-liang had always espoused a highly civilian brand of leadership and had opposed all foreign interference, while Yüan had long tended to be more military and more receptive to foreign influences. He did not find in Yüan's regime the new order for which he was waiting.

Hsi-liang also took the radical step of discouraging his son from serving in office. Pin-hsün, whose whole career lay before him, had early been groomed for public service and had obtained the important post of intendant.[30] Since he had served some time in Chihli and had come to the attention of Yüan Shih-k'ai, it was only natural that Yüan should have appealed to him for political support. Indeed Hsi-liang's former protégés, Ch'en I and Chang Hsi-luan, who were serving Yüan, encouraged the son to follow his own inclinations and serve. But Pin-hsün was well-schooled and filial; he finally followed his father's example and advice and stayed out of public life.[31] It was not until the founding of a new order in 1949 that he came forth and made his father's public papers known to the world.

Hsi-liang's retirement, although based on radical convictions, was not bitter. He refrained from joining those who continually criticized Yüan's regime for falling short of Ch'ing standards. His determination to act according to his own principles without denigrating the efforts of others led one acquaintance to call him a "true worthy." [32]

Hsi-liang also refused an invitation to associate himself with a regional government set up by Chang Tso-lin in Manchuria. Chang, a former Red Beard who had been won over to the Ch'ing and had risen in the official hierarchy, gradually became the most powerful man in Manchuria after 1912. According to Chin-liang, Chang "warmly admired Hsi[-liang] and respected his incorruptibility." [33] Perhaps wishing to honor Hsi-liang for his past administration of Manchuria or perhaps hoping to persuade him to participate in the regional government, Chang repeatedly offered him "hundreds of square li" of newly opened lands. Completely indifferent to personal wealth or regional power, Hsi-liang only "thanked him and refused." [34]

Hsi-liang also refrained from joining or encouraging any of the various movements for Manchu or Mongol autonomy after 1912. He had played no part in his friend Chin-liang's plan to create a small Manchu state, the Republic of Great Peace (*ta-t'ung kung-ho-kuo*) in the homeland of the Manchus, Ch'ang-pai-shan, Kirin.[35] He also showed no sympathy for the Mongols who declared their independence of China, perhaps because he felt that they would find their greatest autonomy within the Chinese order. He was admired by Manchu loyalists and remained a Mongol to his death, but his posthumous title, Wen-ch'eng (accomplished and sincere) was wholly Chinese.[36]

Hsi-liang was above all a Chinese patriot, loyal to his own concept of a moral sovereign ruling over a Chinese world. He would have his sovereign demonstrate legitimacy by deriving his mandate from the Chinese people and show flexibility by adapting his programs to the changing times. In 1917 he addressed himself to this vision of a sovereign in a deathbed memorial to the infant Emperor P'u-yi:

> In 1911 my heart had not died but my strength had ebbed away; a wasting illness was wracking my breast and has continued to do so for these past six years. Now the weight of my old affliction is growing heavier and I know that I shall not get up again.
>
> I presume to think that the emperor in his palace is still high and serene, sincere and wise, and that in his minority he must be devoting himself energetically to his studies. In my crude opinion, remaining close to one's teacher and emphasizing the way are the foundations for achieving virtue; dwelling in retirement and acting according to the times are the means of preserving one's self. I wish only that my emperor may base himself on the natural examples of Yao and Shun, respecting the lessons handed down by his ancestors. If he works hard at the kingly way and makes progress daily without stopping, then, although this be the day of my death, it will be the year of my birth.[37]

His reference to Yao and Shun suggested that the hereditary succession which had dominated most of Chinese history might ultimately give way to the moral succession which had been envisioned in the classics. His invocation of the way and progress implied the need for personal self-cultivation in order to contribute to the creation of a new and vital Chinese world order. Having lived as a Chinese patriot, he died hoping only for the immortality of that world order.

Even as the Ch'ing collapsed and opportunism flourished, Hsi-liang had retained the balance and integrity that had marked his earlier career. Because he was loyal to the state, he had offered to take "important troops to garrison

Luan-chou and protect the capital," but because he was devoted to the people he had asked the court to discipline anyone who should manifest "anti-Chinese feelings." Concerned about relations between the state and the people, he had agreed with those who urged that an early parliament would "do more good than a million soldiers." Worried about holding together the disparate peoples of China, he had doubted that the anti-Manchu republic was meant for "the whole empire." After he had retired, he had refused with thanks those military and regional leaders who asked him to serve and spent the last years of his life "emphasizing the way" as the means for "achieving virtue." The life of a "patriotic worthy" was over, and only its historical significance was left to be assessed.

14: CONCLUSION

As we look back on Hsi-liang's long career, we are struck by his achievements as a resolute statesman. He repeatedly showed calm purposefulness under fire; for example, during the Allied expedition in 1900, the Tibetan revolt in 1905, the Ho-k'ou uprising in 1907, and the An-feng crisis in 1909. Yet two critics, one a colleague and another an acquaintance, remarked that Hsi-liang was "excitable" under pressure and sometimes "impetuous" in making policy. Hsi-liang did indeed express alarm in his secret memorial on "sovereignty" from Honan; he nearly lost control when berating the French consul for intervening in the Ch'uan-Han railway controversy; and he did fly into a rage at an inspector during the opium suppression campaign. These incidents sometimes reflected his inexperience in dealing with novel and complex matters of foreign policy, sometimes merely his determination to preserve China's national autonomy. In at least one case, Hsi-liang staged an outburst to achieve a specific end: he became "very angry" with Willard Straight in order to rush him into the Chin-ai loan against his instructions. Although proud and sometimes impulsive, Hsi-liang was completely in touch with what was going on and knew very well what he wanted to do about it.

Hsi-liang also demonstrated extraordinary honesty and frugality. He refused to honor the empress dowager's chief eunuch or the prince regent's senior statesman with the usual gifts and thereby jeopardized his influence at court. In Szechwan he collected only 39,000 tls. in salary when he could easily have amassed 180,000 more by accepting the customary fees associated with that office. Hsi-liang did occasionally overcome his scruples when it was necessary to get things done. In Szechwan he allowed his secretaries to persuade him to give the grand councillors substantial gifts for New Year's. He did not permit his own fastidiousness to interfere with his use of less upright men, provided they were exceptionally capable. Yet on balance Hsi-liang's integrity must have limited the number of people who felt easy in his company. He seems to have had few friends except his erstwhile patrons Chang Chih-tung and Lu Ch'uan-lin and his one-time subordinates Chin-liang and Cheng Hsiao-hsü. The lack of camaraderie apparently disturbed him little, perhaps because he was a self-contained individual, perhaps because he was happily married.

Hsi-liang's overriding sense of purpose and his general emphasis on probity grew from his larger vision of the Chinese past. The allusions in his writings show that he was attracted not by some stagnant tradition or some pristine culture but by the lessons, vagaries, and dynamics of Chinese history. To be sure, he drew on the seminal Chou ideas of Heaven, the way, and virtue; such key figures as Yao and Shun; and the major schools of thought of Confucius, the Taoists, and the Legalists. But he looked back at these ideas, images, and philosophies through the record of the intervening dynasties. He turned to the Shang and the Ch'in for lessons on dynastic decline; to the Chou and Han for projects of prison reform; to the T'ang for relations between the throne and officials; to the Sung for strategies of resistance on the frontier; to the Ming for evidence of the need for responsible government. He looked to the early Ch'ing for norms in frontier and minority policy and to the late Ch'ing for guidance on the proper balance between central and regional power. Aware of the early nineteenth-century school of statecraft (*ching-shih*), which stressed the need to adapt classical principles to current realities, he paid even more attention to the lessons of late nineteenth-century events like the Ili crisis and the Sino-Japanese War. Showing both flexibility and growth, he changed his own assessment of the Boxer uprising and of the representative councils after 1909. Perhaps because he knew and loved history, he was able to work with its major currents rather than against them.

This immersion in Chinese history colored Hsi-liang's awareness of the world outside China. Like most officials of his time, he learned no foreign languages and never traveled abroad. His knowledge of Japan and the West was garnered largely from official accounts, the press, and subordinates who had studied abroad. Receptive to the "new learning" (*hsin-hsüeh*), he was quite ready to make use of technological and scientific developments that he thought could benefit China. He kept a model steam locomotive in his office in Szechwan and turned to foreign medical advice to combat the pneumonic plague in Manchuria. He instructed his own son to learn English and he sent many young men abroad to study, but he intended for them to use their new knowledge to serve China. Although in favor of equal and dignified exchanges with foreigners about Western learning (*hsi-hsüeh*), he deplored the mindless copying of foreign styles and habits as useless and demeaning. While he established good relations with some individual diplomats and advisors, he remained always on guard against foreigners as a group. His suspicions were confirmed by long years of dealing with foreigners who used their superior power to try to dominate the Chinese.

Hsi-liang knew that the Westerners' great strength derived mostly from their economic development—especially from their recent industrial growth. Taking account of these Western achievements, he urged his fellow Chinese to dig mines, build railways, and set up factories. Yet he did not wish to replicate the Western system, under which merchants and manufacturers, many of whom he considered "fat speculators," were able to control the economy and place private profits ahead of public benefits. He continued to emphasize agriculture as the basis of the economy and the foundation of the people's welfare. He recognized that the Westerners had succeeded in releasing great reserves of energy among their own people, and he led his countrymen to emulate some of their accomplishments. Yet he threw his greatest energies into such reforms as the opium suppression campaign and he continued to stress moral determination in domestic matters. "In the affairs of the empire, a firm spirit can accomplish much." He rejected the Western assumption, shared by some Chinese of his day, that overseas expansion was the chief index of cultural vitality. He seemed to feel that economic sufficiency and cultural stability were more in tune with Chinese values and, indeed, with the resources and requirements of a finite world.

In certain matters, Hsi-liang believed that some Chinese values were superior to those of the West. He acknowledged the usefulness of Western parliaments and Western socialism; but he warned that even the adoption of a parliament might not keep the people's minds from "flowing away," and he cautioned that even the noble goal of socialism had to be adjusted to the realities of the Chinese social system. In both these matters, he praised the foreigners primarily for attaining the Chinese ideal of "uniting high and low" in pursuit of common goals. He favored a responsive government that would merit the support of "public opinion" and the "people's feelings." He tried to maintain a "light government" by resisting tax increases. When this proved impossible, he recognized the need to allow the taxpayers to participate in government. At first he talked of "self-government" in the sense of Chinese rather than foreign rule and involved the people merely in projects to preserve Chinese sovereignty. Later he showed increasing faith in the people's ability to manage their own affairs, and he moved from "self-strengthening" to "self-management" to "self-construction." During the parliamentary crisis he proposed "self-government," this time in the sense of rule by the people. Hsi-liang sometimes referred to patriots as "bandits" and to the common people as "ignorant," but these were exceptions to his usual demonstrations of confidence in the people. Rooted in fundamental Chinese notions of sovereignty, his populism grew as a means of rallying the people in defense of China and reached its height in an effort to establish popular rule in the space of a few months.

Hsi-liang also thought that China had something to teach the rest of the world about dealing with minority races and conducting interstate relations. He soon overcame his own Mongol origins, dropping all reference to them after his first few memorials, and thereafter acted as a Chinese in dealing with the minorities. To be sure, he seems to have adopted the Chinese presumption that the Han people's more sophisticated technological development indicated a higher culture. He assumed that Han Chinese could be ruled by appealing to their minds while the frontier peoples had to be controlled with laws and regulations. He also made the debatable judgment that the Shan chiefs were oppressive and out of touch with their own people. Yet he did not go as far in his assumption of superiority or in his paternalism as did many other officials faced with managing relations between the Han and the minorities. It was foreign pressure on the frontier more than Han chauvinism which caused him to characterize some minorities as "barbarians" and to extend closer control over their affairs. Unlike many officials, Hsi-liang flatly rejected the Western model of overseas empire, suggesting that it was contrary to China's traditions and needs. Instead he pursued his own very Chinese minority policy, which drew on the ancient cliché of being "kind to the young and the weak" and involved an acute awareness of the political, linguistic, and cultural differences among the different peoples called Chinese. When he expressed respect for the Buddhism of the Mongols of Manchuria, he suggested that he wished to revitalize the broadest kind of Chinese order to serve as a model for the rest of the world.

In his effort to achieve this revitalization, Hsi-liang adopted the three strategies that characterized the principal phases of his career. He relied on resistance when his material resources were limited and the foreign threat was immediate and overwhelming. The Allied troops were not only "at the gate" but through the door: "we do not dare to allow them to advance further." The invasion was a gross violation of foreign concepts of national sovereignty and was particularly offensive to China. "Since China was the first independent country to appear, it has special independent authority." China had to react immediately and forcefully. "If we do not devise laws and establish regulations, I fear that those above will have nothing to stand by and those below nothing to protect." In the face of foreign imperialism, Hsi-liang and his countrymen worried about the "guest usurping the place of the host," about "losing the country," and about the "death" of the nation: resistance—not some trivial antiforeignism—was the only possible reaction. The burden was not on China to overcome its antiforeignism, but on the West to halt an encroachment that made resistance the only rational response.

Hsi-liang turned to expansion when he had more resources available and when the foreign advance was less immediate or sustained. There was a need for expansion in some fields simply to realize latent Chinese capacities. Expansion of education was the foundation for "molding the people of the country," and teacher training was "the basis for expanding education." Expansion was necessary in other areas, quite apart from its intrinsic merits, to preempt them from the foreigners. "If we do not immediately advocate that officials establish a company to collect Chinese shares to protect our rights and the matter is allowed to drag along, we will not keep authority in our hands, and we will either have to borrow foreign funds or permit others to build [the railroad]." There was also a call for expansion to reestablish the status quo that foreigners had disturbed, directly or indirectly. "We must extend the command of Heaven in order to suppress the rebellion and restore order." Hsi-liang adopted expansion to meet the West on its own terms. If the Western nations could expand overseas simply to extend their influence, surely China could expand on her own continent in order to secure her territory. In dealing with the Western empires, Hsi-liang and his countrymen learned not the value of being "nationalist" in a Western sense but the need to expand Chinese control as a measure of self-defense.

When resources were scarce and domestic problems preeminent, Hsi-liang took a radical tack against internal adversaries. In regard to social ills that harmed the general interest, radicalism could involve a certain ruthlessness. "Where the body is weak and the craving strong, the prohibition of opium may be painful, but still we must not have pity and must help cut off the fixation with selfish desires." In the case of small states that might be pulled out of the orbit of Chinese influence, radicalism entailed an effort to attract them back by ensuring their autonomy. "Replacing the chiefs with such officials is meant to benefit the people; it is clearly never the wish of the chiefs. If there is resistance at every turn, then I fear that they will only be encouraged in their tendency to look outward and will only rush to advance their plans for causing trouble." By words and actions, Hsi-liang demonstrated that a Chinese could be radical not only in a Western way but in Chinese ways as well. While open to new ideas, he seems to have found the sources of his radicalism primarily in history. Perhaps it was his keen sense of the past that freed him from any monolithic "culturalism" and enabled him to select among various traditions and to act in accordance with his times.

When he was forced to make policy under tremendous stress, as in Manchuria, Hsi-liang combined these three approaches in significant ways. In foreign affairs he was preoccupied with resistance: he was driven to using diplomacy as a means of defending China's integrity, not as a necessary attribute of the modern state nor as a tool for expanding Chinese influence abroad. Even when he relied on the balance of power to protect China, he placed little faith in it: "Although it is true that all countries [of the West] are out for their private gain and benefit [and thus can be used against one another], yet in bringing harm to East Asia, they are all together." Hsi-liang did adopt expansion in frontier policy, but he was careful to share the burden with the foreigners. Speaking of the Americans he said, "In borrowing their money, . . . we will also be borrowing their influence; they will exchange their influence for our rights and we will use their influence to strengthen our frontier." He preferred radicalism in minority policy, showing again that the Chinese had their own idea of the proper relationship between a great power and a smaller neighbor. Regarding the Mongols he said: "Some say that the area is distant and provisioning difficult, but in the whole world there is not a country without troops." This observation was radical in a day when Western countries deprived their colonies of armies, and it remains radical today when some supposedly sovereign states are not allowed to maintain respectable military forces.

Hsi-liang integrated the three approaches in politics and world view as well. He resisted centralization, despite the argument that it was "modern": "If some evil arises, a rescript can be sent in the morning and the official obliged to take off his hat in the evening; so what is the problem?" He also resisted the militarization implicit in the Luan-chou mutiny, by proposing to lead troops under civilian control to "garrison Luan[-chou] and protect the capital." He expanded the economy, as had many statesmen before him, commenting: "What the state cannot do, I have advocated that the people manage in the hope of making at least a beginning." He worked for the extension of political power to new groups by agreeing that "if a short scheme of the constitution be first of all proclaimed to the people, . . . [it] will do more good than a million soldiers." He was radical in his effort to recreate the ancient utopia: once a constitution was completed, there would be "no nobles or base persons, no higher or lower, and all will have to accept administration according to the laws, rooting out their private selfishness." It was a radicalism based on a certain concept of the self, not a reaction against "revolution," which led Hsi-liang to retirement after 1912. As he advised the infant emperor, "remaining close to one's teacher and emphasizing the way are the foundations for achieving virtue; dwelling in retirement and acting according to the times are the means of preserving one's self."

By standing firm on his fundamental convictions even as he altered the means of carrying them out, Hsi-liang revealed his understanding of the Chinese national revolution. The key idea in Chinese nationalism was China (*chung-kuo,* the central kingdom), which implied both the country (*kuo-chia*) and the world (*t'ien-hsia*). "Nationalist thinking" (*kuo-chia chih ssu-hsiang*) had developed during the war against Japan on behalf of Korea. It was thus by definition an antiforeign movement to preserve both China and the tributary states. Chinese nationalism was the defense of Chinese territory from foreigners who would encroach upon it without accepting the changing Chinese concept of cultural identity. It meant the integration and consolidation of the Chinese world order in reaction against outside pressure. Because the West betrayed its own notions of international equality and justice in its dealings with China, Hsi-liang regarded it more as a threat than as a model. Under these circumstances, China would have to refashion its own concept of world order to create a new model for civilized interstate relations. This task—to make China the "central country" again—was at the heart of Hsi-liang's nationalism.

Hsi-liang had equally firm ideas about the Chinese revolution. Here the important concept was change (*i* or *ko*), which included change from above (*kai-ko,* reform) and change from below (*ko-ming,* rebellion). The revolution might come from above, but if it did not, it would certainly come from below. In the political sphere it would involve "communication between high and low" and "responsible government"; in the social realm it would aim toward the goals of "neither noble or base persons" or, more practically, "equal grain" for the peasantry. While China's long history and sense of place would contribute to political solidarity, its relative poverty would make possible new achievements in social equality. The revolution grew from the problems of population growth and Western impact, but it also sprang from the Chinese past. The Chinese revolution was, in short, the intensification of a long radical tradition and the acceleration of a long rebel heritage toward the ends of political participation and social equity. An effort to recreate the "golden age" was fundamental to Hsi-liang's notion of revolution.

Hsi-liang's life and thought take on greater importance when placed in the context of his times. In comparison with the better-known thinkers of his day, Hsi-liang emerges as more successful than the scholar K'ang Yu-wei; more political than the translator Yen Fu; more typical than the intellectual Liang Ch'i-ch'ao; and more practical than the anti-Manchu Sun Yat-sen. Measured against contemporary statesmen, he was closer to the people than Chang Chih-tung; more influential than Li Ping-heng; more capable in civil affairs than Yüan Shih-k'ai; and more loyal to the Ch'ing than Chang Chien. Just as his relative obscurity was balanced by his great power, so his virtual absence from the history books was outweighed by his imprint on his own times. His impact suggests that he stood for something much larger than himself.

Hsi-liang shared some of his most important ideas and tendencies with other leading thinkers and statesmen. K'ang Yu-wei and Chang Chih-tung also demonstrated the modes of action that we have called resistance, expansion, and radicalism. K'ang advocated resistance during the wars against France and Japan; he was expansionist in his view of the three stages of history and in his extension of the idea of Grand Harmony to all the world; he was radical in his desire for rapid reforms and his willingness to dismantle institutions to achieve social justice. Chang Chih-tung was also a leading proponent of resistance during the French and Japanese wars; he planned great expansionary programs in education and transportation; and he was radical in his emphasis on hewing to the "mean" in political action and on preserving the "essence" of China even while borrowing from the West. That these men had a vision and were determined to realize it distinguished them from lesser Chinese officials and from foreign statesmen of their day.

Hsi-liang's concept of the national revolution meshed well with the prevailing currents of the decade after 1900. The Ch'ing and the Alliance as well as other forces in Chinese politics like the constitutionalists, the military, students, women, workers and the peasantry agreed in emphasizing "rights recovery" and "responsible government" as their most important goals. These groups all wanted to preserve China's national integrity and to deal with the problems of political and social organization. Operating in the mainstream of Chinese life, these groups achieved change through successive waves, from the resistance of the Reform and Boxer movements, through the expansion of the court and provincial reforms, to the radicalism of the movements for an "early parliament" and for "equal grain." Collectively these waves constituted a critical phase in the larger history of the Chinese national revolution. Far from being the beginning of the national revolution, 1911 was merely a collapse that brought an end to a decade of ferment and change.

Taking a larger view of the Chinese national revolution, we find that Chinese nationalism had developed long before the first decade of the twentieth century. The problem of China's identity in the world outside Asia arose as early as the Jesuit and Russian contacts in the seventeenth century. Despite their efforts to deal equitably with the Chinese, the Jesuits and Russians in fact asserted the superiority of Western ways and tried to dominate large portions of China's culture and territory. Their encroachment was only the first step in a long march that brought outright Western imperialism during the nineteenth century. More recently the Japanese, Americans, and Russians have tried to create successive new orders in Asia but have succeeded only in clashing with the force of Chinese nationalism. A revived China is now regaining full sovereignty over its territory and building a new culture that may provide a fresh direction for East Asia in the future. This new culture will draw on the rich legacy of Chinese civilization as well as on the experience of the outside world.

The contours of the Chinese revolution are equally large; an understanding of them requires a perspective at least as broad as that on Chinese nationalism. In a sense, the Chinese revolution was manifested in the establishment of efficient Manchu government in the seventeenth century and in the rebellion of the White Lotus in the eighteenth. This pattern of change from above and below, reflecting both internal and external forces, persisted during the nineteenth century with the self-strengthening movement and the massive mid-century uprisings, including that of the Taipings. During the first half of the twentieth century, the revolution further accelerated and intensified, from the first decade through the May Fourth and May Thirtieth movements, the United Front and Yenan periods, to the founding of the People's Republic in 1949. The revolution has reached fever pitch during the last two decades through land reform, collectivization, the Great Leap Forward, and the Great Proletarian Cultural Revolution. Even today the Chinese continue to grapple with the fundamental issues of popular participation and social equality that have underlain the revolution from the beginning. Given the enormity of the task, they may well be right in predicting that the revolution will continue for another century.

The general direction of this national revolution may be better understood in light of some important precedents of earlier Chinese history. China first confronted a vital foreign culture with the arrival of Buddhism from India during the early centuries of the Christian era. The Chinese of the T'ang and Sung periods reacted to the Buddhist influence by rejecting some of its institutions and religious ideas and by accepting some of its humanitarian impulses and philosophical ideas. Chinese of more recent centuries have responded to Western culture in similar ways. They have rejected many Western institutions and religious beliefs but taken over certain social ideas and scientific concepts. China faced its first complete military defeat by a foreign people who did not respect Chinese culture when the Mongols used their superior military technology to conquer the Sung in the thirteenth century. Chinese of the Yüan and Ming periods reacted by resisting and expelling the Mongols even as they accepted some of their military techniques. Similarly in recent centuries the Chinese have resisted Western military encroachment and ousted the foreigners even as they have adopted some Western military techniques. The most important characteristic of the recent period is that the Westerners tried to play a dual role in China, arriving not only as cultural transmitters but also as military conquerors. This dual quality of Western influence has of course had a profound impact on the nature of China's reaction.

Precedents for the recent revolution also may be found in earlier centuries of Chinese history. The examination system of the Sui and T'ang began to open the channels of political participation to men who had no ties to the aristocracy or the bureaucracy. Later, population growth and gross misrule decreased political mobility and contributed to a series of rebellions which brought down the Yüan dynasty in the fourteenth century. This sequence prefigured the reconstitution of the examination system and the resulting accessibility of official positions in the early Ch'ing followed by population growth and political chaos which ended in declining mobility and the uprisings of the early twentieth century. The system of "equal fields" of the Sui and T'ang, designed primarily to increase tax revenues, resulted also in a measure of social justice throughout part of China. When this system was disrupted by growing population and rising governmental indifference in later dynasties, the potential for social conflict increased and finally burst forth in the bitter uprisings of the late Ming. During the recent period this pattern was approximated when the early Ch'ing enforced a certain rough justice in the countryside, but the late Ch'ing and republic failed to deal with rising population and growing political disorder and ultimately were confronted by a series of social uprisings which culminated in the Cultural Revolution. An important aspect of this recent revolution is the complex interrelationship between soaring population growth and massive industrial development. While the Chinese may allow their numbers to grow and may meet their economic needs through rapid industrialization, they may also strive instead for a stable population and economic sufficiency.

The earliest period of Chinese history offers further insights into the current national revolution. The Chinese first achieved cultural unity in the Shang, in the second millennia B.C., and they had their first political revolution with the founding of the Chou in the twelfth century B.C. Cultural unity led to national unity and political revolution to social revolution with the founding of the Ch'in dynasty in the third century B.C. These currents developed more fully during the great Han which became the model for all subsequent Chinese dynasties. The pattern of this early period supports Hsi-liang's claims that China was the "first independent country to appear" and that it was well acquainted with the need to "change according to the times." An extraordinary sense of place and of time, transmitted through the ages by means of the unique Chinese language, has made China the most continuous, although ever-changing, civilization in the world.

Just as one can trace the national revolution through three periods of Chinese history, so one can find elements of the three strategies of resistance, expansion and radicalism in these periods. The early schools of Confucius, the Legalists, and the Taoists contributed in different ways to the modes of resistance, expansion, and radicalism. In foreign affairs, the Han founder Kao-tsu was in one way a resister, his grandson Wu-ti was the supreme expansionist, and successors such as the Hsüan emperor were in effect radicals. Later the T'ang critic Han Yü emerged as an intellectual resister, the Sung synthesizer Chu Hsi as a sort of expansionist, and the Ming statesman Wang Yang-ming as one form of radical. In the military field, the Ming founder T'ai-tsu seems to have served mainly as a resister, his son and successor Yung-lo as an expansionist, and later emperors, sometimes simply by default, as radicals. In recent times, the scholar Liang Ch'i-ch'ao was perhaps primarily a resister, the writer Ch'en Tu-hsiu an expansionist and the historian Li Ta-chao a radical. In the military and foreign spheres, Mao Tse-tung has been the resister, Liu Shao-ch'i the expansionist, and Lin Piao the radical. While these characterizations are far too brief and simple to explain the complex realities of these Chinese lives, they may suggest the relevance of Hsi-liang's experience to the larger question of continuity and change in Chinese history.

Today, when the Chinese national revolution seems to pervade the whole of Chinese life, it may be well to remember that the Chinese have had mixed feelings about those epochs, events, and personalities that may be associated with the national revolution. They have long been ambivalent in interpreting the Ch'in dynasty which brought a harsh authoritarianism along with national unification and social change. They have criticized the Sung for its isolationism as well as praised it for its cultural florescence and social mobility.

They have attacked the Ming for its despotism as well as gloried in its political unity and social order. They have embraced the People's Republic because it has restored their pride but they also have regretted the accompanying identity crisis and social disorder. For most Chinese in most periods, the national revolution has been something of an unfortunate aberration, temporarily necessary but eventually unsatisfying. Continually the Chinese have hoped to go beyond it to those various utopias which, whether posited in the past or projected into the future, have never ceased to attract them.

Hsi-liang's career suggests, finally, that the future of the Chinese national revolution will depend on Western actions as well as on Chinese ideals. If Western intellectuals continue to assert the superiority of their ideas and foreign states try to maintain their domination over China, the national revolution will go on, complete with the resistance, expansion, and radicalism that outsiders profess to deplore. If Westerners acknowledge the value of Chinese civilization and terminate their military containment of China, the Chinese national revolution may gradually subside. Just as China will continue to learn from the rest of the world, so the West may begin to learn from China. This result would have pleased Hsi-liang, who died hoping for just that kind of a civilized world order.

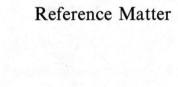

Reference Matter

ABBREVIATIONS USED IN THE NOTES

Full references to the major archives are given below. For the published works listed here, complete citations will be found in the bibliography.

BH
: H. Brunnert · and V. Hagelstrom, *Present Day Political Organization of China.*

CCWCSL
: Wang Yen-wei, comp.; Wang Liang, ed., *Ch'ing-chi wai-chiao shih-liao* (Kuang-hsü and Hsüan-t'ung periods designated by the addition of KH or HT).

CWH
: Chang Chih-tung, *Chang Wen-hsiang-kung ch'üan-chi.*

FO
: Great Britain, Foreign Office Archives, Public Record Office, London.

HL
: Chung-kuo k'o-hsüeh-yüan, comp., *Hsi-liang i-kao tsou-kao.*

HTSL
: Liu Chia-yeh-t'ang, comp., *Hsüan-t'ung cheng-chi shih-lu.*

Hummel
: Arthur Hummel, ed., *Eminent Chinese of the Ch'ing Period.*

IHT
: Ming-Ch'ing tang-an-kuan, comp., *I-ho-t'uan tang-an shih-liao.*

KHSL
: *Ta Ch'ing Te-tsung ching (Kuang-hsü) huang-ti shih-lu.*

KWT
: Chung-yang yen-chiu-yüan, comp., *K'uang-wu tang.*

MAE
: France, Ministère des Affaires Etrangères, Archives, Quai d'Orsay, Paris.

Morse
: Hosea Ballou Morse, *The International Relations of the Chinese Empire*, vol. 3.

NCH
: *North China Herald.*

Shen Yün-lung
: Shen Yün-lung, ed., *Chin-tai chung-kuo shih-liao ts'ung-k'an.*

THL
: Wang Hsien-ch'ien et al., eds., *Shih-erh ch'ao Tung-hua-lu.*

WWP
: Republic of China, Chung-yang yen-chiu-yüan, Wai-wu-pu tang, Nan-kang.

NOTES

Introduction

1 Hsiao Kung-ch'üan, "K'ang Yu-wei and Confucianism," *Monumenta Serica* 18 (1959): 96–212; Joseph R. Levenson, *Liang Ch'i-ch'ao and the Mind of Modern China*; Benjamin Schwartz, *In Search of Wealth and Power: Yen Fu and the West*; Hao Chang, *Liang Ch'i-ch'ao and Intellectual Transition in China, 1890–1907*; Maurice Meisner, *Li Ta-chao and the Origins of Chinese Marxism*.

2 Lloyd Eastman, *Throne and Mandarins: China's Search for a Policy During the Sino-French Controversy, 1880–1885*; Immanuel C. Y. Hsü, *The Ili Crisis: A Study of Sino-Russian Diplomacy*; Paul A. Cohen, *China and Christianity: The Missionary Movement and the Growth of Chinese Antiforeignism, 1860–1870*; John Schrecker, *Imperialism and Chinese Nationalism: Germany in Shantung*; John K. Fairbank, ed., *The Chinese World Order: Traditional China's Foreign Relations*; Ho Ping-ti and Tang Tsou, eds., *China in Crisis*, vol. 2.

3 Vincent Shih, "Some Chinese Rebel Ideologies," *T'oung Pao* 44 (1956): 151–226; Yuji Muramatsu, "Some Themes in Chinese Rebel Ideologies," in Arthur F. Wright, ed., *The Confucian Persuasion*, pp. 241–67; Harold R. Isaacs, *The Tragedy of the Chinese Revolution*; (for the theme of revolution from below, see also works by Chalmers Johnson, John Israel, William Hinton, and Mark Selden in the bibliography); Franz Michael and Chang Chung-li, *The Taiping Rebellion: History and Documents*, vol. 1, *History*; (for the idea of revolution from above, see also works by Franz Shurmann, Ezra Vogel, A. Doak Barnett, and John Lindbeck in the bibliography); James P. Harrison, "Chinese Communist Interpretations of the Chinese Peasant Wars," in Albert Feuerwerker, ed., *History in Communist China*, pp. 189–215; Harold Schiffrin, *Sun Yat-sen and the Origins of the Chinese Revolution*.

4 Mary C. Wright, *The Last Stand of Chinese Conservatism*; Meribeth Cameron, *The Reform Movement in China, 1898–1912*; Chester Tan, *The Boxer Catastrophe*; Michael Gasster, *Chinese Intellectuals and the Revolution of 1911*; Mary B. Rankin, *Early Chinese Revolutionaries*; Mary C. Wright, ed., *China in Revolution: The First Phase, 1900–1913*; Ho and Tsou, *China in Crisis*, vol. 1, bks. 1 and 2.

5 James B. Crowley, ed., *Modern East Asia: Essays in Interpretation*.

6 Edward Friedman and Mark Selden, eds., *America's Asia: Dissenting Essays on Asian-American Relations*.

7 Chao Erh-sun, ed., *Ch'ing-shih kao* [Draft history of the Ch'ing], 236: 1a–3a; Chang Ch'i-yün, ed., *Ch'ing-shih* [History of the Ch'ing]; *HL*, pp. 1–5.

8 Chou I-fu (Chou Hsün), *Shu-hai ts'ung-t'an* [A discussion of matters in Szechwan], 3:50a; Fei Hsing-chien, *Chin-tai ming-jen hsiao-chuan* [Short biographies of famous people of recent times], p. 181; Chin-liang, *Kuang-Hsüan*

hsiao-chi [Short tales of the Kuang(-hsü) and Hsüan(-t'ung periods)], p. 149; see also Chang Chi-hsü, *Chang Wen-hsiang kung chih-O chi* [A record of Chang Wen-hsiang's administration of Hupeh], p. 12.

9 *HL*, no. 1215, p. 1344; Chang, *Ch'ing-shih*, vol. 4, pp. 3992–4003.

10 Calhoun to Secretary (1 May 1911), U. S. Department of State, *Records Relating to the Internal Affairs of China, 1910–1911* (microfilm), 893.00/528 (hereafter cited as USDS 893.00).

11 C. P. Fitzgerald, *The Chinese View of Their Place in the World*; Hisayuki Miyakawa, "The Confucianization of South China," in Wright, *The Confucian Persuasion*, pp. 21–46; Harold Wiens, *China's March toward the Tropics*; Joseph R. Levenson, ed., *European Expansion and the Counter-Example of Asia, 1300–1600*; Owen Lattimore, *Inner Asian Frontiers of China*.

12 For the use of "radicalism" in this sense, see Etienne Balazs, *Chinese Civilization and Bureaucracy*, pp. 175, 197; James T. C. Liu, *Reform in Sung China*, p. 115; Laurence A. Schneider, *Ku Chieh-kang and China's New History*, p. 2; Jonathan Spence, "Ch'ing and Modern China" (unpublished manuscript cited with the author's permission), pp. 75–76; for some of the experiences and values on which a radical could draw, see Jean Chesneaux, "Egalitarian and Utopian Traditions in the East," in Joseph R. Levenson, ed., *Modern China*, pp. 76–89.

Chapter 1

1 Unless otherwise indicated, this description of Hsi-liang's rise to power is based on *HL*, p. 1; for a description of the banners (the military and administrative system with which the Manchus ruled China), see BH, no. 718; for background on the Buriat Mongols, see David M. Farquhar, "The Ch'ing Administration of Mongolia up to the Nineteenth Century," p. 39; C. R. Bawden, *The Modern History of Mongolia*, pp. 136, 244.

2 Chin-liang, *Chin-shih jen-wu chih* [A record of personalities of modern times], p. 288; Chang Keng, comp., *Kan-su hsin t'ung-chih* [The new local history of Kansu], 52: 35a.

3 Chou, *Shu-hai*, 3: 54.

4 *NCH*, vol. 68, p. 187.

5 Information supplied the author by Professor Kuo T'ing-yee, director, Institute of Modern History, Academia Sinica, Nan-kang, Taiwan.

6 Fang Chao-ying and Tu Lien-che, eds., *Tseng-chiao Ch'ing-ch'ao chin-shih t'i-ming pei-lu fu-yin-te* [Revised edition of the index to inscriptions of recipients of the Chin-Shih degree under the Ch'ing dynasty], p. 204; Ho Ping-ti, *The Ladder of Success in Imperial China*, p. 236.

7 Fei, *Chin-tai*, p. 181; Hummel, p. 140.

8 Ho Ping-ti, *Studies in the Population of China, 1368–1953*, p. 233.

9 *CWH*, 4: 21.

10 *HL*, p. 4; Hummel, p. 750; Hsiao Kung-ch'üan, *Rural China, Imperial Control in the Nineteenth Century*, p. 204.

11 Hummel, pp. 27–31.

12 *CWH*, 4: 21.

13 Ibid.

14 Ibid., 4: 29b–31b; 7: 35–38; Chin-liang, *Chin-shih*, p. 288.

15 Cited in Su Yün-feng, "Chang Chih-tung yü wan-Ch'ing chiao-yü kai-ko" [Chang Chih-tung and late Ch'ing educational reforms], (Chung-yang yen-chiu yüan, Chin-tai shih yen-chiu-so, 1969 unpublished manuscript, consulted courtesy of the author), p. 47. All translations from the Chinese are my own unless otherwise indicated.

16 *CWH*, 4: 31b–39a. Although contrary to the statutes, this practice was widespread. Ch'ü T'ung-tsu, *Local Government in China under the Ch'ing*, p. 25.

17 Chou, *Shu-hai*, 3: 54.

18 *THL*, pp. 1332, 1710.

19 *HL*, no. 277, p. 280.

20 Li Ping-heng, *Li Chung-chieh kung tsou-i* [The memorials of Li Chung-chieh], 8:16.

21 Ibid.

22 For Chang's attitudes during the Ili crisis, see Hsü, *The Ili Crisis*, pp. 70–77; for his attitudes during the Sino-French War, see Eastman, *Throne and Mandarins*, pp. 26–29, 98–107, 195–222.

23 Hummel, p. 745; Wu Hsiang-hsiang, "Ts'en Ch'un-hsüan," in Ts'en Ch'un-hsüan, *Lo-chai Man-pi* [Rambling notes from the study of Lo], pt. 2, pp. 1–3, in *Chung-kuo hsien-tai shih-liao ts'ung-shu* [Library of Chinese contemporary historical materials], ed. Wu Hsiang-hsiang.

24 Li, *Li Chung-chieh*, 8: 16b.

25 Hsiao I-shan, *Ch'ing-tai t'ung-shih* [A comprehensive history of the Ch'ing period], 3: 1222–31.

26 For background on Li, see Hummel, pp. 464–71; K. C. Liu, "The Confucian as Patriot: Li Hung-chang's Formative Years 1823–1866," *Harvard Journal of Asiatic Studies*, 30 (1970): 5–45; K. C. Liu, "Li Hung-chang in Chihli: The Emergence of a Policy, 1870–1875," in *Approaches to Modern Chinese History*, ed. Albert Feuerwerker et al., pp. 68–104. For the charges of corruption, see Hummel, p. 469; J. O. P. Bland, *Li Hung-chang*, pp. 218–50.

27 A comprehensive history of the Sino-Japanese War is yet to be written. See Hilary Conroy, *The Japanese Seizure of Korea*; Morse, chaps. 1–2; John K. Fairbank, Edwin O. Reischauer, Albert M. Craig, *East Asia: The Modern Transformation*, pp. 378–84.

28 Fan Tang-shih, *Fan Po-tzu shih-wen-chi* [The poems and essays of Fan Po-tzu], pp. 3–7.

29 Fei, *Chin-tai*, p. 410.

30 For Hsi-liang's retrospective view in 1910, see *HL*, no. 1147, p. 1263.

31 Li, *Li Chung-chieh*, 9: 30b. Yü-hsien's severity was immortalized in a novel by one of his subordinates, Liu T'ieh-yün, *The Travels of Lao Ts'an*, translated and annotated by Harold Shadick, chap. 4.

32 Cohen, *China and Christianity*, chaps. 3–5.

33 Hummel, p. 407.

34 *IHT*, pp. 1–7.

35 Shan-tung li-shih hsüeh-hui (Shantung Historical Association), comp., *Shan-tung chin-tai shih tzu-liao* [Materials on the modern history of Shantung], pp. 34, 38, 44.

36 *CCWCSLKH*, 127: 17a.

37 *NCH*, vol. 59, p. 1031.

38 Schrecker, *Imperialism and Chinese Nationalism*, pp. 19–23, 57.

39 *CCWCSLKH*, 127: 21–22.

40 Chin-liang, *Chin-shih*, p. 288.

41 *THL*, pp. 3995, 4015.

42 Schrecker, *Imperialism and Chinese Nationalism*, pp. 35–39.

43 Hummel, pp. 702–705; Cameron, *The Reform Movement*, pp. 35–45; Immanuel C. Y. Hsü, *The Rise of Modern China*, pp. 423–57.

44 Hsiao Kung-ch'üan, "Weng T'ung-ho and the Reform Movement of 1898," *Tsing Hua Journal of Chinese Studies*, n. s., 1, no. 2 (April 1957): 121–27, 134; William Ayers, *Chang Chih-tung and Educational Reform in China*, chap. 6.

45 Hsiao Kung-ch'üan, "The Philosophical Thought of K'ang Yu-wei: An Attempt at a New Synthesis," *Monumenta Serica* 21 (1962): 129–93; and idem, "The Case for Constitutional Monarchy: K'ang Yu-wei's Plan for the Democratization of China," *Monumenta Serica* 24 (1965): 1–83.

46 Hummel, pp. 295–300; for a popular but unreliable account, see J. O. P. Bland and E. Backhouse, *China under the Empress Dowager*.

47 Hummel, pp. 405–09; 950–53.

48 Fei, *Chin-tai*, pp. 128–30.

49 *HL*, no. 1, p. 1; no. 2, p. 2; *THL*, p. 4285.

50 *HL*, no. 3, p. 3.

51 *HL*, no. 33, p. 31.

Chapter 2

1 *HL*, no. 33, p. 32.

2 Wang Shu-huai, *Wai-jen yü wu-hsü pien-fa* [Foreigners and the reforms of 1898], esp. pp. 99–118; Li Shou-k'ung, "Pa-kuo lien-chün ch'i-chien Tz'u-hsi kui-cheng Te-tsung chih chiao-she" [Diplomacy concerning the return of government to the emperor during the Allied invasion], *Ta-lu tsa-chih* 23, no. 7 (1961): 11–14; 23, no. 8 (1961): 23–29.

3 Ayers, *Chang Chih-tung*, p. 144.

4 *THL*, p. 4595.

5 *CWH*, 162: 11b–12b; Wang Erh-min, "Ch'üan-pien shih-ch'i chih nan-sheng tzu-pao" [The southern provinces' self-protection during the Boxer uprising], *Ta-lu tsa-chih* 25, no. 5 (1962): 160; *NCH*, vol. 66, p. 546.

6 For background on the Boxer movement, see Tan, *The Boxer Catastrophe*, chaps. 2–3; for a nationalistic interpretation, see Jerome Ch'en, "The Nature and Characteristics of the Boxer Movement—a Morphological Study," *Bulletin of the School of Oriental and African Studies* 23 (1960): 287–308; for the Allied expeditions, see Morse, chaps. 10–11.

7 Wang, "Ch'üan-pien," p. 160.

8 Tan, *The Boxer Catastrophe*, chaps. 4–5.

9 *CWH*, 51: 8a–9a; 162: 18a–19b; *HL*, no. 13, p. 9; interview with Professor Wang Erh-min, Institute of Modern History, Academia Sinica, Nan-kang, Taiwan, 1969.

10 Fei, *Chin-tai*, p. 145.

11 *CWH*, 51: 18a–20a; 164: 31b–32a.

12 *CWH*, 51: 28a.

13　*KHSL*, 479: 6a.
14　For information on these troops, see *HL*, nos. 37, 38, 46; for the context, see Ralph Powell, *The Rise of Chinese Military Power, 1895–1912*, pp. 116 ff.; Hummel, p. 406.
15　Tan, *The Boxer Catastrophe*, chap. 6.
16　*HL*, no. 55, p. 49; *KHSL*, 474: 3b.
17　Morse, pp. 240–43; Great Britain, Foreign Office, Parliamentary Papers, *China*, no. 362 (20 September 1900), p. 174 (hereafter cited as British Parliamentary Papers, *China*).
18　Alfred Count von Waldersee, *A Field-Marshal's Memoirs*, condensed and translated by F. Whyte, p. 209.
19　Liu K'un-i, *Liu K'un-i i-chi* [The posthumous manuscripts of Liu K'un-i], p. 2596; *IHT*, pp. 727–28.
20　British Parliamentary Papers, *China*, no. 179, p. 108.
21　E. H. Edwards, *Fire and Sword in Shansi: The Story of the Martyrdom of Foreigners and Chinese Christians*, p. 117.
22　*IHT*, pp. 774, 876–77; Tan, *The Boxer Catastrophe*, p. 72.
23　*CWH*, 167: 13b–14a; 168: 18a.
24　Satow to Wai-wu-pu, 19 and 30 November 1900, WWP, *Chiao-wu, chiao-an tang* [Mission affairs, archives of mission cases]; *NCH*, vol. 66, p. 741; *HL*, no. 105, p. 104; *IHT*, p. 790.
25　Consul at Hankow to Ministère, 4 January 1901, MAE, Chine, Politique Etrangère, Relations avec les Puissances, vol. 20.
26　*IHT*, p. 834; *KHSL*, 475: 1b.
27　*IHT*, pp. 680, 779–80; *CWH*, 167: 12b–13. For the record of Li's strategy as effected in Chahar, see Lo Tun-jung, ed., *Keng-tzu kuo-pien-chi* [A record of the great uprising of 1900], pp. 95, 216, 218.
28　*HL*, no. 46, pp. 40–41; *CWH*, 167: 13b–14a.
29　Sun Tzu, *The Art of War*, translated and introduced by S. B. Griffith, pp. 131–32.
30　*IHT*, p. 680.
31　*KHSL*, 472: 3b–4.
32　Ibid., 3a.
33　Morse, pp. 316–20.
34　*IHT*, pp. 745–46; *KHSL*, 472: 17b; 473: 5a; *HL*, no. 59, pp. 52–54.
35　Morse, p. 316; *IHT*, pp. 741, 748, 754.
36　*IHT*, p. 790, emphasis added.
37　*KHSL*, 473: 4b; *IHT*, p. 870.
38　General Voyron, *Rapport sur l'expédition de Chine, 1900–1901*, pp. 215–18.
39　*HL*, no. 65, p. 58.
40　*IHT*, p. 784; Voyron, *Rapport*.
41　For a study based on German records, see Kawai Kazuo, "The Boxer Protocol Negotiations" (Ph.D. diss., Stanford University, 1939), p. 186.
42　Ibid., p. 188.
43　*KHSL*, 478: 6a; Chef d'Etat Majeur (in Peking) (15 March 1901), Fonds: Chine, 1900–1901, 09–44, Section Outre-Mer, Service Historique de L'Armée de Terre, Chateau de Vincennes, Vincennes, France (hereafter cited as Service Historique).
44　*KHSL*, 477: 22a; see also Tan, *The Boxer Catastrophe*, pp. 216–23.

45 Kazuo, "The Boxer Protocol," p. 187; German fear of conflict with the other powers and censure from America also played a role.
46 Ch'i Pen-yu, "Patriotisme ou trahison de la Patrie?" reprinted from *Hung-ch'i* in *Pekin Information*, vol. 15, pp. 5–17.
47 Italian and American Ministers to Wai-wu-pu, 19 January 1901, WWP, *Chiao-wu, chiao-an tang.*
48 *NCH*, vol. 66, p. 397.
49 *HL*, no. 15, p. 11; no. 71, p. 63; no. 75, pp. 66–67.
50 Edwards, *Fire and Sword*, pp. 113–16.
51 *NCH*, vol. 66, pp. 445–46.
52 *IHT*, pp. 919, 969.
53 *KHSL*, 479: 7b.
54 *HL*, pp. 1–2. On the other hand, Li too worked to keep the Allies from invading Shansi. *IHT*, p. 1039.
55 Annex to Pichon to Ministère, January 1901, MAE, Chine, Politique Etrangère, Relations avec les Puissances, vol. 20.
56 *KHSL*, 479: 6b.
57 Ibid., 476: 18a; *IHT*, pp. 963–65.
58 *CWH*, 168: 7.
59 Ts'en, *Lo-chai*, pp. 8–9.
60 *KHSL*, 479: 1a.
61 Ts'en, *Lo-chai*, pp. 9–10; Edwards, *Fire and Sword*, pp. 120–22; Kazuo, "The Boxer Protocol," app. D, pp. 467–70; *IHT*, pp. 925–27, 1021, 1026, 1029–30, 1037–38; Kenneth S. Latourette, *A History of Christian Missions in China*, p. 521; William Hinton, *Fanshen*, pp. 60–68.
62 For one example of such resistance, see Frederick Wakeman, *Strangers at the Gate: Social Disorder in South China, 1839–1861.*
63 Colleagues included Sung Ch'ing and Ma Yü-k'un, who had fought valiantly against the Japanese; subordinates included Wan Pen-hua and Liu Kuang-ts'ai, who invoked the model of Yüeh Fei. Wang Yao-huan, "Chin-tung fang-chün chi-lüeh" [Outline record of the defense army of eastern Shansi], in *I Ho T'uan* [The Boxers], ed. Chien Po-tsan, ts'e 3, pp. 317 ff.; Hellmut Wilhelm, "From Myth to Myth: The Case of Yüeh Fei's Biography," in *Confucian Personalities*, ed. A. Wright and D. Twitchett, pp. 156–60; Li Hung-chang, *Li Wen-chung kung tien-kao* [The draft telegrams of Li Hung-chang], 31: 1b–2a; 34b–35a; 39b.
64 This was true, for example, of Chao Erh-feng, Ts'ai Nai-huang, Hsü Han-tu, and Sheng-yün, whose names will appear later in this study. *HL*, no. 75, pp. 66–67; no. 292, p. 303.
65 *HL*, no. 79, pp. 71–72; Wang Yung-chou, comp., *Ching-hsing hsien-chih* [Local history of Ching-hsing district], p. 742; Voyron, *Rapport*, p. 178; Baillaud to Voyron, 27 January 1901, Service Historique. For a definition of the "local elite" in the early Ch'ing, see Jonathan Spence, *Ts'ao Yin and the K'ang-hsi Emperor: Bondservant and Master*, pp. 43–46, 65–81.

Chapter 3

1 Hu Chün, *Chang Wen-hsiang kung (Chih-tung) nien-p'u* [A chronological biography of Chang Chih-tung] (Taipei reprint, in Shen Yün-lung, no. 47), 4: 11a.

2 Fei, *Chin-tai*, p. 232.

3 Ibid., p. 233.

4 BH, 820D; Chang, *Ch'ing-shih*, 127: huang-ho [Yellow River], 1; Cameron, *The Reform Movement*, p. 45; Ch'ang-tu Hu, "The Yellow River Administration in the Ch'ing Dynasty," *Journal of Asian Studies* 14, no. 4 (August 1955): 505–13.

5 *HL*, no. 122, p. 119; no. 135, p. 131; for reform of the grain tributary system, see Chang Che-lang, *Ch'ing-tai ti ts'ao-yün* [Grain transport in the Ch'ing period], p. 86.

6 *KHSL*, 494: 2b.

7 Harold Hinton, *The Grain Tributary System of China (1845–1911)*, p. 74.

8 *HL*, nos. 135, 185, 186, 187, 190; *KHSL*, 496: 12b.

9 *HL*, no. 189, pp. 184–85.

10 *HL*, no. 156, p. 152.

11 *HL*, no. 181, pp. 176–77.

12 Morse, pp. 351–53; *NCH*, vol. 66, p. 789; Chi-ming Hou, *Foreign Investment and Economic Development in China, 1840–1937*, pp. 42–43.

13 *HL*, no. 156, pp. 153–54; no. 171, pp. 168–69; no. 174, pp. 170–71; no. 202, pp. 201–02; no. 221, p. 219.

14 *NCH*, vol. 68, p. 17.

15 Latourette, *A History*, pp. 521–22; WWP, *Chiao-an, chiao-an-tang, Ho-nan Wu-an, An-yang, Hua-hsien teng p'ei-shang* [Mission affairs, archives of mission cases, the indemnities for Wu-an, An-yang, Hua-hsien and other places in Honan].

16 *NCH*, vol. 68, p. 966.

17 Hsiao, *Rural China*, p. 443.

18 *NCH*, vol. 68, p. 1016.

19 *HL*, no. 213, pp. 212–13; no. 253, p. 253; *THL*, p. 4821.

20 *HL*, no. 196, p. 196.

21 *KHSL*, 486: 6a; 498: 5a; *NCH*, vol. 68, p. 910.

22 *HL*, no. 213, pp. 212–13.

23 *NCH*, vol. 68, pp. 753, 966, 968–69, 1015–17, 1063, 1163; Ch'eng T'ing-heng, comp., *Ta-ming hsien-chih* [Local history of Ta-ming district], p. 542.

24 *HL*, no. 156, pp. 153–54; no. 211, pp. 210–11; Shen T'ung-sheng, *Kuang-hsü cheng-yao* [Administrative compendium of the Kuang-hsü period], 27: 71a–73a.

25 *HL*, no. 254, pp. 254–55.

26 *HL*, no. 219, p. 218.

27 *HL*, no. 269, p. 270.

28 *HL*, no. 223, pp. 220–21; no. 228, pp. 226–28; no. 229, pp. 228–29.

29 *HL*, no. 233, p. 231.

30 Ibid.

31 Ibid.

32 Ibid.

33 Ibid.

34 *HL*, no. 325, pp. 340–43.

35 Ibid.

36 *NCH*, vol. 71, p. 555.

37 *HL*, nos. 136, 188, 223, 230, 272; *NCH*, vol. 68, p. 187.

38 Fei, *Chin-tai*, p. 213.

39 For background, see Ellsworth Carlson, *The Kaiping Mines*, pp. 1–46; Li En-han, *Wan Ch'ing ti shou-hui k'uang-ch'üan yün-tung* [The late Ch'ing movement to recover mining rights], pp. 3–14; for the agreement, see *KWT*, pp. 1630–34; an imperfect translation appears in John V. A. MacMurray, ed., *Treaties and Agreements With and Concerning China*, vol. 1, pp. 131–34.

40 *Yü-pei k'uang-wu chiao-she shih-mo-chi* [A complete record of the diplomacy over the mines of north Honan]; *KWT*, pp. 1623, 1625, 1626.

41 Hummel, pp. 964–65; Shen, *Kuang-hsü cheng-yao*, pp. 70b–71a.

42 *THL*, p. 4775.

43 *HL*, no. 203, p. 203.

44 *KWT*, pp. 1672, 1694–701.

45 *HL*, no. 203, p. 204.

46 Han Kuo-chün, *Chih-sou nien-p'u* [A chronological biography of Han Kuo-chün], pp. 6b–7a.

47 *KWT*, p. 1665.

48 *KWT*, p. 1671.

49 *KWT*, p. 1664.

50 Wright, *China in Revolution*, pp. 15–16; *KWT*, pp. 1725–36, 1792, 1801–30, 1847.

51 *KWT*, pp. 86–90; Li, *Wan Ch'ing*, p. 19.

52 *CCWCSLKH*, 155: 3b.

53 For a biography of Sheng, see Albert Feuerwerker, *China's Early Industrialization: Sheng Hsüan-huai (1845–1916) and Mandarin Enterprise*, chap. 3.

54 Sheng Hsüan-huai, *Yü-chai ts'un-kao* [The telegrams of Sheng Hsüan-huai], 57: 11.

55 *CCWCSLKH*, 157: 10b, 16a.

56 *KWT*, p. 1672.

57 Percy Kent, *Railway Enterprise in China*, pp. 128–29.

58 *HL*, no. 204; *KWT*, pp. 1613–14, 1620, 1915–19.

59 *KWT*, pp. 1917–18.

Chapter 4

1 *HL*, no. 286, p. 293; *NCH*, vols. 67–68, passim; vol. 69, p. 1392; Jean Chesneaux, *Les sociétés secrètes en Chine (19e et 20e siècles)*, pp. 152–53.

2 *HL*, no. 270, p. 271; no. 276, pp. 276–77.

3 *HL*, no. 276, pp. 276–77.

4 *HL*, no. 276, pp. 278–79; no. 305, p. 316.

5 *HL*, no. 286, pp. 293–98; no. 284, p. 291; no. 301, pp. 310–13; *KHSL*, 512: 6. Neither the creation of districts nor the encouragement of colonization was to "strengthen the frontier" let alone to "set Mongol against Han." Cf. Sechin Jagchid, "Wai Meng-ku ti 'tu-li,' 'tzu-chih,' ho 'ch'e-chih' " [Outer Mongolia's "independence," "self-government," and "secession"], in *Chung-kuo hsien-tai shih ts'ung-k'an* [Selected writings on modern Chinese history], ed. Wu Hsiang-hsiang, ts'e 4, p. 52; Wang Shu-tang, *China, Land of Many Nationalities*, p. 7.

6 *HL*, no. 276, pp. 278–79; no. 299, p. 309; no. 314, pp. 325–26.

7 *HL*, no. 277, p. 280; no. 278, p. 281.

8 *HL*, no. 280, p. 293; no. 281, pp. 288–89; Carlson, *The Kaiping Mines*, pp. 23,

47–71; Li, *Wan Ch'ing*, pp. 6–7; Jagchid, "Wai Meng-ku," p. 51; *KWT*, pp. 711–13.

9 *HL*, no. 281, p. 288.
10 Ibid.; *NCH*, vol. 70, p. 600.
11 Chang, *Ch'ing-shih*, lieh-chuan 303, fan-pu 1, Kharach'in; *HL*, no. 281, p. 288.
12 *HL*, no. 281, p. 288.
13 *HL*, no. 278, p. 281.
14 Ibid.
15 *HL*, no. 280, pp. 283–87.
16 Ibid., articles 1, 2, 12, 18.
17 *HL*, no. 304, pp. 315–16; *KWT*, p. 723; *THL*, pp. 5013–14; Intelligence Diary, period ending 8 December 1903, FO 17/1653.
18 *KWT*, p. 723.
19 *HL*, no. 278, p. 281.
20 *NCH*, vol. 70, p. 284; Intelligence Diary, periods ending 16 February 1903, 3 March 1903, FO 17/1617.
21 *THL*, p. 4984; *KHSL*, 513: 3a, 6a; *NCH*, vol. 70, p. 689; Hsü K'o, *Ch'ing-pai lei-ch'ao* [Miscellaneous writings of the Ch'ing period], section 35, p. 70.
22 *HL*, no. 300, p. 310.

Chapter 5

1 *NCH*, vol. 66, pp. 445–46; British Parliamentary Papers, *China*, no. 138, pp. 89–90. Contrast the view that xenophobia necessarily entails disrespect for the law. Edward Rhoads, "Nationalism and Xenophobia in Kwangtung (1905–1906): The Canton Anti-American Boycott and the Lienchow Anti-Missionary Uprising," *Harvard Papers on China*, vol. 16, p. 154.
2 *NCH*, vol. 79, p. 568; vol. 81, p. 301.
3 Contrast the view that "blind antiforeignism" was incompatible with nationalism. Akira Iriye, "Public Opinion and Foreign Policy: The Case of Late Ch'ing China," in Feuerwerker, *Approaches*, pp. 223–25.
4 Bons d'Anty to Dubail, 23 September 1903, MAE, Chine, Politique Intérieure, Dossier Général, vol. 7 (hereafter in this chapter cited as MAE, Dossier Général).
5 Ibid.
6 Fox to Jordan, 5 February 1907, FO 228/1660.
7 Fox to Jordan, 31 March 1907, FO 228/1660.
8 *NCH*, vol. 74, p. 653; Goffe to Satow, 25 May 1905, 1 July 1905, FO 228/1591.
9 For a brief account of the antiforeign agitation of the 1890s and its suppression, see Schiffrin, *Sun Yat-sen*, p. 215.
10 Hosie to Satow, 28 November 1903, FO 228/1499; Bons d'Anty to Dubail, 23 September 1903, MAE, Dossier Général, vol. 7.
11 Bons d'Anty to Dubail, 23 May 1904, 23 July 1904, 28 March 1905, MAE, Dossier Général, vols. 7, 8.
12 Hosie to Satow, 28 November 1903, FO 228/1499; Goffe to Satow, 1 July 1905, FO 228/1591; Goffe to Carnegie, 3 July 1906, FO 228/1629.
13 Bons d'Anty to Dubail, 23 May 1904, MAE, Dossier Général, vol. 7; Campbell to Satow, 1 April 1905, FO 228/1591.

14 Bons d'Anty to Dubail, 23 May 1904, 23 July 1904, MAE, Dossier Général, vol. 7.

15 Goffe to Satow, 1 July 1905, 6 September 1905, FO 228/1591; Goffe to Carnegie, 3 July 1906, FO 228/1629.

16 Goffe to Satow, 31 December 1905, FO 228/1591; *HL*, no. 406, pp. 438-41; no. 471, pp. 509-11.

17 *HL*, no. 428, pp. 460-62; no. 442, pp. 475-77; no. 507, pp. 551-52; no. 558, pp. 608-10; no. 573, pp. 629-34; Goffe to Satow, 30 May 1905, 1 July 1905, 10 October 1905, FO 228/1591; *Tung-fang tsa-chih* [The eastern miscellany], vol. 1, no. 2, pp. 56-58 (hereafter cited as *Tung-fang*).

18 Bons d'Anty to Legation, 10 October 1904, MAE, Dossier Général, vol. 7; Campbell to Satow, 1 April 1905, FO 228/1591.

19 Hosie to Satow, 9 January 1905, FO 228/1591.

20 *NCH*, vol. 73, p. 1424; lower- as well as upper-class Szechwanese responded to these appeals. *Tung-fang*, vol. 1, no. 8, nw. 103; interview with the Szechwanese scholar and former Nationalist Minister of Finance Liu Hang-ch'en, Taipei, 1969 (hereafter cited as interview with Liu Hang-ch'en).

21 Hosie to Satow, 9 January 1905, FO 228/1591; Doire to Bapst, 16 January 1907, MAE, Chine, Politique Extérieure, Dossier Général, vol. 10.

22 *NCH*, vol. 75, p. 336.

23 Levenson (*Liang Ch'i-ch'ao*, p. 119) and Chang (*Liang Ch'i-ch'ao*, p. 145) stress China's "traditional" orientation toward civil pursuits.

24 *HL*, no. 362, p. 387.

25 *HL*, no. 501, p. 544.

26 *HL*, no. 327, p. 345; *KHSL*, 520: 20b; 521: 8a; BH, nos. 655, 656.

27 Hosie to Satow, 5 January 1904, FO 228/1549; BH, no. 656.

28 *HL*, no. 403, p. 437; no. 444, pp. 479-80.

29 *KHSL*, 547: 1b; *HL*, no. 501, pp. 544-46; Powell, *The Rise of Chinese Military Power*, pp. 231, 233. His successor was later forced to ask for another delay. Hsien-cheng pien-ch'a-kuan, *Cheng-chih kuan-pao* [Official journal of politics], 5: 370.

30 *HL*, nos. 367, 459, 497, 509, 527; *KHSL*, 559: 14b.

31 Chou, *Shu-hai*, 3: 50b, 53a. The other was the Ch'uan-Han railway; see chap. 6 of this book.

32 *NCH*, vol. 75, p. 588.

33 *HL*, no. 343, pp. 367-68; no. 361, pp. 386-87; no. 508, pp. 552-53.

34 Thomas L. Kennedy, "The Kiangnan Arsenal, 1895-1911: The Decentralized Bureaucracy Responds to Imperialism," *Ch'ing-shih wen-t'i* 2, no. 1 (October 1969): 17-34.

35 *HL*, no. 362, pp. 387-89.

36 *KHSL*, 525: 5.

37 For the argument that regionalism weakened the Ch'ing response to imperialism, see Stanley Spector, *Li Hung-chang and the Huai Army*.

38 *HL*, no. 362, pp. 387-89; no. 413, pp. 446-47.

39 *NCH*, vol. 81, p. 180.

40 Hosie to Satow, 9 January 1905, FO 228/1591; *NCH*, vol. 75, p. 588; Campbell to Satow, 1 April 1905, FO 228/1591.

41 *HL*, no. 511, p. 556; no. 564, p. 621; Chou, *Shu-hai*, 2: 19a; Hosie to Satow, 9 January 1905, FO 228/1591; Campbell to Satow, 1 April 1905; Goffe to Satow, 10 October 1905, 4 April 1906, FO 228/1591.

42 *HL*, no. 548, pp. 600–01; *KHSL*, 564: 2b; Chou, *Shu-hai*, 2: 18b; *NCH*, vol. 81, p. 180; Chang, *Ch'ing-shih*, vol. 3, p. 1727; Fox to Jordan, 31 March 1907, FO 228/1660; Wang Chien-ch'ing, *Pa-hsien-chih* [Local history of Pa-hsien district], ts'e 2: pt. 1, p. 5a.

43 Wolfgang Franke, *The Reform and Abolition of the Traditional Chinese Examination System*, p. 53.

44 Bons d'Anty to Dubail, 23 September 1903, MAE, Dossier Général, vol. 7.

45 Ho, *The Leader of Success*, pp. 226, 237; *KHSL*, 519: 13.

46 *NCH*, vol. 76, p. 616. Even Chang Chih-tung later had some second thoughts about the abolition of the examination system. Ayers, *Chang Chih-tung*, p. 245.

47 *Tung-fang*, vol. 1, no. 4, chiao-yü, p. 102; vol. 2, no. 2, chiao-yü, p. 29.

48 *HL*, no. 372, pp. 400–01; *Tung-fang*, vol. 1, no. 4, chiao-yü, p. 102. There were two other medical schools in the empire, one at Pao-ting and one at Canton. Powell, *The Rise of Chinese Military Power*, p. 236.

49 Goffe to Satow, 31 December 1905, FO 228/1591.

50 *HL*, no. 341, p. 362.

51 Chang Chung-lei, "Ch'ing-mo Min-ch'u Ssu-ch'uan ti chün-shih hsüeh-t'ang chi Ch'uan-chün p'ai-hsi" [The military schools at the end of the Ch'ing and the beginning of the republic and military cliques in the Szechwan army], in *Hsin-hai ko-ming hui-i-lu* [Memoirs of the revolution of 1911], ed. Chung-kuo jen-min cheng-chih hsieh-shang hui-i ch'üan-kuo wei-yüan hui wen-shih tzu-liao yen-chiu wei-yüan hui [Committee on Written Historical Materials of the National Committee of the Chinese People's Political Consultative Conference], (Peking, 1961–), 3: 346–47 (hereafter cited as Chung-kuo jen-min, *Hsin-hai ko-ming hui-i-lu*).

52 *HL*, no. 341, p. 363; this has been called "muscular Confucianism." See Schwartz, *In Search of Wealth and Power*, pp. 15–16.

53 *HL*, no. 341, p. 363; no. 528, p. 581.

54 Campbell to Satow, 1 April 1905, FO 228/1591; *HL*, no. 450, pp. 488–89; no. 577, pp. 644–45.

55 *HL*, pp. 645–47; Samuel Chu, *Reformer in Modern China: Chang Chien, 1853–1926*, pp. 166–68; Goffe to Jordan, 8 October 1906, 31 December 1906, FO 228/1629; Fox to Jordan, 31 March 1907, FO 228/1660.

56 For the movement to study abroad, see Yi-chü Wang, *Chinese Intellectuals and the West, 1872–1949*, pp. 41–98; Fang Chao-ying, *Ch'ing-mo Min-ch'u yang-hsüeh hsüeh-sheng t'i-ming lu ch'u-chi yi-yi mou-shih ts'ung-pien* [List of students who studied abroad during the late Ch'ing and early Republic]; Robert A. Scalapino, "Prelude to Marxism: The Chinese Student Movement in Japan, 1900–1910," in Feuerwerker, *Approaches*, pp. 190–215.

57 "Ssu-ch'uan-sheng liu-hsüeh Jih-pen kuan-fei sheng tiao-ch'a-piao" [Table summarizing data on Szechwanese government fellowship students in Japan], circa 1908, in Chiao-yü pu tang [Archives of the Ministry of Education], Musan, Taiwan (hereafter cited as Ministry of Education Archives).

58 *HL*, no. 479, p. 522; *NCH*, vol. 77, p. 610.

212

NOTES TO PAGES 54–58

59 *HL*, no. 374, pp. 401–02; "Liu-Pi kuan-fei hsüeh-sheng li-li ch'ing ts'e" [A record of government fellowship students sent to Belgium], circa 1908, Ministry of Education Archives.

60 *HL*, no. 370, pp. 399–400; *NCH*, vol. 72, p. 797; *Tung-fang*, vol. 1, no. 4, shih-p'ing, p. 12.

61 *HL*, no. 410, pp. 443–44; Goffe to Satow, 1 July 1905, FO 228/1591; Fox to Jordan, 24 January 1907, FO 228/1660.

62 *Hsüeh-pu tsou-tzu chi-yao* [Collection of memorials of the ministry of education], circular of 13 March 1906, microfilm, Institute of Modern History, Academia Sinica.

63 Ibid., circular of 25 March 1906.

64 *HL*, no. 518, p. 563.

65 *HL*, no. 518, pp. 563–64. The use of *huan-ch'iu* suggested that Chinese culture should be admired throughout the globe. *Tz'u-hai*, pp. 1930, 1942–43.

66 *HL*, no. 518, p. 564.

67 *HL*, nos. 517, 518, 519; *KHSL*, 558: 3b.

68 Doire to Monsieur le Ministre, 19 December 1906, MAE, Dossier Général, vol. 9.

69 *HL*, no. 578, p. 648. A recent study makes the same criticism. Wang, *The Chinese Intellectuals*, pp. 497–503.

70 *HL*, no. 337, pp. 357–58.

71 *HL*, no. 479, p. 521.

72 *HL*, no. 346, p. 371; no. 479, p. 520; no. 481, p. 524.

73 *HL*, no. 480, p. 524; no. 479, pp. 520–21.

74 Fox to Jordan, 24 January 1907, 31 March 1907, FO 228/1660; Goffe to Satow, 4 April 1905, FO 228/1660.

75 *NCH*, vol. 70, p. 886; *HL*, no. 409, pp. 443–44.

76 *HL*, no. 487, p. 529; *Tung-fang*, vol. 2, no. 9, chiao-yü, p. 250.

77 Bons d'Anty to Legation, 23 July 1904, 10 October 1904, MAE, Dossier Général, vol. 7; Goffe to Carnegie, 9 July 1906, FO 228/1629.

78 Goffe to Satow, 22 May 1906, FO 228/1691; Pien Chung-fan, " 'Ch'ung-ch'ing jih-pao,' ch'uang-pan jen Pien Hsiao-wu lieh-shih shih-shu" [The story of the martyr Pien Hsiao-wu, founder of the *Chungking Daily*], Chung-kuo jen-min, *Hsin-hai ko-ming hui-i-lu* 3: 336–38.

79 Chang Shen-k'ai, *Ho-ch'uan hsien-chih* [Local history of Ho-ch'uan district], 62: 29a; interview with Liu Hang-ch'en.

80 *HL*, nos. 418, 479, 485, 486, 489, 560; Chou, *Shu-hai*, 2: 47a; *Tung-fang*, vol. 1, no. 2, chiao-yü, pp. 254–56; no. 6, chiao-yü, p. 145; no. 8, chiao-yü, p. 195.

81 Chou, *Shu-hai*, 3: 45a; *Tung-fang*, vol. 1, no. 9, chiao-yü, p. 215; no. 12, chiao-yü, p. 281; vol. 2, no. 11, chiao-yü, p. 293. Buddhist opposition was exceptional. *HL*, no. 490, pp. 532–33.

82 Chou, *Shu-hai*, 3: 45a. Despite the misgivings of Chu Teh's foster father, Chu Teh himself was educated in these schools. Agnes Smedley, *The Great Road: The Life and Times of Chu Teh*, p. 75.

83 *Tung-fang*, vols. 1, 2, chiao-yü, Ssu-ch'uan, passim.

Chapter 6

1 Lee En-han, "China's Response to Foreign Investment in Her Mining Industry," *Journal of Asian Studies* 28, no. 1 (1968): 55–56; *KWT*, pp. 2626–30, 2648–49,

2862–78; *HL*, no. 348, pp. 373–74; Hosie to Satow, 23 May 1904, FO 228/1549; Hosie to Satow, 9 January 1905, FO 228/1591; Goffe to Satow, 4 April 1906, FO 228/1629; FO 228/2486, passim; WWP, *K'uang-wu tang-an, Ko-kuo k'uang-wu, Fa-shang Hua-li kung-ssu* [Mining archives, the mining affairs of all countries, the French Hua-li company), 1914.

2   *KWT*, pp. 2631–37; 2851–70; 2941; *HL*, no. 348, pp. 373–74; Bons d'Anty to Legation, 22 August 1903, MAE, Chine, Industrie et Travaux Publics, Mines, Sseu-tch'ouan, vol. 6; Goffe to Satow, 19 May 1906, 6 July 1906, 16 August 1906, FO 228/2342; Hsi-liang to Goffe, 1 December 1906, enclosed in Goffe to Jordan, 15 December 1906, FO 228/2342; Wang, *Pa-hsien chih*, 9: 24b; 16: 2b.

3   Inspectorate General of Customs, *Decennial Reports, 1902–1911* (Shanghai, 1913), p. 268 (hereafter cited as *Decennial Reports*).

4   *HL*, no. 348, p. 374; no. 375, p. 405; no. 543, pp. 596–97; Hosie to Satow, 5 January 1904, FO 228/1549.

5   Chou, *Shu-hai*, 2: 20; *HL*, no. 375, p. 404.

6   Fox to Jordan, 31 March 1907, FO 228/1660; *Decennial Reports*, pp. 268–69.

7   *HL*, no. 375, pp. 404–05.

8   *HL*, no. 448, p. 483; Goffe to Satow, 1 July 1905, FO 228/1591; Chang Chung-li, *The Income of the Chinese Gentry*, pp. 176–78.

9   Fox to Hosie, 9 May 1907, FO 228/1660; Wang, *Pa-hsien chih*, 14: 7a; *Decennial Reports*, p. 262.

10   For the licentiate's own story, see Chang, *Ho-ch'uan hsien-chih*, 18: 1–21; 19: 1–4; 20: 1–28; 62: 29a; *Tung-fang*, vol. 1, no. 9, chiao-yü, pp. 244–45.

11   *Decennial Reports*, p. 269; interview with Liu Hang-ch'en.

12   For local elite support for this position, see *Tung-fang*, vol. 1, no. 9, shih-yeh, pp. 142–45.

13   *Decennial Reports*, p. 269; Fox to Jordan, 8 March 1907, FO 228/1660.

14   Feuerwerker, *China's Early Industrialization*, chap. 3; Chu, *Reformer in Modern China*, chap. 3.

15   There were precedents for "self-management," for a Ch'uan-Han line, and for a "self-managed" line in Szechwan. See Kent, *Railway Enterprise*, pp. 2–3; Chang Kia-ngan, *China's Struggle for Railroad Development*, p. 45; *Ch'i-chiang hsü-chih* [Local history of Ch'i-chiang, continued], 3: 31b.

16   Ling Hung-hsün, "Ch'uan-Han t'ieh-lu," in *Chung-hua min-kuo k'ai-kuo wu-shih-nien wen-hsien* [Documents on the fiftieth anniversary of the founding of the republic of China], ed. Chung-hua min-kuo k'ai-kuo wu-shih-nien wen-hsien pien-tsuan wei-yüan-hui [Committee on the Compilation of Documents on the Fiftieth Anniversary of the Founding of the Republic of China] (Taipei, 1963–), ts'e 8, p. 680; Memorandum by Lieutenant-Colonel C. C. Manifold to the Secretary, Political and Secret Department, India Office, 10 December 1903, FO 17/1654 (hereafter cited as Manifold Memorandum).

17   Conger to Prince of Ch'ing, 12 August 1903, U.S., Department of State, *Foreign Relations of the United States*, vol. 9, p. 175; Chou K'ai-ch'ing, *Ssu-ch'uan yü hsin-hai ko-ming* [Szechwan and the revolution of 1911], p. 43.

18   *CWH*, 66: 22–23.

19   Ibid.

20   Hillier to Cameron, 30 June 1903, enclosed in Hong Kong and Shanghai Banking Corporation to Foreign Office, 21 August 1903, FO 17/1620.

21   de Marteau to Société Française d'Explorations Minières en Chine, 2 July 1903, MAE, Chine, Industrie et Travaux Publics, Chemins de Fer, Ligne de Sseu-tch'ouan, vol. 1 (hereafter cited as MAE, Ligne de Sseu-tch'ouan).

22   Hillier to Cameron, 30 June 1903, FO 17/1620; Dubail to Delcassé, 16 November 1903, MAE, Direction Politique, vol. 7.

23   Yoshihiro Hatano, "The Background of the Railway Nationalization Policy of the Late Ch'ing Period: The Reason Why the Policy was Taken Up," *Research Conference on the Chinese Revolution of 1911*, no. 7, p. 22.

24   *HL*, no. 323, pp. 339–40. The statutes of the Peking-Kalgan line provided for it to be built by the Chinese engineer Chan T'ien-yu, who had already built a smaller line without foreign assistance. Ling Hung-hsün, *Chan T'ien-yu hsien-sheng nien-p'u* [A chronological biography of Chan T'ien-yu], pp. 37–38.

25   Feuerwerker, *China's Early Industrialization*, p. 68.

26   "Ching-kao ko-sheng tzu-pan t'ieh-lu-che" [A respectful warning to the self-managed railways of all provinces], editorial in the *Wai-chiao pao*, in *Tung-fang*, vol. 2, no. 10, chiao-t'ung, p. 85.

27   Chao, *Ch'ing-shih kao*, 155: chiao-t'ung, 1, 10a; Morse, app. B.

28   Arthur Lewis Rosenbaum, "Chinese Railway Policy and the Response to Imperialism: The Peking-Mukden Railway, 1895–1911," *Ch'ing-shih wen-t'i* 3, no. 1 (1969): 70; see also idem, "China's First Railway: The Imperial Railways of North China, 1880–1911" (Ph.D. diss., Yale University, 1972). Cited with permission of the author.

29   *CWH*, 189: 23–24a; Ting Chen-to's memorial of 16 April 1905, enclosed in Wilkinson to Lansdowne, 20 April 1905, FO 17/1680; Fox to Jordan, 4 March 1907, FO 228/1660; Ch'üan Han-sheng, "T'ieh-lu kuo-yu wen-t'i yü hsin-hai ko-ming" [The railway nationalization question and the revolution of 1911], in Wu, *CHS Ts'ung-k'an*, ts'e 1, p. 120.

30   Tai Chih-li, *Ssu-ch'uan pao-lu yün-tung shih-liao* [Historical materials on the railway protection movement in Szechwan], no. 2, p. 2; *KHSL*, 517: 13b.

31   *HL*, no. 363, p. 390.

32   Ibid.

33   *HL*, no. 473, p. 512.

34   *HL*, no. 371, p. 400; Fei, *Chin-tai*, pp. 319–20.

35   *HL*, no. 371, p. 400; Chungking extract, 2 April 1904, MAE, Ligne de Sseu-tch'ouan, vol. 1.

36   *HL*, no. 522, pp. 568–71; Fei, *Chin-tai*, pp. 313–14.

37   Chou, *Shu-hai*, 3: 50b; Chou K'ai-ch'ing, ed., *Ssu-ch'uan wen-hsien* [Documents on Szechwan], no. 62, p. 20; interview with Liu Hang-ch'en.

38   Hillier to Cameron, 30 June 1903, enclosed in Hong Kong and Shanghai Banking Corporation to Foreign Office, 21 August 1903, FO 17/1620; Procès-verbal, 9 August 1903, WWP, *K'uang-wu tang, Ssu-ch'uan k'uang-wu* [Mining archives, Szechwan mining], ts'e 2; F. A. Campbell to Chinese Central Railways Ltd., 15 March 1904, FO 17/1654; Dubail to Ministère, 1 June 1904, MAE, Ligne de Sseu-tch'ouan, vol. 1; Prince of Ching to Conger, 30 January 1904, enclosed in

Fletcher to Secretary of State, 14 July 1909, U.S., Department of State, *Foreign Relations*, 1909, pp. 175–76; E-tu Zen Sun, *Chinese Railways and British Interests, 1898–1911*, p. 110.

39   Bons d'Anty to Dubail, 30 June 1904, MAE, Ligne de Sseu-tch'ouan, vol. 1.

40   Hosie to Satow, 4 May 1904, enclosed in Satow to Lansdowne, 2 June 1904, FO 17/1749; Bons d'Anty to Dubail, 13 and 30 June 1904, MAE, Ligne de Sseu-tch'ouan, vol. 1.

41   Tai, *Ssu-ch'uan pao-lu*, no. 6, pp. 5–6; no. 7, pp. 6–7.

42   *HL*, no. 473, p. 512.

43   C. C. Manifold, "Report on Political Relations in Ssu-ch'uan Likely to Affect the Railway and Trade" (1904), FO 17/1763 (hereafter cited as Manifold Report).

44   Sheng, *Yü-chai*, 66: 33a; 67: 1b–2a.

45   Hosie to Satow, 28 December 1904, FO 17/1763.

46   *HL*, no. 374, pp. 402–03.

47   Chou, *Shu-hai*, 1: 1a; 2: 50b; 3: 51a.

48   Regulations of July 1904, enclosed in Hosie to Satow, 4 July 1904, FO 228/1549.

49   Chou, *Shu-hai*, 3: 54b. Hsi-liang declined to take customary fees (*kuei-fei*) that could have equaled 180,000 tls. a year. Chang, *The Income*, pp. 12–14, 32.

50   Han Suyin, *The Crippled Tree*, p. 138; Wu Chin-hang, "Ssu-ch'uan Hsin-hai ko-ming chien-wen lu" [A record of what I saw and heard during the revolution of 1911 in Szechwan], Chung-kuo jen-min, *Hsin-hai ko-ming hui-i-lu*, vol. 3, p. 99.

51   Hosie to Satow, 28 December 1904, enclosed in Satow to Lansdowne, 4 February 1905, FO 17/1763; Goffe to Satow 4 May 1905, enclosed in Satow to Lansdowne, 1 June 1905, FO 17/1763; Wang, *Pa-hsien chih*, 14: 6b; *NCH*, vol. 76, p. 675.

52   Chou, *Shu-hai*, 3: 52a.

53   Bons d'Anty to Dubail, 10 December 1904, MAE, Ligne de Sseu-tch'ouan, vol. 2; Tai, *Ssu-ch'uan pao-lu*, no. 10, p. 9.

54   Tai, *Ssu-ch'uan pao-lu*, no. 10, p. 9.

55   Ibid.

56   Ibid., no. 11, pp. 17–29.

57   Ibid., no. 10, p. 11.

58   Ibid.

59   *NCH*, vol. 73, p. 1247.

60   *HL*, no. 422, p. 455; title 3, articles 23–35, in "Ch'uan-Han t'ieh-lu tsung-kung-ssu chi-ku chang-ch'eng" [Regulations for the collection of shares for the Ch'uan-Han railway], in Tai, *Ssu-chu'an pao-lu*, no. 14, p. 35 (hereafter cited as "Chi-ku chang-ch'eng").

61   Articles 2, 3, 6, 7, 12–15, in "Ch'uan-Han t'ieh-lu an-tsu ch'ou-ku hsiang-hsi chang-ch'eng" [Detailed regulations for levying grain according to rent for the Ch'uan-Han railway], *Tung-fang*, vol. 2, no. 7, chiao-t'ung, p. 73; Chou, *Shu-hai*, 2: 51a; 3: 51b.

62   John Lossing Buck, *Land Utilization in China*, pp. 195–96; *NCH*, vol. 72, p. 1081; Chou, *Shu-hai*, 3: 52a.

63   Articles 39, 40, 45, in "Chi-ku chang-ch'eng," p. 38.

64   Chou, *Shu-hai*, 3: 52b–53a; Tai, *Ssu-ch'uan pao-lu*, no. 16, p. 43.

65   He expected to get 15,000,000 tls. from rent shares, 3,200,000 from contributions,

and 1,280,000 from state funds and the opium tax for a total of 19,480,000 tls.

66 *HL*, no. 422, p. 455; article 5, in "Chi-ku chang-ch'eng," p. 33.

67 Tai, *Ssu-chuan pao-lu*, no. 13, pp. 31–32.

68 Manifold Memorandum.

69 Ibid.; title 2, article 4 of regulations, enclosed in Manifold Report; *NCH*, vol. 72, p. 1111.

70 Brett to Satow, 22 October 1904, FO 228/1549; Tai, *Ssu-ch'uan pao-lu*, no. 5, p. 5. The merchants of eastern Szechwan may have favored this section for commercial reasons; Wang, *Pa-hsien chih*, 14: 6b; Vice-consul to Bapst, 23 April 1908, MAE, Ligne de Sseu-tch'ouan, vol. 4.

71 *CWH*, 191: 32.

72 Chou, *Shu-hai*, 3: 51a.

73 *HL*, no. 422, p. 455.

74 Ibid.

75 "Proclamation Issued by the Governor-General of Szechwan Inviting Subscriptions for Shares in the Szechwan-Hankow Railway," translation enclosed in Satow to Lansdowne, 4 February 1905, FO 17/1763.

76 Bons d'Anty to Dubail, 15 March 1905, MAE, Ligne de Sseu-tch'ouan, vol. 2; Campbell to Satow, 25 March 1905, enclosed in Satow to Lansdowne, 3 May 1905, FO 17/1763.

77 Bons d'Anty to Legation, 15 November 1904, MAE, Ligne de Sseu-tch'ouan, vol. 1.

78 *HL*, no. 470, p. 509; no. 502, p. 546; interview with Liu Hang-ch'en; Bons d'Anty to Dubail, 20 June 1905, MAE, Ligne de Sseu-tch'ouan, vol. 2; Bons d'Anty to Dubail, 31 August 1905, MAE, Ligne de Sseu-tch'ouan, vol. 3; Doire to Bapst, late 1906, MAE, Ligne de Sseu-tch'ouan, vol. 3.

79 *HL*, no. 460, pp. 497–98; no. 502, pp. 546–47.

80 *Tung-fang*, vol. 2, no. 7, chiao-t'ung, p. 63.

81 Chou, *Ssu-ch'uan yü hsin-hai*, pp. 69–71.

82 Ibid., pp. 72–73.

83 *KHSL*, 548: 6b.

84 *CWH*, 194: 28b–29b.

85 Ibid., 66: 24a; 194: 28b; 195: 7a–8a, 22b–23.

86 Ibid., 66: 22b–26b.

87 *HL*, no. 515, pp. 559–61.

88 Bons d'Anty to Legation, 15 November 1904, MAE, Ligne de Sseu-tch'ouan, vol. 1.

89 Bons d'Anty to Dubail, 15 May 1905, MAE, Ligne de Sseu-tch'ouan, vol. 2; Chou, *Ssu-ch'uan yü hsin-hai*, p. 71; Tai, *Ssu-ch'uan pao-lu*, no. 10, p. 15; Campbell to Satow, 13 February 1905, enclosed in Satow to Lansdowne, 3 March 1905, FO 17/1763.

90 Bons d'Anty to Dubail, 14 April 1905, MAE, Ligne de Sseu-tch'ouan, vol. 2; Goffe to Satow, 18 April 1905, FO 228/1591; Clavery to Rouvier, 23 June 1905, MAE, Ligne de Sseu-tch'ouan, vol. 2; Bons d'Anty to Dubail, 30 September 1905, MAE, Ligne de Sseu-tch'ouan, vol. 3; Chou, *Shu-hai*, 3: 52.

91 Bons d'Anty to Dubail, 25 July 1905, MAE, Ligne de Sseu-tch'ouan, vol. 2.

92 *CWH*, 193: 29a, 29b.

93   *CWH*, 195: 27–28, 32a; de la Batie to Bapst, 6 October 1906, MAE, Ligne de
     Sseu-tch'ouan, vol. 3.
94   *HL*, no. 582, pp. 657–58.
95   *HL*, no. 515, pp. 559–60.
96   *HL*, no. 355, pp. 379–80; no. 522, pp. 568–71; no. 538, p. 592; Chou, *Shu-hai*, 2:
     19b; Fei, *Chin-tai*, pp. 313–14.
97   Fox to Jordan, 31 March 1907, FO 228/1660; Doire to Bapst, late 1906, MAE,
     Ligne de Sseu-tch'ouan, vol. 3; Doire to Bapst, 14 January 1907, MAE, Ligne de
     Sseu-tch'ouan, vol. 4; Fei, *Chin-tai*, p. 81; Chou, *Shu-hai*, 3: 54b; interview with
     Liu Hang-ch'en.
98   Chou, *Ssu-ch'uan yü hsin-hai*, p. 73; Tai, *Ssu-ch'uan pao-lu*, no. 18, p. 57.
99   *HL*, no. 515, p. 559.
100 Tai, *Ssu-ch'uan pao-lu*, no. 17, p. 52.
101 Chou, *Ssu-ch'uan yü hsin-hai*, p. 73; Doire to Bapst, 10 November 1906, Bapst to
     Ministère, 29 November 1906, MAE, Ligne de Sseu-tch'ouan, vol. 3.
102 *HL*, no. 582, articles 8–11, p. 654.
103 Tai, *Ssu-ch'uan pao-lu*, nos. 25, 26, pp. 72–73; interview with Liu Hang-ch'en.
104 Tai, *Ssu-ch'uan pao-lu*, no. 17, pp. 47, 51.
105 Doire to Bapst, 5 November 1906, MAE, Ligne de Sseu-tch'ouan, vol. 3.
106 *HL*, no. 574; Chou, *Ssu-ch'uan yü hsin-hai*, p. 73; Tai, *Ssu-ch'uan pao-lu*, no. 17, p.
     51; Doire to Bapst, 16 October, 5 November 1906, MAE, Ligne de Sseu-tch'ouan,
     vol. 3.
107 Doire to Bapst, 24 November 1906, MAE, Ligne de Sseu-tch'ouan, vol. 3.
108 Wang Ti, "Ssu-ch'uan t'ao Man-chou hsi" [A Szechwanese manifesto proclaim-
     ing military action against the Manchus], in Chung-kuo jen-min, *K'ai-kuo
     wen-hsien*, ts'e 16, p. 263; interview with Liu Hang-ch'en.
109 For the Commercial Regulations of 1903 defining merchant-management, see Li,
     Wan Ch'ing, p. 96.
110 Regulations of the Association, *Chung-wai jih-pao* (15 September 1906), trans-
     lated and enclosed in Doire to Bapst, 5 November 1906, MAE, Ligne de
     Sseu-tch'ouan, vol. 3.
111 Tai, *Ssu-ch'uan pao-lu*, no. 17, p. 45; no. 18, p. 55.
112 Doire to Bapst, 5 November 1906, MAE, Ligne de Sseu-tch'ouan, vol. 3.
113 *HL*, no. 582, pp. 653–57.
114 Doire to Bapst, 14 May 1907, MAE, Ligne de Sseu-tch'ouan, vol. 4; Tai,
     Ssu-chuan pao-lu, p. 73.
115 Hu Tung-chao, "Report on the Construction of the Railroad in Szechwan,"
     translated and enclosed in Bons d'Anty to Boissonnas, 26 December 1907, MAE,
     Ligne de Sseu-tch'ouan, vol. 4; Shih T'i-yüan, "Hui Ch'eng-tu pao-lu yün-tung"
     [Memoirs of the railway protection movement in Chengtu], Chung-kuo jen-min,
     Hsin-hai ko-ming hui-i-lu, vol. 3, p. 43.
116 Ch'üan, "T'ieh-lu kuo-yu wen-t'i," pp. 218–20; Tai, *Ssu-ch'uan pao-lu*, no. 27, pp.
     73–74, no. 28, pp. 75–76; Marie-Claire Bergère, "The Role of the Bourgeoisie," in
     Wright, *China in Revolution*, p. 233; Chou, *Ssu-ch'uan yü hsin-hai*, pp. 96–98.
117 Hatano, "The Background of the Railway Nationalization Policy," pp. 27–32.
118 Fei, *Chin-tai*, p. 226; Tai, *Ssu-ch'uan pao-lu*, no. 10, p. 15; nos. 32, 37, 38;

Consul-General to Boissonnas, 4 May 1909, MAE, Ligne de Sseu-tch'ouan, vol. 4.

119   Sun, *Chinese Railways*, p. 99; *CWH*, 70: 35–37.
120   Rosenbaum, "Chinese Railway Policy," pp. 59–60; *Morse*, pp. 90, 99–100; Sun, *Chinese Railways*, p. 98.
121   Tai, *Ssu-ch'uan pao-lu*, no. 60; Charles Hedtke, "The Genesis of the Revolution in Szechwan," *Research Conference on the Chinese Revolution of 1911*, p. 68.
122   Chou, *Ssu-ch'uan yü hsin-hai*, p. 73; Ch'üan, "T'ieh-lu kuo-yu wen-t'i," p. 215; Chou, *Shu-hai*, 2: 17b.
123   Chou, *Ssu-ch'uan yü hsin-hai*, pp. 43–44; Hatano, "The Background of the Railway Nationalization Policy," pp. 18–19.
124   Goffe to Satow, 19 May 1905, enclosed in Satow to Lansdowne, 13 June 1905, FO 17/1763.
125   Manifold Memorandum.
126   *Decennial Reports*, p. 262.
127   Chao Ching-hsüeh, "The Chengtu-Chungking Railway Completed," *People's China* 14 (1952): 26–28.

Chapter 7

1   Alastair Lamb, *Britain and Chinese Central Asia: The Road to Lhasa, 1767 to 1905*, chap. 10.
2   *HL*, no. 326, p. 344.
3   Tieh-tseng Li, *Tibet, Today and Yesterday*, pp. 40–55; Tsepon W. D. Shakabpa, *Tibet, A Political History*, pp. 113–55; Wiens, *China's March*, p. 231; *Ssu-ch'uan ch'üan-t'u* [A complete map of Szechwan] (n. p., n. d.), Sterling Memorial Library, Yale University.
4   Li, *Tibet*, pp. 62, 64, 80–81; Shakabpa, *Tibet*, pp. 172, 187, 198–200; Lamb, *Britain and Chinese*, chap. 7.
5   Li, *Tibet*, p. 64.
6   *KHSL*, 519: 6b.
7   Hosie to Satow, 19 October 1903, enclosed in Satow to Curzon, 17 November 1903, FO 17/1748.
8   *NCH*, vol. 71, p. 1269.
9   Wu Feng-p'ei, *Ch'ing-tai Hsi-tsang shih-liao ts'ung-k'an* [Library of historical materials on Tibet in the Ch'ing period], chi 1, pt. 1.
10   Wu Feng-p'ei, *Ch'ing-chi ch'ou-tsang tsou-tu* [Memorials on late Ch'ing Tibetan policy], ts'e 3, chi 1, chüan 1, pp. 1–4, 6, 8.
11   *Han-pao*, translated in Intelligence Diary (24 November 1903), FO 17/1653; cf. Lu Hsing-ch'i, "Hsi-tsang chiao-she chi-yao" [An outline of diplomacy on Tibet] (Taipei: Meng-tsang wei-yüan-hui, unpublished manuscript, 1954), p. 26b (Consulted courtesy of Mr. Lo Hui-min of the Meng-tsang wei-yüan-hui, Taipei).
12   Hosie to Satow, 19 October 1903, in Satow to Curzon, 17 November 1903, FO 17/1748; Litton to Lansdowne, 14 April 1904, FO 17/1748.
13   Bons d'Anty to Dubail, 20 June 1903, MAE, Chine, Politique Intérieure, Dossier Général, vol. 7; Intelligence Diary, 19 January 1904, FO 17/1645; Chou, *Shu-hai*, 2: 4a, 5b; Fei, *Chin-tai*, pp. 454–55.
14   *KHSL*, 520: 20; 523: 4b; 527: 4; 520: 19; 521: 4b; *HL*, no. 342, pp. 365–66;

Hosie to Satow, 5 January 1904, enclosed in Satow to Curzon, 10 February 1904, FO 17/1748; Hosie to Satow, 9 April 1904, FO 228/1549.

15 *HL*, no. 342, pp. 365–67; *KHSL*, 519: 8b; Goffe to Satow, 28 February 1906, FO 228/1629.

16 *HL*, no. 342, pp. 366–67.

17 *HL*, no. 342, p. 366; no. 375, p. 405; Hosie, "Report on the Province of Szechwan," 5 February 1904, FO 17/1665; Bons d'Anty to Direction des Affaires Politiques, 5 December 1904, MAE, Chine, Politique Intérieure, Thibet, vol. 3 (hereafter cited as MAE, Thibet); WWP, K'uang-wu, *Ssu-ch'uan ko-k'uang ch'üan-an* [Mining affairs: A complete record of all mining cases in Szechwan], ts'e 1, p. 4216; Lamb, *Britain and Chinese*, p. 274.

18 *HL*, no. 375, p. 404; Hosie to Satow, 29 February 1904, FO 228/1549; Hosie to Satow, 20 May 1904, FO 228/1549.

19 *HL*, no. 347, pp. 371–72; no. 344, pp. 368–70.

20 Younghusband to Viceroy, 31 January 1904, enclosed in India Office to Foreign Office, 5 February 1904, FO 17/1748.

21 Wu, *Ch'ing-chi ch'ou-tsang*, 1: 9, 10; Younghusband to Secretary to the Government of India, 29 December 1903, in India Office to Foreign Office, 1 February 1904; Nepalese Representative to Lhasa to Ravenshaw, 5 April 1904, enclosed in Secretary to the Government of India to Foreign Department, 7 May 1904, FO 17/1749.

22 Wu, *Ch'ing-chi ch'ou-tsang*, 1: 14, 19, 21; Shakabpa, *Tibet*, pp. 208–09; Sang-p'i, Ts'ai-wang-jen-tseng, et al., "Hui-ku hsin-hai ko-ming ch'ien-hou ti Hsi-tsang ch'ing-k'uang" [Memoirs of conditions in Tibet before and after the Hsin-hai revolution], Chung-kuo jen-min, *Hsin-hai ko-ming hui-i-lu*, vol. 3, p. 510.

23 Wu, *Ch'ing-chi ch'ou-tsang*, 1: 21, 23; *NCH*, vol. 73, p. 814; Lamb, *Britain and Chinese*, pp. 302–03.

24 Wu, *Ch'ing-chi ch'ou-tsang*, 1: 21, 31, 36.

25 Fu Sung-mu, *Hsi-k'ang chien-sheng chi* [A record of the founding of Hsi-k'ang province], p. 38.

26 *HL*, no. 395, pp. 425–26; *KHSL*, 535: 10a.

27 Fu, *Hsi-k'ang*, p. 35.

28 Moyes [of the China Inland Mission] to Hosie, 25 March 1903, enclosed in Hosie to Townley, 10 April 1903, FO 228/1499; Alexander Hosie, "Report on a Journey to the Eastern Frontier of Thibet," British Parliamentary Papers, *China*, no. 1 (1905), pp. 38–39.

29 Hosie to Satow, 21 December 1904, FO 17/1754; Hosie, "Journey," p. 55; *NCH*, vol. 71, p. 842.

30 Fu, *Hsi-k'ang*, 25a; extracts from a private letter, enclosed in Campbell to Satow, 20 March 1905, enclosed in Satow to Lansdowne, 3 May 1905, FO 17/1754; letter of Moyes, enclosed in Goffe to Satow, 21 April 1905, FO 17/1754.

31 *NCH*, vol. 72, p. 1109.

32 *HL*, no. 358, p. 382; Chou, *Shu-hai*, 3: 39–42.

33 *KHSL*, 528: 7b–8a; Chou, *Shu-hai*, 3: 41a; Goffe to Satow, 31 May 1905, enclosed in Satow to Lansdowne, 23 June 1905, FO 17/1755.

34 *HL*, no. 496, pp. 538–40; Bons d'Anty to Direction des Affaires Politiques, 2 May

1905, MAE, Thibet, vol. 4; Letter from Moyes, enclosed in Goffe to Satow, 21 April 1905, FO 17/1754.

35 Chou, *Shu-hai*, 3: 41a; *HL*, no. 439, p. 473; no. 443, p. 477; Wilkinson to Lansdowne, 30 June 1905, FO 17/1755.

36 Wu, *Ch'ing-chi ch'ou-tsang*, 1: 7–8.

37 *HL*, no. 443, p. 477.

38 *KHSL*, 535: 7b.

39 *HL*, no. 438, pp. 470–71.

40 *HL*, no. 439, pp. 472–73.

41 *HL*, no. 443, pp. 477–78; extracts, enclosed in Goffe to Satow, 3 May 1905, enclosed in Satow to Lansdowne, 30 May 1905, FO 17/1754; extract enclosed in Goffe to Satow, 12 May 1905, enclosed in Satow to Lansdowne, 9 June 1905, FO 17/1755; Wilkinson to Lansdowne, 30 June 1905, FO 17/1755.

42 *HL*, no. 439, pp. 472–73.

43 Ibid.; Fei, *Chin-tai*, p. 363; Chou, *Shu-hai*, 3: 56–57.

44 Letter from Moyes, enclosed in Goffe to Satow, 21 April 1905, FO 17/1754.

45 Extracts, enclosed in Goffe to Satow, 12 May 1905, enclosed in Satow to Lansdowne, 9 June 1905, FO 17/1755.

46 *HL*, no. 452, p. 490; no. 453, p. 491.

47 *HL*, no. 443, pp. 477–79.

48 *HL*, no. 455, pp. 492–93; *KHSL*, 547: 1b.

49 *HL*, no. 443, pp. 478–79; no. 425, p. 458; no. 475, p. 516; Chou, *Shu-hai*, 3: 57b.

50 *HL*, no. 452, p. 490.

51 Goffe to Satow, 25 April 1905, enclosed in Satow to Lansdowne, 26 May 1905, FO 17/1754; Goffe to Satow, 31 May 1905, enclosed in Satow to Lansdowne, 23 June 1905, FO 17/1755.

52 Annex no. 2, enclosed in Bons d'Anty to Legation, 25 May 1905, enclosed in Consul at Chungking to Direction des Affaires Politiques, 2 June 1905, MAE, Thibet, vol. 4.

53 *KHSL*, 543: 12.

54 Bons d'Anty to Legation, 2 May 1905, enclosed in Dubail to Delcassé, 30 April 1905, MAE, Thibet, vol. 4.

55 Extracts, enclosed in Goffe to Satow, 12 May 1905, enclosed in Satow to Lansdowne, 9 June 1905, FO 17/1755.

56 Bons d'Anty to Legation, 25 May 1905, enclosed in French Consul at Chungking to Direction des Affaires Politiques, 2 June 1905, MAE, Thibet, vol. 4.

57 Hsi-liang to Wai-wu-pu, 25 April 1905; Ch'ing to Dubail, 7 May 1905, enclosed in Dubail to Delcassé, 10 May 1905, MAE, Thibet, vol. 4; *HL*, no. 474, p. 514.

58 Wu, *Ch'ing-chi ch'ou-tsang*, 2: 2–6; *HL*, no. 474, pp. 512–13; Hsi-liang to Wai-wu-pu, 1 August 1905, translated and enclosed in Wai-wu-pu to Dubail, 3 August 1905, annex no. 1 in Dubail to Delcassé, 5 August 1905, MAE, Thibet, vol. 4.

59 Extracts, enclosed in Goffe to Satow, 18 August 1905, FO 17/1755.

60 *HL*, no. 536, p. 590.

61 *HL*, no. 536, pp. 588–89; Chou, *Shu-hai*, 3: 41b.

62 Chou, *Shu-hai*, 3: 56b–57a; Intelligence Report, 31 December 1905, enclosed in Goffe to Satow, 31 December 1905, FO 228/1591.

63 *KHSL*, 549: 1–2.
64 *KHSL*, 548: 8b.
65 *HL*, no. 510, p. 555; Shakabpa, *Tibet*, p. 225; letter of 9 February 1906 enclosed in Goffe to Satow, 22 February 1906, FO 228/1629.
66 *HL*, no. 510, p. 555; Shakabpa, *Tibet*, p. 225.
67 Hauchecorne to Direction des Affaires Politiques, 29 December 1905, MAE, Thibet, vol. 4; *HL*, no. 510, p. 555; no. 533, pp. 584–85; *KHSL*, 546: 16b–17a; *Chung-wai jih-pao*, translated and enclosed in Goffe to Carnegie, 21 June 1906, FO 228/1629; Shakabpa, *Tibet*, p. 225.
68 *HL*, no. 533, pp. 585–86; Shakabpa, *Tibet*, p. 225.
69 Eric Teichman, *Travels of a Consular Officer in Eastern Tibet*, p. 37; *HL*, no. 533, pp. 584–85.
70 Shakabpa, *Tibet*, p. 225; Wu, *Ch'ing-chi ch'ou-tsang*, 2: 11–12, 21–24; Goffe to Carnegie, 9 June 1906, FO 228/1629.
71 *HL*, no. 533, p. 584.
72 Goffe to Carnegie, 18 June 1906, FO 228/1629.
73 Fu, *Hsi-k'ang*, pp. 7–8; enclosure in Goffe to Jordan, 29 December 1906, FO 228/1629.
74 Intelligence Report, 30 June 1907, enclosed in Fox to Jordan, 30 June 1907, FO 228/1660.
75 Fu, *Hsi-k'ang*, pp. 38b–39a; Fei, *Chin-tai*, pp. 303–04.
76 *HL*, no. 438, p. 471.
77 Ibid., pp. 470–71.
78 Ibid.
79 Ibid.
80 *KHSL*, 543: 19b; 549:4; Wu, *Ch'ing-chi ch'ou-tsang*, 2: 16–17.
81 *HL*, no. 500, p. 453; no. 474, p. 514; no. 344, p. 368.
82 Hsi-liang to Wai-wu-pu, 19 July 1905, translated and enclosed in Dubail to Delcassé, 21 July 1905, MAE, Thibet, vol. 4; article 13 of the Pa-t'ang missionary settlement, enclosed in Hauchecorne to Legation, 14 January 1906, MAE, Thibet, vol. 4; Hsi-liang to Wai-wu-pu, 23 February 1906, WWP, *Chiao-wu, Ssu-ch'uan chiao-wu, Pa-t'ang fan-fei chiang-hai Fa-chiao-shih* [Mission affairs, Szechwan mission affairs, the case of the Tibetan bandits' killing the French missionaries].
83 *HL*, no. 540, p. 594; *KHSL*, 564: 2b; Fu, *Hsi-k'ang*, p. 52.
84 *Chung-wai jih-pao*, translated and enclosed in Goffe to Carnegie, 21 June 1906, FO 228/1629; Intelligence Report, 31 December 1906, enclosed in Goffe to Jordan, 31 December 1906, FO 228/1629; Goffe to Jordan, 9 January 1907, FO 228/1660; Fox to Jordan, 23 February 1907, FO 228/1660.
85 *HL*, no. 581, pp. 651–52; enclosure in Goffe to Jordan, 29 December 1906, FO 228/1629.
86 Fu, *Hsi-k'ang*, p. 51b.
87 Louis T. Sigel, "Ch'ing Tibetan Policy (1906–1910)," *Harvard Papers* 20 (1966): 193.
88 Chang to Wai-wu-pu, 5 November 1905, Wai-wu-pu to Hsi-liang, 1 January 1906, WWP, *Hsi-tsang tang* [Tibetan archives].
89 Chang to Wai-wu-pu, 25 February 1906, 17 March 1907, WWP, *Hsi-tsang tang*.
90 Fei, *Chin-tai*, p. 181.

91 Chou, *Shu-hai*, 3: 54.
92 Fu, *Hsi-k'ang*, pp. 51–55, 57–61; Teichman, *Travels*, pp. 23–33; Sigel, "Ch'ing Tibetan Policy," pp. 194–99; Latourette, *A History*, pp. 580, 653.
93 Tai, *Ssu-ch'uan pao-lu*, no. 10, p. 13; Chang, *Ho-ch'uan hsien-chih*, 62: 29a.
94 Goffe to Jordan, 9 January 1906, FO 228/1660; interview with Liu Hang-ch'en.
95 Fei, *Chin-tai*, pp. 382–83, 454–55.
96 *Wai-chiao-pao, Chung-wai jih-pao, Shih-min-pao, Shih-pao,* and *Nan-fang-pao* in *Tung-fang*, vol. 1, no. 2, she-shuo, pp. 32–34; no. 6, she-shuo, pp. 120–23; no. 8, chün-shih, pp. 309–11; vol. 2, no. 2, chün-shih, pp. 188–94; no. 6, she-shuo, pp. 207–14; Huang Chi-lu, comp., *Chung-kuo jih-pao, 1904–1908,* vol. 1, p. 0286.
97 Peter Fleming, *Bayonets to Lhasa*, p. 301.

Chapter 8

 1 Wilkinson to Jordan, 23 July 1907, FO 228/1665.
 2 Hsien-cheng pien-ch'a-kuan, *Cheng-chih kuan-pao*, vol. 3, p. 339; *HL*, no. 705, p. 774.
 3 Ottewill to Jordan, 19 February 1908, FO 228/1700; *HL*, no. 630, p. 700; no. 655, p. 719; no. 672, pp. 739–40; Feng-hsü, *Hao-an tsou-kao* [Draft memorials of Hao-an], p. 171.
 4 Ottewill to Jordan, 24 August, 2 September 1908, FO 228/1700; Wilton to Jordan, 23 September 1908, FO 228/1696.
 5 Wilkinson to Jordan, 13 July 1907, FO 228/1665; *HL*, no. 586, p. 661; no. 691, pp. 759–60; *KHSL*, 574: 5; *NCH*, vol. 83, p. 523; vol. 84, p. 144.
 6 Jonathan Spence, *To Change China: Western Advisers in China, 1620–1960*, p. 290.
 7 *NCH*, vol. 87, p. 32.
 8 *HL*, no. 604, p. 677.
 9 Litton to Satow, 12 August 1905, enclosed in Litton to Lansdowne, 13 August 1905, FO 17/1755; Fei, *Chin-tai*, p. 231.
10 *HL*, no. 586, p. 662.
11 *HL*, no. 604, p. 677.
12 *KHSL*, 576: 14b–15a.
13 Ibid.
14 *HL*, no. 606, p. 681.
15 *HL*, no. 611, p. 686.
16 Ibid.
17 Hummel, pp. 742–46; Wright, *The Last Stand*, pp. 113–17.
18 *HL*, no. 606, pp. 681–82; no. 611, p. 686; no. 658, p. 722.
19 *HL*, no. 595, p. 670.
20 Intelligence Report, enclosed in Wilkinson to Jordan, 18 April 1908, FO 228/1696.
21 *HL*, no. 653, p. 718.
22 For a biography of Pai, see Fei, *Chin-tai*, p. 363.
23 Extract from *Chung-kuo jih-pao* of May 1908, appended to Ch'en Ch'un-sheng, "Wu-shen Ho-k'ou ch'i-i chi" [Record of the 1908 Ho-k'ou uprising], in Chung-kuo jen-min, *K'ai-kuo wen-hsien*, pien 1, ts'e 13, section 5, p. 396.
24 Consul-General to Jordan, 20 August 1907, FO 17/1665.
25 *NCH*, vol. 85, p. 685.

26 *HL*, no. 657, pp. 721–22.
27 *HL*, no. 606, p. 682; no. 611, p. 686; no. 658, p. 722; no. 663, p. 731.
28 *HL*, no. 595, p. 669; no. 746, p. 806.
29 *HL*, no. 636, p. 705. For a "regionalist" interpretation, see William R. Johnson, "China's 1911 Revolution in the Provinces of Yunnan and Kweichow" (Ph.D. diss., University of Washington, 1962), p. 26.
30 Chang, "Ch'ing-mo Min-ch'u," p. 348; Intelligence Report, enclosed in Wilkinson to Jordan, 18 April 1908, FO 228/1696; *HL*, nos. 633, 701, 812.
31 Chang, "Ch'ing-mo Min-ch'u," p. 348; Hsien-cheng pien-ch'a-kuan, *Cheng-chih kuan-pao*, vol. 2, p. 67.
32 *HL*, no. 636, pp. 704–05.
33 *HL*, no. 748, pp. 807–08.
34 *HL*, no. 663, p. 730; no. 637, p. 707; Intelligence Report, enclosed in Wilton to Jordan, 8 January 1909, FO 228/1733.
35 *HL*, no. 677, pp. 747–48.
36 *HL*, no. 586, p. 662; no. 604, p. 677; no. 636, p. 704; no. 663, pp. 729-30; no. 817, p. 874. For an independent appraisal of the quality of troops transferred from Szechwan, see Miu Kuo-chang, *Hsüan-wei hsien-chich-kao* [Draft history of Hsüan-wei district], 1934 (Taipei reprint, 1967), p. 92.
37 Chang, *Ch'ing-shih*, vol. 3, p. 1638.
38 *HL*, no. 636, p. 705; no. 637, p. 707; Intelligence Report, enclosed in Wilton to Jordan, 8 January 1909, FO 228/1733.
39 *HL*, no. 636, p. 705; Intelligence Report, enclosed in Wilton to Jordan, 8 January 1909, FO 228/1733.
40 *HL*, no. 636, p. 705; no. 637, pp. 706–07; no. 663, p. 731; no. 748, pp. 807–08; no. 789, p. 839; no. 812, pp. 865–66; Wilton, "Report on the Lu chun of Yunnan," enclosed in Wilton to Jordan, 21 September 1909, FO 228/1733.
41 *HL*, no. 636, p. 706; no. 586, p. 662; no. 602, pp. 674–75; no. 663, p. 731; Wilton, "Report on the Lu chun"; Wright, *China in Revolution*, p. 29.
42 *HL*, no. 665, p. 733; Yoshihiro Hatano, "The New Armies," in Wright, *China in Revolution*, p. 372; cf. Johnson, "China's 1911 Revolution in Yunnan," p. 28.
43 Chung-kuo k'o-hsüeh-yüan, comp., *Yün-nan Kuei-chou hsin-hai ko-ming tzu-liao* [Materials on the 1911 revolution in Yunnan and Kweichow], p. 81; *HL*, no. 586, p. 661.
44 *HL*, no. 821, p. 876; *NCH*, vol. 89, p. 51; Wilton, "Report on the Lu chun."
45 Li Ken-yüan, *Hsüeh-sheng nien-lu* [A chronological biography of (Li) Hsüeh-sheng], in Shen Yün-lung, no. 14, 1: 3b.
46 Wright, *China in Revolution*, p. 15.
47 Chen Ching-jen, "Opium and Anglo-Chinese Relations," *Chinese Social and Political Science Review* 19 (1935–36): 386–88.
48 Hsin-pao Chang, *Commissioner Lin and the Opium War*, app. A.
49 Chen, "Opium," pp. 388–92; Chang, *Commissioner Lin*, p. 16.
50 John K. Fairbank, *Trade and Diplomacy on the China Coast*; Masataka Banno, *China and the West, 1858–1861* (Cambridge: Harvard University Press, 1964).
51 Jonathan Spence, "Opium Smoking in Ch'ing China" (unpublished draft cited with permission of the author).

52 Chen, "Opium," pp. 395, 418, 421–23; Cameron, *The Reform Movement*, pp. 137–39; Chang, *Commissioner Lin*, pp. 34–36.
53 Su, "Chang Chih-tung," p. 48.
54 Ibid.
55 *CWH*, 7: 35b.
56 Ibid., 35b, 36b.
57 Ibid., 36a.
58 Cited in Chen, "Opium," p. 428.
59 Cameron, *The Reform Movement*, p. 139.
60 Ibid., p. 149; Morse, p. 438; Chou, *Shu-hai*, 3: 52b.
61 Cameron, *The Reform Movement*, pp. 140–42.
62 Chen, "Opium," p. 422.
63 *HL*, no. 579, p. 650.
64 Ibid., pp. 650–51; Alexander Hosie, *On the Trail of the Opium Poppy*, 2: 272; S. A. M. Adshead, "The Opium Trade in Szechwan, 1881–1911," *Journal of Southeast Asian History* 7, no. 2 (September 1966): 93–99.
65 Hosie, *On the Trail*, p. 273; Wilkinson to Jordan, 20 September 1907, FO 228/2420.
66 W. H. Wilkinson, "Anti-Opium Regulations in Yunnan Province and their Observance," enclosed in Wilkinson to Jordan, 14 August 1907, FO 228/2420 (hereafter cited as Wilkinson, "Anti-Opium").
67 Wilton to Jordan, 17 August 1908, FO 228/2423.
68 *HL*, no. 757, p. 814.
69 Hosie, *On the Trail*, p. 274; Wilkinson, "Anti-Opium."
70 Cited in Chen, "Opium," p. 423.
71 *HL*, no. 699, p. 768; Wilkinson, "Anti-Opium."
72 Ottewill to Jordan, 31 May 1907, FO 228/2417.
73 Wilton to Jordan, 1 September, FO 228/2423.
74 *HL*, no. 699, p. 768; Ottewill to Jordan, 24 October 1907, FO 228/2421; Consul-General, "Memorandum: Opium Reports by Members of the China Inland Mission," enclosed in Consul-General to Jordan, 10 January 1908, FO 228/2422 (hereafter cited as Consul-General, "Memorandum").
75 Wilkinson, "Anti-Opium"; *HL*, no. 699, p. 768.
76 Wilkinson, "Anti-Opium"; Memorial of Governor-General Shen Ping-k'un, translated and enclosed in Rockhill to Secretary of State, 21 May 1909, U.S. Department of State, *Foreign Relations*, 1909, pp. 104–06.
77 Wilton, "Opium Report," enclosed in Wilton to Jordan, 17 August 1908, FO 228/2423 (hereafter cited as Wilton, "Opium Report").
78 *HL*, no. 699, p. 769; Wilton to Jordan, 8 January 1909, FO 228/1733.
79 *HL*, no. 699, p. 768.
80 Consul-General, "Memorandum."
81 Ibid.; Wilkinson to Jordan, 14 August 1907, FO 228/2420.
82 Consul-General, "Memorandum"; Ottewill to Jordan, 14 September 1907, FO 228/2420.
83 Ottewill to Jordan, 24 October 1907, FO 228/2421.
84 Wilkinson, "Anti-Opium."
85 *HL*, no. 699, p. 769.

86 Wilton, "Opium Report."
87 *HL*, no. 699, pp. 769–70.
88 *HL*, no. 699, p. 770; Wilton to Jordan, 17 August 1908, FO 228/2423.
89 Consul-General, "Memorandum."
90 Consul-General, "Memorandum"; Wilton to Jordan, 1 September 1908, FO 228/2423; Bourgeois to Ministère, 5 January 1909, MAE, Direction des Affaires Politiques et Consulaires, Chine, Questions Sociales, Opium, vol. 5 (hereafter cited as MAE, Opium).
91 Wilton to Jordan, 11 September 1908, FO 228/2423.
92 Wilton, "Opium Report"; Soulié to Ministère, 29 March 1908, 24 October 1908, MAE, Opium, vol. 4.
93 Wilton, "Opium Report for Period Ending December 31, 1908," enclosed in Wilton to Jordan, 12 January 1909, FO 228/2424 (hereafter cited as Wilton, "Opium Report for 1908").
94 Ibid.; Wilton to Jordan, 1 September 1908, FO 228/2423.
95 Wilton to Jordan, 1 September 1908, FO 228/2423.
96 Soulié, "La Prohibition de l'opium au Yunnan," enclosed in Bourgeois to Ministère, 24 October 1908, MAE, Opium, vol. 4 (hereafter cited as Soulié, "La Prohibition").
97 *HL*, no. 790, p. 840.
98 Bourgeois to Ministre, 22 June 1908, MAE, Chine, Mines, Yunnan, vol. 4.
99 *HL*, no. 757, pp. 814–15.
100 *NCH*, vol. 88, p. 496.
101 *HTSL*, 4: 23.
102 U.S., Department of State, *Foreign Relations*, 1909, pp. 104–06.
103 *NCH*, vol. 88, p. 475; vol. 89, pp. 21, 51, 142.
104 Wilton, "Opium Report for 1908."
105 Soulié, "La Prohibition."
106 Wilton, "Opium Report for 1908."
107 Wilton to Jordan, 1 September 1908, FO 228/2423.
108 Ibid.
109 Ottewill to Jordan, 24 July 1908, FO 228/2423.
110 *HL*, no. 579, p. 651.
111 Ch'ung Ch'ien, comp., *Ch'u-hsiung hsien-chih* [Local history of Ch'u-hsiung district], p. 106; *HTSL*, 5: 50; Bourgeois to Ministre, 5 January 1909, MAE, Opium, vol. 5.
112 Chung-kuo shih-hsüeh-hui, *Hsin hai ko-ming* [The revolution of 1911], comp. Ch'ai Te-keng, et al., vol. 3, pp. 488–89; *NCH*, vol. 90, p. 673; Wilton to Jordan, 11 January 1909, FO 228/1733.
113 Hosie, *On the Trail*, pp. 276–77; Morse, p. 438.
114 Leonard P. Adams II, "China: The Historical Setting of Asia's Profitable Plague," in Alfred McCoy (with Cathleen B. Read and Leonard P. Adams II) *The Politics of Heroin in Southeast Asia*, (New York: Harper & Row, 1972), pp. 376–83.
115 Hosie, *On the Trail*, pp. 276–77; U.S., Department of State, *Foreign Relations*, 1909, p. 105.
116 Cameron, *The Reform Movement*, p. 136.

117 Ibid., p. 158; Li, *Hsüeh-sheng*, 1: 13a.
118 An En-p'u, comp., *Chao-t'ung hsien-chih-kao* [Draft history of Chao-t'ung district], p. 187.
119 Hosie, *On the Trail*, p. 277.

Chapter 9

 1   Still using "native methods," it produced 80 percent of national output in the 1920s. Hsieh Hsiao-chung, *Yün-nan yu-chi* [Travels in Yunnan], in Shen Yün-lung, no. 9, pp. 119–20.
 2   E-tu Zen Sun, "Mining Labor in the Ch'ing Period," in Feuerwerker, *Approaches*, pp. 57–58, n. 37.
 3   Ting Chen-to to Wai-wu-pu, 13 January 1905, WWP, *Yün-nan Ko-Meng ch'ang-fei-t'u fen-chieh yang-kuan-an* [The case of the Ko(-chiu) and Meng(-tzu) factory bandits' burning and plundering the foreign customs in Yunnan].
 4   MacMurray, *Treaties and Agreements*, pp. 911–14; Chung-hua, *K'ai-kuo wen-hsien*, pien 1, ts'e 9, pp. 687–91.
 5   K. J. Frost to His Majesty's Secretary of State, 18 October 1906, FO 228/2640; *KWT*, p. 3284.
 6   *KWT*, pp. 3284–86.
 7   E-tu Zen Sun, "Ch'ing Government and the Mineral Industries before 1800," *Journal of Asian Studies* 27, no. 4 (August 1968): 838, n. 11; *NCH*, vol. 84, pp. 108, 291; vol. 90, p. 494.
 8   *KWT*, pp. 3288–89.
 9   Réau to Bapst, 3 January 1908, MAE, Chine, Mines, Yunnan, vol. 4.
10   *KWT*, pp. 3290–91.
11   *KWT*, pp. 3292, 3303, 3307; *KHSL*, 579: 11b–13a; Collins to Li Ching-hsi, May 1910, FO 228/2640.
12   *KWT*, pp. 3305–06.
13   Réau to Bapst, 3 January 1908, MAE, Chine, Mines, Yunnan, vol. 4.
14   *KWT*, p. 3305.
15   Réau to Bapst, 3 January 1908, MAE, Chine, Mines, Yunnan, vol. 4; *KWT*, p. 3306.
16   *KWT*, p. 3304; U.S., Department of State, *Foreign Relations*, 1909, p. 106; Lee, "China's Response," p. 66.
17   *KWT*, p. 3288.
18   *KWT*, p. 3310.
19   *KWT*, p. 3304.
20   Morse, pp. 90–91; annex to a letter from Peking, 11 June 1908, MAE, Chine, Industrie et Travaux Publics, Ligne du Yunnan, vol. 14 (hereafter cited as MAE, Ligne du Yunnan); Wilkinson to Jordan, 24 September 1907, FO 228/2638.
21   Company accounts, enclosed in Wilkinson to Jordan, 20 January 1908, FO 228/2638 (hereafter cited as "Accounts").
22   *HL*, no. 586, p. 663.
23   *HL*, no. 653, p. 717; Wilkinson to Chief Secretary, 5 August 1907, FO 228/2638.
24   Wilkinson to Chief Secretary, 20 January 1908, enclosed in Wilkinson to Jordan, 20 January 1908, FO 228/2638.
25   Ibid.; Wilkinson to Chief Secretary, 5 August 1907, FO 228/2638.

26 Translated and enclosed in Wilkinson to Jordan, 28 September 1907, FO 228/2638.

27 "Accounts"; *NCH*, vol. 83, p. 713; Wilkinson to Chief Secretary, 5 August 1907, FO 228/2638; *HL*, no. 741, pp. 802–03; Hsien-cheng pien-ch'a-kuan, *Cheng-chih kuan-pao*, vol. 5, p. 223.

28 *HL*, no. 735, p. 797.

29 Translated and annexed to Consulat de Canton to Department, 14 January 1908, MAE, Ligne du Yunnan, vol. 14.

30 Ibid.

31 Ottewill to Jordan, 3 November 1907, 23 November 1907, FO 228/2638.

32 Translated and enclosed in Wilkinson to Jordan, 28 September 1907, FO 228/2638.

33 Ottewill to Jordan, 23 November 1907, FO 228/2638; Wilkinson to Jordan, 28 September 1907, 19 October 1907, FO 228/2638.

34 *HL*, no. 735, p. 796. Estimates of the amount raised ranged between 700,000 and 8,000,000 tls. Intelligence Report, 30 June 1909, enclosed in Wilton to Jordan, 7 July 1909, FO 228/1733; Bourgeois to Pichon, 26 August 1908, MAE, Ligne du Yunnan, vol. 15; Johnson, "China's 1911 Revolution in Yunnan," p. 97.

35 *HL*, no. 735, p. 797.

36 Intelligence Report in Wilton to Jordan, 8 January 1909, FO 228/1733.

37 Ibid.; *HL*, no. 735, p. 797; Bourgeois to Ministre, 17 January 1909, MAE, Ligne de Sseu-tch'ouan, vol. 4.

38 Ottewill to Jordan, 19 October 1908, FO 228/2638; Bapst to Pichon, 29 February 1908, MAE, Ligne du Yunnan, vol. 14.

39 Litton to Foreign Office, 4 February 1905, FO 17/1680; Wilkinson to Jordan, 13 September 1907, FO 228/2638; Hsi-liang to Wilkinson, 23 September 1907, FO 228/2638.

40 Wilkinson to Jordan, 28 September 1907, FO 228/2638.

41 Arnould, "Rapport sur le chemin de fer du Sseu-tch'ouan-Yunnan-fou" (2 December 1907), MAE, Chine, Chemins de fer, Lignes de Sseu-tch'ouan, vol. 4 (hereafter cited as Arnould, "Rapport").

42 Chung-kuo k'o-hsüeh-yüan, *Yün-nan Kuei-chou*, pp. 10–11; Ottewill to Jordan, 25 April 1907, FO 228/2638.

43 Arnould, "Rapport"; *NCH*, vol. 85, pp. 288, 466, 591; vol. 86, p. 521; *HL*, no. 777, p. 832; Wilkinson to Chief Secretary, 15 January 1908, enclosed in Wilkinson to Jordan, 20 January 1908, FO 228/1696; Sly to Jordan, 11 May 1908, FO 228/1696.

44 Note by Réau, 7 August 1907, MAE, Ligne du Yunnan, vol. 13; annex to letter from Peking, 6 November 1908, MAE, Ligne du Yunnan, vol. 14.

45 [Illegible] to Ministre des Colonies, 29 May 1908, MAE, Ligne du Yunnan, vol. 14; Bapst to Pichon, 27 August 1908, MAE, Ligne du Yunnan, vol. 15; Wilkinson to Jordan, 22 April 1908, FO 228/1696.

46 Dépêche Coloniale, 28 February 1908, MAE, Ligne du Yunnan, vol. 14; Extract from *Chou Min Hsin Pao*, 20 July 1908, translated in MAE, Ligne du Yunnan, vol. 15; [Illegible] to Ministre des Colonies, 29 May 1908, MAE, Ligne du Yunnan, vol. 14; Vice-Consul to Ministre, 24 April 1908, MAE, Ligne du Yunnan, vol. 14.

47 Bapst to Pichon, 28 January 1909, MAE, Ligne du Yunnan, vol. 15; Boissonas to Pichon, 15 February 1909, MAE, Ligne du Yunnan, vol. 15. The French finished the line in 1910. Sénat no. 23, MAE, Ligne du Yunnan, vol. 15; Morse, p. 91.

48 Chang Ta-i, "T'ung-meng-hui Yün-nan fen-pu chih ch'eng-li chi ch'i huo-tung" [The founding of the Yunnan branch of the revolutionary alliance and its activities], in Chung-hua, K'ai-kuo wen-hsien, pien 1, ts'e 12, p. 130. For general accounts of the founding of the Alliance, see Hsüeh, Huang Hsing, chap. 4; Schiffrin, Sun Yat-sen, chap. 12. Most numbers of Yunnan Miscellany have been reprinted in Chung-kuo k'o-hsüeh-yüan, Yün-nan tsa-chih hsüan-chi [Selections from Yunnan Miscellany].

49 Yang Ta-chu, "Yün-nan ko-ming hsiao-shih" [A brief history of the revolution in Yunnan], in Chung-hua, K'ai-kuo wen-hsien, pien 1, ts'e 12, p. 123.

50 Chang, "T'ung-meng-hui Yün-nan fen-pu," pp. 130–31.

51 Lü Chih-i, "Yang Chen-hung shih-lüeh" [Biography of Yang Chen-hung], in Chung-hua, K'ai-kuo wen-hsien, pien 1, ts'e 12, p. 144; Yang, "Yün-nan ko-ming," p. 123.

52 Lü, "Yang Chen-hung," p. 144; Yang, "Yün-nan ko-ming," p. 123; Chang, "T'ung-meng-hui Yün-nan fen-pu," p. 131.

53 Yang, "Yün-nan ko-ming," pp. 123–24; Chang, "T'ung-meng-hui Yün-nan fen-pu," p. 132.

54 Chung-kuo K'o-hsüeh-yüan, Yün-nan Kuei-chou, p. 80; HL, no. 604, p. 678.

55 Chang, "T'ung-meng-hui Yün-nan fen-pu," pp. 132–33; Wilton to Jordan, 8 January 1909, FO 228/1733.

56 HL, no. 660, p. 724; Chung-kuo k'o-hsüeh-yüan, Yün-nan Kuei-chou, p. 80.

57 HL, no. 632, p. 702; no. 660, pp. 725–27; no. 816, pp. 869–73; Department of Foreign Affairs to Wilkinson, 18 June 1907, FO 228/1665; Wilton to Jordan, 8 January 1909, FO 228/1733.

58 HL, no. 695, p. 764; Wu Cho-ju et al., comps., Hsin-p'ing hsien-chih [A history of Hsin-p'ing district], p. 143.

59 Ottewill to Jordan, 5 November 1907, FO 228/1669; HL, no. 720, p. 786.

60 Miu, Hsüan-wei hsien-chih kao, p. 801; Chang, "T'ung-meng-hui Yün-nan fen-pu," p. 133.

61 Tsou Lu, "T'ung-meng-hui Yün-nan chih-pu chih huo-tung" [The activities of the Yunnan branch of the revolutionary alliance], in Chung-hua, K'ai-kuo wen-hsien, pien 1, ts'e 12, p. 128.

Chapter 10

1 Lü, "Yang Chen-hung," p. 144; Yang, "Yün-nan ko-ming," p. 124; Chang, "T'ung-meng-hui Yün-nan fen-pu," p. 132; Ottewill to Jordan, 25 April 1907, FO 228/1669; Ottewill to Wilkinson, 17 May 1907, FO 228/1669.

2 Lü, "Yang Chen-hung," p. 144; Wilton to Jordan, 31 July 1907, FO 228/1669.

3 HL, no. 646, p. 712; Wilton to Jordan, 31 July 1907, FO 228/1669; Yang, "Yün-nan ko-ming," p. 124.

4 Memorandum of conversation between Shih Hung-shao and the Chinese writer, 18 September 1907, FO 228/1665.

5 KHSL, 579: 11b–13a; Wilton to Jordan, 31 July 1907, FO 228/1669; Wilkinson to Jordan, 26 October 1907, FO 228/1665.

6   *HL*, no. 663, p. 732; Ottewill to Jordan, 5 November 1907, FO 228/1669.

7   *KHSL*, 579: 9b; Ottewill to Jordan, 20 June 1908, FO 228/1700.

8   For a map of these states, see Yao Wen-tung, *Yün-nan k'an-chieh ch'ou-pien chi* [A record of border demarcation and frontier policy in Yunnan], in Shen Yün-lung, no. 179.

9   *HL*, no. 718, p. 784.

10 For the Shan, see Wiens, *China's March*, p. 300.

11 Wang Tu, "Tiao An-jen chuan" [Biography of Tiao An-jen], in Chung-hua, *K'ai-kuo wen-hsien*, pien 1, ts'e 12, p. 139.

12 Feng Tzu-yu, *Ko-ming i-shih* [Reminiscences of the revolution], 1: 90–91; 2: 249.

13 Ibid., 1: 90; Wang, "Tiao An-jen chuan," p. 139; "The Conditions and Circumstances of Japanese at Kangai," enclosed in Rose to Jordan, 15 April 1909, FO 228/1733. For a biography of one of these advisers, see Marius B. Jansen, "Oi Kentaro (1843–1922): Radicalism and Chauvinism," *Far Eastern Quarterly* 2, no. 3 (May 1952): 305–16.

14 Ottewill to Jordan, 4 September 1908, FO 228/1700; "The Conditions and Circumstances of Japanese at Kangai."

15 Ottewill to Jordan, 5 September 1908, 15 September 1908, FO 228/1700.

16 *HL*, no. 773, p. 828.

17 Rose to Jordan, 21 February 1909, FO 228/1733.

18 Ottewill to Jordan, 19 February 1908, FO 228/1700; Wilton to Jordan, 29 March 1909, FO 228/1733.

19 *HL*, no. 773, p. 828.

20 Ottewill to Jordan, 4 September 1908; Ottewill to Chief Secretary, June 1908, FO 228/1700.

21 Ottewill to Jordan, 19 February 1908, FO 228/1700.

22 Intelligence Report, enclosed in Ottewill to Jordan, March 1908, FO 228/1700; Ottewill to Jordan, 29 July 1908, FO 228/1700.

23 *HL*, no. 619, p. 692; Ottewill to Jordan, 4 September 1908, FO 228/1700.

24 *KHSL*, 594: 4b–5a; *HL*, no. 773, p. 827.

25 *HL*, no. 773, pp. 828–29.

26 Ibid.

27 Ibid.

28 *HL*, no. 805, p. 860; no. 824, p. 880.

29 Wilton to Jordan, 26 February 1909, FO 228/1733.

30 Chang, "T'ung-meng-hui Yün-nan fen-pu," p. 135.

31 Tsou, "Yün-nan chih pu chih huo-tung," p. 129; Ottewill to Jordan, 29 October 1908, FO 228/1700.

32 Tsou, "Yün-nan chih pu chih huo-tung," p. 129.

33 Ibid.; Lü, "Yang Chen-hung," p. 147.

34 Feng, *Ko-ming i-shih*, 2: 259; Johnson, "China's 1911 Revolution in Yunnan and Kweichow," p. 100.

35 Hsüeh, *Huang Hsing*, pp. 56–57, 65–70.

36 Feng, *Ko-ming i-shih*, 2: 216–21.

37 Chung-hua, *K'ai-kuo wen-hsien*, pien 1, ts'e 13, p. 390.

38 Department, 30 December 1907, MAE, Chine, Politique Extérieure, Relations

avec la France, Yunnan, vol. 11 (hereafter cited as MAE, Relations avec la France, Yunnan).

39 WWP, *Chung-Fa Yüeh-nan chiao-she tang, Yin-tu ko-ping Liang Hsiu-ch'un an* [Archives of Sino-French diplomacy concerning Vietnam, the extradition case of Liang Hsiu-ch'un].

40 Bourgeois to Pichon, 4 February 1909, MAE, Relations avec la France, Yunnan, vol. 14.

41 See *Chung-hsing jih-pao* [The China Arise Gazette], in Chung-hua, *K'ai-kuo wen hsien*, pien 1, ts'e 13, pp. 426–30.

42 Sly to Jordan, 13 May 1908, FO 228/2639.

43 Délégué to Ministre, 31 December 1907, MAE, Chine, Mines, Yunnan, vol. 4.

44 Soulié to Direction Politique, 8 May 1908, MAE, Chine, Politique Intérieure, Dossier Général, vol. 13 (hereafter cited as MAE, Dossier Général).

45 Ibid.; Feng, *Ko-ming i-shih*, 5: 226.

46 Chung-hua, *K'ai-kuo wen-hsien*, pien 1, ts'e 13, pp. 388–90, 398, 404; Feng, *Ko-ming i-shih*, 5: 227.

47 Carlisle to Secretary of State for Foreign Affairs, 8 May 1908, FO 228/2639; Chung-hua, *K'ai-kuo wen-hsien*, pien 1, ts'e 13, p. 388.

48 Chung-hua, *K'ai-kuo wen-hsien*, pien 1, ts'e 13, p. 411. While the original document included the word "socialism" (*she-hui chu-i*), a more recent Kuomintang copy used the word "social" (*she-hui*). Ibid., pp. 391–92.

49 Carlisle to Secretary of State, 13 May 1908, FO 228/2639; Soulié to Direction Politique, 8 May 1908, MAE, Dossier Général, vol. 13; Chung-hua, *K'ai-kuo wen-hsien*, pien 1, ts'e 13, p. 400; Soulié to Direction Politique, MAE, Dossier Général, vol. 13.

50 Chung-hua, *K'ai-kuo wen-hsien*, pien 1, ts'e 13, p. 400.

51 Ibid., p. 389.

52 *London and China Telegraph*, 16 June 1908, MAE, Dossier Général, vol. 13; Hsüeh, *Huang Hsing*, p. 70.

53 "Ho-k'ou ch'i-i," in Chung-kuo shih-hsüeh-hui, *Hsin-hai ko-ming*, vol. 3, p. 269.

54 *HL*, no. 803, p. 849.

55 "Ho-k'ou ch'i-i," p. 270.

56 Ibid., p. 272.

57 Hen Hai, "Yün-nan ko-ming-chün chih chan-chieh" [The victories of the Yunnan revolutionary army], Chung-hua, *K'ai-kuo wen-hsien*, pien 1, ts'e 13, p. 412.

58 "Ho-k'ou ch'i-i," pp. 270–71, 274–75, 278–79.

59 Ibid., pp. 269, 271–74, 276–78.

60 *Chung-hsing jih-pao*, in Chung-hua, *K'ai-kuo wen-hsien*, pien 1, ts'e 13, p. 412.

61 "Ho-k'ou ch'i-i," p. 282.

62 Chung-hua, *K'ai-kuo wen-hsien*, pien 1, ts'e 13, p. 400.

63 Ibid., p. 393.

64 Ibid., pp. 389, 392, 399.

65 Carlisle to Secretary of State, 13 May 1908, FO 228/2639.

66 Réau to Bapst, 27 May 1908, MAE, Chine, Industrie et Travaux Publics, Chemin de Fer, Yunnan, vol. 14.

67 "Ho-k'ou ch'i-i," p. 280; Vasselle to Gouverneur-Général, 7 May 1908; Bonheure

to Ministre des Colonies, 10 May 1908; Bonheure to Ministère, 15 May 1908; Réau to Ministre, 21 May 1908, MAE, Relations avec la France, Yunnan, vol. 11.

68 "Ho-k'ou ch'i-i," p. 292.
69 Weiss to Renault, 14 May 1908, MAE, Relations avec la France, Yunnan, vol. 11.
70 Chung-hua, K'ai-kuo wen-hsien, pien 1, ts'e 13, p. 404; Feng, Ko-ming i-shih, 5: 225.
71 Chung-hua, K'ai-kuo wen-hsien, pien 1, ts'e 13, p. 398; Feng, Ko-ming i-shih, 5: 225.
72 Hsüeh, Huang Hsing, p. 71.
73 "Ho-k'ou ch'i-i," p. 273; Chung-hua, K'ai-kuo wen-hsien, pien 1, ts'e 13, p. 396.
74 "Ho-k'ou ch'i-i," p. 285.
75 Ibid., pp. 274–75, 278–81, 283, 287, 290.
76 Ibid., pp. 278–79; Sly to Jordan, 13 May 1908, FO 223/2639; Chung-hua, K'ai-kuo wen-hsien, pien 1, ts'e 13, p. 389.
77 "Ho-k'ou ch'i-i," pp. 274–75, 290–91, 293, 297, 300, 310–11; HL, no. 723, p. 787; NCH, vol. 87, p. 478.
78 Chung-hua, K'ai-kuo wen-hsien, pien 1, ts'e 13, p. 384.
79 Yang, "Yün-nan ko-ming," p. 125; Chang, "T'ung-meng-hui Yün-nan fen-pu," p. 132; Tsou, "Yün-nan chih pu chih huo-tung," p. 128; Chung-kuo jen-min, Hsin-hai ko-ming hui-i-lu, vol. 3, p. 481.
80 Ambassador in Tokyo to Pichon, 28 May 1908, MAE, Relations avec la France, Yunnan, vol. 11; Chang, "T'ung-meng-hui Yün-nan fen-pu," p. 133.
81 Ta-t'ung jih-pao, 10 May 1908, enclosed in MAE, Dossier Général, vol. 13; China Mail, Hong Kong Telegraph, South China Morning Post, enclosed in Liébert to Ministre, 17 May 1908, Relations avec la France, Yunnan, vol. 12; NCH, vol. 87, p. 446.
82 Chang, "T'ung-meng-hui Yün-nan fen-pu," pp. 133–34; Chung-hsing jih-pao, in Chung-hua, K'ai-kuo wen-hsien, pien 1, ts'e 13, pp. 147–49.
83 Chung-hua, K'ai-kuo wen-hsien, pien 1, ts'e 13, pp. 147–49.
84 Chang, "T'ung-meng-hui Yün-nan fen-pu," pp. 133–34; Chung-hua, K'ai-ku wen-hsien, pien 1, ts'e 13, pp. 147–49; Ambassador in Tokyo to Pichon, 28 May 1908, MAE, Relations avec la France, Yunnan, vol. 11.
85 Lü, "Yang Chen-hung," p. 145.
86 Chung-hua, K'ai-kuo wen-hsien, pien 1, ts'e 13, p. 413; Wang, "Tiao An-jen chuan," p. 139.
87 For later conflict between the Shan and the Alliance, see Wang, "Tiao An-jen chuan," pp. 139–40; Johnson, "China's 1911 Revolution in Yunnan," pp. 102–06.
88 HL, no. 676, p. 745. For O-erh-t'ai's programs, see Kent C. Smith, "Ch'ing Policy and the Development of Southwest China: Aspects of O-erh-t'ai's Governor-Generalship, 1726–1731" (Ph.D. diss., Yale University, 1970), chap. 3 (cited with the author's permission).
89 Chung-yang jih-pao, 16 May 1908, in MAE, Dossier Général, vol. 13.
90 "Ho-k'ou ch'i-i," pp. 299–300, 306. For San-Meng, see Wiens, China's March, p. 311; Hsieh, Yün-nan, pp. 263–64; Yao, Yün-nan k'an-chieh, pp. 5–6.
91 Feng, Ko-ming i-shih, 2: 218–19; Chung-kuo jen-min, Hsin-hai ko-ming hui-i-lu, vol. 3, p. 471.
92 London and China Telegraph, 16 June 1908, MAE, Dossier Général, vol. 12.

93 Feng, *Ko-ming i-shih*, 2: 217; 5: 225–26; Chung-hua, *K'ai-kuo wen-hsien*, pien 1, ts'e 13, p. 402.

94 Lapeyrouie to Résident Supérieur de Laos, 10 March 1908, MAE, Relations avec la France, Yunnan, vol. 12.

95 Chung-hua, *K'ai-kuo wen-hsien*, p. 394.

96 "Ho-k'ou ch'i-i," pp. 285, 290–91.

97 Ibid., pp. 282, 302–03, 306–07; *NCH*, vol. 87, p. 546; Chung-hua, *K'ai-kuo wen-hsien*, pien 1, ts'e 13, p. 394; Carlisle to Secretary of State, 27 May 1908, FO 228/2639.

98 Hsi-liang to Bourgeois, 8 June 1908, MAE, Relations avec la France, Yunnan, vol. 12.

99 Ibid.; *HL*, no. 767, p. 822.

100 *Shun-t'ien jih-pao*, 11 August 1908, enclosed in MAE, Relations avec la France, Yunnan, vol. 13.

101 Note for the Minister in Peking, 8 June 1908, MAE, Relations avec la France, Yunnan, vol. 12.

102 Ibid.

103 *Shun-t'ien jih-pao*, 4 July 1908; Gerery to Pichon, 27 June 1908; Liu to Pichon, 27 June 1908, MAE, Relations avec la France, Yunnan, vols. 12, 13.

104 *Pei-ching jih-pao*, 1 July 1908; *Shun-t'ien jih-pao*, 23 June 1908; *Chung-yang jih-pao* 28 June 1908, MAE, Relations avec la France, Yunnan, vols. 12, 13.

105 *Ling-hai-pao*, 9 July 1908; *Pei-ching jih-pao*, 7 July 1908, MAE, Relations avec la France, Yunnan, vol. 13; *NCH*, vol. 88, p. 170; *Chung-yang jih-pao*, 26 June 1908, MAE, Relations avec la France, Yunnan, vol. 13.

106 Adee to Rockhill, 15 August 1908, United States National Archives, Records of the Department of State, Foreign Affairs Division, China, 15076/494; Grey to Minister, 18 June 1908, FO 228/2639.

107 Pichon to Ministre, 11 June 1908, Bapst to Ch'ing, 24 June 1908, Bonheure to Colonies, 4 July 1908, *Matin*, 9 July 1908, Pichon to Colonies, 16 July 1908, Ministère to Ministre, 29 July 1908, Bapst to Ch'ing, 19 August 1908, Pichon to Ministère des Colonies, 5 September 1908, Pichon to Bapst, 3 October 1908, Ch'ing to Bapst, 1 November 1908, *Times*, 16 January 1909, MAE, Relations avec la France, Yunnan, vols. 12–14; Note for Ministre, 5 March 1909, MAE, Ligne du Yunnan, vol. 15.

108 *NCH*, vol. 88, p. 92.

Chapter 11

1 Shen Yün-lung, "Hsü Shih-ch'ang p'ing-chuan" [A critical biography of Hsü Shih-ch'ang], in *Chuan-chi wen-hsüeh* [Biographical literature], vol. 14, no. 5, p. 59.

2 *NCH*, vol. 90, pp. 62, 410, 688, 754.

3 Wilton to Jordan, 25 February 1909, FO 228/1733; *HL*, no. 828, p. 883.

4 *HL*, no. 398, p. 431.

5 Ibid., pp. 430–31.

6 MacMurray, *Treaties and Agreements*, pp. 549–55; C. Walter Young, *The International Relations of Manchuria*, pp. 49–53.

7 Shen, "Hsü Shih-ch'ang," vol. 13, no. 6, p. 60.

8   Ning Wu, "Tung-pei hsin-hai ko-ming chien-shu" [A description of the 1911 revolution in the northeast], in Chung-kuo jen-min, *Hsin-hai ko-ming hui-i-lu*, vol. 5, p. 540.
9   MacMurray, *Treaties and Agreements*, pp. 552, 791.
10 *CCWCSLHT*, 4:6–9a.
11 Ibid., 4: 13b–14a, 22b; 5: 12–13a, 14–15; 6: 4b–5.
12 Ibid., 6: 28b–29; Hsu Shuhsi, *China and Her Political Entity*, pp. 321–22.
13 *CCWCSLHT*, 5: 6a, 36, 39b, 40–41a; 6: 32b–35; MacMurray, *Treaties and Agreements*, pp. 790–98.
14 *CCWCSLHT*, 7: 1–2a.
15 Ibid., 5: 33–35, 43b–44; 6: 37–41; 8: 7b–11a, 40–47; MacMurray, *Treaties and Agreements*, pp. 790–91; 796–97.
16 *CCWCSLHT*, 8: 33–34a.
17 *NCH*, vol. 92, p. 419.
18 Fei, *Chin-tai*, p. 233; Shen, "Hsü Shih-ch'ang," vol. 15, no. 5, p. 59; *NCH*, vol. 92, pp. 477, 500.
19 Ts'ao Ju-lin, *I-sheng chih hui-i* [Memoirs of a life], pp. 80–81.
20 Chang Mu-an, "Chi-lin chiu-wen hui-i-lu" [Memoir of things heard long ago in Chi-lin], in Chung-kuo jen-min, *Hsin-hai ko-ming hui-i-lu*, vol. 5, pp. 573–75.
21 *CCWCSLHT*, 4: 33.
22 *NCH*, vol. 92, pp. 515, 543.
23 *CCWCSLHT*, 8: 19, 47–48.
24 Ibid.; Chung-kuo k'o-hsüeh-yüan, comp., *Chin-tai tung-pei jen-min ko-ming yün-tung shih* [A history of the recent revolutionary movement of the people of the northeast], p. 183; *NCH*, vol. 92, pp. 563, 602, 645, 666, 667, 703, 710, 722; vol. 93, pp. 50, 77, 78, 247.
25 *Tung-fang*, vol. 7, no. 6, fu-lu ti-ssu, p. 25.
26 *CCWCSLHT*, 10: 4b–7a.
27 Ibid., 10: 7.
28 Ibid., 10: 7b–8a.
29 Ibid., 8: 36; 9: 32b–33; 14: 1–2a; 19: 5b–6a; Ts'ao, *I-sheng*, pp. 83–84; *HL*, no. 906, p. 973; no. 997, pp. 1087–88; MacMurray, *Treaties and Agreements*, pp. 788–89.
30 *CCWCSLHT*, 18: 23b–25a; Shen, "Hsü Shih-ch'ang," vol. 14, no. 1, pp. 66–67.
31 *KWT*, vol. 6, pp. 3745, 3755, 3785.
32 *CCWCSLHT*, 7: 44b; MacMurray, *Treaties and Agreements*, pp. 793–95.
33 Ts'ao, *I-sheng*, p. 84.
34 Shen, "Hsü Shih-ch'ang," vol. 14, no. 3, p. 79; *HL*, no. 1021, p. 1117; no. 1065, pp. 1163–64.
35 *HTSL*, 17: 3b–5.
36 *HL*, no. 830, pp. 884–86; *Sheng-ching shih-pao* [Mukden Times], no. 777, p. 5 (hereafter cited as *Sheng-ching*); *HTSL*, 15: 18b–19.
37 *HL*, no. 918, pp. 983–85; no. 995, pp. 1084–85.
38 *HL*, no. 852, pp. 905–06.
39 Robert L. Irick, "The Chinchow-Aigun Railroad and the Knox Neutralization Plan in Ch'ing Diplomacy," *Harvard Papers*, vol. 13, p. 83.
40 *CCWCSLHT*, 3: 17b–18; *HTSL*, 11: 31.

41 *HL*, no. 837, pp. 890–91; no. 841, pp. 893–94; Sun, *Chinese Railways*, p. 151.
42 *HL*, no. 867, pp. 928–30.
43 *HL*, no. 898, p. 959.
44 Irick, "The Chinchow-Aigun," p. 84; *HTSL*, 10: 50. For background on Hsü's efforts and plans, see Michael H. Hunt, "Frontier Defense and the Open Door: Manchuria in Chinese-American Relations, 1895–1911" (Ph.D. diss., Yale University, 1971), pp. 147–218, 237–39 (cited with the author's permission).
45 The Kirinese had raised 1.7 million tls., but the Fengtienese were unable to raise 2 million tls. for a short commercial line. *Sheng-ching*, no. 766, p. 5.
46 *NCH*, vol. 89, p. 339; cf. *HL*, p. 2.
47 *HL*, no. 889, p. 950.
48 Herbert Croly, *Willard Straight*, pp. 303–05; *HL*, no. 898, pp. 959–62; MacMurray, *Treaties and Agreements*, pp. 800–02; see also Hunt, "Frontier Defense and the Open Door," pp. 241–42.
49 *HL*, no. 898, pp. 959–60; *HTSL*, 20: 4.
50 *HL*, no. 898, p. 960; *CCWCSLHT*, 7: 48a; 9: 34b.
51 MacMurray, *Treaties and Agreements*, pp. 800–02, articles 5, 6.
52 *NCH*, vol. 92, pp. 441, 483; vol. 93, pp. 179, 460.
53 *NCH*, vol. 92, p. 666; Irick, "The Chinchow-Aigun," pp. 90–91; *HTSL*, 20: 4b.
54 Irick, "The Chinchow-Aigun," p. 88.
55 Ts'ao, *I-sheng*, p. 84.
56 Shen, "Hsü Shih-ch'ang," vol. 14, no. 5, pp. 55–56.
57 *NCH*, vol. 92, p. 270; vol. 94, p. 35; Irick, "The Chinchow-Aigun," pp. 94, 98, 110; Hsu, *China*, p. 339.
58 Irick, "The Chinchow-Aigun," p. 98; Shen, "Hsü Shih-ch'ang," vol. 14, no. 5, pp. 55–56.
59 See map 4 in this book; Stephen R. MacKinnon, "Liang Shih-i and the Communications Clique," *Journal of Asian Studies* 29, no. 3 (May 1970): 581–91.
60 Feng Kang, ed., *San-shui Liang Yen-sun hsien-sheng nien-p'u* [Chronological biography of Liang Yen-sun], 1: 86–87; for Liang's bias against Hsi-liang, see Ibid., p. 86; cf. Chin-liang, *Kuang-Hsüan*, pp. 135–38. Liang's successor favored the Chin-ai, Sheng, *Yü-chai*, 75: 13; 76: 6a–7b.
61 *CCWCSLHT*, 10: 42–44. For further documentation on the ministries' debate over the Chin-ai, see Hunt, "Frontier Defense and the Open Door," pp. 243–45.
62 Shen, "Hsü Shih-ch'ang," vol. 14, no. 5, p. 59; Irick, "The Chinchow-Aigun," pp. 97–98.
63 *HL*, no. 934, pp. 1006–08; no. 936, pp. 1009–10; no. 1045, p. 1140; no. 1098, pp. 1203–04.
64 Willard Straight Diary, 20 December 1909, p. 42, Willard Straight Papers, Olin Library, Cornell University (hereafter cited as Straight Papers).
65 *HL*, no. 935, pp. 1008–09.
66 Irick, "The Chinchow-Aigun," pp. 96, 98; *CCWCSLHT*, 12: 19–21, 24, 28a, 35b–36.
67 Sun, *Chinese Railways*, pp. 151–52.
68 *CCWCSLHT*, 10: 4b.
69 Ibid., 12: 47; Sun, *Chinese Railways*, p. 160.

70   Charles Chia-hwai Chu, "The China Policy of the Taft-Knox Administration, 1909–1913" (Ph.D. diss., University of Chicago, 1956), pp. 188, 205–06. For a slightly different interpretation of American failings, see Hunt, "Frontier Defense and the Open Door," pp. 255–61.

71   *CCWCSLHT*, 13: 34b–35.

72   Ibid., 14: 16b–17; see also Hunt, "Frontier Defense and the Open Door," p. 280.

73   Sun, *Chinese Railways*, pp. 162–63; E. B. Price, *The Russo-Japanese Treaties of 1907–1916 Concerning Manchuria and Mongolia*, pp. 42–43.

74   Chu, "The China Policy," p. 221; *CCWCSLHT*, 15: 33.

75   Chu, "The China Policy," p. 226.

76   *CCWCSLHT*, 15: 16a, 18.

77   *HL*, no. 1086, p. 1184.

78   *HL*, no. 1099, pp. 1204–06; *Tung-fang*, vol. 7, no. 9, chi-tsai, 3, pp. 237–39.

79   Chu, "The China Policy," pp. 257, 262, 264, 268; *CCWCSLHT*, 16: 32–34; Straight to Fischer, 19 December 1910, Straight Correspondence, Straight Papers; MacMurray, *Treaties and Agreements*, p. 851; see also Hunt, "Frontier Defense and the Open Door," p. 283.

80   Chu, "The China Policy," chap. 4, 5: Morse, p. 99; see also Hunt, "Frontier Defense and the Open Door," pp. 287–88, 290–92.

81   Chu, "The China Policy," p. 126; Fletcher to Cloud, 30 September 1909, United States National Archives, Records of the Department of State, Mukden Post Records, Legation to Mukden (1908–09).

82   *HL*, no. 994, pp. 1083–84; *KWT*, vol. 6, p. 3946.

83   Owen Lattimore, *The Mongols of Manchuria*, map facing title page.

84   Hsü Shih-ch'ang, *Tung-san-sheng cheng-lüeh* [The administration of the three eastern provinces], 2: hsia, 41–44, 45–62a, 77–83a.

85   *HL*, no. 988, p. 1074.

86   *CCWCSLHT*, 5: 15b–16a.

87   *HL*, no. 919, pp. 985–86.

88   *HL*, no. 1125, p. 1238; no. 1135, p. 1253.

89   *HL*, no. 970, p. 1053.

90   Ibid.

91   *HL*, no. 919, p. 985.

92   *HL*, no. 970, pp. 1053–54.

93   *HL*, no. 988, p. 1074.

94   Ibid.

95   Hsü, *Tung-san-sheng*, 2: shang, 17–18; 84–85a; *HL*, no. 937, p. 1010.

96   Lattimore, *The Mongols*, pp. 206–07; Hsü, *Tung-san-sheng*, 2: shang, 6–7a, 36–44b; *HL*, no. 850, pp. 901–04; nos. 1017, 1018, 1019.

97   Chung-kuo k'o-hsüeh-yüan, *Chin-tai tung-pei*, p. 175.

98   *HL*, no. 879, p. 943; no. 951, pp. 1032–33; no. 953, pp. 1034–37; *Sheng-ching*, no. 767, p. 3; no. 769, p. 5.

99   *CCWCSLHT*, 17: 28–30; Chung-kuo k'o-hsüeh-yüan, *Chin-tai tung-pei*, p. 177.

100 Robert H. G. Lee, *The Manchurian Frontier in Ch'ing History*, pp. 123, 137.

101 Lattimore, *The Mongols*, pp. 86–87.

102 *HTSL*, 10: 50b–51a; 18: 2b–6a.

103   *HL*, no. 979, p. 1062; Lee, *The Manchurian Frontier*, p. 122; Lattimore, *The Mongols*, p. 119.

104   *Feng-t'ien tzu-i-chü ti-i-tz'u pao-kao shu* [Report of the first session of the Fengtien provincial assembly], 3: 43–49; *HL*, no. 1050, pp. 1144–46; no. 1123, p. 1236; Lattimore, *The Mongols*, p. 125.

105   Hsü, *Tung-san-sheng*, 2: shang, 10–11a, 45–61; *HL*, no. 979, pp. 1062–64; no. 1108, p. 1216; Lattimore, *The Mongols*, pp. 119–20.

Chapter 12

  1   *NCH*, vol. 96, pp. 777–78; Shen, "Hsü Shih-ch'ang," vol. 14, no. 5, p. 59; Ts'ao, *I-sheng*, p. 85; Chin-liang, *Kuang-Hsüan*, p. 112.
  2   Chin-liang, *Kuang-Hsüan*, p. 92; *NCH*, vol. 95, p. 39.
  3   *Tung-fang*, vol. 7, no. 4, wen-chien, 1, p. 49; Fei, *Chin-tai*, p. 82.
  4   Shen, "Hsü Shih-ch'ang," vol. 14, no. 5, p. 59; *NCH*, vol. 92, p. 601.
  5   Shen, "Hsü Shih-ch'ang," vol. 14, no. 5, p. 59.
  6   *NCH*, vol. 95, p. 59.
  7   *HL*, no. 1031, pp. 1126–27.
  8   *NCH*, vol. 96, pp. 7, 384; Shen, "Hsü Shih-ch'ang," vol. 14, no. 5, p. 59.
  9   Wang, *The Chinese Intellectuals*, p. 255.
 10   *NCH*, vol. 95, p. 418.
 11   Shen, "Hsü Shih-ch'ang," vol. 14, no. 5, p. 59; BH, nos. 369a, 818; *HL*, no. 874, pp. 935–36; no. 1182, p. 1306; no. 1206, p. 1336; Bertaud to Pichon, 31 August 1910, MAE, Chine, Politique Intérieure, Manchourie, vol. 1; *NCH*, vol. 96.
 12   Shen Nai-cheng, "Ch'ing-mo chih tu-fu chi-ch'üan, chung-yang chi-ch'üan, yü 't'ung-shu pan-kung' " [The concentration of authority in the governors-general and governors, the centralization of authority and the institution of "All affairs in one office" during the late Ch'ing], *She-hui k'o-hsüeh* [Social Science] 2 (1937): 311–41.
 13   Lee, *The Manchurian Frontier*, pp. 151, 155; Shen, "Hsü Shih-ch'ang," vol. 13, no. 4, p. 34; vol. 14, no. 3, p. 78.
 14   *HL*, no. 854, p. 914.
 15   *HL*, no. 1031, p. 1127.
 16   Chung-kuo k'o-hsüeh-yüan, *Chin-tai tung-pei*, p. 198; Hsüeh, *Huang Hsing*, pp. 72–74.
 17   Feng Tzu-yu, *Chung-hua min-kuo k'ai-kuo ch'ien ko-ming-shih* [The history of the revolution prior to the founding of the Chinese republic], 3: 141; *HL*, no. 1129, pp. 1242–46; *NCH*, vol. 93, p. 403; vol. 95, p. 239.
 18   Chung-kuo k'o-hsüeh-yüan, *Chin-tai tung-pei*, p. 199; *Tung-fang*, vol. 7, no. 2, chi-tsai 3, pp. 45–46.
 19   Chung-kuo k'o-hsüeh-yüan, *Chin-tai tung-pei*, p. 200.
 20   Vidya Prakash Dutt, "The First Week of Revolution: The Wuchang Uprising," in Wright, *China in Revolution*, esp. pp. 384–85; Ernest P. Young, "The Reformer as Conspirator: Liang Ch'i-ch'ao and the 1911 Revolution," in Feuerwerker, *Approaches*, pp. 252–53.
 21   Shen, "Hsü Shih-ch'ang," vol. 14, no. 1, p. 67.
 22   Ning, "Tung-pei hsin-hai ko-ming," p. 537.
 23   Li, *Hsüeh-sheng*, 1: 15b–16a.

24 Ning, "Tung-pei hsin-hai ko-ming," p. 542.

25 Ibid.; Chung-kuo k'o-hsüeh-yüan, *Chin-tai tung-pei*, p. 201.

26 *HL*, no. 1201, p. 1324; *NCH*, vol. 96, p. 617.

27 *HL*, no. 869, pp. 931–32; no. 917, p. 983; no. 929, pp. 1001–02; no. 1014, pp. 1104–08; no. 1201, p. 1324; Shen, "Hsü Shih-ch'ang," vol. 14, no. 4, pp. 56–57.

28 *HL*, no. 866, p. 926.

29 *HL*, no. 853, p. 913; no. 870, p. 932; no. 1013, pp. 1104–07; Lee, *The Manchurian Frontier*, p. 171; BH, no. 656 C, F.

30 Feng Yü-hsiang, *Wo-ti sheng-huo* [My life], p. 122.

31 *HL*, no. 870, p. 932; no. 1131, p. 1249; *Tung-fang*, vol. 7, no. 12, wen-chien, 2, p. 21; Lee, *The Manchurian Frontier*, p. 171.

32 Lee, *The Manchurian Frontier*, pp. 140–46, 149; Shen, "Hsü Shih-ch'ang," vol. 14, no. 5, p. 59; *HL*, no. 853, p. 911; no. 856, p. 915; no. 859, pp. 917–22; no. 865, pp. 925–26; no. 926, p. 999; no. 928, pp. 1000–01; no. 1037, p. 1132; no. 1081, pp. 1179–80; no. 1104, p. 1210; no. 1157, p. 1273; no. 1160, p. 1275; Chin-liang, *Kuang-Hsüan*, pp. 121–22, 139–40, 143–44.

33 *HL*, no. 879, p. 943; no. 880, p. 944; no. 881, pp. 944–45; no. 949, pp. 1028–30; Shen, "Hsü Shih-ch'ang," vol. 13, no. 5, p. 36: *Sheng-ching*, no. 781, p. 5; Chai Wen-hsüan et al., comps., *Feng-t'ien t'ung-chih*, 135: 50–55; Han, *Chih-sou nien-p'u*, 9b–12a.

34 *HL*, no. 853, pp. 910–14; *NCH*, vol. 90, p. 559; *Sheng-ching*, no. 765, p. 2; no. 767, p. 2; no. 768, p. 5.

35 Shen, "Hsü Shih-ch'ang," vol. 14, no. 3, p. 82; *HL*, no. 848, p. 898; no. 853, p. 913; no. 866, p. 927; no. 895, p. 955; no. 1036, p. 1131; no. 1096, pp. 1200–01; no. 1131, p. 1250; no. 1160, pp. 1276–77; *Sheng-ching*, no. 777, p. 5; Han, *Chih-sou nien-p'u*, pp. 11b–12a; *Feng-t'ien tzu-i-chü*, 2: 41.

36 *HL*, no. 932, p. 1004; no. 1131, p. 1251.

37 *Feng-t'ien tzu-i-chü*, 2: 11–15, 16–38, 42–46; 3: 36–38; *HL*, no. 933, pp. 1005–06; no. 1161, p. 1279; no. 1177, pp. 1299–1300; no. 1178, p. 1301; no. 1179, p. 1302; no. 1180, pp. 1302–04; *NCH*, vol. 96, p. 195.

38 *Feng-t'ien tzu-i-chü*, 2: 100–04; *HL*, no. 914, pp. 980–81; no. 1160, p. 1276; Chung-kuo k'o-hsüeh-yüan, *Chin-tai tung-pei*, p. 166; *NCH*, vol. 97, p. 303.

39 *HL*, no. 1160, p. 1275; *Feng-t'ien tzu-i-chü*, 2: 38–40, 71–75, 97–99, 104–11; Chung-kuo k'o-hsüeh-yüan, *Chin-tai tung-pei*, p. 167.

40 Chung-kuo k'o-hsüeh-yüan, *Chin-tai tung-pei*, pp. 154–56.

41 Ibid., pp. 156, 166; *Feng-t'ien tzu-i-chü*, 2: 55; *Tung-fang*, vol. 7, no. 2, tiao-ch'a, 1, pp. 9–11. Even scholars who question the "oppression" thesis regard the loss of these mines to Japan as "tragic." Hou, *Foreign Investment*, pp. 69–70.

42 Hsien-cheng yen-chiu hui [Constitutional Research Association], ed., *Hsien-cheng tsa-chih* [Constitutional Magazine], vol. 2, pp. 124–26. Other officials were equally skeptical at that time. Ibid., vol. 2, pp. 95–131.

43 *HL*, no. 899, pp. 964–65; no. 1021, p. 1116; no. 1034, pp. 1129–30; no. 1109, p. 1219; no. 1161, p. 1278; Lee, *The Manchurian Frontier*, p. 156; P'eng-yüan Chang, "The Constitutionalists," in Wright, *China in Revolution*, p. 148.

44 *Feng t'ien tzu-i-chü*, table facing 1: 34; 2: 58–62; 3: 5–12, 18–23, 131–33; *HL*, no. 956, p. 1043.

45 *NCH*, vol. 97, p. 259; *HL*, no. 1021, p. 1108; no. 1109, p. 1220; Wang, *The Chinese Intellectuals*, p. 256; Chang, "The Constitutionalists," p. 166; Calhoun to Secretary, 21 November 1910, U.S., Department of State, *Records Relating to the Internal Affairs of China*, 893.00/482 (hereafter cited as USDS).

46 Wang, *The Chinese Intellectuals*, p. 255.

47 Chang P'eng-yüan, *Li-hsien-p'ai yü hsin-hai ko-ming* [The constitutionalists and the revolution of 1911], pp. 63, 77; *NCH*, vol. 93, pp. 309–10, 329, 365, 700.

48 Li Shou-k'ung, "Ko-sheng tzu-i-chü lien-ho-hui yü hsin-hai ko-ming" [The association of provincial assemblies and the revolution of 1911], in Wu, *CHS ts'ung-k'an*, ts'e 3, p. 330.

49 Chang, "The Constitutionalists," pp. 162–63; Calhoun to Secretary, 21 November 1910, USDS 893.00/482.

50 Fei, *Chin-tai*, p. 410; Hsien-cheng, *Hsien-cheng tsa-chih*, vol. 1, pp. 1–2. For a biography of Cheng, see Howard Boorman, ed., *Biographical Dictionary of Republican China*, 1: 270.

51 *HL*, no. 1031, p. 1126.

52 Li, "Ko-sheng tzu-i-chü," pp. 338–40, 343; Chang, "The Constitutionalists," pp. 162–65; Calhoun to Secretary, 21 November 1910, USDS 893.00/482; *NCH*, vol. 97, pp. 104–05.

53 Chung-hua, *K'ai-kuo wen-hsien*, pien 1, ts'e 8, hsia, pp. 633–35.

54 Ibid., p. 635. By "no responsibility" in the Ming, Hsi-liang may have referred to the abolition of the prime ministership in 1380; by the "warning of Yin" he alluded to the fall of the first historical Chinese dynasty in 1027 B. C.

55 *NCH*, vols. 93–97, esp. vol. 97, pp. 182, 227, 231; *Tung-fang*, vol. 7; Li, "Ko-sheng tzu-i-chü," pp. 344–45; Chang, "The Constitutionalists," pp. 165–66; Calhoun to Secretary, 21 November 1910, USDS 893.00/482; Shen, "Hsü Shih-ch'ang," vol. 14, no. 5, p. 59.

56 Translated and enclosed in Calhoun to Secretary, 21 November 1910, USDS 893.00/482.

57 Ibid.; *NCH*, vol. 97, p. 259.

58 Li, "Ko-sheng tzu-i-chü," p. 345; *Tung-fang*, vol. 7, no. 11, chi-tsai, 1, p. 155; *NCH*, vol. 97, pp. 324, 359, 384, 483.

59 Notes of the Chinese secretary of the American Legation who attended the session, in Calhoun to Secretary, 21 November 1910, USDS 893.00/482; *HL*, no. 957, p. 1043; Li, "Ko-sheng tzu-i-chü," p. 346; Chang, "The Constitutionalists," p. 168; Fischer to Secretary, 6 December 1910, USDS 893.00/487.

60 Bertaud to Pichon, 13 December 1910, MAE, Chine, Politique Intérieure, Dossier Général, vol. 22; Ning, "Tung-pei hsin-hai ko-ming," p. 541.

61 *HL*, no. 1147, p. 1262.

62 Ibid., p. 1263.

63 *HL*, no. 1139, p. 1256.

64 *HL*, no. 1147, p. 1263.

65 Li, "Ko-sheng tzu-i-chü," pp. 347–48; Fischer to Secretary, 28 December 1910, USDS 893.00/494; *NCH*, vol. 97, pp. 756, 796; Chung-kuo shih-hsüeh-hui, *Hsin-hai ko-ming*, vol. 3, p. 533.

66 Consul-General to de Margerie, 26 December 1910, MAE, Chine, Politique

Intérieure, Dossier Général, vol. 22; Chung-kuo Shih-hsüeh-hui, *Hsin-hai ko-ming*, vol. 3, pp. 533–34; Chang, "The Constitutionalists," pp. 168–73; Li, "Ko-sheng tzu-i-chü, pp. 353–54.

67 Chung-kuo k'o-hsüeh-yüan, *Chin-tai tung-pei*, p. 161; Ichiko Chūzō, "The Role of the Gentry: An Hypothesis," in Wright, *China in Revolution*, p. 304.
68 *Feng-t'ien tzu-i-chü*, 2: 91–94; *Tung-fang*, vol. 7, no. 6, fu-lu, 4, p. 27; *Sheng-ching*, no. 775, p. 5.
69 *Feng-t'ien tzu-i-chü*, 2: 68.
70 Ibid., 2: 68–71.
71 Ibid., 2: 87–90.
72 Ibid., 2: 57; *NCH*, vol. 96, p. 195; *HL*, no. 1161, p. 1279.
73 Chung-kuo k'o-hsüeh-yüan, *Chin-tai tung-pei*, pp. 169, 172.
74 Ibid., p. 172.
75 *HL*, no. 996, p. 1086; *Feng-t'ien tzu-i-chü*, 3: 51–52.
76 *Tung-fang*, vol. 7, no. 6, chi-tsai, 3, pp. 139–42; no. 8, chi-tsai, 3, pp. 140–42.
77 *HL*, no. 1142, p. 1268.
78 *HL*, no. 1148, pp. 1263–64.
79 *HL*, no. 1173, p. 1294; *NCH*, vol. 102, p. 11. See also Han, *Chih-sou nien-p'u*, pp. 13–14a; *HL*, nos. 1151, 1188, 1198, 1199, 1201, 1202; cf. Chung-kuo k'o-hsüeh-yüan, *Chin-tai tung-pei*, p. 160; Feng, *Wo-ti sheng-huo*, p. 135.
80 *HL*, no. 1187, p. 1310; no. 1206, p. 1336; Li, "Ko-sheng tzu-i-chü," pp. 354, 357; Chang, "The Constitutionalists," p. 168.

Chapter 13

1 Li Chien-nung, *The Political History of China, 1840–1928*, trans. and ed. Ssu-yu Teng and Jeremy Ingalls, p. 247.
2 Chao, *Ch'ing-shih-kao*, 236: 3a; for Ts'en, see Young, "The Reformer," p. 260; for Yüan, see Ernest P. Young, "Yüan Shih-k'ai's Rise to the Presidency," in Wright, *China in Revolution*, p. 421.
3 Chang, *Ch'ing-shih*, vol. 4, pp. 3992–4003; *NCH*, vol. 101, p. 181.
4 Chin-liang, *Kuang-Hsüan*, p. 148.
5 Li, *The Political History*, pp. 251–52.
6 Chin-liang, *Kuang-Hsüan*, p. 148.
7 Chung-kuo k'o-hsüeh-yüan, *Chin-tai tung-pei*, pp. 204–05; Feng, *Wo-ti sheng-huo*, pp. 142–44; Young, "The Reformer," p. 251; *NCH*, vol. 101, p. 230; Li, *The Political History*, p. 253.
8 Young, "The Reformer," pp. 253–54.
9 Chang, *Ch'ing-shih*, vol. 1, p. 382.
10 Chin-liang, *Kuang-Hsüan*, p. 149.
11 Percy Kent, *The Passing of the Manchus*, pp. 151–56, 240–42; Li, *The Political History*, p. 249.
12 *NCH*, vol. 101, p. 449.
13 Chang, *Ch'ing-shih*, vol. 1, p. 382.
14 Kent, *The Passing*, pp. 168–69.
15 *HTSL*, 64: 8–9a; *NCH*, vol. 101, pp. 366, 466.
16 Yüan Shih-k'ai and Sun Yat-sen also courted foreign support. Young, "Yüan

Shih-k'ai's Rise," p. 429; Harold Z. Schiffrin, "The Enigma of Sun Yat-sen," in Wright, *China in Revolution*, pp. 467–73.

17 *NCH*, vol. 101, p. 519; Kent, *The Passing*, p. 242.

18 *NCH*, vol. 101, p. 450; Chin-liang, *Kuang-Hsüan*, p. 149.

19 Chung-kuo k'o-hsüeh-yüan, *Chin-tai tung-pei*, p. 211; Wright, *The Last Stand*, pp. 12 ff.; *NCH*, vol. 101, pp. 503, 508.

20 Li, *The Political History*, p. 259; *NCH*, vol. 101, p. 714.

21 *HL*, no. 1207, p. 1337; no. 1210, p. 1340; *NCH*, vol. 102, p. 26.

22 *HL*, no. 1208, p. 1338; no. 1209, pp. 1339–40.

23 Chung-kuo k'o-hsüeh-yüan, *Hsin-hai ko-ming*, vol. 5, p. 377; *HL*, no. 1212, pp. 1341–42; Chung-hua, *K'ai-kuo wen-hsien*, pien 2, ts'e 5, p. 411.

24 Kent, *The Passing*, pp. 299–300; Li, *The Political History*, pp. 262–63.

25 Li, *The Political History*, p. 267.

26 Chung-kuo shih-hsüeh-hui, *Hsin-hai ko-ming*, vol. 5, pp. 331–32.

27 Chin-liang, *Kuang-Hsüan*, p. 149.

28 For a discussion of types of Chinese eremitism, see Frederick W. Mote, "Confucian Eremitism in the Yüan Period," in Wright, *The Confucian Persuasion*, pp. 202–40.

29 Fei, *Chin-tai*, p. 233.

30 Hsien-cheng pien-ch'a-kuan, *Cheng-chih kuan-pao*, 3: 130.

31 Fei, *Chin-tai*, p. 233; *HL*, p. 3.

32 Fei, *Chin-tai*, p. 233.

33 For a biography of Chang, see Boorman, *Biographical Dictionary*, 1: 115–22; Chin-liang, *Kuang-Hsüan*, p. 152.

34 Chin-liang, *Kuang-Hsüan*, p. 152.

35 Ibid., p. 142.

36 Chao, *Ch'ing-shih-kao*, 236: 3a; Thurston Griggs, "The *Ch'ing Shih Kao*: a Bibliographical Summary," *Harvard Journal of Asiatic Studies* 18, no. 1 (1955): 105–10.

37 *HL*, no. 1215, p. 1344.

GLOSSARY

The following list is complete except for personal names in Hummel, terms in BH, place names in Playfair, and Chinese names or terms found in Western texts for which no Chinese equivalents could be found.

ai-kuo-che 愛國者
An-feng 安奉
an-liang ch'ou-ku 按糧抽穀
an-liang chüan-shu 按糧捐輸
an-tsu ch'ou-ku 按租抽穀
Chan T'ien-yu 詹天佑
Chang-ch'ia 張恰
Chang Hsi-luan 張錫鑾
Chang Hsün 張勳
Chang I 張毅
Chang-i 張翼
Chang Jen-chün 張人駿
Chang Lo-ch'eng 張羅澄
Chang Shao-tseng 張紹曾
Chang Shih-en 章世恩
Chang Te-ch'ing 張德卿
Chang Tso-lin 張作霖
Chang Yin-t'ang 張蔭堂
Chang Yün-ch'ing 張濬卿
Chao Erh-sun 趙爾巽
Chao Fan 趙藩
Chen-kuo 鎮國
Ch'en Chung-hsin 陳鍾信
Ch'en I 陳宧
Ch'en Jung-ch'ang 陳榮昌
Cheng Hsiao-hsü 鄭孝胥
ch'eng-shen 城紳
Ch'eng Te-ch'üan 程德全
Ch'eng-tu jih-pao 成都日報
Ch'eng Ying 承瀛
Chi-chang 吉長
Chi-hui 吉會

Chi-liang 繼良
ch'i-hsia ch'a-shih 旗下差使
Ch'i Tsu-yi 祁祖彝
Chiang-ch'ia 江卡
chiang-ling 將領
Ch'iang 羌
Chiao-yü kuan-pao 教育官報
Ch'iao Shu-nan 喬樹枏
chien tu-pan 簡督辦
Ch'ien-Tsang 前藏
chih-t'ai 制臺
Chin-ai 錦愛
Chin-liang 金梁
Chin-t'ao 錦洮
chin-t'ieh 津貼
chin-yen-hui 禁煙會
Chin-Yü 津榆
Ch'in Li-shan 秦力山
Ch'in Shu-sheng 秦樹聲
Ching-feng 京奉
Ching-shih 經世
ching-tzu 勁字
Ch'ing-pi 清弼
chiu-hsü 救恤
chiu-kuo pao-chung 救國保種
chiu-liao 舊僚
ch'iu-chih tsung-chü 求治總局
Chou Hsün 周詢
Chou K'o-ch'ang 周克昌
Chou-li 周禮
Chou Shan-p'ei 周善培
Chou Yün-hsiang 周雲祥

241

Chu Ch'i-ch'ien 朱啓鈴
chu-ch'üan 主權
Chu Shou-p'eng 朱壽朋
Chu Teh 朱德
Ch'uan-Han 川漢
Ch'uan-Han t'ieh-lu tsung kung-ssu
　川漢鐵路總公司
ch'üan-chü 全局
ch'üan-kung-chü 勸工局
chün kuo-min hsüeh-t'ang 軍國民學堂
Chung-hsing jih-pao 中興日報
chung-hsüeh 中學
Chung-hua k'ai-kuo 中華開國
Chung-hua kuo-min-chün cheng-fu
　中華國民軍政府
Chung-kuo 中國
Chung-kuo chih t'u-ti 中國之土地
Chung-kuo jih-pao 中國日報
Chung-wai jih-pao 中外日報
Chung-yang jih-pao 中央日報
Ch'ung 充
erh-ssu jen 二四人
fan-li 藩籬
Fan Tang-shih 范當世
fan-yi sheng-yüan 繙譯生員
fang-ying 防營
Fang Yu-sheng 方友升
Fei Tao-ch'un 費道純
Feng-ch'üan 鳳全
Feng-hsü 馮煦
Fu 福
Fu-an 福安
Fu-ch'eng 福成
Fu-shun 撫順
Han Hung 韓宏
Han Kuo-chün 韓國鈞
Ho-ch'eng 和成
ho-pan 合辦
Hou-Tsang 後藏
Hsi Hsiao-fa 席小發
Hsi-liang 錫良
Hsiang-ch'eng 卿城
hsiang-shen 鄉紳
hsiang-yüeh 鄉約
Hsin-fa 新法
hsin-hung chih-chang 心紅紙張

Hsin Yün-nan 新雲南
Hsing-Tien meng 醒滇夢
Hsiung Ch'eng-chi 熊成基
Hsiung Hsi-ling 熊希齡
Hsiung-nu 凶奴
Hsü Han-tu 許涵度
Hsü Lien 徐濂
Hu Ching-i 胡景伊
Hu Chün 胡峻
Hu Han-min 胡漢民
Hu-lu-tao 胡蘆島
Hu Tung-ch'ao 胡棟朝
hua-ku 華股
Hua-yi 華益
Hua-ying 華英
huan-chi 宦積
huan-ch'iu 環球
Huang Hsing 黃興
Huang Ming-t'ang 黃明堂
Huang Pa 黃伯
hui-kuan 會館
hui-pan 會辦
Hung-hu-tzu 紅鬍子
I Ho Yüan 頤和園
i-hsüeh 義學
i-lao 遺老
Ijuin 伊集院
I-Wan 易萬
kai-liang 改良
kai-tsao 改造
kai-t'u kuei-liu 改土歸流
kan-ssu-hui 敢死會
Kao-tien 高店
Kao Yen 高岩
Ko-chiu 箇舊
ko-ming 革命
k'o-chü 科舉
Kuan Fu-ch'en 關弗臣
Kuan Jen-fu 關仁甫
kuan tsung-pan 官督辦
kuan-tu min-pan 官督民辦
Kuei-lin 桂霖
K'uei-shun 奎順
kung-chü 公局
kung-fei 公費
kung-min pao-lu-hui 公民保路會

kung-wei 拱衛
kuo-chia 國家
kuo-chia chu-i 國家主義
kuo-hui ch'ing-yüan tai-piao-t'uan
　國會請願代表團
kuo-min 國民
kuo-min chih i-lun 國民之議論
Kuo-pao 國報
kuo-su 國俗
kuo-t'i 國體
Lan T'ien-wei 藍天蔚
Li Chi-hsün 李稷勳
Li Ching-hsi 李經羲
Li-ho 禮和
Li Ken-yüan 李根源
li-mu 吏目
Li Po 李白
Li Po-tung 李伯東
Li Sheng 李升
liang 糧
Liang Shih-i 梁士詒
lien-chuang-she 聯莊社
lien-Jih 聯日
Lien-yü 聯豫
Liu Kuang-ts'ai 劉光才
Liu-sheng hsüeh-sheng t'ung-hsiang-hui
　留省學生同鄉會
Liu T'ing-shu 劉廷恕
Lo Chin-pao 羅進寶
Lo Tu 羅度
lu-chün hsüeh-shu 陸軍學術
Lu Ch'uan-lin 鹿傳霖
Lu Chung-tai 陸鍾岱
Lu-Han 蘆漢
Lu Yao-t'ing 陸耀廷
Lung Chi-kuang 龍濟光
Lung-hsing 隆興
Lung-wang-tung 龍王洞
Lung Yü-kuang 龍裕光
Ma Tien-hsüan 馬殿選
Ma Wei-ch'i 馬維騏
Meng En-yüan 孟恩遠
Mi-yün 密雲
Miao 苗
min-chien 民間
Min Li-sung 閔立松

mu-fu 幕府
Na-t'ung 那桐
Namti 南溪
Ni Ssu-ch'ung 倪嗣沖
Ou-hsi 歐西
pa-ch'i shu-yüan 八旗書院
Pai Chin-chu 白金柱
pao-chia 保甲
Pao-Tien-hui 保滇會
pao-ts'un-hui 保存會
pao-wei-tui 保衛隊
Pei-ching jih-pao 北京日報
Pei-yang kuan-pao 北洋官報
Pen-hsi-hu 本溪湖
Pin-hsün 斌循
Pin-t'u 賓圖
Po-li 波里
pu-chu kuo-chia chih yung 補助國家之用
P'u-liang 溥良
P'u Tien-chün 蒲殿俊
San-chan 三瞻
San-meng 三猛
San-tien-hui 三點會
Sang-p'i 桑披
Shan 山
shang-wu tsung-chü 商務總局
she-hui chu-i chih min-chu kuo-chia
　社會主義之民主國家
shen-pao-cheng 紳保正
Shen Ping-k'un 沈秉堃
shen tsung-pan 紳總辦
shen-tung 紳董
sheng kuo-chia chih ssu-hsiang
　生國家之思想
Sheng-yün 升允
shih 士
shih 詩
Shih-hsü 世續
Shih Tien-chang 施典章
shou 收
shu-yüan 書院
Shun 舜
Shun-t'ien jih-pao 順天日報
Ssu-ch'uan hsüeh-pao 四川學報
Ssu-ch'uan kuan-pao 四川官報
Su Lun-yüan 蘇掄元

Sui-fu 綏府
Sun P'u 孫璞
Sun Shu-hsün 孫樹勳
Sun Tien-k'uei 孫殿魁
Sung Chiao-jen 宋教仁
Sung-shou 松壽
Ta-kung-pao 大公報
Ta-tao-hui 大刀會
Ta-t'ung jih-pao 大同日報
ta-t'ung kung-ho-kuo 大同公和國
tai-chi 台吉
T'ai-ch'uan 泰川
T'ai Shan 泰山
T'ai-tsu 太祖
Taiping 太平
T'ang Shou-ch'ien 湯壽潛
Tao-sheng 道勝
T'ao-k'o-t'ao 套克套
Te-ko 德格
Te-erh-ko 德爾格
ti-kuo chu-i 帝國主義
Tiao An-jen 刁安仁
Tien-Ch'uan 滇川
Tien-nan chao-pao 滇南朝報
T'ien-pao-shan 天寶山
Tien-Shu 滇蜀
Tien-Shu T'eng-yüeh t'ieh-lu kung-ssu
　滇蜀騰越鐵路公司
Tien-Yüeh 滇越
t'ien-hsia 天下
t'ien-tsu-hui 天足會
Ting Chen-to 丁振鐸
Ting-ling 丁零
T'ing-yung 廷雍
Ts'ai Ao 蔡鍔
Ts'ai Nai-huang 蔡乃煌
tsang-wen hsüeh-t'ang 藏文學堂
Ts'ao K'un 曹琨
Tseng-hou 增厚
tsu 租
tsu-ku 租股
Ts'ui Hsiang-k'uei 崔祥奎
tsung-li 總理
tsung-she tang 宗社黨
tsung-tung 總董
Tu Fu 杜甫

tu-li 獨立
tu-pan 督辦
Tu Te-yü 杜德輿
t'u-fa 土法
t'u-mu 土目
t'uan-chang 團長
tung-wen hsüeh-t'ang 東文學堂
Tung-ya 東亞
T'ung-chih 同治
t'ung-hsiang hui 同鄉會
t'ung-kuan 同官
t'ung-ling 統領
T'ung-meng-hui 同盟會
t'ung-nien 同年
tzu-chi 字寄
tzu-hsiu 自修
tzu-pan 自辦
Wan Pen-hua 萬本華
Wang Chen-pang 王鎮邦
Wang Ching-hsüan 王靜軒
Wang Ch'üan-shan 王荃善
Wang Ho-shun 王和順
Wang Hung-t'u 王鴻圖
Wang P'eng-yün 王鵬運
wang-tao 王道
Wei Ching-t'ung 魏景桐
Wen-ming yen-shuo-hui 文明演說會
Wu Ching-lien 吳景濂
Wu Hsi-chen 吳錫珍
Wu K'un 吳琨
Wu Lu-chen 吳祿貞
wu-pei-chün 武備軍
Wu-t'ai 烏泰
Yang Chen-hung 楊振鴻
yang-jen 洋人
yang-kuan 洋官
Yang Ta-chu 楊大鑄
Yao 堯
Yeh Erh-k'ai 葉爾愷
Yen-chih 延祉
Yen Hsi-shan 閻錫山
Yin 殷
Yu-t'ai 有泰
Yü-feng 豫豐
Yü Lien-san 俞廉三
Yü Man-tzu 于蠻子

yü-min 愚民

Yü-nan 豫南

yü-pei li-hsien kung-hui 預備立憲公會

Yü Yin-lin 于蔭霖

Yüeh Han 粵漢

Yün-nan Ching-kao 雲南警告

Yün-nan kung-hsüeh-hui 雲南公學會

Yün-nan liu-Jih t'ung-hsiang-hui 雲南留日同鄉會

yung-ying 勇營

BIBLIOGRAPHY

The following list includes all sources mentioned in the notes except the major archives, for which full references appear in the list of abbreviations preceding the notes. All works, whether Chinese or Western, primary or secondary, are cited in one list alphabetized by author, editor, or compiler. Anonymous works are alphabetized by title.

Adshead, S. A. M. "The Opium Trade in Szechwan, 1881–1911." *Journal of Southeast Asian History* 7, no. 2 (1966): 93–99.

An, En-p'u 安恩溥, comp. *Chao-t'ung hsien-chih-kao* 昭通縣志稿 [Draft history of Chao-t'ung district (Yunnan)]. 9 chüan. 1936. Reprint. Taipei, 1967.

Ayers, William. *Chang Chih-tung and Educational Reform in China*. Cambridge: Harvard University Press, 1971.

Balazs, Etienne. *Chinese Civilization and Bureaucracy*. New Haven: Yale University Press, 1964.

Banno, Masataka. *China and the West, 1858–1861*. Cambridge: Harvard University Press, 1964.

Barnett, A. Doak, ed. *Chinese Communist Politics in Action*. Seattle: University of Washington Press, 1969.

Bawden, C. R. *The Modern History of Mongolia*. New York: Praeger, 1968.

Bergère, Marie-Claire. "The Role of the Bourgeoisie." In *China in Revolution: The First Phase, 1900–1913*, edited by Mary C. Wright, pp. 229–95. New Haven: Yale University Press, 1968.

Bland J. O. P., and Backhouse E. *China under the Empress Dowager*. 1910. Reprint. Taipei, 1962.

———. *Li Hung-chang*. London: Constable and Co., 1917.

Boorman, Howard, ed. *Biographical Dictionary of Republican China*, vol. 1. New York: Columbia University Press, 1967.

Brunnert, H., and Hagelstrom, V. *Present Day Political Organization of China*. Translated from the Russian by A. Beltchenko and E. Moran. Peking, 1910.

Buck, John Lossing. *Land Utilization in China*. Nanking: University of Nanking, 1937.

Cameron, Meribeth E. *The Reform Movement in China, 1898–1912*. Stanford: Stanford University Press, 1931.

Carlson, Ellsworth. "The Kaiping Mines. 1887–1912." Cambridge: Harvard University, 1958. Mimeographed.

Chai, Wen-hsüan 翟文選 et al., comps. *Feng-t'ien t'ung-chih* 奉天通志 [Local history of Fengtien]. Shen-yang, 1934.

Chang, Che-lang 張哲郎. *Ch'ing-tai ti ts'ao-yün* 清代的漕運 [Grain transport in the Ch'ing period]. Taipei: Chia-hsin shui-ni kung-ssu wen-hua chi-chin-hui, 1969.

Chang, Chi-hsü 張繼煦. *Chang Wen-hsiang kung chih-O-chi* 張文襄公治鄂記 [A record of Chang Wen-hsiang's administration of Hupeh]. Taipei: K'ai-ming shu-tien, 1966.

Chang, Ch'i-yün 張其昀, ed. *Ch'ing-shih* 清史 [History of the Ch'ing]. Taipei: Kuo-fang yen-chiu-yüan, 1962.

Chang, Chih-tung 張之洞. *Chang Wen-hsiang kung ch'üan-chi* 張文襄公全集 [The collected works of Chang Wen-hsiang]. 1928. Reprint. Peiping, 1937; Taipei, 1963.

Chang, Chung-lei 張仲雷. "Ch'ing-mo Min-ch'u Ssu-ch'uan ti chün-shih hsüeh-t'ang chi Ch'uan-chün p'ai-hsi" 清末民初四川的軍事學堂及川軍派系 [The military schools at the end of the Ch'ing and the beginning of the republic and military cliques in the Szechwan army]. In Chung-kuo jen-min, *Hsin-hai ko-ming hui-i-lu*, 3:345–64.

Chang, Chung-li. *The Income of the Chinese Gentry*. Seattle: University of Washington Press, 1962.

Chang, Hao. *Liang Ch'i-Ch'ao and Intellectual Transition in China, 1890–1907*. Cambridge: Harvard University Press, 1971.

Chang, Hsin-pao. *Commissioner Lin and the Opium War*. Cambridge: Harvard University Press, 1964.

Chang, Hui-ch'ang 張惠昌. "Chüeh-ch'ü Ch'uan-Han t'ieh-lu kung-ssu ti ling-tao ch'üan" 攫取川汉鐵路公司的領得權 [The seizure of leadership over the Ch'uan-Han railway company]. In his "Li-hsien-p'ai-jen ho Ssu-ch'uan tzu-i-chü 立宪派人和四川諮議局 [The constitutionalists and the Szechwan provincial assembly]. In Chung-kuo jen-min *Hsin-hai ko-ming hui-i-lu*, 3: 145–73.

Chang Keng 長庚, comp. *Kan-su hsin t'ung-chih* 甘肅新通志 [The new local history of Kansu]. 80 chüan. n.p., 1909.

Chang, Kia-ngan. *China's Struggle for Railroad Development*. New York, 1943.

Chang, Mu-an 張穆安. "Chi-lin chiu-wen hui-i-lu" 吉林舊聞回憶錄 [Memoir of things heard long ago in Chi-lin]. In Chung-kuo jen-min, *Hsin-hai ko-ming hui-i-lu,* 5: 572–80.

Chang, P'eng-yüan. "The Constitutionalists." In *China in Revolution: The First Phase 1900–1913*, edited by Mary C. Wright, pp. 143–83. New Haven: Yale University Press, 1968.

————. 張朋園. *Li-hsien-p'ai yü hsin-hai ko-ming* 立憲派與辛亥革命 [The constitutionalists and the revolution of 1911]. Taipei: Shang-wu yin-shu-kuan. 1969.

Chang, Shen-k'ai 張森楷. *Ho-ch'uan hsien-chih* 合川縣志 [Local history of Ho-ch'uan district (Szechwan)]. 83 chüan. n.p., 1920.

Chang, Ta-i 張大義. "T'ung-meng-hui Yün-nan fen-pu chih ch'eng-li chi ch'i huo-tung" 同盟會雲南分部之成立及其活動 [The founding of the Yunnan branch of the revolutionary alliance and its activities]. In Chung-hua, *K'ai-kuo wen-hsien*, pien 1, ts'e 12, pp. 129–37.

Chao, Ching-hsüeh. "The Chengtu-Chungking Railway Completed." *People's China* 14 (1952):26–28.

Chao, Erh-sun 趙爾巽, ed. *Ch'ing-shih kao* 清史稿 [Draft history of the Ch'ing]. Peking: kuan-nei edition, 1927.

Chen, Ching-jen. "Opium and Anglo-Chinese Relations." *Chinese Social and Political Science Review* 19 (1935–36):386–437.

Ch'en, Ch'un-sheng 陳春生. "Wu-shen Ho-k'ou ch'i-i chi" 戊申河口起義記 [Record of the 1908 Ho-k'ou uprising]. In Chung-hua, *K'ai-kuo wen-hsien,* pien 1, ts'e 13, pp. 390–96.

Ch'en, Jerome. "The Nature and Characteristics of the Boxer Movement—a Morphological Study." *Bulletin of the School of Oriental and African Studies* 23 (1960): pp. 287–308.

Ch'eng, T'ing-heng 程廷恒, comp. *Ta-ming hsien-chih* 大名縣志 [Local history of Ta-ming district (Chihli)]. 31 chüan. n.p., 1934.

Chesneaux, Jean. "Egalitarian and Utopian Traditions in the East." In *Modern China,* edited by Joseph R. Levenson. London: Macmillan Co., 1971. pp. 76–89.

———. *Les sociétés secrètes en Chine (19e et 20e siècles).* Paris: René Julliard, 1965.

Chiao-yü pu tang [Archives of the ministry of education] ,Musan, Taiwan.

Ch'i-chiang hsü-chih 綦江續志 [Local history of Ch'i-chiang, continued (Szechwan)]. n.p., n.d.

Ch'i Pen-yu. "Patriotisme ou trahison de la Patrie?" Reprinted from *Hung-ch'i* [Red Flag], *Pekin Information* 15 (1967): 5–17.

Chin-liang 金梁. *Chin-shih jen-wu-chih* 近世人物志 [A record of personalities of modern times]. 1934. Reprint. Taipei, 1955.

———. *Kuang-Hsüan hsiao-chi* 光宣小記 [Short tales of the Kwang(-hsü) and Hsüan (-t'ung) periods]. n.p., 1933.

"Ching-kao ko-sheng tzu-pan t'ieh-lu-che" 敬告名省自辦鐵路者 [A respectful warning to the self-managed railways of all provinces]. From *Wai-chiao-pao* 外交報, in *Tung-fang,* vol. 2, no. 10 (1905), chiao-t'ung, pp. 85–87.

China, Inspectorate General of Customs. *Decennial Reports, 1902–1911.* Shanghai, 1913.

Chou, I-fu 周宜甫 [Chou Hsün 周詢]. *Shu-hai t'sung-t'an* 蜀海叢談 [A discussion of matters in Szechwan]. 1935. Taipei reprint. In Shen Yün-lung, no. 7.

Chou, K'ai-ch'ing 周開慶. *Ssu-ch'uan yü hsin-hai ko-ming* 四川與辛亥革命 [Szechwan and the revolution of 1911]. Taipei: Ssu-ch'uan wen-hsien yen-chiu-she, 1952.

———. *Ssu-ch'uan wen-hsien* 四川文獻 [Documents on Szechwan], no. 62 (1968).

Chu, Charles Chia-hwai. "The China Policy of the Taft-Knox Administration, 1909–1913." Ph. D. dissertation, University of Chicago, 1956.

Chu, Samuel C. *Reformer in Modern China: Chang Chien, 1853–1926.* New York: Columbia University Press, 1965.

Ch'ü, T'ung-tsu. *Local Government in China under the Ch'ing.* Cambridge: Harvard University Press, 1962.

Ch'üan, Han-sheng 全漢昇. "Ch'ing-chi t'ieh-lu chien-she ti tzu-pen wen-t'i" 清季鐵路建設的資本問題 [The question of capital for establishing railways in the late Ch'ing]. *She-hui k'o-hsüeh lun-tsung* 社會科學論叢 [Journal of Social Science], no. 4 (1953), pp. 1–16.

———. "T'ieh-lu kuo-yu wen-t'i yü hsin-hai ko-ming" 鐵路國有問題與辛亥革命 [The railway nationalization question and the revolution of 1911]. In Wu, *CHS Ts'ung-k'an,* ts'e 1, pp. 209–271.

Ch'ung, Ch'ien 崇謙, comp. *Ch'u-hsiung hsien-chih* 楚雄縣志 [Local history of Ch'u-hsiung district (Yunnan)]. 12 chüan. 1910. Reprint. Taipei, 1957.

Chung-hsing jih-pao 中興日報 [The China Arise Gazette], in *K'ai-kuo·wen-hsien,* pien 1, ts'e 13, pp. 414–30.

Chung-hua min-kuo k'ai-kuo wu-shih nien wen-hsien pien-tsuan wei-yüan-hui 中華民國開國五十年文獻編纂委員會 [Committee on the Compilation of Documents on the Fiftieth Anniversary of the Founding of the Republic of China], ed. *Chung-hua min-kuo k'ai-kuo wu-shih-nien wen-hsien* 中華民國開國五十年文獻 [Documents on the fiftieth anniversary of the founding of the republic of China]. 1 pien. 16 vols. Taipei, 1963–.

Chung-kuo jen-min cheng-chih hsieh-shang hui-i ch'üan-kuo wei-yüan-hui wen-shih tzu-liao yen-chiu wei-yüan-hui 中國人民政治協商會議全國委員會文史資料研究委員會 [Committee on Written Historical Materials of the National Committee of the Chinese People's Political Consultative Conference], ed. *Hsin-hai ko-ming hui-i-lu* 辛亥革命回憶錄 [Memoirs of the revolution of 1911]. 6 vols. Peking, 1961–.

Chung-kuo k'o-hsüeh-yüan 中國科學院 [Chinese Academy of Science], comp. *Chin-ta i tung-pei jen-min ko-ming yün-tung shih* 近代東北人民革命運動史 [A history of the recent revolutionary movement of the people of the northeast]. Ch'ang-ch'un: Chi-lin jen-min ch'u-pan-she yin-hang, 1960.

————. *Hsi-liang i-kao tsou-kao* 錫良遺稿奏稿 [The posthumous manuscripts and draft memorials of Hsi-liang]. 2 vols. Peking: Chung-hua shu-chü, 1959.

————. *Hsin-hai ko-ming tzu-liao* 辛亥革命資料 [Materials on the 1911 revolution]. Peking: Chung-hua shu-chü, 1961.

————. *Yün-nan Kuei-chou hsin-hai ko-ming tzu-liao* 雲南貴州辛亥革命資料 [Materials on the 1911 revolution in Yunnan and Kweichow]. Peking: K'o-hsüeh ch'u-pan-she, 1959.

————. *Yün-nan tsa-chih hsüan-chi* 雲南雜誌選集 [Selections from the *Yunnan Miscellany*]. Peking: K'o-hsüeh ch'u-pan-she, 1958.

Chung-kuo shih-hsüeh-hui 中國史學會 [Chinese Historical Association], ed. *Hsin-hai ko-ming* 辛亥革命 [The revolution of 1911]. Compiled by Ch'ai Te-keng 柴德賡 et al. 8 vols. Shanghai: Jen-min ch'u-pan-she, 1957.

Chung-wai jih-pao 中外日報 [Universal Gazette]. In *Tung-fang,* vol. 1, no. 6 (1904), she-shuo, pp. 120–23.

Chung-yang yen-chiu-yüan 中央研究院 [The Central Institute of Research–Academia Sinica], comp. *K'uang-wu-tang* 礦務檔 [Archives of mining affairs]. 8 vols. Taipei: Chung-yang yen-chiu-yüan, 1960.

Cohen, Paul A. *China and Christianity: The Missionary Movement and the Growth of Chinese Antiforeignism, 1860–1870.* Cambridge: Harvard University Press, 1963.

Conroy, Hilary. *The Japanese Seizure of Korea.* Philadelphia: University of Pennsylvania Press, 1960.

Croly, Herbert, *Willard Straight,* New York, 1924.

Crowley, James B., ed. *Modern East Asia: Essays in Interpretation.* New York: Harcourt, Brace, and World, 1970.

Dreyer, June. "China's Minority Nationalities in the Cultural Revolution." *The China Quarterly,* no. 35 (1968), pp. 96–109.

Dutt, Vidya Prakash. "The First Week of Revolution: The Wuchang Uprising." In *China in Revolution: The First Phase, 1900–1913*, edited by Mary C. Wright, pp. 383–416. New Haven: Yale University Press, 1968.

Eastman, Lloyd. *Throne and Mandarins: China's Search for a Policy During the Sino-French Controversy, 1880–1885*. Cambridge: Harvard University Press, 1967.

Edwards, E. H. *Fire and Sword in Shansi: The Story of the Martyrdom of Foreigners and Chinese Christians*. New York: F. H. Revell, 1903.

Fairbank, John K., and Teng, Ssu-yü, eds. *China's Response to the West: A Documentary Survey, 1839–1923*. New York: Atheneum, 1963.

Fairbank, John K., ed. *The Chinese World Order: Traditional China's Foreign Relations*. Cambridge: Harvard University Press, 1968.

Fairbank, John K. *Trade and Diplomacy on the China Coast*. Cambridge: Harvard University Press, 1953.

Fairbank, John K.; Reischauer, Edwin O.; and Craig, Albert M. *East Asia: The Modern Transformation*. Boston: Houghton Mifflin, 1965.

Fan, Tang-shih 范當世. *Fan Po-tzu shih-wen-chi* 范伯子詩文集 [The poems and essays of Fan Po-tzu]. Taipei: Hua-wen shu-chü, 1966.

Fang, Chao-ying 房兆楹 and Tu Lien-che 杜聯喆, eds. *Tseng-chiao Ch'ing ch'ao chin-shih t'i-ming pei-lu fu-yin-te* 增校清朝進士題名碑錄附引得 [Revised edition of the index to inscriptions of recipients of the Chin-shih degree under the Ch'ing dynasty]. Cambridge: Harvard University Press, 1941.

Fang, Chao-ying, ed. 房兆楹 *Ch'ing-mo Min-ch'u yang-hsüeh hsüeh-sheng t'i-ming lu ch'u-chi yi-yi mou-shih ts'ung-pien* 清末民初洋學學生題名錄初輯一宜楙室叢編 [List of students who studied abroad during the late Ch'ing and early republic]. Nan-kang: Chung-yang yen-chiu-yüan, 1962.

Farquhar, David M. "The Ch'ing Administration of Mongolia up to the Nineteenth Century." Ph. D. dissertation, Harvard University, 1960.

Fei, Hsing-chien 費行簡. *Chin-tai ming-jen hsiao-chuan* 近代名人小傳 [Short biographies of famous people of recent times]. n.d. Taipei reprint, 1968. In Shen Yün-lung, no. 78.

Feng-hsü 馮煦. *Hao-an tsou-kao* 蒿盦奏稿 [The draft memorials of Hao-an]. n.p., 1923. Taipei reprint, 1968.

Feng Kang 鳳岡, ed. *San-shui Liang Yen-sun hsien-sheng nien-p'u* 三水梁燕孫先生年譜 [Chronological biography of Liang Yen-sun]. n.p., 1939.

Feng-t'ien tzu-i-chü ti-i-tz'u pao-kao shu 奉天諮議局第一次報告書 [Report of the first session of the Fengtien provincial assembly]. 3 chüan. n.p., circa 1910.

Feng, Tzu-yu 馮自由. *Chung-hua Min-kuo k'ai-kuo ch'ien ko-ming-shih* 中華民國開國前革命史 [The history of the revolution prior to the founding of the Chinese republic]. Chungking, 1944.

————. *Ko-ming i-shih* 革命逸史 [Reminiscences of the revolution]. 5 vols. Chungking, 1942.

Feng, Yü-hsiang 馮玉祥. *Wo-ti sheng-huo* 我的生活 [My life]. Chungking, 1944.

Feuerwerker, Albert, *China's Early Industrialization: Sheng Hsüan-huai (1845–1916) and Mandarin Enterprise*. Cambridge: Harvard University Press, 1958.

Feuerwerker, Albert, ed. *History in Communist China*. Cambridge: Massachusetts Institute of Technology Press, 1968.

Feuerwerker, Albert, et al., eds. *Approaches to Modern Chinese History*. Berkeley and Los Angeles: University of California Press, 1967.

Fitzgerald, C. P. *The Chinese View of their Place in the World*. Oxford: Oxford University Press, 1964.

Fleming, Peter, *Bayonets to Lhasa*. New York: Harper and Brothers, 1961.

France. Service Historique de l'Armée de Terre, Chateau de Vincennes, Vincennes, Section Outre-Mer. Fonds: Chine, 1900–1901.

Franke, Wolfgang. *The Reform and Abolition of the Traditional Chinese Examination System*. Cambridge: Harvard University Press, 1960.

Friedman, Edward, and Selden, Mark, eds. *America's Asia: Dissenting Essays on Asian-American Relations*. New York: Random House, 1971.

Friters, Gerard M. *Outer Mongolia and Its International Position*. Baltimore: Johns Hopkins Press, 1949.

Fu, Sung-mu 傅嵩姝. *Hsi-k'ang chien-sheng-chi* 西康建省記 [Record of the founding of Hsi-k'ang province]. Reprint. Taipei 1968.

Gasster, Michael. *Chinese Intellectuals and the Revolution of 1911*. Seattle: University of Washington Press, 1969.

Gillin, Donald G. *Warlord: Yen Hsi-shan in Shansi Province, 1911–1949*. Princeton: Princeton University Press, 1967.

Great Britain. Foreign Office. Parliamentary Papers. *China*, 1900–01, 1904–05.

Griggs, Thurston. "The *Ch'ing Shih Kao*: A Bibliographical Summary." *Harvard Journal of Asiatic Studies* 18, no. 1 (1955): 105–23.

Griswold, A. Whitney. *The Far Eastern Policy of the United States*. New York: Harcourt, Brace and Co., 1938.

Han, Kuo-chün 韓國鈞. *Chih-sou nien-p'u* 止叟年譜 [A chronological biography of Han Kuo-chün]. Taipei reprint, in Shen Yün-lung, no. 9.

Han, Suyin. *The Crippled Tree*. New York: G. P. Putnam's Sons, 1965.

Harrison, James P. "Chinese Communist Interpretations of the Chinese Peasant Wars." In *History in Communist China*, edited by Albert Feuerwerker, pp. 189–215. Cambridge: Massachusetts Institute of Technology Press, 1968.

Harvard Papers on China. Harvard University, East Asian Research Center, 16 vols. (1962)–.

Hatano, Yoshihiro. "The Background of the Railway Nationalization Policy of the Late Ch'ing Period: The Reason Why the Policy Was Taken Up." *Research Conference on the Chinese Revolution of 1911*. Portsmouth: Joint Committee on Contemporary China. 1965.

———. "The New Armies." In *China in Revolution: The First Phase, 1900-1913*, edited by Mary C. Wright, pp. 365–82. New Haven: Yale University Press, 1968.

Hedtke, Charles. "The Genesis of Revolution in Szechwan." *Research Conference on the Chinese Revolution of 1911*. Portsmouth: Joint Committee on Contemporary China, 1965.

Hen, Hai 恨海. "Yün-nan ko-ming-chün chih chan-chieh" 雲革命軍之戰捷 [The victories of the Yunnan revolutionary army]. In Chung-hua, *K'ai-kuo wen-hsien*, pien 1, ts'e 13, pp. 412–14.

Hinton, Harold. *The Grain Tributary System of China (1845–1911)*. Cambridge: Harvard University Press, 1956.

Hinton, William. *Fanshen*. New York: Monthly Review Press, 1966.

Ho, Ping-ti, and Tsou, Tang, eds. *China in Crisis*. 3 vols. Chicago: The University of Chicago Press, 1968.

Ho, Ping-ti. *The Ladder of Success in Imperial China*. New York: Columbia University Press, 1962.

————. *Studies in the Population of China, 1368–1953*. Cambridge: Harvard University press, 1959.

Hou, Chi-ming. *Foreign Investment and Economic Development in China, 1840–1937*. Cambridge: Harvard University Press, 1965.

Hosie, Sir Alexander. *On the Trail of the Opium Poppy*. London: George Philip and Son, 1914.

Hsiao, I-shan 蕭一山. *Ch'ing-tai t'ung-shih* 清代通史 [A comprehensive history of the Ch'ing period]. 5 vols. Taipei: Shang-wu yin-shu kuan, 1963.

Hsiao, Kung-ch'üan. "K'ang Yu-wei and Confucianism." *Monumenta Serica*, 18 (1959): 96–212.

————. *Rural China: Imperial Control in the Nineteenth Century*. Seattle: University of Washington Press, 1960.

————. "Weng T'ung-ho and the Reform Movement of 1898." *Tsing Hua Journal of Chinese Studies*, n. s., 1, no. 2 (1957): 111–245.

Hsieh, Hsiao-chung 謝曉鐘. *Yün-nan yu-chi* 雲南遊記 [Travels in Yunnan]. n.p., 1923. In Shen Yün-lung, no. 9.

Hsien-cheng pien-ch'a-kuan 憲政編查館 [Constitutional Printing Office], comp. *Cheng-chih kuan-pao* 政治官報 [Official journal of politics]. 48 vols. 1907-11. Reprint. Taipei, 1965.

Hsien-cheng yen-chiu hui 憲政研究會 [Constitutional Research Association], ed. *Hsien-cheng tsa-chih* 憲政雜誌 [The constitutional magazine], 2 vols. 1905–06.

Hsu, Shuhsi. *China and Her Political Entity*. New York, 1926.

Hsü, Immanuel C. Y. *The Ili Crisis: A Study of Sino-Russian Diplomacy*. Oxford: Clarendon Press, 1965.

————. *The Rise of Modern China*. Oxford: Oxford University Press, 1970.

Hsü, K'o 徐珂, comp. *Ch'ing-pai lei-ch'ao* 清稗類鈔 [Miscellaneous writings of the Ch'ing period]. Shanghai: Shang-wu yin-shu kuan yin-hang, 1917.

Hsü, Shih-ch'ang 徐世昌, comp. *Tung-san-sheng cheng-lüeh* 東三省政略 [The administration of the three eastern provinces]. 12 vols. Reprint. Taipei, 1956.

Hsüeh-pu tsou-tzu chi-yao 學部奏咨輯要 [Collection of memorials and communications of the ministry of education]. 1905–06. Microfilm. Institute of Modern History, Academia Sinica.

Hsüeh, Chün-tu. *Huang Hsing and the Chinese Revolution*. Stanford: Stanford University Press, 1961.

Hu, Chün 胡鈞. *Chang Wen-hsiang kung (Chih-tung) nien-p'u* 張文襄公 (之洞) 年譜 [A chronological biography of Chang Wen-hsiang or Chang Chih-tung]. Taipei reprint, in Shen Yün-lung, no. 47.

Huang, Chi-lu 黃季陸, comp. *Chung-kuo jih-pao, 1904–1908* 中國日報, [The Chinese Daily, 1904–1908]. Taichung: Chung-kuo Kuo-min-tang, 1969.

Hummel, Arthur, et al., eds. *Eminent Chinese of the Ch'ing Period (1644–1912)*. 2 vols. Washington, D.C.: Government Printing Office, 1943–44.

Hunt, Michael. "Frontier Defense and the Open Door: Manchuria in Chinese American Relations, 1895–1911." Ph. D. dissertation, Yale University, 1971.

Ichiko Chūzō, "The Role of the Gentry: An Hypothesis." In *China in Revolution: The First Phase, 1900–1913*, edited by Mary C. Wright, pp. 279–317. New Haven: Yale University Press, 1968.

Irick, Robert L. "The Chinchow-Aigun Railroad and the Knox Neutralization Plan in Ch'ing Diplomacy." *Harvard Papers on China*, 13 (1959): 80–112.

Iriye, Akira, "Public Opinion and Foreign Policy: The Case of Late Ch'ing China." In *Approaches to Modern Chinese History*, edited by Albert Feuerwerker, et al., pp. 216–38. Berkeley and Los Angeles: University of California Press, 1967.

Isaacs, Harold R. *The Tragedy of the Chinese Revolution*. Stanford: Stanford University Press, 1951.

Israel, John. *Student Nationalism in China, 1927–1937*. Stanford: Stanford University Press, 1966.

Jagchid, Sechin 札奇斯欽. "Wai Meng-ku ti 'tu-li', 'tzu-chih', ho 'ch'e-chih'." 外蒙古的'獨立'自治'和'撤治' [Outer Mongolia's "Independence," "Self-Government," and "Secession"]. In Wu, *CHS ts'ung-k'an*, ts'e 4, pp. 39–141.

Jansen, Marius B. "Oi Kentaro (1843–1922); Radicalism and Chauvinism," *Far Eastern Quarterly* 2 (1952): 305–16.

Johnson, Chalmers. *Peasant Nationalism and Communist Power: The Emergence of Revolutionary China, 1937–1945*. Stanford: Stanford University Press, 1962.

Johnson, William R. "China's 1911 Revolution in the Provinces of Yunnan and Kweichow." Ph. D. dissertation, University of Washington, 1962.

Kazuo, Kawai. "The Boxer Protocol Negotiations." Ph. D. dissertation, Stanford University, 1939.

Kennedy, Thomas L. "The Kiangnan Arsenal, 1895–1911: The Decentralized Bureaucracy Responds to Imperialism." *Ch'ing-shih wen-t'i* 2, no. 1(1969): 17-37.

Kent, Percy. *The Passing of the Manchus*. London: E. Arnold, 1912.

———. *Railway Enterprise in China*. London: E. Arnold, 1907.

Lamb, Alastair. *Britain and Chinese Central Asia: the Road to Lhasa, 1767 to 1905*. London: Routledge and Kegan Paul, 1960.

Latourette, Kenneth S. *A History of Christian Missions in China*. New York: Macmillan Co., 1929.

Lattimore, Owen. *Inner Asian Frontiers of China*. New York: American Geographical Society, 1940.

———. *The Mongols of Manchuria*. New York, 1934.

Lee, En-han. "China's Response to Foreign Investment in Her Mining Industry." *Journal of Asian Studies* 28 (1968): 55-76.

Lee, Robert H. G. *The Manchurian Frontier in Ch'ing History*. Cambridge: Harvard University Press, 1970.

Levenson, Joseph R., ed. *European Expansion and the Counter-Example of Asia, 1300–1600*. Englewood Cliffs, N.J.: Prentice-Hall, 1967.

Levenson, Joseph R. *Confucian China and Its Modern Fate*. 3 vols. Berkeley: University of California Press, 1958, 1964, 1965.

————. *Liang Ch'i-ch'ao and the Mind of Modern China.* Cambridge: Harvard University Press, 1953.

Li Chien-nung. *The Political History of China, 1840–1928.* Translated and edited by Ssu-yu Teng and Jeremy Ingalls. Princeton: Princeton University Press, 1956.

Li, En-han 李恩涵. *Wan-Ch'ing ti shou-hui k'uang-ch'üan yün-tung* 晚清的收回礦權運動 [The late Ch'ing movement to recover mining rights]. Taipei: Chung-yang yen-chiu-yüan, Chin-tai shih yen-chiu so, 1963.

Li, Hung-chang 李鴻章. *Li Wen-chung kung tien-kao* 李文忠公電稿 [The draft telegrams of Li Hung-chang]. 1908, Reprint. Taipei, 1962.

Li, Ken-yüan 李根源. *Hsüeh-sheng nien-lu* 雪生年錄 [A chronological biography of (Li) Hsüeh-sheng], in Shen Yün-lung, no. 14.

Li, Ping-heng 李秉衡. *Li Chung-chieh kung tsou-i* 李忠節公奏議 [The memorials of Li Ping-heng]. 2 vols. 1920, Reprint. Taipei, 1968.

Li, Shou-k'ung 李守孔. "Ko-sheng tzu-i-chü lien-ho-hui yü hsin-hai ko-ming" 各省諮議局聯合會與辛亥革命 [The association of provincial assemblies and the revolution of 1911]. In Wu, *CHS ts'ung-k'an,* ts'e 3, pp. 321–73.

————. "Pa-kuo lien-chün ch'i-chien Tz'u-hsi kuei-cheng Te-tsung chih chiao-she" 八國聯軍期間慈禧歸政德宗之交涉 [Diplomacy concerning the return of government to Te-tsung during the allied invasion]. *Ta-lu tsa-chih* 大陸雜誌 [Continental Miscellany], vol. 23 (1961), nos. 7, 8.

Li, Tieh-tseng. *Tibet, Today and Yesterday.* New York: Bookman Associates, 1960.

Lindbeck, John M. *China: Management of a Revolutionary Society.* Seattle: University of Washington Press, 1970.

Ling, Hung-hsün 凌鴻勛. *Chan T'ien-yu hsien-sheng nien-p'u* 詹天佑先生年譜 [A chronological biography of Chan T'ien-yu]. Taipei: Chung-kuo kung-ch'eng-shih hsüeh-hui, 1962.

————. "Ch'uan-Han t'ieh-lu" 川漢鐵路 [The Ch'uan-Han railway], in Chung-hua, *K'ai-kuo wen-hsien,* pien 1, ts'e 8, pp. 680–81.

Liu Chia-yeh-t'ang 劉嘉業堂 [The Chia-yeh library of the Liu family]. *Ta-Ch'ing Hsüan-t'ung cheng-chi shih-lu* 大清宣統政紀實錄 [The political annals of the Hsüan-t'ung reign of the great Ch'ing dynasty]. 43 chüan in 16 ts'e. 1934. Reprint. Taipei, 1964.

Liu, James T. C. *Reform in Sung China.* Cambridge: Harvard University Press, 1959.

Liu, Kwang-ching. "The Confucian as Patriot: Li Hung-chang's Formative Years (1823–1866)." *Harvard Journal of Asiatic Studies* 30 (1970): pp. 5–45.

————. "Li Hung-chang in Chihli: The Emergence of a Policy, 1870–1875." In *Approaches to Modern Chinese History, edited* by Albert Feuerwerker, et al., pp. 68–104. Berkeley and Los Angeles: University of California Press, 1967.

Liu, K'un-i 劉坤一. *Liu K'un-i i-chi* 劉坤一遺集 [The posthumous manuscripts of Liu K'un-i]. 6 vols. Peking: Chung-hua shu-chü, 1959.

"Liu-Pi kuan-fei hsüeh-sheng lü-li ch'ing ts'e" 留比官費學生履歷清冊 [A record of government fellowship students sent to Belgium]. Circa 1908. Chiao-yü pu tang 教育部檔 [Archives of the Ministry of Education]. Musan, Taiwan.

Liu, T'ieh-yün. *The Travels of Lao Ts'an.* Translated and annotated by Harold Shadick. Ithaca: Cornell University Press, 1952.

Lo, Tun-jung 羅惇融, ed. *Keng-tzu kuo-pien chi* 庚子國變記 [A record of the great uprising of 1900]. Taipei, 1965.

Lu, Hsing-ch'i 陸與棋. "Hsi-tsang chiao-she chi-yao" 西藏交涉紀要 [An outline of diplomacy on Tibet]. Mimeographed. Taipei: Meng-tsang wei-yüan hui, 1954.

Lü, Chih-i 呂志伊. "Yang Chen-hung shih-lüeh" 楊振鴻事略 [Biography of Yang Chen-hung]. In Chung-hua, *K'ai-kuo wen-hsien,* pien 1, ts'e 12, pp. 144–47.

MacKinnon, Stephen R. "Liang Shih-i and the Communications Clique." *Journal of Asian Studies* 29 (1970): 581–602.

MacMurray, John V. A., ed. *Treaties and Agreements with and Concerning China.* 2 vols. New York, 1921.

McCoy, Alfred W. (with Cathleen B. Read and Leonard P. Adams II). *The Politics of Heroin in Southeast Asia.* New York: Harper & Row, 1972.

Meisner, Maurice. *Li Ta-chao and the Origins of Chinese Marxism.* Cambridge: Harvard University Press, 1967.

Michael, Franz, and Chang Chung-li. *The Taiping Rebellion: History and Documents.* Vol. 1. *History.* Seattle: University of Washington Press, 1966.

Ming-Ch'ing Tang-an kuan 明清檔案館, comp. *I-ho-t'uan tang-an shih-liao* 義和團檔案 史料 [Historical materials in the Boxer archives]. 2 vols. Peking: Chung-hua shu-chü, 1959.

Minogue, K. R. *Nationalism.* New York: Basic Books, 1967.

Miu, Kuo-chang 繆果章. *Hsüan-wei hsien-chih-kao* 宣威縣志稿 [Draft history of Hsüan-wei district (Yunnan)]. 12 chüan. Reprint. Taipei, 1967.

Miyakawa, Hisayuki. "The Confucianization of South China." In *The Confucian Persuasion,* edited by Arthur F. Wright, pp. 21–46. Stanford: Stanford University Press, 1960.

Morse, Hosea Ballou. *The International Relations of the Chinese Empire.* Vol. 3. *The Period of Subjection, 1894–1911.* Shanghai, 1918. Reprint. Taipei, n.d.

Muramatsu, Yuji. "Some Themes in Chinese Rebel Ideologies." In *The Confucian Persuasion,* edited by Arthur F. Wright, pp. 241–67. Stanford: Stanford University Press, 1960.

Nan-fang-pao 南防報 [Southern Defense Gazette], in *Tung-fang,* vol. 2, no. 6 (1906), she-shuo, pp. 207–16.

Ning, Wu 寧武. "Tung-pei hsin-hai ko-ming chien-shu" 東北辛亥革命簡述 [A description of the 1911 revolution in the northeast], in Chung-kuo jen-min, *Hsin-hai ko-ming hui-i-lu,* vol. 5, pp. 536–45.

Nivison, David S. "Protest against Conventions and Conventions of Protest." In *The Confucian Persuasion,* edited by Arthur F. Wright, pp. 177–201. Stanford: Stanford University Press, 1960.

North China Herald. 46 vols. Shanghai, 1901–1912.

Pien, Chung-fan 卞仲璠. "'Ch'ung-ch'ing jih-pao' ch'uang-pan jen Pien Hsiao-wu lieh-shih shih-shu" 重慶日報創辦人卞小吾烈士事遂 [The story of the martyr Pien Hsiao-wu, founder of the *Chungking Daily*], in Chung-kuo jen-min, *Hsin-hai ko-ming hui-i-lu,* vol. 3, pp. 336–39.

Playfair, G. M. H. *Cities and Towns of China.* 1910. Reprint. Taipei, 1964.

Powell, Ralph. *The Rise of Chinese Military Power, 1895–1912.* Princeton: Princeton University Press, 1955.

Price, E. B. *The Russo-Japanese Treaties of 1907–1916 concerning Manchuria and Mongolia.* Baltimore, 1933.

Rankin, Mary B. *Early Chinese Revolutionaries.* Cambridge: Harvard University Press, 1971.

Reid, John Gilbert. *The Manchu Abdication and the Powers, 1908–1912.* Berkeley and Los Angeles: University of California Press, 1935.

Remer, Charles F. *A Study of Chinese Boycotts.* Baltimore, 1935.

Rhoads, Edward. "Nationalism and Xenophobia in Kwangtung (1905–1906): The Canton Anti-American Boycott and the Lienchow Anti-Missionary Uprising." *Harvard Papers on China,* vol. 16 (1962), pp. 154–197.

Rosenbaum, Arthur Lewis, "China's First Railway: The Imperial Railways of North China, 1880–1911." Ph.D. dissertation, Yale University, 1972.

————. "Chinese Railway Policy and the Response to Imperialism: The Peking-Mukden Railway, 1895–1911." *Ch'ing-shih wen-t'i* 2, no. 1 (1969): 38–70.

Sang-p'i, Ts'ai-wang-jen-tseng 桑頗才旺仁增, et al. "Hui-ku hsin-hai ko-ming ch'ien-hou ti Hsi-tsang ch'ing-k'uang 回顧辛亥革命前後的西藏情況 [Memoirs of conditions in Tibet before and after the Hsin-hai revolution]. In Chung-kuo jen-min, *Hsin-hai ko-ming hui-i-lu,* vol. 3, pp. 510–15.

Savina, F. M. *Histoire des Miao.* Hong Kong: Imprimerie de la Société des Missions Etrangères de Paris, 1930.

Scalapino, Robert A. "Prelude to Marxism: The Chinese Student Movement in Japan, 1900–1910." In *Approaches to Modern Chinese History,* edited by Albert Feuerwerker, et al., pp. 190–215. Berkeley and Los Angeles: University of California Press, 1967.

Schiffrin, Harold Z. "The Enigma of Sun Yat-sen." In *China in Revolution: The First Phase, 1900–1913,* edited by Mary C. Wright, pp. 443–74. New Haven: Yale University Press, 1968.

————. *Sun Yat-sen and the Origins of the Chinese Revolution.* Berkeley and Los Angeles: University of California Press, 1968.

Schneider, Laurence. *Ku Chieh-kang and China's New History.* Berkeley and Los Angeles: University of California Press, 1971.

Schrecker, John E. *Imperialism and Chinese Nationalism: Germany in Shantung.* Cambridge: Harvard University Press, 1971.

Schurmann, Franz. *Ideology and Organization in Communist China.* Berkeley and Los Angeles: University of California Press, 1966.

Schwartz, Benjamin. *In Search of Wealth and Power: Yen Fu and the West.* Cambridge: Harvard University Press, 1964.

Selden, Mark. *The Yenan Way in Revolutionary China.* Cambridge: Harvard University Press, 1971.

Shakabpa, Tsepon W. D. *Tibet: A Political History.* New Haven: Yale University Press, 1967.

Shan-tung li-shih hsüeh-hui 山東歷史學會 [Shantung Historical Association], comp.

Shan-tung chin-tai shih tzu-liao 山東近代史資料 [Materials on the modern history of Shantung]. Tsinan, 1961. Reprint. Tokyo, 1965.

Shen, Nai-cheng 沈乃正. "Ch'ing-mo chih tu-fu chi-ch'üan, chung-yang chi-ch'üan, yü 't'ung-shu pan-kung.'" 清末之督撫集權中央集權與"同署辦公" [The concentration of authority in the governors-general and governors, the centralization of authority and the institution of "all affairs in one office" during the late Ch'ing]. *She-hui k'o-hsüeh* 社會科學 [Social Science] 2 (1937): 311–42.

Shen, T'ung-sheng 沈桐生. *Kuang-hsü cheng-yao* 光緒政要 [Administrative compendium of the Kwang-hsü period]. 34 chüan in 30 ts'e. Shanghai: Ch'ung-i t'ang shih-yin, 1909.

Shen, Yün-lung 沈雲龍, comp. *Chin-tai Chung-kuo shih-liao ts'ung-k'an* 近代中國史料叢刊 [Library of historical materials on modern China]. 570 vols. Taipei: Wen-hai shu-chü, 1966–.

———. "Hsü Shih-ch'ang p'ing-chuan" 徐世昌評傳 [A critical biography of Hsü Shih-ch'ang]. *Chuan-chi wen-hsüeh* 傳記文學 [Biographical Literature], chüan 13 (1968), nos. 1–6, chüan 14 (1969), nos. 1–5.

Sheng-ching shih-pao 盛京時報 [Mukden Times]. Nos. 761–1344. 1909–1912. National Diet Library, Tokyo, Japan.

Sheng, Hsüan-huai 盛宣懷. *Yü-chai ts'un-kao* 愚齊存藁 [The telegrams of Sheng Hsüan-huai]. 2 vols. 1939. Reprint. Taipei, 1963.

Sheridan, James E. *Chinese Warlord: The Career of Feng Yü-hsiang*. Stanford: Stanford University Press, 1966.

Shih, T'i-yüan 石體元. "I Ch'eng-tu pao-lu yün-tung" 億成都保路運動 [Memoirs of the railway protection movement in Chengtu], in Chung-kuo jen-min, *Hsin-hai ko-ming hui-i-lu,* vol. 3, pp. 42–67.

Shih-min-pao 時敏報 [The Times], in *Tung-fang,* vol. 1, no. 8 (1904), chün-shih, pp. 309–13.

Shih-pao 時報 [Eastern Times], in *Tung-fang,* vol. 2, no. 3 (1905), nei-wu, pp. 37–39.

Shih, Vincent. "Some Chinese Rebel Ideologies." *T'oung Pao* 44, (1956): 151–226.

Sigel, Louis T. "Ch'ing Tibetan Policy (1906–1910)." *Harvard Papers on China*, vol. 20 (1966), pp. 177–201.

Smedley, Agnes. *The Great Road: The Life and Times of Chu Teh*. London: John Calder, 1958.

Smith, Kent C. "Ch'ing Policy and the Development of Southwest China: Aspects of Ortai's Governor-Generalship, 1726–1731." Ph. D. dissertation, Yale University, 1970.

Spector, Stanley. *Li-Hung-chang and the Huai Army*. Seattle: University of Washington Press, 1964.

Spence, Jonathan. "Ch'ing and Modern China." Unpublished manuscript, 1972.

———. "Opium Smoking in Ch'ing China." Unpublished manuscript, 1971.

———. *To Change China: Western Advisors in China,* 1620–1960. Boston: Little, Brown and Co., 1969.

———. *Ts'ao Yin and the K'ang-hsi Emperor: Bondservant and Master*. New Haven: Yale University Press, 1966.

"Ssu-ch'uan-sheng liu-hsüeh Jih-pen kuan-fei sheng tiao-ch'a-piao" 四川省留學日本官費

生調查表 [Table summarizing data on Szechwanese government fellowship students in Japan], circa 1908. Chiao-yu pu tang 教育部檔 [Archives of the Ministry of Education]. Musan, Taiwan.

Straight, Willard. The Willard Straight Papers. Olin Library, Cornell University, Ithaca.

Su, Yün-feng 蘇雲峯. "Chang Chih-tung yü Wan-Ch'ing chiao-yü kai-ko 張之洞與晚清教育改革 [Chang Chih-tung and late Ch'ing educational reforms]. Nan-kang: Institute of Modern History unpublished manuscript, 1968.

Sun, E-tu Zen. Chinese Railways and British Interests, 1898–1911. New York: Columbia University Press, 1954.

———. "Ch'ing Government and the Mineral Industries before 1800." Journal of Asian Studies 27, no. 4 (1968): 835–45.

———. "Mining Labor in the Ch'ing Period." In Approaches to Modern Chinese History, edited by Albert Feuerwerker, et al., pp. 45–67. Berkeley and Los Angeles: University of California Press, 1967.

Sun Tzu. The Art of War. Translated and introduced by S. B. Griffith. Oxford: Clarendon Press, 1963.

Ta Ch'ing Te-tsung ching (Kuang-hsü) huang-ti shih-lu 大清德宗景(光緒)皇帝實錄 [Veritable records of Te-tsung in the Kwang-hsü reign of the great Ch'ing]. Mukden, 1938. Reprint. Taipei, 1964.

Tai, Chih-li 戴執禮, ed. Ssu-ch'uan pao-lu yün-tung shih-liao 四川保路運動史料 [Materials on the railroad protection movement in Szechwan]. Peking: K'o-hsüeh ch'u-pan-she, 1959.

Tan, Chester. The Boxer Catastrophe. New York: Columbia University Press, 1955.

Teichman, Eric. Travels of a Consular Officer in Eastern Tibet. Cambridge: At the University Press, 1922.

Ts'ao, Ju-lin 曹汝霖. I-sheng chih hui-i 一生之回憶 [Memoirs of a life]. Hong Kong: Ch'un-ch'iu tsa-chih-she, 1966.

Ts'en, Ch'un-hsüan 岑春煊. Lo-chai man-pi 樂齊漫筆 [Rambling notes from the study of Lo]. In Wu, CHS ts'ung-shu. Taipei, 1962.

Tsou, Lu 鄒魯. "T'ung-meng-hui Yün-nan chih-pu chih huo-tung" 同盟會雲南之部之活動 [The activities of the Yunnan branch of the revolutionary alliance]. In Chung-hua, K'ai-kuo wen-hsien, pien 1, ts'e 12, pp. 127–29.

Tsou, Tang. America's Failure in China. Chicago: Chicago University Press, 1963.

Tung-fang tsa-chih 東方雜誌 [The eastern miscellany]. 6 vols. Shanghai, 1904–10.

United States. Department of State. Foreign Relations of the United States, 1903–1909. 8 vols.

———. Records Relating to the Internal Affairs of China, 1910–1911. Microfilm. Sterling Memorial Library, Yale University, New Haven.

United States National Archives, Records of the Department of State, Foreign Affairs Division, China.

Vogel, Ezra. Canton Under Communism: Programs and Politics in a Provincial Capital, 1949–1968. Cambridge: Harvard University Press, 1969.

Voyron, Genéral. Rapport sur l'expédition de Chine, 1900–1901. Paris: Charles-Lavauzelle, n.d.

Wai-chiao-pao 外交報 [Foreign Relations Gazette], in *Tung-fang,* vol. 1, no. 2 (1904), she-shuo, pp. 32–34.

Wakeman, Frederick. *Strangers at the Gate: Social Disorder in South China 1839–1861.* Berkeley and Los Angeles: University of California Press, 1966.

Waldersee, Alfred Count von. *A Field-Marshal's Memoirs.* Condensed and translated by F. Whyte. London: Hutchinson and Co., 1924.

Wang, Chien-ch'ing 王鑑清. *Pa-hsien-chih* 巴縣志 [Local history of Pa-hsien district]. 23 chüan. n.p., 1939.

Wang, Erh-min 王爾敏. "Ch'üan-pien shih-ch'i chih nan-sheng tzu-pao" 拳變時期之南省自保 [The southern provinces' self-protection during the Boxer uprising], *Ta-lu tsa-chih* 大陸雜誌 [Continental Miscellany], vol. 25 (1962), nos. 3–6.

Wang, Hsien-ch'ien 王先謙. *Hsü Shou-t'ang shih-wen-chi* 虛受堂詩文集 [Collected poems and essays of the Hsü Shou Hall]. n.p., n.d.

_____, et al., eds. *Shih-erh ch'ao Tung-hua-lu* 十二朝東華錄 [Tung-hua records of twelve reigns]. 220 chüan. Shanghai, 1909. Reprint. Taipei, 1963.

Wang, Shu-huai 王樹槐. *Wai-jen yü wu-hsü pien-fa* 外人與戊戌變法 [Foreigners and the reforms of 1898]. Taipei: Chung-yang yen-chiu-yüan, Chin-tai shih yen-chiu so, 1965.

Wang, Shu-tang. *China, Land of Many Nationalities.* Peking: The Foreign Languages Press, 1955.

Wang, Ti 皇帝. "Ssu-ch'uan t'ao Man-chou hsi" 四川討滿洲檄 [A Szechwanese manifesto proclaiming military action against the Manchus], in Chung-hua, *K'ai-kuo wen-hsien,* pien 1, ts'e 16, pp. 256–67.

Wang, Tu 王度. "Tiao An-jen chuan" 刁安仁傳 [Biography of Tiao An-jen], in Chunghua, *K'ai-kuo wen-hsien,* pien 1, ts'e 12, pp. 139–140.

Wang, Yao-huan 王燿煥. "Chin-tung fang-chün chi-lüeh" 晉東防軍紀略 [Outline record of the defense army of eastern Shansi]. In *I-Ho-T'uan* 義和團 [The Boxers], edited by Chien Po-tsan 翦伯贊, ts'e 3, pp. 315–22. 4 vols. Shanghai, 1951.

Wang, Yen-wei 王彥威, comp., Wang Liang 王亮, ed. *Ch'ing-chi wai-chiao shih-liao, Kuang-hsü ch'ao, Hsüan-t'ung ch'ao* 清孝外交史料光緒朝,宣統朝 [Historical materials on foreign relations in the late Ch'ing, Kwang-hsü, and Hsüan-t'ung periods]. Peiping, 1932–1933. Reprint. Taipei, 1964.

Wang, Yi-chü. *Chinese Intellectuals and the West, 1872–1949.* Chapel Hill: University of North Carolina Press, 1966.

Wang, Yung-chou 王用舟, comp. *Ching-hsing hsien-chih* 井陘縣志 [Local history of Ching-hsing district (Hopei)]. 16 pien. n.p., 1934.

Wiens, Harold J. *China's March toward the Tropics.* Hamden, Conn.: Shoe String Press, 1954.

Wilhelm, Hellmut. "From Myth to Myth: The Case of Yüeh Fei's Biography." In *Confucian Personalities,* edited by A. Wright and D. Twitchett, pp. 146–61. Stanford: Stanford University Press, 1962.

Wright, Arthur F., and Twitchett, D., eds. *Confucian Personalities.* Stanford: Stanford University Press, 1962.

———., ed. *The Confucian Persuasion.* Stanford: Stanford University Press, 1960.

Wright, Mary C. "Introduction: The Rising Tide of Change," in Wright, *China in Revolution,* pp. 1–63.

————. *The Last Stand of Chinese Conservatism: The T'ung-chih Restoration, 1862–1874*. Stanford: Stanford University Press, 1962.

Wright, Mary C., ed. *China in Revolution: The First Phase, 1900–1913*. New Haven: Yale University Press, 1968.

Wu, Chin-hang 吳晉航. "Ssu-ch'uan hsin-hai ko-ming chien-wen lu" 四川辛亥革命見聞錄 [A record of what I saw and heard about the revolution of 1911 in Szechwan]. In Chung-kuo jen-min, *Hsin-hai ko-ming hui-i-lu*, vol. 3, pp. 99–110.

Wu, Cho-ju 吳卓如, et al., comps. *Hsin-p'ing hsien-chih* 新平縣志 [Local history of Hsin-p'ing district (Yunnan)]. 8 chüan. Reprint. Taipei, 1967.

Wu, Feng-p'ei 吳豐培, ed. *Ch'ing-chi ch'ou Tsang tsou-tu* 清季籌藏奏牘 [Memorials on late Ch'ing Tibetan policy]. 3 vols. Peiping: Kuo-li Pei-p'ing yen-chiu-yüan, 1938.

————. *Ch'ing-tai Hsi-tsang shih-liao ts'ung-k'an* 清代西藏史料叢刊 [Library of historical materials on Tibet in the Ch'ing period]. Peiping: Kuo-li Pei-p'ing yen-chiu-yüan, 1938.

Wu, Hsiang-hsiang 吳相湘, ed. *Chung-kuo hsien-tai shih-liao ts'ung-shu* 中國現代史料叢書 [Library of Chinese contemporary historical materials]. 16 vols. Taipei, 1962–.

————. *Chung-kuo hsien-tai shih ts'ung-k'an* 中國現代史叢刊 [Selected writings on modern Chinese history]. 6 ts'e. Taipei, 1960–1964.

Yang, Ta-chu 楊大鑄. "Yün-nan ko-ming hsiao-shih" 雲南革命小史 [A brief history of the revolution in Yunnan]. In Chung-hua, *K'ai-kuo wen-hsien*, pien 1, ts'e 12, pp. 123–27.

Yao, Wen-tung 姚文棟. *Yün-nan k'an-chieh ch'ou-pien-chi* 雲南勘界籌邊記 [A record of border demarcation and frontier policy in Yunnan]. Taipei reprint, 1968. In Shen Yün-lung, no. 179.

Young, C. Walter. *The International Relations of Manchuria*. Chicago: University of Chicago Press, 1929.

Young, Ernest P. "The Reformer as a Conspirator: Liang Ch'i-ch'ao and the 1911 Revolution." In *Approaches to Modern Chinese History*, edited by Albert Feuerwerker, et al., pp. 239–67. Berkeley and Los Angeles: University of California Press, 1967.

————. "Yuan Shih-k'ai's Rise to the Presidency." In *China in Revolution: The First Phase, 1900–1913*, edited by Mary C. Wright, pp. 419–42. New Haven: Yale University Press, 1968.

Yü-pei k'uang-wu chiao-she shih-mo-chi 豫北礦務交涉始末記 [A complete record of the diplomacy over the mines of north Honan]. 2 ts'e. Taipei, n.d.

INDEX

Advisers: in Szechwan arsenal, 52; in Szechwan schools, 53–54; Japanese surveyors in Szechwan, 67; Japanese in Yunnan schools, 88; few in Yunnan, 88; Hsi-liang's attitude toward, 88, 189; in Manchurian agricultural reform, 167

Agriculture: reformed in Manchuria, 167; as base, 190

Aigun, Heilungkiang, 145–46

Allied expeditions, 28, 188, 191; Hsi-liang resists, 13, 16–24; relieve legations, 16; pressure on Shansi, 17–23; in Chihli, 17–24; planned for Shensi, 21–22; advance into Shansi, 24

Allied villages (*lien-chuang she*): in Honan, 28

Allies, 16–24 passim, 45, 60

America. *See* United States

American Group: and Willard Straight, 147; and development loan, 149; withdraws from Chin-ai line, 152; and Manchurian development loan, 153

An-feng line (An-tung to Mukden), 146, 174, 188; controversy over, 141–42, 143, 144, 145

An-tung: Japanese railway in, 141, 147; peasant riots in, 177–78

Anglo-French expedition of 1860, 183

Anhui, 118

Antiforeignism, xii, 130, 193; defined, xii, 209*nn*1,3; in Shantung, 6; of Li Pingheng, 6; of Yü-hsien, 6; of Hsi-liang, 47–49, 87–88; in Kham, 75; of Ts'ui Hsiang-k'uei, 93; of Ko-chiu mine workers, 103; of Yunnanese peasants, 108–09; of Yang Chen-hung, 116; and radicalism, 128; use of term, 191; in Szechwan, 209*n*9

Anti-Manchu: agitators and Hsi-liang, xvi; in *Chungking Daily*, 56; exploitation of corruption charges, 68; radicals focus on Yunnan, 85; propaganda suppressed in Yunnan, 112; movement set back, 116. *See also* Revolutionary Alliance; Secret societies; Sun Yat-sen

Antiopium associations (*chin-yen-hui*), 97; Hsi-liang encouraged, 96

Anzer, Johann (Catholic bishop): estab-

lishes mission in Ts'ao-chou, 6; wants German base at Chiao-chou, 7

Arsenal: important reform of, in Szechwan, 50; modest reform of, in Yunnan, 92

Association for Lectures on Culture, 110

Association for Yunnanese, 110

Banditry, 184, 190; and Boxers, 8, 16, 21, 24, 36, 124, 163; in Jehol, 13, 36–38; in Szechwan, 48, 53; in Manchuria, 157, 164

Banner: Bordered Blue and Hsi-liang, 1, 178, 180; in Jehol, 39; academy (*pa-ch'i shu-yüan*), 53; Affairs Bureau, 166; reform, 166; system, 202*n*1

Banque d'Annam, 123, 126

Barbarians, 79, 191; Hsi-liang on, 77, 82. *See also* Minorities

Bargas: and T'ao-k'o-t'ao, 157; and colonization, 157–58

Belgium: Hsi-liang sends students to, 54; and Chin-ai line, 152

Berlin, 66

Bismarck, Otto von, 162

Bons d'Anty: as French Consul in Szechwan, 48; on Christians and missionaries, 48; and Catholics, 49; and Hsi-liang, 49, 62–63; and Ch'uan-Han line, 62; and Feng-hsü, 62, 63

Boxer indemnities, 13, 32, 45; resisted in Honan, 26, 27–30; and Honan military reforms, 28; taxes to pay, 29

Boxer movement, xii, 13, 28, 36, 163, 189, 195; Hsi-liang's view of, 15, 16; weak in south, 16; and siege of Peking legations, 16; Hsi-liang suppresses in Shansi, 18; settlement suspends examinations, 28; Court prefers another to parliament, 173; nationalistic interpretation of, 204*n*6

Boycott, anti-French, 133; anti-Japanese, 143–44

Braves: in Yunnan, reorganization of, 89, 92

Buddhism: priests' status in China, 30; and Szechwan educational reform, 56; of Tibet, 77; of Shan, 116; of Mongols, 154, 155, 191; arrival from India, 196

Bureau to Encourage Manufacturing, 58